". . . a guidebook along the tough and challenging road to higher profits and growth—where signposts are in the language of cash. . . ."

To maximize business profits—maximize liquidity and the equity potential for creating liquidity. This is the essence of *The Strategy of Cash,* a book that demonstrates how to create and maintain a "liquidity environment" of maximum cash productivity and equity expansion. Its purpose is to help managers achieve the company's maximum compounded rate of earnings growth while preserving an invulnerable balance sheet position.

To accomplish this, the book

- formulates and demonstrates a basic *liquidity concept* which describes how profits are maximized by the intensive creation of corporate cash and equity

- applies external and internal *cash-generating strategies* that logically emerge from the basic liquidity concept

- provides a complete arsenal of specific cash-generating and equity-generating *implementation strategies,* that shape the liquidity environment from which maximum profits and growth necessarily flow

The author argues that *cash* is the core principle of all business activity, the central organizing concept from which managers derive the fullest understanding of the functioning of their firms and the most fruitful strategies for maximizing profits. He advocates further that the liquidity approach gathers all of the cash-generating weapons into a unified conceptual and strategic framework, and directs them with maximum force to the creation of profits. And, using cash productivity formats and tables that are illu gestive, he helps municate profit-b to allow each con tactical problems i

The Strategy of Ca only for senior offic managers of large and smaller companies. It is also directed to assistant controllers, assistant treasurers,

(Continued on back flap)

The Strategy of Cash

WILEY SERIES ON SYSTEMS AND CONTROLS FOR FINANCIAL MANAGEMENT

Edited by Robert L. Shultis and Frank M. Mastromano

THE STRATEGY OF CASH

**A LIQUIDITY APPROACH TO MAXIMIZING
THE COMPANY'S PROFITS**

S. D. SLATER

President, Amadon Corporation

Boston Massachusetts

A WILEY-INTERSCIENCE PUBLICATION

JOHN WILEY & SONS, New York • London • Sydney • Toronto

000490

Copyright © 1974, by John Wiley & Sons, Inc.

All rights reserved. Published simultaneously in Canada.

No part of this book may be reproduced by any means, nor
transmitted, nor translated into a machine language without the written permission of the publisher.

Library of Congress Cataloging in Publication Data:

Slater, S   D   1927–
    The strategy of cash.

    (Wiley series on systems and controls for financial
management)
    "A Wiley-Interscience publication."
    1. Corporations—Cash position.   I.   Title.

HG4028.C45S56 1974   658.1'55   74-9811
ISBN 0-471-79640-9

Printed in the United States of America
10 9 8 7 6 5 4 3 2 1

TO EVE, DON, AND JULIA

SERIES PREFACE

No one needs to tell the reader that the world is changing. He sees it all too clearly. The immutable, the constant, the unchanging of a decade or two ago no longer represent the latest thinking—on *any* subject, whether morals, medicine, politics, economics, or religion. Change has always been with us, but the pace has been accelerating, especially in the postwar years.

Business, particularly with the advent of the electronic computer some 20 years ago, has also undergone change. New disciplines have sprung up. New professions are born. New skills are in demand. And the need is ever greater to blend the new skills with those of the older professions to meet the demands of modern business.

The accounting and financial functions certainly are no exception. The constancy of change is as pervasive in these fields as it is in any other. Industry is moving toward an integration of many of the information gathering, processing, and analyzing functions under the impetus of the so-called systems approach. Such corporate territory has been, traditionally, the responsibility of the accountant and the financial man. It still is, to a large extent—but times are changing.

Does this, then, spell the early demise of the accountant as we know him today? Does it augur a lessening of influence for the financial specialists in today's corporate hierarchy? We think not. We maintain, however, that it is incumbent upon today's accountant and today's financial man to learn *today's* thinking and to *use today's* skills. It is for this reason the Wiley Series on Systems and Controls for Financial Management is being developed.

Recognizing the broad spectrum of interests and activities that the series title encompasses, we plan a number of volumes, each representing the latest thinking, written by a recognized authority, on a particular facet of the financial man's responsibilities. The subjects contemplated for discussion within the series range from production accounting systems to planning, to corporate records, to control of cash. Each book is an in-depth study of one subject within this group. Each is intended to be a practical, working tool for the businessman in general and the financial man and accountant in particular.

ROBERT L. SHULTIS
FRANK M. MASTROMANO

CONTENTS

Management's wealth-creating imperative...Maximizing
stockholders' wealth: the causal sequence...Maximizing Pi:
the percentage increase of equity...Pi as the central organizing concept of business enterprise

The manager as investment manager: maximizing balance-
sheet velocity...The seven SCALDER sources of corporate
cash...The liquidity environment: cash velocity and synergy...Maximizing cash to maximize profits...Cash return on
equity (CRE)...CRE and the cash productivity factor...
Some technical pitfalls: "net income" and dividend leakage

ECA: equity created by acquisition...Liquidity ECA cash
availability...ECO: equity created by public offerings...
Equity formation and cash productivity

$Pi = CRE \times ECO \times ECA$...Implementing Pi: the strategy of
maximum cash productivity

PART IV: GENERATING COST CASH

PART V: ASSET SOURCES OF CASH

Discounting cash flow for maximum return...Evaluating investment cash return...The net cash impact of alternative projects...Capital costs and payback...Locating the cutoff rate of return...Payback and risk

PART VI: IMPLEMENTING THE STRATEGY OF MAXIMUM CASH PRODUCTIVITY

The Cash Productivity Plan: CRE versus ECO and ECA...The cash planning sequence...Delineating our planning environment...Establishing the Pi growth rate...The Cash Productivity Guide (Pi Frame)...Organizing to construct the Cash Productivity Plan...Determining our maximum-impact direction...Preparing the functional resource plans...The financial plan...The interim and base year Plans...Visualizing and actualizing target year 5...Qualities of an achievable Plan

Structuring cash productivity objectives...Characteristics of cash-effective objectives...Formats for administering objectives...Interim cash productivity reviews...Organizing to achieve the Cash Productivity Plan...Charting the organizational structure...Recruiting cash-motivated people...Position guides for organizational clarity...Effective policies and procedures

The substance of motivation...The cash contribution ratio as performance gauge...Evaluating and rewarding cash productivity...Promotion as the engine of the motivational system...Cumulating promotional incentives

PART VII: SAFEGUARDING CASH PRODUCTIVITY: CONTROLLING RESULTS AGAINST PLAN

Quantitative controls: financial versus nonfinancial...

Nonquantitative "controls": eyeball-to-eyeball...The three tiers of cash control: forecast, analyze, prevent...Forecasting cash variances...The functional forecast...Forecasting net cash impact and cash velocity...Projecting balance-sheet cash...The forecasted income statements and balance sheets...The CRE basis of cash forecasting

TABLES, CHARTS, AND FIGURES

Chapter 12

Chapter 13

Chapter 15

Chapter 16

Chapter 17

Chapter 18

Chapter 19

The Strategy of Cash

PART 1

THE CREATION OF CASH, PROFITS, AND CORPORATE WEALTH

CHAPTER 1

INTRODUCTION: THE STRATEGY OF CASH AS A MANAGERIAL ALTERNATIVE

To maximize business profits, maximize liquidity and the equity potential for creating liquidity. In this cryptic remark is compressed the entire subject matter of the many chapters to follow. It will be elaborated, tested, and applied to actual business situations in a hundred different ways.

What it means, as a managerial pattern and approach, is that our job in running the business is to create and maintain a "liquidity environment" of maximum cash productivity and equity expansion. Then our company will necessarily achieve its maximum compounded rate of earnings growth while preserving an invulnerable balance sheet position.

That this must be our fundamental concept and strategy, actually our sole legitimate concern as business managers, is the thesis of *The Strategy of Cash*. The book is therefore organized and written to accomplish three things:

1. To formulate and demonstrate a basic *liquidity concept*, which describes how profits are maximized by the intensive creation of corporate cash and equity.

2. To apply the external and internal *cash-generating strategies* that logically emerge from the basic liquidity concept.

3. To provide a complete arsenal of specific cash-generating and equity-generating *implementation strategies*, which shape the liquidity environment from which maximum profits and growth necessarily flow.

Cash is thus seen as the core principle of all business activity. It is the central organizing concept from which we derive the fullest understanding of the functioning of our firm, and the most fruitful strategies for maximizing its profits. We are in business solely and simply to generate and reinvest *cash* at the highest attainable rate. Nothing else we could possibly do is of greater benefit to our employees, suppliers, stockholders, customers, and the community at large.

The liquidity approach gathers all of our cash-generating weapons into a unified conceptual and strategic framework, and directs them with maximum force to the creation of profits. It is plainly a much better mousetrap, it seems to me, among the alternative managerial approaches. My conviction about it has strengthened during the past two decades of involvement with many scores of companies of almost every description and size—as investment analyst, investment banker, and company president. Gradually and even painfully I have rejected all the conventional management patterns in favor of the liquidity strategy.

During these years it has seemed apparent that the elements producing success in a company and those undermining profits were always rooted in cash generation. To whatever extent a company was organized to build cash productivity, it grew rapidly, profitably, and without impairment to the soundness of its balance sheet. Where a company was an inefficient cash producer, it lost out in one way or another in the competitive battle for survival.

This is not to say that conventional methods of managing and building a business are wrong; they are not. The strategy of cash actually incorporates various components of existing methods, as will become evident, though usually with different ends in view. It is only that even a partial liquidity emphasis—applying just a few of its key elements—always seems to build profits disproportionately. The output far exceeds the input.

So it is probably time to single out liquidity as an identifiable managerial approach, and apply *all* the elements of the strategy as an integrated and unified whole. This I have sought to do as a business manager and Boston financial adviser to managers, drawing entirely from my own experience and theirs. It has required the building of a practical conceptual framework that departs abruptly from the customary business pattern; creating a system of ideas to be housed usefully within that framework; and developing or urging specific implementing strategies to give maximum profit-generating impact to both the framework and the ideas.

The reader will therefore find the going difficult in many places unless he uses the Glossary at the end of the book. New perspectives and approaches have required new terms to describe and communicate them. Acronyms have been used extensively to aid the communication process. Abbreviations abound, to avoid tiresome repetition of lengthy phrases. So the reader is urged to use the Glossary not merely as a handy reference from time to time, but as a constant companion and indispensable working tool.

The orientation of this book is uniformly one of strategy, not tactics. It attempts to help management create the profit-maximizing liquidity environment, and identify the major cash-generating problems and opportunities. Once they are identified, we can readily enlist in-house operating specialists or outside consultants to provide the tactical solutions. From the strategic standpoint, that is, a problem identified is a problem three-quarters solved.

The cash-productivity formats and tables used throughout the book should be valuable aids in their own right. But they are essentially illustrative and suggestive—and deliberately unsophisticated—rather than recommendations in behalf of particular mechanical procedures. This is the area of tactics, not strategy. Not only should each company solve its tactical problems in its own way, but each company is on a higher or lower level of sophistication than other companies. So, for both reasons, formats and mechanical procedures for implementing cash strategies should vary widely. In short, my tactical illustrations help develop and communicate the strategies rather than advocate any particular type of tactical implementation of them.

But the book is written not merely for the "generals" and senior officers of companies large and small, and their financial managers. It is perhaps even more specifically for those armies of corporate noncoms and junior officers who intend to be generals some day. I hope it will also be useful to management's advisers, particularly their attorneys and accountants, and to the future managers now toiling in the vineyards of our business administration colleges.

Yet *The Strategy of Cash* is really just a guidebook along the tough and challenging road to higher profits and growth—where signposts are in the language of cash—and makes no pretensions to being anything more. It is being started in Scotland over an extended summer holiday, and its value may be akin to that of my family's guidebook through this exquisite country: It makes no pretensions to being a history book, a geography book, or anything other than an itinerary that helps us set our travel objectives and decide how best to achieve them.

The Strategy of Cash is meant to be such an itinerary, and to be used as such, in the poorly charted and hazardous country through which the business manager travels.

S. D. Slater

Boston, Massachusetts

CHAPTER 2

CASH AND THE CREATION
OF CORPORATE WEALTH

The private business corporation is a wealth-creating institution for its stockholders. This is the reason it was founded in the first place, and the reason for its continued existence.

It has many secondary or resultant community-welfare justifications, of course, such as providing useful goods and services and employing people. But the business firm is the institutionalized expression and manifestation of its owners, who perpetuate it for its profit-generating and wealth-creating capability. Always paramount is the value of their investment and what is happening to that value over time.

MANAGEMENT'S WEALTH-CREATING IMPERATIVE

This is why management's ability is ultimately defined and measured solely in terms of its ability to create wealth for the owners of the business. Their wealth is measured pragmatically if ruthlessly by the present cash-realizable value of their shares of stock in the company, which usually means market price. So our job as managers is to augment stockholders' wealth, or the long-term market valuation of their shares. A management that thinks there is any other definition or gauge of its ability is deluding itself: it is necessarily on a collision course with its stockholders, its more intelligent and aggressive competitors, or both.

This wealth-creating imperative applies with equal force to managers who are also the owners of the business. They risk their capital to make it grow, and their wealth-creating motivation as managers is exceedingly high. Lacking an adequate growth opportunity in the business, they would inevitably scale down or eliminate their investment by selling shares or even the entire company. Whether they remained as managers or not, their capital would be redirected to more promising opportunities elsewhere. Management's paramount consideration as owners is identical to that of nonmanagement owners: the wealth-creating potential of the business.

Stockholders' wealth—from which the corporation and its management derive their existence and purpose—is therefore the supremely important focus upon which all business activity converges. But what do we mean by the value of the company's stock, by which we measure wealth? Shares fluctuate constantly in price (or in sales value for a private company), much of which is beyond management's control. So we must be realistic and evaluate stockholders' wealth in terms of long-term average price movements, both absolutely and in relation to general stock market averages.

This is admittedly a gray area and somewhat subjective. But let us assume that our stock this year has been trading at an average price of $50, and ten years ago the average annual price was $10. If during that period the general market has not done nearly as well, we can safely make some very affirmative statements about management's wealth-creating capabilities in behalf of its stockholders.

MAXIMIZING STOCKHOLDERS' WEALTH: THE CAUSAL SEQUENCE

Let us therefore look at the sequence of factors that determine share values, or ownership wealth, whose augmentation is the sole function of top management:

1. The *price/earning ratio* of the shares. It independently affects the price, of course, but management's influence on this factor alone is more often illusory than real. Intensive stockholder relations or even outright market manipulation may produce artificial bulges in the price, but they are rarely if ever permanent or reliable.

2. *Earnings per share*. We can exert a durable impact on the price / earnings ratio and share prices only by maintaining a long-term upward trend in share earnings. Everything we do to create market-value wealth for our stockholders must therefore focus on earnings per share, and have an impact on and be reflected in this essential calculation.

3. *Return on equity*, or net income/stockholders' investment. *Equity* is the company's assets minus liabilities, or the stockholders' net investment at depreciated book cost. It is simply book value, net worth, or net asset value. *Return on equity* is the ratio net income/equity. This third causal

factor in our sequence has a proximate or immediate relationship to earnings per share. If we increase the earnings' return on stockholders' investment, by increasing earnings but not the number of shares outstanding, we increase earnings per share. Throughout the book we actually use the term, and concept, cash return on equity (CRE).

4. *Equity formation* powerfully influences earnings per share and stockholders' wealth. We must not only maximize the return on stockholders' equity, but also create and otherwise introduce into the corporation *additional* equity per share (apart from the equity increments resulting from retained earnings). Equity creation is accomplished by various strategies, which we discuss in detail later, such as acquiring other companies or the public offering of new shares.

By influencing these four closely related factors, therefore, we influence the market valuation of ownership equity. It is a sequence that begins with equity formation and return on equity, which are causes, and ends with earnings per share and the price/earnings ratio, which are the effects. Let us look first at the two causal factors.

MAXIMIZING PI: THE PERCENTAGE INCREASE OF EQUITY

It might even be useful to invent an entirely new concept to combine the familiar idea of return on equity with the unfamiliar one of equity formation. This would tell us the rate at which equity per share is increasing, from all causes. Let us call it *percentage increase of equity* per share (PIE), or simply *Pi*.

Pi is maximized when we maximize both the external and internal creation of equity: Equity per share that is increasing at the maximum rate from external sources such as acquisitions and the public sale of stock is generating earnings (retained equity) at the maximum rate. In our causal sequence, it must then follow that we will have maximized earnings per share, and secondarily the price/earnings ratio and thereby market price. So Pi is really what the manager's job is all about in his crucial role of maximizing stockholders' wealth.

And Pi is also the all-important consideration for the stockholder. It is the increase in his equity per share from *all* sources, not just retained earnings. With Pi at its maximum rate, the company is generating the maximum earnings *return* on equity, and this equity is itself growing at the maximum rate from all sources.

Pi thus exerts a *multiple* impact on earnings per share, and is therefore an exceedingly potent concept and strategy of business management. It is the heart of the strategy of cash.

PI AS THE CENTRAL ORGANIZING CONCEPT OF BUSINESS ENTERPRISE

Maximizing long-run Pi is the entire rationale, the meaning, the purpose, and the justification of a business firm—and its managers—because the firm is the institutionalized expression of stockholders' wealth.

The private enterprise economic system could not continue to exist, let alone function properly, if this were not so. Investors would then neither place nor keep capital in equity form. Of the many categories of risk investments, the equity type is by definition the riskiest. The only possible justification for exposing our capital to maximum risk is the opportunity, whether eventually realized or not, of maximum total return. A lesser risk will settle for a lesser return. But maximum risk can never be justified or compensated by anything less that the potential for maximum return.

Without a maximum-return potential, funds would not be exposed to pure equity risks. They would tend to flow into investments situated toward the safer edge of the risk continuum, which ranges from maximum risks at one end to very safe first mortgages and bonds at the other. In other words, there would be no stockholders. And without stockholders, there would be no stockholders' wealth in the form of private business firms, no business managers, and no private enterprise economic system.

In fact, equity funds would not be risked in business firms and the private business system could not exist even if it were merely *questioned* that the purpose of the firm is the maximization of ownership wealth. It would be as if the ultimate purpose of doctors and the medical profession were no longer to maximize the good health of patients. Even if this ultimate objective were merely questioned, patients would tend inevitably to look elsewhere and the medical system as we know it would cease to exist. An absurd illustration such as this must be used to demonstrate the total absurdity of a private business system in which the maximization of Pi is not the implicit central organizing concept.

Our private economic system thus functions on the basis of, and solely because of, the unquestioned institutionalized expectation on the part of everyone that maximum-risk equity capital in the care of business management is being exposed to maximum-profit opportunities. It is a private enterprise system of wish-fulfillment based on Pi—or, perhaps not inappropriately, Pi-in-the-sky.

This is entirely apart from the very pragmatic wealth-creating imperative of the individual business firm, as noted earlier. The management that consistently generates a below-normal total return on equity will eventually be brought down by its more efficient and aggressive competitors, if it is not first downed by its own stockholders.

Debt capital, too, would not flow into business firms except for the institutionalized conviction that they exist to maximize total return on their equity investments. At bottom, all debt financing is based on margin of safety. Only part of the lender's inducement to advance funds is the expectation of sufficient cash flow to service the principal and interest requirements. The bulk of his inducement is the expectation that cash flow will be sufficiently in excess of the debt service requirement to provide him with a protective margin of safety.

The lender insists on the margin-of-safety incentive because he has no capital-gain incentive, as do the suppliers of equity money. He has only the protection of his capital and a stream of fixed interest payments. So the size of his anticipated margin of safety largely determines whether he will lend, in what amount, at what terms, for how long, and at what borrowing cost.

For the general lending *system* to exist and function, therefore, lenders must look upon business firms (conceptually and empirically) as profit-maximizing engines. They exist to maximize return on equity and Pi, not merely to limp along generating "enough" return to service debt and pay some dividends. This institutionalized conviction, that business exists to maximize Pi, gives the lending system its institutionalized margin of safety on which is based its willingness to commit debt funds to the business *system*. Without it, there could be no private lending institutions as we know them, no debt capital, and therefore no private business enterprise.

Business management is thus paid to maximize stockholders' wealth by maximizing Pi. This totally describes *what* our job is, and immediately raises the question "how?" The answer, which we will now explore, is that we must confine ourselves exclusively to—and in fact redefine our professional responsibilities solely in terms of—cash productivity.

CHAPTER 3

MAXIMIZING CASH PRODUCTIVITY

To maximize stockholders' wealth, management must exert a decisive influence on a sequence of four causal factors: the price-earnings ratio, earnings per share, return on equity, and equity formation. Return on equity and equity formation together constitute the supremely important profit-generating concept and strategy of Pi, or the percentage increase of equity, upon which the entire structure of stockholders' wealth is built.

In this chapter we examine the corporate liquidity environment that maximizes the first half of Pi, *cash return on equity* (CRE). Then Chapter 4 looks into its second half, *equity formation*, and its role in the production of cash and earnings. In Chapter 5 we combine or synthesize cash return on equity and equity formation into the grand strategy of Pi. As the all-inclusive cash-generating basis for maximizing earnings per share, Pi serves as the core theme around which all the cash-productivity sections of the book are developed.

THE MANAGER AS INVESTMENT MANAGER: MAXIMIZING BALANCE SHEET VELOCITY

To formulate a truly effective strategy of cash, we must first redefine the top manager's role. He is no other than an investment manager whose portfolio is the corporate balance sheet. And his investment objective is the maximum production of *cash* from that balance sheet.

On the liability side of the balance sheet are his sources of debt and equity cash. And on the asset side are all the current and fixed investments of that cash. The manager's entire responsibility and sole function is to maximize the *liquidity velocity* of that balance sheet. That is, he maximizes the force, velocity, and profitability at which cash circulates within the corporate system—from the productive sources of cash to its reinvestment at maximum return, back to cash production, and so on ad infinitum.

By thus maximizing liquidity velocity, the manager maintains and nourishes a *liquidity environment*. This, we will see, automatically maximizes profits because changes in liquidity velocity precisely determine changes in profits.

There are three general sources of cash productivity available to management as the investment manager of the balance sheet. First, the *external* sources of cash on the liability side, such as long-term debt ($+L$, for leverage) and the sale of stock or other forms of equity ($+E$). Second, internal *operating* cash provided by retained earnings ($+E$), also on the liability side. This comes from sales cash ($+S$) on the one hand and cost control or reductions ($-C$) on the other. And third, from the asset side of the balance sheet, we generate *asset* cash ($-A$) from the control or liquidation of assets. Then we reinvest ($+R$) the cash from these three sources, promptly and productively, to generate still more cash.

Corporate management, as investment managers, thus generates cash externally from $+L$ and $+E$ and internally from $+S$, $-C$, and $-A$. And it *reinvests* ($+R$) that cash at the maximum rate of return available within its own business or from the acquisition of other businesses.

THE SEVEN *SCALDER* SOURCES OF CORPORATE CASH

So management's job focuses narrowly on maximizing the velocity of balance sheet liquidity, by maximizing cash productivity from all five external and internal sources: sales, costs, assets, leverage, and equity ($+S-C-A+L+E$). Its sixth source is reinvestment ($+R$), so our liquidity acronym becomes SCALER. And we have a seventh source of cash, akin to external equity financing but strategically distinct from it: cash generation from developmental *acquisitions* and mergers ($+D$). And so we have *SCALDER*.

To burn this cash-productivity acronym into our memory, we might tell ourselves that a *scalder* is a device or tool used for burning. It sprays boiling liquid or superheated steam on surfaces, such as those of industrial metals and public buildings, to smooth or clean them.

In these seven ways we maximize both cash return on stockholders' equity (CRE) and equity formation, thereby maximizing the percentage increase of equity (Pi). Let us elaborate a bit on each source:

1. *Leverage* cash ($+L$). External cash provided mainly by the many varieties of intermediate and long-term debt financing available to our company. (The subject of Chapter 6.)

2. *Equity* cash (+E). External cash provided directly by the private or public sale of stock and indirectly (or potentially) by the equity formation caused by a public offering. (Chapter 7.)

3. *Acquisition* cash (+D). External cash and liquidity supplied directly by the acquired company in a merger. Or it is provided indirectly (potentially) by the equity formation resulting from an acquisition, from which additional cash can be generated. (Chapter 8.)

4. *Sales* cash (+S or Sc). External cash provided by stepped-up marketing, product development, international sales, and other efforts that increase the gross volume of sales (+S). And internal cash supplied by the increased productivity or cash yield of gross sales, which we can call sales cash (Sc). (The subject of all of Part Three.)

5. *Cost* cash (−C). Internal cash provided by cost control and reduction, which is a dollar-for-dollar contributor to the company's pretax cash flow. This is true both for absolute and relative cost control, the latter being the situation in which costs are kept from rising as rapidly as sales. As the ratio sales/costs increases, cost cash is generated. (Part Four.)

6. *Asset* cash (−A). Internal cash provided by asset control and reduction, both absolutely and relatively, as the turnover ratio sales/assets increases. The control of major cash-absorbing assets such as inventories, slow receivables, idle or underutilized plant and equipment, and the assets locked into low-profit products. (Chapter 17.)

7. *Reinvestment* cash (+R). Internal cash supplied by the reinvestment, for maximum cash payback, of all the cash we generate from the six preceding +S−C−A+L+D+E sources. It is the additional and compounded cash-generating impact produced by the generated cash that we reinvest or apply to the uses of funds, +C, +A, −L, and −E. Cash is allocated to those reinvestment uses, and only to those uses, that will provide the maximum cash return from among all the available alternatives. (Chapter 18.)

THE LIQUIDITY ENVIRONMENT: CASH VELOCITY AND SYNERGY

Management is thus charged, above all, with maintaining a liquidity environment. Cash is generated with maximum force from all the sources, and simultaneously reinvested in those applications, that will produce the highest cash payback.

Again, three crucial elements determine the liquidity velocity (and cash productivity) of our liquidity environment: (1) the *force* with which our business is now producing cash, especially because of high ratios of S/C, S/A, and L/A; (2) the *speed* and efficiency with which the cash is reinvested at maximum return; (3) the *payback* profitability of the projects in which the cash is invested.

In the narrow sense, "cash velocity" is the second component of liquidity velocity—the speed at which cash circulates from the productive $-C + S - A + L$ sources of cash to its reinvestment (R) at maximum return, and back to cash production. High cash velocity means that there is no dilution of cash productivity from dividend payments (called leakage), idle cash, low-return temporary investments, or other losses or delays in putting it to work at maximum return.

"Liquidity velocity" thus expresses in dynamic terms what "liquidity environment" expresses in static terms. The liquidity environment prevails when cash is circulating at maximum force, velocity, and return, from sources to applications, and back to sources. We increase profits by increasing the speed and efficiency at which cash circulates, as surely as we do by increasing either of the other two elements of the liquidity environment—the force of present cash production and the profitability of investment projects.

The liquidity environment is also influenced strongly by an extraordinary phenomenon involving the interaction of primary and secondary cash productivity. We might call this *cash synergism*, defining synergism from the dictionary as "a united action of different agents or organs, producing a greater effect than the sum of the various individual actions."

In this process, an increase in primary cash productivity from the sources we have discussed also simultaneously strengthens the company's ability to generate cash from various *secondary* or derivative sources. Additional borrowings ($+L$) are now supported by the increased cash-flow debt capacity. Or the sale of equity securities and the acquisition of profitable or cash-rich companies are now made possible by the more generous flow of primary cash.

So an increase in the primary cash productivity of our corporate environment tends to produce a more-than-proportional increase in total cash productivity, as the secondary flow of cash is unleashed. And when the secondary cash is reinvested productively, the resulting new primary cash generates *additional* secondary cash, which in turn is reinvested; and so on.

The total cash impact is thus mutually interactive and cumulative, with the generation of primary and secondary cash reinforcing each other. As this synergistic process moves forward with cumulative force, substantial overall cash production can often result from the relatively modest initial increment in primary cash.

MAXIMIZING CASH TO MAXIMIZE PROFITS

Cash, not "profits," is the focus of our entire discussion and analysis throughout the book. Management's exclusive concern is maximizing *cash* productivity from the seven SCALDER sources.

Cash is the secret weapon in building a company into a substantial and powerful corporation. There are two questions that management must constantly be asking and answering creatively: First, are we generating the highest possible after-tax *cash* return on our equity? Second, are we investing that cash at the highest possible *cash* return on each investment made in our business or in the acquisition of other businesses?

Cash is really the only tool a corporation has to produce more cash, simply because it is hard and spendable dollars. Nothing else is, by definition. Reinvesting these dollars promptly according to the dictates of liquidity velocity, at the highest possible rate of return, produces still more cash. This in turn is reinvested at the maximum rate of return; and so forth. Over the years, if we thus generate cash and reinvest that cash at the highest possible percentage return, the company obviously is growing at its highest possible *compounded* rate. We have created a liquidity environment of maximum velocity: it is the point of maximum cash productivity (MCP).

Thus cash is not our most powerful weapon, but our *only* weapon for producing profits and growth. Our company is a "cash machine," pure and simple, that produces cash from the seven basic $+S-C-A+L+D+E+R$ sources. The skill with which we operate the machine so as to maximize cash output from all these sources determines the company's success. It is that simple. Nothing else management does with its time really matters in the end. But failure to do this much can be harmful or even disastrous.

CASH RETURN ON EQUITY (CRE)

We can now begin to quantify these relationships, starting with the expression $CSA = MCP$. But first we must define the term *expression*, of which we will have many examples throughout the book. It is *not* a mathematical formula as such, but a bit of shorthand to make clear in an abbreviated way certain crucial concepts and ideas used frequently in developing the strategy of cash. An expression is thus an entirely valid description of business relationships, both static and dynamic, that neither makes arithmetical claims nor needs to. For instance, the expression $CRE = -C + S - A + L(R)$ tells us that cash return on equity emerges from cost control, sales increase, asset control, leverage, and the reinvestment of cash. This is true, even though the expression is not a formula and has no mathematical pretensions. It is an invaluable conceptual, or idea, framework for describing the process of internal cash productivity.

So back to the expression $CSA = MCP$. As we have seen, CSA refers to the only sources of internal cash available to our company: cost reduction

$(-C)$, sales increase $(+S)$, and asset reduction $(-A)$. And MCP is maximum cash productivity. It is the condition that exists when costs and assets are held to a minimum in relation to sales volume; so we are generating internal cash at the maximum compounded rate.

Now we must add to the process of internal cash productivity, or $-C+S-A$, the cash factors $+R$ and $+L$. By introducing $+R$, we simply recognize the reinvestment or recirculation of the internal cash produced by CSA. It broadens our expression to $CSA(R)=MCP$.

To this must be added the external cash generation of leverage $(+L)$, or borrowings, which provide an additional pool of cash to the internal CSA pool. The larger combined supply of cash now tends to generate more cash income on a fixed equity base, thereby increasing our return on equity. Given two identical companies generating the same amount of internal cash from CSA, the one that uses the additional leverage cash will earn the higher return on equity. This of course assumes the normal situation in which the additional leverage cash employed in the business earns more than its interest cost.[1] For example:

	Assets (000) 1	Debt (000) 2	Equity (000) 3	Cash Earnings (000) 4	CRE 5
1. Now	$ 5,000	$ 0	$5,000	$600	12%
2. Borrow $5,000	10,000	5,000	5,000	800	16%

Line 1. Our company has $5,000,000 of total assets (column 1) which normally earn about 12%, or $600,000 a year (column 4). Since we have no debt, our equity is also $5,000,000 (column 3), and cash return on equity (CRE) from $600,000 a year is therefore also 12% (column 5).

Line 2. Now we borrow $5,000,000 at 8% interest (column 2), raising our total assets to $10,000,000. Earnings continue at the customary 12% return on total assets, or $1,200,000 a year. After interest costs of $400,000, cash earnings are $800,000. But with only $5,000,000 of equity, which has not changed, earnings of $800,000 provide a return of 16%, not 12%. Return on equity (column 5) has increased substantially solely because of the leverage.

[1]We make this assumption throughout the book—that cash provided by leverage earns more than its interest cost. This is the only rational assumption, since otherwise it would be irrational to borrow.

Having thus added leverage, and satisfied all the requirements of CRE (which term now replaces MCP), our expression for maximizing return on equity is CSAL(R) = CRE.

It is worth noting the crucial role of assets, or −A, in this expression. Suppose we had excluded A entirely, so that our expression were CSL(R). This describes a management that is generating cash from −C and +S, but not from −A. It is utilizing leverage cash. And the cash from CSL is being reinvested (R) to generate still more cash. But it is *not* controlling the growth of its assets (−A), which is a separate and important source of cash, as we see later. So reinvestment applications are being deprived of a certain amount of asset cash, and to that extent cash return on equity has been diminished.

Companies everywhere function this way, without a systematic asset control effort. The A in our expression represents the constant pressure we must exert on all the balance sheet assets if CRE is to be maximized. The asset cash is thereby released and reinvested in projects yielding maximum cash returns, thus increasing the turnover ratio, sales/assets. And turnover exerts a major if not the strongest influence on CRE.

To work easily with the all-important CRE tool, let us now convert the expression (or idea framework) CSAL(R) into a usable formula.

CRE AND THE CASH PRODUCTIVITY FACTOR

The expression CSAL(R) can be converted to the actual arithmetic formula for CRE, which is cash flow (S−C) divided by equity (A−L). Or it can be converted into a much more revealing and versatile substitute that we will call the *cash productivity factor* (CPF).

Arithmetically, that is, CRE is simply turnover multiplied by profit margin, or sales/equity × cash flow/sales. For instance:

1.	Sales (S)	$2,000,000
2.	Cash flow	200,000
3.	Equity	1,000,000
4.	Assets (A)	2,000,000
5.	Debt (L)	1,000,000
6.	CRE (2 ÷ 3)	20%
7.	Profit margin (2 ÷ 1)	10%
8.	Turnover (1 ÷ 3)	200%

$$\text{CRE (6)} = \text{turnover (8)} \times \text{profit margin (7)}$$

$$20\% = 200\% \times 10\%$$

Now let us do the same thing but express CRE in terms of C, S, A, and L. Substituting $S - C$ for cash flow and $A - L$ for equity, we have

$$\mathrm{CRE} = \frac{\text{cash flow}}{\text{sales}} \times \frac{\text{sales}}{\text{equity}}$$

$$= \frac{S - C}{S} \times \frac{S}{A - L}$$

$$= \frac{200}{2000} \times \frac{2000}{1000}$$

$$= 10\% \times 2$$

$$= 20\%$$

Or, simply, $$\mathrm{CRE} = \frac{S - C}{A - L}$$

$$= \frac{200}{1000}$$

$$= 20\%$$

$\mathrm{CRE} = S - C / A - L$ is about as close as any actual computation of CRE can get to the CSAL factors that determine it. But it is not close enough. It conceals more than it reveals; is arithmetically clumsy to work with; and still leaves us with CRE, which is essentially a resultant or effect, not a cause. Cash return on equity tells us what happened, but not what *made* things happen.

What made things happen—and the very foundation of the strategy of cash—is *cash productivity*. This can be measured by the *cash productivity factor* (CPF). It is an extraordinarily versatile and revealing substitute, or proxy, for CRE that exposes all the cash forces converging on and *producing* it.

CPF being a measure of the total causal influence on CRE, we use the two terms interchangeably. Both are developed from CSAL(R) as follows:

$$\mathrm{CPF} = -C + S - A + L(R) \quad \text{becomes}$$

$$\left(\frac{S}{C} \times \frac{S}{A} \times \frac{L}{A} \right)(R)$$

We have merely restated $-C + S - A + L$ with similar effect as the ratios S/C, S/A, and L/A. An increase in S or L in relation to C or A, depending upon the ratio, increases cash productivity (CPF) and probably also cash return on equity.

The expression $CPF = (S/C \times S/A \times L/A)(R)$ tells us that cash return on equity (which it represents) is produced by the interaction of cost cash (S/C), asset cash (S/A), and leverage cash (L/A). And the combined pool of cash is reinvested (R) at a measurable cash payback and liquidity velocity. The CPF expression is a conceptual, or idea, framework for describing management's critically important task of striving always to maximize cash return on equity.

By dropping the R, which is merely descriptive, we have an actual arithmetic computation for the cash productivity factor:

$$CPF = \frac{S}{C} \times \frac{S}{A} \times \frac{L}{A}$$

We can work easily with any *one* of these three causal ratios, as we will see time and again. And we can study their behavior in conjunction with their corresponding subratios down the line in every corner of our organization. They are simple to interpret and apply: *up* is good (cash-generating); *down* is bad (cash-absorbing).

Cash productivity is increased by an increase in the numerators S and L, as noted, or by a decrease in the denominators C and A. Also, cash productivity declines if the numerators S and L decline or if the denominators C and A increase. So we will call S/C, S/A, and L/A *cash contribution ratios (CCRs)*.

The cash productivity factor (CPF) quantifies and measures the combined (unweighted) impact of these three ratios on cash return on equity by computing their *products* in simple multiplication. For instance, from our previous example:

$$CPF = \frac{S}{C} \times \frac{S}{A} \times \frac{L}{A}$$

$$= \frac{2000}{1800} \; \frac{2000}{2000} \; \frac{1000}{2000}$$

$$= 1.11 \quad 1.00 \quad 0.50$$

$$= 0.55$$

$$CRE = \frac{S-C}{A-L}$$

$$= \frac{200}{1000}$$

$$= 20\%$$

Here we see that CRE of 20% was produced by CPF of 0.55.

A change in any *one* cash contribution factor changes CPF, and CRE. Let us assume, simplistically, $+S$ of \$200,000:

$$CPF = \frac{S}{C} \times \frac{S}{A} \times \frac{L}{A}$$

$$= \frac{2200}{1800} \frac{2200}{2000} \frac{1000}{2000}$$

$$= 1.22 \quad 1.10 \quad 0.50$$

$$= 0.67$$

$$CRE = \frac{S-C}{A-L}$$

$$= \frac{400}{1000}$$

$$= 40\%$$

CPF thus rises from 0.55 to 0.67, which increases CRE from 20% to 40%. Or let us assume $-A$ of \$200,000:

$$CPF = \frac{2000}{1800} \times \frac{2000}{1800} \times \frac{1000}{1800}$$

$$= 1.11 \quad 1.11 \quad 0.56$$

$$= 0.69$$

$$CRE = \frac{200}{800}$$

$$= 25\%$$

CPF has now increased from the original 0.55 to 0.69, but CRE only rises from 20% to 25%. An asset reduction thus had a slightly stronger impact on CPF than did the earlier sales increase (0.69 versus 0.67). But the asset reduction had a much milder impact on CRE than did the sales increase (25% versus 40%):

	Start	$+S$	$-A$
CPF	0.55	0.67	0.69
CRE	20%	40%	25%

The cash productivity factor (CPF) and cash return on equity (CRE) thus tend to move together up or down, but at different rates. This is because CPF, as a measure of the company's total cash productivity, weights the three cash contribution ratios (CCRs) equally. But CRE weights them very unequally, giving the heaviest emphasis to S/C.

CPF and CRE could therefore conceivably move in opposite directions for a while. For instance, CPF could be driven up by a huge increase in debt ($+L/A$), whose excessive interest costs undermine the profit margin ($-S/C$) and *CRE*. In its impact on CRE, this increase in CPF is a malignant rather than benign generation of cash. CPF is thus a conceptual and strategic substitute for CRE—indispensable in pursuing the strategy of cash—but not an arithmetic substitute.

That is, $CPF = S/C \times S/A \times L/A$ is an arithmetic statement of the *quantity* of cash productivity that our business derives from these three CCR sources, which productivity normally tends to have a corresponding *qualitative* impact on CRE—in the same direction but not usually to the same extent.

We therefore can and do use CRE in place of CPF in the expression (not the arithmetic formula) $CRE = (S/C \times S/A \times L/A)(R)$. This expression is applicable to the business as a whole and, as noted, to *each* of its organizational components and subcomponents down the line. We can generate cost cash in any section of the company by increasing sales-to-costs ($+S/C$) or reducing costs-to-sales ($-C/S$). And we can produce asset cash by increasing sales generated from our present assets ($+S/A$) or by reducing assets without reducing sales proportionally ($-A/S$).

To the extent that this cash is produced and promptly reemployed in high-priority cash return projects, CRE is increased. To the extent that the additional cash flow supports higher leverage, or $+L/A$, there is a further secondary inflow of debt cash that will also be invested in high-return projects. And to the extent that there ensues a synergistic cash effect, or cumulative interaction between primary and secondary cash, the increase in total cash productivity (and CRE) will be that much more than proportional to the original cash productivity.

To summarize, the cash productivity factor (CPF) quantifies the combined (unweighted) cash impact that the three cash contribution ratios (CCRs) have on CRE, by computing their products in simple multiplication. Because of this three-dimensional causal influence that cash productivity exerts on CRE, we measure the impact of cash strategy primarily in terms of the cash productivity factor (CPF)—and only secondarily in terms of CRE. Three-dimensional cash productivity is the cause of which unidimensional CRE is the effect.

SOME TECHNICAL PITFALLS: "NET INCOME"
AND DIVIDEND LEAKAGE

The strategy of cash requires that we deal with operating results in accounting terms that have hard cash significance, not in terms that are far removed from spendable cash. *Retained cash flow* meets this requirement better than does net income, which is a fuzzy idea that should not be used for internal management purposes.

Retained cash flow is net income after taxes and dividend payments, but before deducting noncash charges such as depreciation and depletion. It is the accrual-basis cash from operations that management finally has available to reinvest. Net income, however, is computed by adding back to retained cash flow the dividend cash that the corporation is completely and permanently deprived of. Then it is reduced by noncash "expenses" such as depreciation, which do not deprive management of cash.

Depreciation is charged because the net income return *on* assets must exclude any return *of* assets. So net income is reduced by a "depreciation" deduction computed on the basis of recovering the original cost of the asset over its estimated useful life. Otherwise part of the net income would have been a return of capital.

But what remains after deducting depreciation is still not, by a wide margin, net income in the true sense of actual return on investment. In our technologically dynamic business world, management cannot even guess what *kind* of productive assets it will eventually buy many years hence to replace many of its present depreciating assets. And it cannot hope to know *when* an asset will have to be replaced.

So *any* depreciation charge might prove grossly inadequate (and net income overstated) because eventual asset replacements will cost far more than the amount of depreciation accumulated at replacement time. Or "net income" may now be severely understated: depreciation is too high in relation to eventual asset replacement costs, the replacements occurring during massive economic deflation.

Besides, net income serves no useful internal purpose anyway because it is not a measurable quantity of spendable dollars. On the other hand, retained net income plus depreciation cash, or *retained cash flow*, pours into the one general pool of investable cash that is available to management. It is certainly a rough measurement, but at least it makes no claims to being an indication of true income realized from the corporate investment. It is uncluttered with return-of-capital adjustments and hocuspocus that do not mean much in real-world terms.

Dividend policy is a second technical consideration in the implementation of an effective cash strategy. Cash leakage through dividend payments cannot be permitted by a management-board that recognizes its obligation to maximize the growth of its stockholders' investment.

Our only consideration in every corporate decision is: where will a dollar of corporate cash do the most good for our stockholders? That is, where will it provide the highest after-tax return? Dividend policy is an integral part of overall cash management, and demands an identical decision-making procedure.

A dollar of cash will usually produce far greater economic benefits for stockholders if kept within the corporation than if paid to them directly and, after taxes, only partially. The corporate "cash machine" circulates cash from sources to applications and back to sources in order to maximize profits. Dividends subvert that purpose and harm the stockholder, undermining the growth potential of his investment.

The stockholder must pay twice, and heavily, to receive dividends. They are of course not tax deductible to the company, as are interest payments. So at present corporate tax rates, directors must provide about $2.00 of valuable cash before taxes for every $1.00 of dividends they declare. But then the stockholder actually receives, net of *his* taxes, only a fraction of that $1.00. Our progressive individual income tax structure approaches confiscatory rates above the upper-medium income levels. Thus stockholders receiving cash dividend income in fact receive only a modest portion of it. After depriving the corporation of twice the amount of cash and therefore considerable potential enhancement in the value of the equity, dividends give the stockholder relatively little to spend. The procedure is most peculiar, and stockholders should discontinue it if their management-board does not.

The minority of investors who require or can use high taxable income have attractive opportunities available to them in the bond and mortgage markets. And those who need high tax-free income have an equally rewarding opportunity in the municipal bond market. Besides, since capital gain is potential realizable income—simply by periodically selling off required portions of the gain and leaving the original capital intact—there is no problem in any event.

Cash dividends are a harmful relic of ages past, an anachronism in a tax system that has turned them into a ritualistic absurdity. For management to perpetuate this ancient tribal rite may be an admission that it simply has not thought through, with its stockholders, the dividend-paying policy in light of radically different present-day conditions. But to ignore entirely the corrosive implications of cash dividend leakage may well be symptomatic of irresponsibility in the allocation of cash for maximum stockholder benefit.

Our managerial reference point is now seen as the balance sheet, whose cash productivity we seek to maximize by tapping all seven SCALDER sources of cash. Ideally, it is a liquidity environment of maximum velocity and synergy, from which maximum cash (and CRE) necessarily flows. It is neither confusd by "net income" shenanigans nor undermined by dividend leakage.

We can move forward now and look at the extraordinary phenomenon of equity formation, which exerts a powerful cash-productive impact within the comprehensive strategy of Pi.

CHAPTER 4

EQUITY FORMATION AND
THE PRODUCTION OF CASH

Our focus thus far in the development of the strategy of cash has been on maximizing cash return on equity (CRE). This involved three simultaneous processes: (1) generating a pool of cash from the internal sources, $-C+S-A$; (2) adding to the pool with externally generated leverage cash, or $+L$; (3) recirculating the cash $(+R)$ at high velocity among maximum-cash-return investment projects within and outside our business. The entire process was described and summarized by the conceptual expression $CRE=(S/C\times S/A\times L/A)(R)$.

But CRE deals only with the return *on* equity, important as that is. It takes as fixed or given the existing quantity of equity. We should now therefore consider the vital supplementary strategy of *equity formation*: the creation by various means of equity per share, from which additional cash (CRE) will be generated.

Stockholders' wealth and equity formation are *per-share* concepts, of course. We are not really benefited unless there is an enhancement in the value of each share we own. It does not help us much if our company doubles in size through an acquisition, for example, in which so many new shares are offered in payment that each of *our* shares is worth the same afterward as before.

Equity per share is created in four ways. The first and most obvious is by retained earnings, which has been the subject of our discussion of CRE. It is also created by the normal growth of corporate asset values over the years.

But two very productive sources of equity formation are often ignored by operations-oriented managements: the strategy of merger and acquisition and the strategy of public offerings. I have dubbed them, for short, equity created by acquisition (ECA) and equity created by offerings (ECO).

ECA: EQUITY CREATED BY ACQUISITION

When acquiring or merging with another company, we can produce equity per share in two ways: (1) from the manner in which the transaction itself is constructed, or *Transaction ECA*; (2) from the acquired company's liquidity or "cash availability," or *Liquidity ECA*—specifically, when its balance-sheet liquidity exceeds our own.

Let us first look at Transaction ECA. The buying company generates it arithmetically: the equity per share that it picks up by absorbing the selling company exceeds the equity per share of common stock that it offers *for* the selling company.

In its simplest form, an equity-creating transaction is one in which our purchase price is below the selling company's equity (net worth or book value). Regardless of the form of payment, our equity per share benefits by the amount that the equity we acquire is above our purchase price. This needs no elaboration.

But we can also create equity for ourselves if we pay *more* than equity value for the acquisition. This is done by acquiring the company for cash, debt, or other form of payment including common stock, whereby we receive more equity per share than we offer. The following oversimplified but typical example illustrates Transaction ECA.

We agree to acquire ailing Seller Corp. for 40 times its depressed earnings of $50,000, or for $2,000,000 in cash. Though we overpay for earnings, it is really a bargain purchase: the transaction will create substantial equity (and earnings, as we will see later), as follows:

	Assets (000) 1	Debt (000) 2	Equity (000) 3	Number of Shares (000) 4	Equity per Share 5
1. Seller Corp.	$3000	$ 400	$ 2600		
2. Buyer Corp. (us)	2000	1600	400	100	$4
3. Price paid	(2000)		(2000)		
4. Buyer Corp.	$3000	$2000	$1000	100	$10

Line 1. Seller Corp.'s equity is $2,600,000 (column 3), derived from assets of $3,000,000 less debt of $400,000 (columns 1 and 2).

Line 2. We make the purchase via a newly formed entity called Buyer Corp., all of whose 100,000 shares of stock we buy for $400,000 in cash (column 3). Then we have Buyer Corp. borrow $1,600,000 (column 2), which is tied to and well-secured by Seller's equity of $2,600,000. This loan and our original $400,000 gives Buyer $2,000,000 of assets in the form of cash (column 1).

Line 3. As Buyer Corp., we pay the owners $2,000,000 for Seller Corp. (columns 1 and 3).

Line 4. Our initial investment in the 100,000 shares of Buyer was only $400,000, or an equity of $4 a share (on line 2). When the purchase of Seller for cash was completed, Buyer still had only 100,000 shares. But its equity as a merged company had jumped to $1,000,000, or $10 a share. This is Seller's original equity of $2,600,000 plus our equity of $400,000, less the $2,000,000 purchase payment.

The 150% increase in equity from $4 to $10 (column 5) was only partly the result of getting $2,600,000 of Seller's equity for $2,000,000 of cash (column 3). The $600,000 of additional equity is only a 30% gain over the $2,000,000 price paid. Most of the equity creation was accounted for solely by the transaction mechanics of the acquisition, or by Transaction ECA. The use of leverage enabled us to contribute only $400,000 of equity (line 2) to a merged company that ended up with $1,000,000 of equity (line 4).

This is a simplified but entirely realistic illustration of Transaction ECA —equity created by acquisition, due to the form of the transaction. For a problem company with below-normal earnings, such as Seller Corp., it is a fairly typical transaction.

Seller Corp. could actually have been acquired at its net worth of $2,600,000 or even higher, and still have created substantial equity for us. One of the many ways to accomplish this is described by the following:

	Assets (000) 1	Debt (000) 2	Equity (000) 3	Number of Shares (000) 4	Equity per Share 5
1. Good Guys, Inc.	$ 700	$ 0	$ 700	350	$2.00
2. Seller Corp.	3000	400	2600		
3. Price, $2,600,000: 100,000 shares, $2,100,000 of debentures convertible at 10, and warrants to buy 100,000 shares at 10		2100	(2100)	100	

	Assets (000) 1	Debt (000) 2	Equity (000) 3	Number of Shares (000) 4	Equity per Share 5
4. GoodGuys, Inc.	$3700	$2500	$1200	450	$2.67
5. Debentures converted at 10		(2100)	2100	210	
6.	$3700	$ 400	$3300	660	$5.00
7. Warrants exercised at 10	1000		1000	100	
8.	$4700	$ 400	$4300	760	$5.66

Line 1. GoodGuys, Inc., our company, has assets of $700,000 and no debt (to simplify the illustration); so our equity is $700,000 (column 3). With 350,000 shares, equity per share is $2.

Line 2. We buy Seller Corp. with its $3,000,000 of assets and $400,000 of debt, or $2,600,000 of equity.

Line 3. Our price for Seller is its equity value of $2,600,000, consisting of the following package of securities: (1)100,000 shares of GoodGuys common stock, valued at the current market price of 5 (column 4); (2) $2,100,000 principal amount of subordinated debentures convertible into common stock at 10; and (3) warrants to buy 100,000 shares of common at 10.

Line 4. Thereupon, GoodGuys' equity immediately jumps from $2.00 to $2.67 a share (column 5), a gain of 33%. This is because the 100,000 GoodGuys shares we paid (line 3), whose equity was $2.00 a share, constituted only $200,000 of GoodGuys' equity. But we received $500,000 of Seller's equity: its $2,600,000 of equity less the $2,100,000 of debentures we paid for it. The $1,200,000 of combined equity after the transaction (column 3, line 4), less our original equity of $700,000 (line 1), is the $500,000 of equity we received.

Line 8. The conversion of debentures and exercise of warrants, both at 10, eventually increase GoodGuys' equity to $5.66 a share (column 5). This is because the debt was converted and retired (line 5), and the warrant cash was contributed (line 7), at $10 a share. Since the $10 price was much higher than the company's prevailing equity values of $2.67 and $5.00 (column 5), it generated a substantial amount of Transaction ECA.

That is, Seller's former stockholders turned in their debentures and paid cash to exercise their warrants, for GoodGuys' stock valued at $10—which was below its market price but far above equity value.

We acquired Seller for its equity of $2,600,000. So Transaction ECA was dependent not on a bargain purchase, but entirely on the construction of the purchase transaction.

Countless private and public mergers and acquisitions involve the automatic creation of equity per share for the buyer, or Transaction ECA. One need only examine a sampling of the flood of merger prospectuses mailed to public stockholders to get the full flavor of ECA.

The reason ECA can take place is simply that earnings and current share prices, not equity, almost invariably determine a company's acquisition price. Whether or not equity is created by the transaction either goes unnoticed entirely or is not considered to be relevant to the terms of the acquisition. But as we will soon see, equity is extremely relevant and indeed critically important to cash generation, profits, and growth. Equity is the primal source of cash productivity, so the creation of equity is the creation of potential cash.

LIQUIDITY ECA: CASH AVAILABILITY

This is the second type of equity creation accomplished by acquisition. It results from having acquired a company with a balance sheet liquidity potential, or "cash availability," higher than that of *our* balance sheet. Neither the form of payment nor of the transaction influences it. The acquired company's high liquidity, or cash-generating potential, is rooted in its underutilized assets and borrowing power. Such companies are legion among the population of business firms of all types and sizes.

Liquidity is a company's total potential for generating cash, or its cash availability, from all seven SCALDER sources: sales, costs, assets, leverage, acquisitions, equity, and reinvestment. This potential is expressed as

$$CRE = \left(\frac{S}{C} \times \frac{S}{A} \times \frac{L}{A} \right)(R)$$

$$Pi = CRE \times ECO \times ECA$$

A liquid company is typically one with a low or negative CRE and Pi, in which there is substantial room for improvement of cash productivity from all the SCALDER sources. This usually means comparatively low cash contribution ratios of S/C, S/A, and L/A for its industry group; neglected reinvestment opportunities (R); and an unutilized equity-formation potential from public offerings and acquisitions (ECO and ECA).

A low-liquidity company, with low cash availability, is *already* at a high rate of CRE. It has high cash contribution ratios (CCRs), having harnessed and employed (used up) its available SCALDER liquidity. Anything we do to increase its equity per share increases its liquidity—its potential for generating more cash from the increased equity, via the SCALDER sources.

As a liquid company is brought up to full utilization in the hands of the new owners, and the "fat" trimmed, a corresponding amount of cash is produced. By reinvesting this cash in maximum-return projects—itself an area of severe underutilization in this type of company—we can generate large additional returns of cash, equity, and profits.

Acquisition candidates that offer a buyer substantial liquidity, as noted, are those that have high cash-generating potentials from all seven SCALDER sources: $+S$, $-C$, $-A$, $+L$, ECA, ECO, and $+R$. In the order in which we examine them throughout the book, these sources are as follows:

1. *Leverage* cash availability ($+L$). The company has no funded debt, low current liabilities, and heavy actual or potential depreciation cash flow to support large borrowings at favorable rates and terms.

2. *Equity* cash availability ($+E$, or ECO). There is, or could soon be developed, a receptive market for a sizable public offering of the company's stock at prices substantially above equity per share.

3. *Acquisition*, or developmental, cash availability ($+D$, or ECA). The company is or could soon be placed in a strong position to make developmental acquisitions that have high liquidity and corporate development potentials (as opposed to nondevelopmental acquisitions that are mere paper-swapping transactions).

4. *Sales* cash availability ($+S$ and $+Sc$). *External* sales cash availability (S) is evidenced by abnormally low ratios of sales/costs and sales/assets. They provide attractive cash-generating opportunities from the buildup of sales volume to ratio levels approaching those of the firm's most profitable competitors.

Internal sales cash availability means the company's net sales cash (Sc), or sales less variable costs ($S-VC$), is well below the industry norm and provides excellent improvement opportunities.

5. *Cost* cash availability ($-C$). An abnormally narrow profit margin

presents sizable cash-generating opportunities from cost reduction or control.

6. *Asset* cash availability ($-A$). Very low ratios of sales/assets are symptomatic of excessive assets. They reveal substantial room for improvement in inventory turnover, receivables collections, fixed asset utilization, and elsewhere. These assets can be major sources of cash to the new owner following the acquisition. Cost cash availability was the other side of the sales/costs coin from sales cash; asset cash availability is simply the denominator of sales/assets. Both ratios will be increased, and cash thereby generated, either by an increase in sales or by a reduction of costs or assets in relation to sales.

7. *Reinvestment* cash availability ($+R$). Capital spending programs have long been neglected. Small amounts of reinvestment cash, applied to projects almost anywhere in the business, produce abnormally high cash returns. This is the payback-generating funnel into which is poured all the cash produced from the acquired company's other six sources of liquidity, to maximize its CRE.

ECO: EQUITY CREATED BY PUBLIC OFFERINGS

ECO is produced for the same reasons as ECA. In an acquisition, the buyer gains more equity value per share in the form of the acquired company than he gives up in the form of equity per share of stock offered in payment. ECO is generated by a public offering the same way. The company gains more equity per share in the form of net cash proceeds from the underwriting than it gives up in the form of equity per share of the stock it is selling.

All public offerings are priced above, and usually far above, book equity per share. As in ECA, this is because equity is virtually ignored in the pricing procedure in favor of earnings, dividends, and market price. So at the offering, equity per share is automatically increased to a level somewhere between the original equity and the net offering price. The amount of this ECO depends on the extent to which the price exceeds the equity. And it also depends heavily on the percentage of new stock to the total share capitalization outstanding after the sale is completed. The ECO impact is more potent in a large offering than a small one.

We can illustrate ECO with the earlier example of Buyer Corp., in which our original investment of $400,000 was represented by 100,000 shares at 4. After absorbing Seller Corp., the merged company had assets of $3,000,000 and debt of $2,000,000, or equity of $1,000,000. With 100,000 shares, equity per share was $10. This is shown in the following table (on line 1):

	Assets (000)	Debt (000)	Equity (000)	Number of Shares (000)	Equity per Share	Debt/ Equity
1. Merged company	$3000	$2000	$1000	100	$10	200%
2. Offer 200,000 shares at 20	4000		4000	200		
3.	$7000	$2000	$5000	300	$16.67	40%

We eventually boost the depressed earnings to around $200,000 annu-
ally, or $2 a share. The market is good, and we offer publicly an additional
200,000 shares at 10 times earnings, or at 20 (line 2). The 200,000 shares
are worth $10 in equity. At 20, the offering resulted in a jump to $16.67 in
equity per share (line 3). It also reduced the debt/equity ratio from an
excessive 200% after the heavily leveraged merger, to only 40%. If anything,
this illustration of ECO understates the magnitudes involved in the typical
public offering.

As a general rule, maximum equity per share is created by a public
offering when:

1. Total assets are at a maximum, in the sense that the company is fully
leveraged (L/A).
2. Total assets are earning a maximum return (S/A and S/C).
3. The price-earnings ratio is at the maximum attainable level.
4. The public sale involves the highest possible amount of new stock as a
percentage of the post-offering capitalization.

In other words, a fully leveraged company earning a maximum return on
total assets, whose shares are at their maximum price-earnings ratio, will
create the maximum equity per share from a public offering (ECO) if as
many shares as possible are sold.

EQUITY FORMATION AND CASH PRODUCTIVITY

The creation of equity per share is the creation of liquidity, which is the
potential creation of cash and therefore of earnings. This goes to the very
heart of the strategy of cash, and is precisely why it is "a liquidity
approach to maximizing the company's profits."

By expanding equity per share from retained earnings and from equity creation (ECA and ECO), we expand our (liquidity) potential for generating more cash from the expanded equity. This cash-generating potential is exploited via the seven SCALDER sources, which boost earnings per share and the price-earnings ratio, and is finally reflected in higher share prices for the stockholders.

We can perhaps best visualize arithmetically why equity is the primal source of liquidity—the gut substance from which cash productivity ultimately issues forth. Let us do this in terms of the CRE ratio cash flow/equity and its cash productivity factor (CPF) components $S/C \times S/A \times L/A$. An increase in equity increases the denominator of cash flow/ equity, and also the asset (A) denominators of S/A and L/A. Both CRE and CPF are thereby *decreased*, and liquidity by definition is thereby *increased*. That is, we have increased our equity potential for generating cash on the larger equity and asset base: we generate $+CRE$ (or $+$cash flow/equity), and $+CPF$ (especially $+S/A$ and $+L/A$).

Suppose that cash return on equity in our industry is customarily 20%, whereby we generate $200,000 a year on an equity base of $1,000,000. If we increase our equity to $1,250,000, our $200,000 of cash flow now provides a return on equity of only 16%. This decline means that our liquidity (cash-generating potential) has increased, because we still have the identical capability of generating our traditional CRE of 20%. On $1,250,000 of equity, our cash flow capability has now risen to $250,000 a year.

The additional equity supplies the additional liquidity and the additional cash flow via the SCALDER cash-productivity sources. For instance, we can now buy more fixed and current assets to support higher sales ($+S$). We can invest in cost-reducing equipment, or repay high-interest debt, and reduce costs ($-C$). We now have more equity (and cash flow) with which to support additional low-cost debt ($+L$). We can use the additional equity cash (and leverage) to finance a profitable acquisition ($+D$). We can direct the additional equity and leverage cash into maximum-return investments ($+R$). And so forth.

Our equity or ownership investment (E) is thus the underlying basis of SCALDER cash productivity, because it finances the asset (A) and cost (C) investments from which sales (S) are generated. The resulting cash flow supports leverage (L) and acquisitions (D), and the total stream of cash is channeled into maximum-profit reinvestments (R).

Exactly how it is all accomplished is of course the subject of this book, which tackles equity productivity in terms of all seven sources of cash. Each chapter, as we go forward, details fundamental SCALDER strategies for generating cash and earnings out of equity—for maximizing cash return on equity.

In fact, the entire strategy of cash is a continuing dynamic interaction between equity formation and equity productivity (or CRE), directed toward maximizing profits and growth. This is summarized in the comprehensive grand strategy of Pi, which we will talk about next.

CHAPTER 5

PI: THE GRAND STRATEGY OF CASH GENERATION

All that we have been saying about the purpose and function of business management can be compressed symbolically into the sixteenth letter of the Greek alphabet, pi.

Percentage increase of equity (PIE or simply Pi), again, is the rate at which the value of stockholders' equity increases over time. Pi is everything management is trying to do, and excludes everything management is not or should not be trying to do. Business enterprise exists to maximize stockholders' wealth. It can do this only by means of a total process of cash generation, whereby we maximize both the *quantity* (E) and the cash *productivity* (CRE) of equity.

We have seen how this process travels along an interconnected sequence of factors that create stockholders' wealth: equity formation, equity productivity (CRE), earnings per share, and the price-earnings ratio. But only the first two are truly determinative and causal; the latter are essentially derivative and dependent on them.

Pi summarizes the determinative or causal factors—equity formation and equity productivity. In so doing, it becomes the central and universally valid organizing concept and strategy of the profit-making business enterprise. Equity formation and CRE together multiply, in a compounding way, the production of internal and external cash. And cash is the only substance available to management for the production of still more cash. The process at its ultimate extension maximizes the derivative factors—net income per share and the price-earnings valuation of that net income. It thereby maximizes stockholders' wealth.

The concept of Pi brings us again to the elemental image and idea of the corporation as an investment portfolio, to be supervised solely in terms of its balance sheet. We run the company as investment managers of assets and liabilities, pure and simple. And we manage for *total performance*, rather than just for income on the one hand or growth of capital on the other.

This means our objective is always to maximize Pi, or the growth of stockholders' equity, not merely to maximize cash return on equity. We would not be doing our job well, for instance, if we maximized CRE but ignored external equity formation opportunities. And we might be doing our job very well if for a few years we seized some extraordinary equity formation opportunities at the sacrifice of all CRE dollars. *Both* equity formation and CRE are management's total-performance focus.

PI = CRE × ECO × ECA

Pi thus measures the cumulative impact of the interacting cash-generating forces—CRE and equity formation (which is ECO and ECA). It is summarized by the expression, $Pi = CRE \times ECO \times ECA$, within which all of business activity is contained.[1]

CRE in this expression is $(S/C \times S/A \times L/A)(R)$, as already discussed. Pi therefore actually describes three separate, though powerfully interacting, sources or *levels* of cash productivity:

1. $S/C \times S/A$: internal cash productivity.
2. $L/A(R)$: cash return on equity.
3. $ECO \times ECA$: Pi.

The first level or tier is internal cash productivity, or $S/C \times S/A$. It is derived from $-C + S - A$, of course, which are the only sources of internal cash available to operating management.

The second tier is externally generated leverage cash, or L/A. This cash is combined with the internal pool of CSA cash from level 1, and all of it is recirculated at maximum velocity and cash payback (R). Only then do we have all the elements of CRE.

Finally, the third tier of cash productivity is equity creation by public offerings and acquisitions. Here ECO and ECA combine and interact with cumulative impact on CRE, at the first two levels, to yield Pi.

---

[1]Again, expression means an entirely valid description of relationships that neither makes arithmetical claims nor needs to.

IMPLEMENTING PI: THE STRATEGY OF MAXIMUM CASH PRODUCTIVITY

A kind of deadly serious pencil scratching that involves all the elements of a comprehensive strategy of cash is illustrated in Table 1. In a sequence of only nine SCALDER strategies, traced by this not very farfetched example, we increase our company's value more than 1000%—from a market equity of $4,000,000 to $58,000,000.

This Cash Productivity Worksheet is useful both in choosing from among various alternative Pi courses of action and in evaluating past performance. The oversimplified situations depicted here are sometimes deliberately exaggerated to place in sharper focus particular cash-generating strategies. But the astonishing overall corporate growth performance is neither unrealistic nor beyond the reach of any competent management for whom the strategy of cash is central and all-embracing.

The table has nine columns sequenced from left to right in the order in which we normally generate cash and equity. Cash generated in the first three columns (sales and cost columns are not shown) provides retained cash flow (column 4) and cash return on equity (column 5).

Column 7 shows the buildup of equity per share from retained earnings and from ECO and ECA, and is therefore crucial to the entire Pi analysis. Column 9 contains Pi itself—the percentage increase in equity per share (from column 7). Equity rose from $2.50 at the start to $8.04 at the end, so that $Pi = 222\%$.

The sequence of Pi strategies over time is enumerated vertically at the left, on lines 1 to 12.

Line 1. Not shown in this table is that our imaginary company started with sales of $5,000,000 and total cash costs (including taxes) of $4,800,000. Thus retained cash flow (RCF) is $200,000 (column 4). On an equity of $2,500,000 (column 3), CRE is 8% (column 5). With 1,000,000 shares (column 6), equity is $2.50 a share and RCF is $2.00 (columns 7 and 8).

Throughout the example we assume that the company earns retained cash flow at the rate of 10% of total assets; taxes are at 50%; and net income is about 50% of retained cash flow.

Line 2. We launch our SCALDER strategies by generating cost cash ($-C$) of $50,000 and a net sales increase ($+S$) of $100,000. The two strategies together produce $75,000 after taxes (column 4).

Line 3. Now we produce asset cash ($-A$) of $1,000,000 (column 1) by speeding up inventory and receivable turnover, and liquidating some idle fixed assets and an unprofitable subsidiary.

Table 1 The Pi Strategy of Maximum Cash Productivity

SCALDER Strategy	Assets (000) 1	Debt (000) 2	Equity [(1) − (2)] (000) 3	Retained Cash Flow (RCF) (000) 4	CRE [(4) ÷ (3)] 5	Shares (000) 6	Per Share Equity [(3) ÷ (6)] 7	Per Share RCF [(4) ÷ (6)] 8	Pi [from (7)] 9
1. Starting position	$3,000	$500	$2,500	$200	8.0%	1,000	$2.50	$2.00	0%
2. − C of $50,000; + S of $100,000				75					
3. − A: $1,000,000 into cash	− 1,000 + 1,000								
4. CSA subtotal	3,000	500	2,500	275	11.0		2.50	2.75	
5. + R:									
(a) Retained earnings	137		137						
(b) $1,275,000 reinvested at 10%				127					
6. Reinvestment subtotal	3,137	500	2,637	402	15.2		2.64	4.02	6
7. + L: $4,000,000 loan at 7% Interest (after taxes)	4,000	4,000		(140)					
	7,137	4,500	2,637	262					

	(4,000)		(4,000)			100			
8. ECA: (a) We buy	6,500								
(b) Seller Corp.	5,500	1,000	5,500	300					
	9,637	5,500	4,137	562	13.6	1,100	3.76	5.11	50
9. +R: Seller at full profit				350					
10. +E: retained earnings	320		320						
	9,957	5,500	4,457	912	20.5		4.05	8.29	62
11. ECO: 200,000 shares at 30	6,000		6,000			200			
	15,957		10,457			1,300	8.04		222
12. +R: proceeds invested at 10%				600					
+L: borrow $5,000,000 at 7% ETC.	$15,957	$5,500	$10,457	$1,512	14.4%	1,300	$8.04	$11.63	222%

Line 4. After generating the foregoing internal cash from $+S/A$ and $+S/C$, retained cash flow (column 4), after taxes, has risen to $275,000, or $2.75 a share (column 8).

We still have the same $3,000,000 of assets (column 1). But now $1,000,000 of it is in the form of cash available for productive reinvestment, owing to the $-A$ strategy on line 3.

Line 5. (*a*) Net income was assumed to be one-half RCF. So we add half the $275,000 of RCF (column 4), or $137,000, to equity (column 3) and assets (column 1). (*b*) We now reinvest ($+R$) the $1,000,000 of asset cash (no capital gain taxes) and the $275,000 from retained cash flow (column 4). At our assumed return of 10%, this $1,275,000 adds $127,000 to RCF (column 4).

Line 6. CRE (column 5) and equity per share (column 7) have climbed, and RCF (column 8) is up to $4.02.

Line 7. We now borrow ($+L$) $4,000,000 at 7% subject to the acquisition of Seller Corp., on line 8. After-tax interest of 3.5%, or $140,000, is deducted from RCF (column 4).

Line 8. (*a*) The price of Seller Corp. is $5,000,000, consisting of $4,000,000 in cash (columns 1 and 3) and 100,000 shares of our stock at 10 (column 6). (*b*) Seller has assets of $6,500,000, debt of $1,000,000, and equity of $5,500,000 (columns 1, 2, and 3). Its RCF (column 4) is $300,000, or 4.6% of assets.

Thus Transaction ECA results: The acquisition by itself caused equity per share (column 7) to jump from $2.64 to $3.76, or $1.12 a share of ECA. This was only partly due to the discount from its $5,500,000 of equity at which Seller was purchased. ECA was mainly caused by the 100,000-share portion of our purchase price being valued at the market price of 10—and these shares had an equity value of only $2.64 (line 6, column 7).

Our equity price for Seller was thus $264,000 in stock plus the $4,000,000 in cash, or $4,264,000, for which we received equity of $5,500,000. So our equity gain was 29%. Even if Seller's equity had been no more than our purchase price (at market) of $5,000,000, our equity gain (ECA) over the $4,264,000 would still have been 17%.

Line 9. Because Seller's assets of $6,500,000 are producing cash at the rate of only 4.6%, or $300,000 a year, we launch a Liquidity ECA strategy. To develop its high liquidity potential, we launch an intensive cost reduction effort ($-C$), and a far-ranging redeployment of Seller's poorly utilized assets ($-A$). After a while they produce cash at the assumed rate of 10%, or $650,000 ($+R$).

We therefore add an additional $350,000 of RCF (column 4) to the $300,000 already included in this column when we acquired Seller (line 8).

Line 10. We now add $320,000 of retained earnings to equity (column 3) and assets (column 1), summarizing the previous generation of RCF (column 4): $127,000 from reinvesting $1,275,000 (line 5); less $140,000 of interest at 7% on the $4,000,000 loan (line 7); plus $650,000 of RCF from Seller; less 50%, retained earnings being half of RCF.

Equity per share (column 7) has therefore risen to $4.05. But the gain of $0.29 a share since the acquisition, from $3.76 to $4.05, was modest compared with the increase of $1.12 produced by the acquisition itself—in the form of Transaction ECA (or $3.76 less $2.64).

We should now take notice of the impact that all this cash productivity is having on market prices and stockholders' wealth, as follows:

Strategy	Price/RCF (given) 10	Price (10×8) 11	Stockholders' Wealth (Price × 1,000,000 shares) (000) 12
1. At the start	2×	4	$ 4,000
4. CSA subtotal	2	5 1/2	5,500
6. R subtotal	2.5	10	10,000
8. Buy Seller Corp.	3	15 3/8	15,400
10. Seller at full profit	4	33 1/8	33,100
12. Offering completed	5	58	58,000

In column 10 are the assumed ratios of market price to retained cash flow (RCF) at which the shares of the strenghtening company sell. Market prices (column 11) are computed by applying the ratios to RCF (column 8 of Table 1). Stockholders' wealth (column 12) is then simply the price multiplied by the 1,000,000 shares outstanding at the start of the exercise. This is the crucial end product of the comprehensive Pi strategy pursued throughout Table 1, to which we now return.

Line 11. Next comes ECO. The shares are trading at $33\frac{1}{8}$, now that RCF is at $8.29 (column 8) and the price/RCF ratio has risen to 4 (column 10).

So we offer 200,000 shares publicly at 30. This provides a fat $3.99 per share of ECO: $8.04 of equity after the offering, less $4.05 before (column 7). The reason, of course, is that the offering price of 30 was far above the previous equity of $4.05.

Line 12. This is the investment of our underwriting proceeds ($+R$). We continue with our modest assumption that the company can earn cash at

10% of total assets: The $6,000,000 from the offering provides us with $600,000 of additional RCF (column 4).

We now have a much larger equity base to support further leverage. So our next cash-generating strategy might be something on the order of a $5,000,000 private placement of debt securities. Or it might be an acquisition.

And so forth.

At the arbitrary stopping point on line 12, the company has many times its original equity (column 3). This soared from $2,500,000 at the start to about $10,500,000. Retained cash flow (column 4) rose from virtually nothing to an annual rate of $1,500,000.

Equity per share (column 7) more than tripled, from $2.50 to $8.04, most of it contributed by the $1.12 of ECA (line 8) and $3.99 of ECO (line 11). So Pi was ($8.04 − $2.50)/$2.50 = 222%.

Cash return on equity (column 5) fluctuated considerably. It dropped to 13.6% when Seller Corp. was acquired (line 8); rose to 20.5% as the acquisition became more profitable; and dropped to 14.4% after the public offering (line 12). Presumably it will go back to 20.5% or higher when the $5,000,000 of leverage cash (line 12) is put to work. And then we will be earning the high CRE with a much larger and stronger company.

The behavior of CRE was thus always a response to the particular strategy that provided the predominant cash-generating influence at each stage of the Worksheet. Cash return on equity was not an absolute target, an end in itself to be driven constantly higher at the sacrifice of all else. While it fluctuated, stockholders' wealth (column 12) multiplied from $4,000,000 at the start to $58,000,000. And so the purposes of the strategy of cash were admirably served.

Cash return on equity is thus a means to an end within the framework of a comprehensive Pi strategy. It is a relative objective that must be adapted constantly and opportunistically to the requirements of the ultimate objective, Pi. Total performance is what counts. We pursue any powerful strategy, even one that reduces CRE temporarily, that develops major cash-generating potentials for the future. If a sacrifice of CRE serves in its final effect to provide the essential upward impetus to stockholders' wealth, it serves the all-important purpose.

We now turn to the individual cash-producing strategies that implement Pi and generate wealth, starting with leverage cash productivity (+L).

PART 2

EXTERNAL CASH-PRODUCING
STRATEGIES FOR MAXIMIZING PROFITS

CHAPTER 6

GENERATING LEVERAGE CASH

We now have a working conceptual framework within which the cash-creating strategy of Pi can be employed to produce earnings, equity, and ownership wealth. It is a total-cash-management, or *cash system*, approach to the direction of a business for maximum profit.

The component SCALDER cash-generating strategies fit precisely into this systems framework and powerfully implement Pi. So we should examine each of them closely and in logical order. The present Part Two explores the external cash strategies of leverage (L), equity (E), and acquisitions (D). Parts Three and Four will cover sales cash (S) and cost cash (C), respectively. And Part Five will look at the asset cash strategies of asset productivity (A) and reinvestment (R).

Again, these discussions and the accompanying tables will be uniformly strategic, not tactical or operations oriented. Strategy is the lonely province and concern of upper-level management, for whom this book is primarily intended. A good strategist is one who has readily available, and knows exactly where and how to use, good tacticians. If this book ever has a Son of Strategy sequel, let it be something on the order of "The Tactics of Cash." But this is not that book, nor shall the twain meet.

LEVERAGE CASH AND THE MECHANICS OF PRIVATE PLACEMENT

We might as well discuss leverage cash first. It is what most managements think of first when confronted with the need to finance the business. In fact, it is often the only source of supplemental cash productivity that is ever even considered. That the company has not one but *seven* immensely productive sources of external and internal cash comes as a shock or a joke, depending on the prevailing mood.

Leverage cash for the typical company usually means long-term debt capital, such as an issue of convertible bonds or comparable securities sold directly to the lender. Placing our securities privately with one or a few institutional, individual, or corporate investors has some advantages over a public offering. It is generally quicker, easier, less expensive, and more confidential. Our investment banker or other financial guru can assist in some or all of the following six crucial steps:

1. *Research* our company and its prospects, and tailor the most effective long-term financing program for achieving our growth objectives.

2. *Design* the most effective financing instrument or package of securities to meet the company's present capital requirements. We are seeking the lowest cost and most favorable terms consistent with the risks and opportunities inherent in our business. A qualified investment banker is constantly in touch with the market for debt securities. And he has an intimate knowledge of domestic and foreign sources of capital of every variety. Knowing our special requirements and characteristics, he can expertly mesh the needs of borrower and lender to construct the most desirable financing arrangement available at that point in time.

3. *Present* the written financing proposal to the one or two sources of capital exactly suited to it. The report contains the proposed terms and conditions. And it is specifically prepared by the investment banker to answer the questions and meet the objections of the particular investor he will approach. Under this tight procedure, we can normally expect a purchase commitment for the entire issue to be received from the first investor—but certainly no more than the first two or three—to which it is offered.

4. *Negotiate* in our behalf with the prospective investor. Our investment banker tries to get the best interest rate and other provisions of the financing, as set forth in the written report. Again, his daily exposure to the money and capital market is extremely important in representing our best interests. And as a third party, he can be tough with the lender without risking ill will between the two principals.

5. *Assist* the investor, who has made a preliminary purchase commitment, to conclude the financing. He helps him to develop additional facts where needed, meet company personnel, draft the Note Agreement or other documents, and, most important, have a successful closing of the transaction.

6. *Follow up* the financing for both parties. The investment banker's role can prove crucial, for instance, when new requirements of our expanding business call for renegotiating certain provisions of the original agreement.

He keeps the lenders up to date on developments in the company and is always available for questions about its progress or problems.

Because of this vital follow-up service, most institutional and other professional investors prefer to receive financing proposals from an experienced financial intermediary such as an investment banker. They also depend on his screening of potential borrowers. And they benefit from the thorough investigation, information gathering, and other detailed and time-consuming preparation that he performs for them.

THE NATURE OF LEVERAGE CASH

The Pi strategy defines leverage as the cash supplied by all debt and equity securities senior to the ordinary voting common stock. *Any* limitation imposed on the risk, capital gain, income, or voting characteristics of common stock removes it from the common stock category and places it in the leverage category. It is now leverage *to* and for the benefit *of* the common stockholders.

This is because the common stockholder by definition shoulders the ultimate risks and enjoys the ultimate profit potential of the business enterprise. It is from him that the concept of Pi derives its existence and meaning. He is the owner for whom the strategy of cash is pursued. One is either that very special breed of cat known as a common stockholder, pure and simple, or he is not a common stockholder but a leverage investor.

The company's capital structure is a risk-reward continuum along which (above equity) are ranged the degrees of leverage. Pure debt at one end is powerful leverage. But the more a leverage security partakes of the essence of common stock, sharing its risks and rewards, the less leverage it provides *to* the common stock. The terms "leverage" and "debt" therefore have no necessary connection or relationship. A junior straight preferred stock might provide more leverage to the common stock than a fully secured debt security that is convertible into large quantities of the common.

A company could theoretically limp along with equity cash only, its return on equity being the same as return on total assets. But leverage cash can mightily increase return on equity, as we have seen. Using a long pole as a lever and a rock as a pivot or support, a farm boy can lift a barn off its foundations. The longer his pole and the more inflexible it is, the more upward power he exerts under the barn.

The more leverage cash we employ to supplement equity cash, *and* the more it partakes of pure and inflexible leverage characteristics, the more powerful is its upward thrust to return on equity. Pure and inflexible leverage securities do not dilute the common shares or undermine earnings, by claiming either some of those shares or some of their earnings.

We can push the boy-barn analogy a bit further. Too long and inflexible a pole of financial leverage may break, and our corporate barn comes crashing down. For the boy and for our business, leverage enhances both reward and risk. We might even *define* leverage as the augmenting of equity risk: to the precise extent that we contractually shelter a leverage security from the perils of the business, we increase the risk exposure of the common stockholders.

At any point in time, that is, all the security holders together are exposed to a given quantum of total risk. What the leverage security holders gain in the form of guarantees to income and capital, the common stockholder obviously has granted and has given up. If there is too much leverage capital that enjoys many kinds and degrees of safety provisions granted by the common stockholder, the financial structure has become overextended by definition. Cash may become insufficient to service debt, and the structure cracks in the same way that the boy's overextended pole cracks.

THE CRUCIAL INGREDIENTS OF DEBT CAPACITY

Long-term and relatively low-cost leverage capital is the great energizer and perhaps even the basic life force of the profitable and growing company. Our ability to attract external cash on favorable terms ($+L/A$) is no less important to CRE and the success of the company than is our ability to generate internal cash flow ($+S/C$ and $+S/A$). So we must at all times know the effective outer limit of our company's borrowing power, and not finance much above or below it. This is all we mean by debt capacity.

It involves two unrelated questions: How much debt *can* we attract, to maximize return on equity? And how much debt *should* we attract to keep us safely away from the shoals of insolvency? The questions are unrelated because, by mortgaging everything in sight, we usually can attract far more debt capital than we *should* attract.

Three crucial debt capacity ingredients set the outer limit of our ability to borrow prudently: *retained cash flow* ($+S/C$), *asset cash productivity* ($+S/A$), and *equity* (E), in that order of importance.

Let us first dispose of the sacred equity chestnut, or debt/equity. To the extent that debt exceeds equity, creditors have more money at risk in the business than do the owners. But so does the neighborhood bank, which has more money at stake in a mortgaged house than does the owner. Debt/equity is a theoretical or philosophical limitation rather than a practical one. Our debt could exceed equity by a substantial margin and still be well covered by liquid assets. And meanwhile operating cash easily services the interest and amortization requirements. Or we can go broke trying to service a debt load of only half our equity, because we simply do not have enough cash flow.

Nevertheless, our creditors may indeed be philosophically (or perhaps legally) reluctant to invest *much* more heavily than their equity friends, despite the adequacy of cash flow. If so, rightly or wrongly, the extreme debt/equity ratio by itself is an effective borrowing constraint.

But within the far-out debt/equity limit, the crucial ingredient of debt capacity is *cash flow*, closely supported by *asset cash productivity*. We can best discuss them in that order.

In its broadest sense, cash-flow debt capacity is really the total liquidity or *cash availability* of our company. We have the *seven* sources of cash with which to support debt, not just operating cash flow: underutilized borrowing power, public offerings of equity, cash-generating acquisitions, underexploited sales cash potentials, excessive costs to be cut, excessive assets to be liquidated, and neglected reinvestment sources of cash.

But there are four objections to the common practice, conscious or not, of relying on total cash availability as a supporter of debt. First, debt capacity is a depression concept: what is the *least* amount of cash that we will have available for debt service, under the worst possible business conditions? In a severe economic collapse, practically all our cash-availability sources might be made fully productive only after damaging delays, or they could dry up entirely.

The second objection is that, in relying on high corporate liquidity to help support debt, we depend too heavily on one-shot solutions. Many SCALDER sources of excessive liquidity, such as $+L$ or $-A$, will no longer be excessive after they are tapped to support borrowings. They would not provide the continuing flow of debt service cash on which solvency depends.

The third objection is that of prudence. It is chancy to base debt capacity on anything other than the *known* quantity of minimum expectable operating cash flow. This may be too conservative, since there is always *some* excess liquidity to draw upon in a pinch. If so, it might best be thought of as a cushion or margin of safety for debt, in the never ending guessing game about the level to which cash flow will shrink during a long recession or depression.

And finally, there is the profitability objection to maintaining an excessive liquidity potential. This concerns the opportunity cost of not putting it to work productively, which goes to the heart of the strategy of cash. CRE is obviously diminished to the extent that the seven sources of corporate cash are not tapped and reinvested as promptly as possible and at maximum cash return. When we try to justify excessive debt on the grounds that we will have plenty of fat to trim (liquidity to utilize) if cash gets tight, the debt has become prohibitively expensive without our knowing it.

FORECASTING CASH FLOW DEBT CAPACITY

We therefore get back to the hard-core source and substance of debt capacity, which is operating cash flow. This had best be a recession forecast of *total pretax cash flow coverage of total fixed charges*. What is our minimum foreseeable cash flow under the least favorable economic and industry conditions? The answer gives us our debt capacity—our maximum safe level of fixed financing outlays in the form of interest, amortization and rent.

Table 2 presents a five-year debt-capacity computation. It is one way of determining the cash-flow limits of our borrowing power.

Line 4. Pretax cash flow coverage is our cash available before taxes to service all debt charges. It is the total of pretax net income (line 1), noncash charges such as depreciation (line 2), *and* the amount we will pay in interest and financial rent (line 3). This is the rent on all asset and other productive lease commitments (financial leases) that are alternatives to debt financing. It is equivalent to interest and amortization payments.

Line 5. Permissible debt charges, management has ruled, are no more than 50% of pretax cash flow coverage of those charges (line 4). That is, cash flow must cover fixed charges at least two times.

Line 8. Total debt charges are the sum of interest and rent (line 6), and principal repayments multiplied by 2 (line 7). That is, we must provide before taxes (at the 50% rate) *twice* the amount of cash needed for amortization, which is a nondeductible after-tax use of cash.

Line 9. The debt capacity ratio is our permissible debt charges (line 5)—at 50% of cash flow—divided by actual debt charges (line 8). When it is above 100%, we have extra borrowing power—permissible charges exceed actual charges. The ratio increases as cash flow and permissible charges rise in relation to actual charges. It declines when actual charges (line 8) rise in relation to cash flow and permissible charges (line 5).

Line 11. Debt capacity, therefore, is found by applying the debt capacity ratio (line 9) of permissible-to-actual charges, to our present debt (line 10). In year 1, for instance, we apply the 193% ratio to our $800,000 of present debt (line 10) to obtain debt capacity of $1,540,000 (line 11). We have substantial unused borrowing power, even though our debt/equity ratio (line 18) is at 95%.

The debt capacity ratio (line 9) declined steadily from 193% to 131% in year 5: As we increased our debt load (line 13), actual debt charges (line 8) rose more steeply than permissible debt charges (line 5). So excess debt capacity was gradually used up.

The debt/equity ratio (line 18) increased sharply to 150% in year 5, but was not in itself symptomatic of a problem. That is, cash flow debt capacity in year 5 was $2,800,000 (line 11), which still exceeded our debt outstanding (line 13) of $2,630,000.

Lease financing, as noted, is a vital ingredient of cash-flow debt capacity and utilization. It is merely a debt substitute, and must always be treated as such. We kid ourselves if we imagine it makes any difference to our creditors whether we buy the new plant with debt financing or rent it with lease financing. Rental payments over the life of the lease commitment typically exceed the interest and amortization payments on an equivalent loan. The lease uses up at least as much debt capacity as the loan: we are borrowing the asset rather than the money to buy the asset.

Our creditors treat lease-financing rent as the equivalent of interest and amortization, as noted on line 6 of Table 2. We must obviously do the same. Always being "in the shoes of our creditors" is a rule we must not break if a sound relationship is to exist. When creditors—or suppliers, customers, big stockholders—analyze our balance sheet, they capitalize rent. This they do at a risk rate such as the current market yield for the company's debentures. They add the capitalized amount to both sides of the balance sheet, as debt and as an asset. Suppose that our financial rents are $100,000 a year and our borrowing rate is 8%. They add $100,000/0.08, or $1,250,000, both to our debt and our assets before calculating our debt-capacity and liquidity ratios.

When a lease expires, unlike with ownership, we are left without residual asset value. On the other hand, leasing frees our capital for purposes that may (or may not) be more productive than fixed assets. And the rent payments are tax deductible, as is the interest on debt but not the amortization.

To decide whether to lease the asset or buy it against a loan, we compare both arrangements over their lives as to *total after-tax cost.* Rent after taxes, under a lease, is compared to after-tax interest *less* the tax savings

Table 2 Forecasting Leverage Cash Availability

Line		Year (000)					Explanation
	1	2	3	4	5		
Cash Flow							
1. Pretax net income	$300	$340	$400	$460	$520		Given
2. + Depreciation, etc.	100	120	130	150	180		Given
3. + Interest, rent, etc.	32	38	52	68	85		50% of present debt, line 10, assumed to be interest bearing, at 8%
4. Pretax cash flow coverage of debt charges	432	498	582	678	785		Sum of lines 1–3
5. Permissible debt charges	216	249	291	339	392		50% of cash flow coverage, line 4, assumed
Debt Charges							
6. Interest, rent, etc.	32	38	52	68	85		Line 3
7. + Principal repayment ×2	80	95	130	170	213		50% of present debt, line 10, amortizable at 10% annually (×2=pretax requirement)

8. Total debt charges	112	133	182	238	298	Sum of lines 6 and 7
9. Debt capacity ratio	193%	187%	160%	142%	131%	Line 5/line 8
10. Present debt	800	950	1,300	1,700	2,130	Add line 12 each year
11. Debt capacity	1,540	1,790	2,080	2,420	2,800	Line 10 × line 9
12. Increase (decrease) in debt	150	350	400	430	500	Given
13. Debt outstanding	950	1,300	1,700	2,130	2,630	Line 10 + line 12
14. Equity	1,000	1,150	1,320	1,520	1,750	Increased by 50% of pretax net income, line 1
15. Sales	4,300	4,900	5,700	6,500	7,500	Given
16. Debt/sales	22.1%	26.5%	29.8%	32.8%	35.1%	Line 13/line 15
17. Debt capacity/sales	35.8%	36.5%	36.5%	37.2%	37.3%	Line 11/line 15
18. Debt/equity ratio	95%	113%	129%	140%	150%	Line 13/line 14

from depreciation of the asset. Over its life, and considering its discounted or scrap residual value, either renting or owning will require the higher cash outlay.

THE CONSTRAINTS AND HAZARDS OF DEBT/SALES

If cash flow is the primary and crucial ingredient of debt capacity, *asset cash productivity* runs a close and indispensible second. As we will see in Chapter 17, asset cash ($+S/A$) is generated when sales grow at a higher rate than does our investment in assets. The debt required to finance the assets is thereby controlled, in relation to sales ($-L/S$). But when assets grow faster than sales ($-S/A$), debt financing of the assets climbs disproportionately to sales ($+L/S$).

So asset cash productivity is measured by and reflected in the ratio *debt/sales*: When S/A is rising, debt/sales will be under good control; when S/A is declining, debt/sales will climb.

Returning to Table 2, on *line 16*: The debt/sales ratio moved up sharply from 22.1% to 35.1% during the five years, as the excess cash-flow debt capacity was absorbed by additional borrowings.

Line 17. Still, debt/sales never exceeded debt capacity/sales, which remained high and steady at around 36 to 37%. Against this background of substantial cash-flow debt capacity, there may be no harm in a rising debt/sales ratio.

However, what if the debt capacity ratio of permissible to total charges (line 9) is favorable—indicating available borrowing power—but the debt/sales ratio has already climbed to excessive levels? We are then being warned that profit margins are narrowing and are in further danger, promising severe impairment to *future* cash-flow debt capacity.

That is, assets and therefore debt are rising too rapidly in support of increasing sales. This produces a double-barreled increase in costs: both higher interest and (nondeductible) amortization charges on the mounting debt, *and* higher asset-carrying charges. Cash-flow debt capacity, now giving a favorable reading, is in for trouble at the same time that our debt burden is rising. The company is due for a financial squeeze from opposite directions at once: rising debt and a declining capacity to carry it.

The danger is that debt/sales has an arithmetic upward bias on the balance sheet. As the asset side expands in support of higher sales volume, cash to finance the assets comes from the liability and equity side. But equity is relatively fixed and inelastic, rarely augmented by anything other

than some retained earnings. And on the asset side, accumulated depreciation usually has all it can do to maintain existing asset levels, let alone
finance asset expansion.

The financing of net asset growth therefore tends to be drawn largely
from the *debt* portion of the balance sheet. So debt grows at a higher rate
than assets, and becomes oversized and lopsided if not actually dangerous.

Asset growth thus tends to produce a disproportionately large increase
in debt/sales, with unfavorable or even dangerous profit and liquidity-
impairing implications. This may be alleviated or forestalled if and when
the asset investments produce the sales and profit growth for which they
were undertaken. But by then the company probably needs another
massive installation of assets and debt to support its next plateau of
anticipated sales volume.

Its soaring debt/sales ratio narrows the profit *margin*, but not necessarily profits, which may well continue to rise as sales rise, but at a
slower pace. And return on equity probably also continues to rise for a
while. Cash-flow debt capacity was never higher. It is as deceptive as it is
euphoric, because it has a malignant underpinning in the worsening
debt/sales condition. Rising debt and declining debt capacity are now or
soon will be on collision course.

A difficult but solid and durable solution—detailed in Chapter 17 on the
generation of asset cash—is a total managerial devotion to asset control. In
a word, $+S/A$ neutralizes $+L/S$. We neutralize or reduce debt/sales by
increasing sales/assets, as will be demonstrated. The control of assets,
which would otherwise have absorbed debt cash, averts the potential
liquidity and profit-strangulating dangers inherent in sales growth.

LEVERAGE AND RISK

There are also vital *cyclical* considerations in the evaluation of debt limits
and debt capacity. If there is a rule here, it must certainly be that at peaks
in the business cycle, we should replace debt capital with equity capital.
Nothing could be simpler in theory and more difficult in practice. Soaring
stock prices anticipate such a decision-making point in time. They provide
cheap equity money and the maximum amount of ECO (equity created by
offerings), together with a blessed opportunity to eliminate excessive and
high-interest debt.

No other aspect of the strategy of cash could be more obvious and more
compelling—the right thing to do without question or hesitation. Yet the
majority of otherwise intelligently managed companies not only fail to do
this, but choose these very heights to *expand* their business risks and debt

load. There will never be an answer to this profoundest of mysteries in the entire field of corporate finance. Its solution would prevent what is certainly the largest single cause of financial calamity.

The Pi strategy of maximum cash productivity obviously does not advocate risking our solvency by the excessive generation of debt cash (L/A). On the contrary, it is inherently countercyclical, requiring a precautionary contraction of debt when the economy has been strong and is overheating. And it dictates an expansion of leverage following a period of depressed general business conditions. By whatever methods a sophisticated management (or its economic counsel) assesses its cyclical business risks and opportunities, it must obviously make a corresponding countercyclical adjustment of its debt.

Maximizing return on equity, again, is thus not an absolute. It is *risk related*: for any company, the maximum CRE to shoot for is $X\%$ at one stage or level of the business cycle, and $Y\%$ at a different stage. It means that we must realistically contemplate maximizing our return over the course of a *full* business-risk cycle, spanning the best and worst economic conditions. Our preoccupation, always and everywhere, is with *long-term* cash return on equity.

Apart from cyclical risks, leverage cash should be generated or not depending on our effective *cost* of borrowing money in relation to our anticipated return on equity. Interest rates may become too high for the available equity returns, which increases the hazards of borrowing. Underutilization of debt capacity would then be entirely consistent with the overall strategy of maximum cash productivity.

We are now tilting the barn with a long and sturdy lever—generating leverage cash. It is one of our most lucrative and most hazardous sources of profits and growth. To boost the profits and lessen the risk to which leverage exposes us, we must know well (and manipulate skillfully) our cash-flow debt capacity. And we must keep our eyes glued to debt/sales and to the current risk implications of the business cycle. This in a nutshell is leverage cash productivity.

Equity is the second major area of external cash generation, to which we can now turn our attention.

CHAPTER 7

GENERATING EQUITY CASH

A public offering of our stock is both a major source of equity formation, or ECO, and a major source of equity cash. On both counts it is comparable to equity created by acquisitions, or ECA.

As a source of ECO (equity created by offerings) the offering is analogous to Transaction ECA, in that equity per share is created by the transaction itself: the public price is higher than our equity per share. As a source of equity *cash* the offering is analogous to Liquidity ECA: we must first have possession of the cash, as we must of the acquired company's liquidity, to put it to work and create additional earnings and equity.

We have seen that maximum ECO (and ECA) is achieved when three strategic conditions are met. (1) Total assets are at a maximum, in the sense that the company is fully leveraged ($+L/A$). (2) These fully leveraged assets are earning a maximum return, so that CRE and earnings per share are being maximized ($+S/C$ and $+S/A$). (3) The price-earnings ratio is at a maximum. This presumably follows several years of upward-trending earnings per share in an improving general market environment.

In short, we have maximized the cash-generating and wealth-creating potential of our causal sequence: it proceeds from CRE (or $S/C \times S/A \times L/A$), to earnings per share, to price-earnings ratio, to stockholders' wealth. If our company now offers the largest possible amount of new stock at these maximum price levels, either publicly or for another company, equity per share will increase by the largest amount.

Thus maximum cash return on equity maximizes stockholders' wealth, which maximizes the gain in stockholders' equity via ECO or ECA. And since equity is the all-important substance for generating cash (from the SCALDER sources), we are back to CRE; and the circle is closed.

In this way the process of equity formation describes an orbiting course of cumulative and self-reinforcing cash generation—from CRE to stockholders' wealth, to ECO and ECA, and back to CRE. Round and round, and the impact on corporate profits and growth can be prodigious indeed.

THE RATIONALE OF EQUITY CREATION

ECO and ECA are thus identical methods of creating equity instantaneously. In ECO (equity created by offerings), we issue stock to public investors for cash. In ECA (equity created by acquisition), we issue the stock to shareholders of the acquired company in exchange for shares (or assets) of their company, rather than for cash. In both cases, the equity value we receive in the form of cash or stock is higher than the equity per share of the stock we offer. So by developing substantial CRE, and establishing a receptive public market and high price/equity ratio for our stock, we have placed our company in a very strong position to create equity.

The reason ECO and ECA "work" to create equity, as we have noted, is that public security buyers concentrate on current and prospective earnings, dividends, and market price. They virtually ignore equity per share, which in the typical public offering or merger is only a fraction of the offering or exchange price. In an acquisition, particularly, sellers are unconcerned about equity. They want to exchange their stock for the buyer's stock if it benefits them in two ways: (1) its current *market value* is more than that of the shares they surrender and (2) its dividend *income* exceeds the income they now get from their shares.

So the typical seller experiences a dilution of equity in the merger transaction. And the stockholder of the company *offering* shares in an underwriting or merger experiences a corresponding enhancement of his equity per share. This is simply an observable fact, repeated endlessly.

It may or may not be bad for the public sellers of a company thus to relinquish equity value in exchange for a small immediate gain in price and dividends. Their future really depends on the extent to which they participate as stockholders in the capitalization of the combined companies, and the extent to which the companies achieve success together. The success could be considerable if the buyer manages its newly acquired equity as aggressively as it makes acquisitions.

On the other hand, the buyer grants a small premium in price and income to the sellers in exchange for a large gain in an extraordinarily valuable growth asset, equity per share. Its cumulative cash-producing wallop in the form of $+S-C-A+L+D+E+R$ is almost certain to outweigh many times the modest premium granted the sellers.

GENERATING LICO CASH: LEVERAGE IN, CASH OUT

The LICO strategy of "leveraging in" and "cashing out" is grounded in the first of our three conditions for maximizing ECO and ECA—that of maximizing leverage ($+L/A$). But it is an entirely separate strategy, and in itself is highly productive of cash and equity. That is, LICO can be productive even if it has no support whatsoever from the other two conditions—high return on equity and high price-earnings ratio.

The strategic precondition of LICO is the initial absence of leverage. Our company or one we acquire must have a very low debt/equity ratio, or other evidence of high debt capacity. Such an acquisition is often made cheaply because earnings and CRE are depressed by the poor utilization of borrowing power. But though a bargain purchase is always helpful to a buyer, the unique source of LICO's cash-generating impact is simply the initial low level of debt.

We then proceed to "leverage in" by building up debt to the maximum sustainable level. Finally, we "cash out" by selling the company outright or offering its shares publicly. LICO cash will have been generated solely by the leverage that we incurred.

That is, the buyer will pay us a price for the company or its shares based on *earnings*. He is not really concerned with equity and certainly is not influenced by the debt/equity ratio (unless there is real financial strain). So he will pay us about the same price-to-earnings whether our company has debt or not. He ignores and therefore *pays for* our debt. So we might as well sell him the company *with* debt—that we incurred as owners and whose cash we ben•fited from.

Just how we benefit from that debt should become clear in the following two examples of LICO cash productivity, one a public company and the other private. The public company is illustrated in Table 3, in which large quantities of cash are produced *solely* from the LICO effect. It occurs over a five-year period, during all of which we have 100,000 shares outstanding and the earnings rate remains fixed at 5% *of total assets.*

Year 1. Our debt/equity ratio (column 5) is a minimal 20%, satisfying the solitary LICO requirement. On $1,200,000 of assets (column 1), we earn $60,000 (column 4), or $0.60 a share (column 6). The stock of this sluggish outfit is selling at a moderate price-earnings ratio of 11×, or around 6⅝ (columns 9 and 10). And it is at a deep discount of 66% (column 11) from its $10 equity per share (column 7).

The LICO cash potential is negative (column 12): any "cashing out" or sale of stock at the current price would not be at a premium over stockholders' equity.

Year 3. By now we have expanded our debt from $200,000 to $1,200,000 (column 2), where it is 100% of equity (column 5). So total assets have doubled to $2,400,000 (column 1). At our constant 5% return on assets, earnings doubled to $120,000 (column 4). And return on equity jumped from 6 to 10% (column 8).

Table 3   Generating LICO Cash

	Assets (000) 1	Debt (000) 2	Equity (000) 3	Earnings (at 5% of Assets) (000) 4	Debt/ Equity 5	Per Share (100,000 shares)	
						Earnings 6	Equity 7
Year 1	$1200	$200	$1000	$ 60	20%	$0.60	$10
Year 3	2400	1200	1200	120	100	1.20	12
Year 5	6000	4000	2000	300	200	3.00	20

Our stock now begins to reflect the doubling of earnings from $0.60 to $1.20 a share (column 6): its price-earnings ratio climbs from 11× to 14× (column 9), and the price reaches 16¾ (column 10).

That is, as always, the market is not sophisticated, perceptive, thorough, or fair in assigning prices to shares. Our price-earnings ratio increased even though the higher earnings resulted solely from the higher leverage. Except to offset the higher interest charges, we demonstrated no ability whatsoever to generate higher earnings from assets—their return having held to a low 5%.

And, illogically, the market is now paying more for earnings that are riskier, in that the debt/equity ratio has jumped to 100% (column 5). Equity prices, again, slavishly reflect *earnings*, to the exclusion of virtually everything else, including the real reasons for the earnings improvement. And we must act accordingly in formulating and executing cash-generating strategies.

The price/equity ratio (column 11) has now risen from 66 to 140%. So our potential cash productivity from the LICO effect is 40% (column 12). This is simply the price (column 10) over equity (column 7), or 16¾ divided by $12. It means that potential LICO cash is 40% of equity.

For instance, if the company now sold or exchanged 50,000 shares, which has an equity value of 12, it would give up $600,000 of equity value. But it receives 16¾, or a 40% LICO premium. LICO cash productivity is therefore 40% of $600,000, or $240,000. This amount is the $840,000 proceeds of the offering at 16¾, less $600,000 of equity relinquished. Solely because of leverage, therefore, the company is able to generate LICO cash of $240,000.

Year 5. Equity (column 3) has ·grown to $2,000,000 from retained earnings. We have borrowed even more heavily (column 2), and debt/

Table 3 (*Continued*)

| | | | | | Price-Earnings at 11× | | |
| Return on Equity [(4)÷(3)] | Price-Earnings Ratio | Price | Price/ Equity [(10)÷(7)] | LICO Cash Effect [(11)−100%] | Price | Price/ Equity | LICO Cash Effect [(14)−100%] |
8	9	10	11	12	13	14	15
6%	11×	6⅝	66%	Negative	6⅝	66%	Negative
10	14	16¾	140	40%	13¼	110	10%
15	20	60	300	200	33	165	65

equity (column 5) has soared to 200%. Earnings have responded by jumping to $3.00 a share (column 6), *solely* because of the leverage. That is, the leverage-financed total assets are still earning only a modest 5%. Management has shown a remarkable ineptitude in everything but borrowing money.

Futhermore, earnings of $3.00 a share (column 6) are now five times higher than in year 1. We are an authentic growth company, and the stock duly trades at 20 times earnings (column 9), or at *60* (column 10).

With a price/equity ratio of 300% (column 11), the LICO cash effect is the net increase over equity of 200%. Say that we now sell 50,000 shares with an equity of 20, or $1,000,000. LICO cash productivity would be 200% of the $1,000,000, or $2,000,000. In other words, the company sold 50,000 shares at 60, or $3,000,000 of stock, with an equity value of $1,000,000. So $2,000,000 had to originate from something or someplace.

Under the controlled laboratory conditions of our example, the $2,000,000 was produced solely by the LICO effect: we heavily leveraged our narrow equity base to create $2,000,000 of additional value that the market, in its uncomplicated appetite for earnings, gladly paid for and thereby "monetized" for us. It turned the LICO premium into *cash*. The company had leveraged in and cashed out. If management now becomes as skillful in generating earnings from assets, the new owners of the 50,000 shares will be well rewarded indeed.

We can isolate the LICO cash effect even more rigorously, to test it further. In columns 13 to 15, we hold constant the 5% return on total assets, as before. But we also unreasonably assume a constant price-earnings ratio for the five years of soaring earnings. It remains at 11×, instead of rising to 20× as in the previous discussion. The only effect on price must therefore be the growth of debt (column 2).

Nevertheless, our price soars from $6\frac{5}{8}$ to 33 (column 13). And the "pure" LICO cash effect in year 5 is 65% (column 15), or $33/20 - 100\%$. Now the company sells 50,000 shares at 33, whose equity at $20 amounts to $1,000,000. At 65%, our isolated and uninfluenced LICO cash productivity is $650,000.

EQUITY CASH IN PRIVATE TRANSACTIONS

The cash impact of the LICO effect is no less potent in *private*-company transactions. For instance, we have completed negotiations to acquire *Seller Corp.* for 10 times earnings of $50,000 a year, or for $500,000:

	Assets (000)	Liabilities (000)	Equity (000)
1. Buyer Corp. (us)	$100	$ 0	$100
2. Borrows $400,000	400	400	
3. Buyer Corp.	500	400	100
4. Acquires Seller Corp.	1000	200	800
5. For $500,000	(500)		(500)
6. B-S Inc.	$1000	$600	$400
7. Sell B-S Inc.	(1000)	(600)	(400)
8. For $500,000	500		500
9. Us	$500	$ 0	$500

Line 1. We form *Buyer Corp.* and take all its stock for $100,000 in cash.

Line 2. Then we have Buyer borrow $400,000, amply secured by Seller's $800,000 equity (line 4).

Line 3. This loan and our original $100,000 gives Buyer (us) $500,000 in cash to buy Seller.

Line 4. Seller is almost debt-free, which satisfies the sole condition of LICO—minimal initial debt.

Line 5. With its $500,000, Buyer acquires Seller.

We call the combined company *B-S Inc.*, but it is really Seller Corp. plus $400,000 of new debt and minus $400,000 of equity:

Line	Assets (000)	Liabilities (000)	Equity (000)
4. Original Seller Corp.	$1000	$200	$800
6. B-S Inc.	1000	600	400
Difference	$ 0	+$400	−$400

Two years go by. Conglomerator Industries offers to buy B-S Inc. (which is Seller Corp.) from us for 10 times earnings of $50,000, or for exactly our original price of $500,000. Having been unable to increase earnings in two years, we decide to sell.

But instead of breaking even on the transaction, we realize a pretax cash profit of $400,000—directly and solely from the LICO effect: We had originally "leveraged in" on an equity of only $100,000 (line 1), and "cashed out" for $500,000 (line 8). Earnings-oriented Conglomerator paid for our $400,000 debt, which produced the LICO effect and our profit on the transaction.

Our price/equity was $500,000/$100,000. So LICO cash productivity was 400%, the percentage by which the price exceeded the equity. The equity value of our $500,000 selling price having been $100,000, 400% of $100,000 is LICO cash productivity of *$400,000.*

The LICO principle is therefore as forcefully demonstrated in private companies as in public companies. Cash generated from LICO is simply the price we receive over and above the equity, which premium is caused solely by the leverage we introduced in the first place. The identical principle would apply, of course, if we had sold publicly *shares* of B-S Inc., rather than the entire company outright. LICO cash productivity would have been 400% of the equity value of any shares sold.

Let us reduce the LICO effect to a convenient formula, and apply it to our earlier public company example. In year 5 we sold 50,000 shares whose equity per share was $20, for a price of 60:

$$LICO = (price/equity - 100)(shares\ sold \times equity)$$

$$= (60/20 - 100)\ (50,000 \times 20)$$

$$= (200\%)\ (\$1,000,000)$$

$$= \$2,000,000$$

This was our LICO cash productivity from the sale of 50,000 shares. Again, LICO "works" and occurs constantly in public and private transactions because purchasers are concerned with earnings and price. They look at the income statement, not at the balance sheet. If a buyer does happen to look at the balance sheet and equity value, he is most unlikely to be concerned with the debt/equity ratio. Yet two companies may each have an equity of $2,000,000, but the debt of one is $500,000 and the debt of the other is $3,000,000.

It is in these very balance-sheet magnitudes where equity formation and the cash-generating force of LICO are discerned, and where they "work" to produce so decisive an impact within the overall strategy of cash.

We are now ready to move on to the generation of acquisition cash, which is really another—and very potent—aspect or expression of equity formation.

CHAPTER 8

GENERATING ACQUISITION CASH

The acquisition strategy $(+D)$ is an especially prolific supplier of cash because it combines all the cash-generating strategies into one. In the sequence that they normally occur during and after the purchase, these strategies are: (1) Transaction ECA $(+E)$; (2) Liquidity ECA $(-C, -A, +S, \text{ and } +R)$; (3) Leverage $(+L)$; (4) ECO $(+E)$; and (5) LICO $(+E)$. Let us look at them in that order.

GENERATING TRANSACTION ECA

Transaction ECA (equity created by acquisition), as we have seen, provides the initial and automatic increase in our equity per share at the time of the acquisition. It soon blends into Liquidity ECA as the newly acquired equity is made to produce cash via the SCALDER sources.

Transaction ECA is functionally independent of the nature or type of company being acquired. It creates equity per share only because of the way we constructed the securities package offered to the selling stockholders, whereby we receive more equity than we give up.

Even the price we pay is largely irrelevant. We can in fact *overpay* outlandishly for a company and still generate substantial equity. Suppose that Corporation Q has assets of $2,000,000 and debt of $1,000,000, as shown on line 1 of the accompanying table.

Line 2. We buy Seller Corp., with assets of $3,000,000 and debt of $1,000,000.

Line 3. Ours is a fast-growing company with an active market for its stock at around 20. Seller Corp. is only breaking even. So it accepts a price equal to its equity of $2,000,000, payable in 100,000 shares of our stock at 20.

Corporation Q

	Assets (000)	Debt (000)	Equity (000)	Shares (000)	Equity per Share	Equity Value of 500,000 Shares (000)	ECA	Debt/Equity
1. We	$2000	$1000	$1000	500	$2.00	$1000	—	100%
2. Buy Seller Corp.	3000	1000	2000					
3. For $2000 in stock at 20				100				
4. Combined company	$5000	$2000	$3000	600	$5.00	$2500	+150%	67%
5. For $1500 (+75 shares)				575	5.22	2610	+161	
6. For $2500 (+125 shares)				625	4.80	2400	+140	

Line 4. Our equity had been $1,000,000/500,000 shares, or $2 a share (line 1). But the acquisition of Seller's $2,000,000 of equity for 100,000 shares increases our equity to $3,000,000/600,000 shares, or to $5 a share. Therefore the equity value of our original 500,000 shares increases from $1,000,000 (at $2) to $2,500,000 (at $5), or by 150%.

Equity created by acquisition (ECA) did not depend on anything in the nature or makeup of Seller Corp., but rather on the relationship of *our* market price of 20 to *our* equity per share of $2.

Line 5. Nor was the *price* much of an influence on ECA. Had we paid Seller Corp. as little as 75,000 shares, or only $1,500,000 at 20, the equity formation would have been 161%. That is, $3,000,000/575,000 shares = $5.22, which is a gain of 161% over our original equity of $2. And if we had increased the price to 125,000 shares, or to $2,500,000 (line 6), ECA would still have been a substantial 140%.

Each of the three alternative prices for Seller would have given us a large infusion of equity. The enormous price range of $1,500,000 to $2,500,000 did not matter too much.

There were other reasons for accepting the acquisition (on price alone) even if it *were* $2,500,000, and ECA 140%: Before the transaction (line 1), our debt was 100% of the $1,000,000 equity. Afterwards (line 4), debt of $2,000,000 was only 67% of the $3,000,000 equity. So if we borrowed up to 100% of the new equity, $1,000,000 of additional or secondary leverage cash ($+L$) would be generated.

But underutilized borrowing capacity is only one part of Seller's liquidity potential. It also might have substantial cash availability in the form of nonproductive and underutilized assets or excessive costs. This takes us from Transaction ECA to Liquidity ECA.

GENERATING LIQUIDITY ECA

Transaction ECA is the raw and unexploited equity per share we acquire when we absorb the merged company. Liquidity ECA is what we do with this equity. The more liquidity in the acquired company, and the less we pay for it in the purchase price, the more Liquidity ECA we will derive from the acquisition. But since the purchase price tends to be low when liquidity is high—because then earnings are depressed—we have a double-barreled reason for seeking out high-liquidity companies.

A sluggish, depressed, sleepy, or even sick company can provide the liquidity-oriented buyer with extraordinary opportunities to improve things and generate cash. And it is on the bargain counter. We have seen how such high-liquidity candidates offer cash availability from all seven sources:

1. *Leverage* cash, from low debt or high depreciation cash flow.
2. Later on, *equity* from a public offering.
3. Equity from *acquisitions*.
4. *Sales*, which are too low in relation to assets and can be improved.
5. *Costs*, which are too high and can be reduced.
6. *Assets*, which are excessive in relation to sales and can be reduced or can produce more sales.
7. *Reinvestment* sources of cash, which have been long and sadly neglected.

The most compact and precise expression of the cash availability of an acquisition candidate is our Pi expression, which summarizes all seven SCALDER sources:

$$CRE = \left(\frac{S}{C} \times \frac{S}{A} \times \frac{L}{A} \right)(R)$$

$$Pi = CRE \times ECO \times ECA$$

All these ratios and relationships should be deficient. After all, this is the cash-availability opportunity we are seeking. To the extent that any one of them is above rock bottom, the liquidity available to a new owner is diminished.

The Pi expression (percentage increase of equity) says plainly that we must have the courage to buy a company with *no* cash return on equity (CRE), for a price low enough to reflect that unhappy circumstance. We are thus buying extremely low S/C and S/A ratios, compared with those of its profitable industry competitors. Its leverage (L/A) capacity is no doubt poorly used, if at all. And reinvestment projects (R) have been suffering from long and severe neglect.

By applying even a modicum of energy and talent to these three ratio areas, and to reinvestment, CRE has nowhere to go but up. Since other companies in the industry are doing much better, so can our acquired company. Certainly we can do no worse than elevate its CRE to *our* level.

Later, when internal cash has begun to flow and percolate, we can go to work aggressively on equity formation through ECO and ECA. In this way, we have concentrated the full force of Pi on the acquired company's cash-generating potential.

It gets us back to the unique and exclusive role of business management as investment manager of the balance sheet. Our objective always, in our own company, is to maximize the liquidity velocity and cash productivity described in that statement and summarized by the Pi expression. The same balance-sheet management and Pi strategy are fully available to select and structure promising acquisitions and to build their profits.

The post-acquisition consolidated balance sheet combines the two companies; we plan to bring their balance sheet onto ours. Pro forma, the two together must show substantially increased cash availability from *both* the asset and the liability sides. Are there idle or underutilized assets per share from which we can generate large pools of cash? This we will do either by increasing sales in relation to assets or by decreasing assets in relation to sales. And is there substantial cash availability per share on the liability side: from increased borrowings as a primary source of leverage cash? And from secondary leverage to be generated when underutilized assets are made productive, which will enlarge the company's cash flow debt capacity? Can the retained earnings section be made more cash productive by the reduction of excessive costs and the development of sales cash?

It is thus an intensive analytical search for *potential cash* lurking in the balance sheet of our acquisition candidate. We are of course helped by large items of actual cash and the equivalent, but this is rare. Working capital as a whole should be fairly liquid, if possible, containing little that may be sluggish such as in-process inventories. And our search is helped by substantial fixed-asset liquidity in the form of underutilized land and buildings or unprofitable but salable divisions and subsidiaries.

Less noticeable but surprisingly fruitful are "off-statement" assets not on the balance sheet, though often referred to in the footnotes. These are intangibles with a high cash value, such as potential tax credits, hidden assets, assets long ago written off, and forgotten mineral or other rights.

All these areas of our search comprise the *statics* of cash availability: Where exactly is the primary cash located? But we are also probing into the *dynamics* of balance-sheet cash production, or its synergism:

Asset and leverage cash availability are closely interconnected in terms of primary and secondary productivity, as we have seen. Our analytical probings should shuttle back and forth from the left to the right side of the statement, and back again. We are searching both for cash availability on either side, *and* the contact points where asset and leverage cash are interactive and mutually supportive in the total cash-generating effort. Primary cash flow supports secondary leverage cash, which produces more primary cash, and back again. For instance, we might discover a large potential tax credit, or a source of additional tax-sheltered noncash charges such as depreciation. Each is the discovery *both* of a primary cash source and of a secondary leverage source to be based upon it.

FROM CASH AVAILABILITY TO CASH PRODUCTIVITY

All the subsequent chapters of the book develop and apply specific procedures for bringing a company—our own or an acquisition—from high cash availability to high cash productivity. This *is* the strategy of cash. So we need not dwell on it separately here.

In particular, we will examine the host of strategies for maximizing the cash contribution ratios, S/C and S/A, in every corner, nook and cranny of the business. These strategies uncover and eliminate pockets of excessive cost and asset cash everywhere, down to the minutest function and unit of the organization.

All the pockets of cash in the high-liquidity acquisition must be wrung out and the cash recirculated in maximum-payback projects. In this sense, the company is a great, soft sponge swollen with water. We squeeze it hard to get rid of the water, and the sponge is lean and tough again. Then we can reuse the precious water. The high-liquidity acquisition is bloated with potential cash that nobody really notices. It must be squeezed out by maximizing the cash contribution ratios S/C and S/A, and of course L/A, and made productive again via +R.

This means that cash is rechanneled at maximum velocity and payback within the company or into the purchase of other companies. But a management that neglected its cash contribution ratios also neglected its internal projects. It will have a vast and enticing selection of very-high-return investment opportunities in its own business crying for cash. They include capital investments, research projects, new product developments, marketing programs, and so on. In such a company, small amounts of reinvestment cash, applied almost anywhere in the business, produce abnormally high cash returns.

As we travel the bumpy road from cash availability to cash productivity, we will greatly enhance per-share earnings and wealth if we preserve and exploit a common-share "funnel effect." This means holding the common stock capitalization to its smallest possible number of shares, like the narrow apex of a funnel, through which all the Pi strategies direct their flow of cash. The narrow-capitalization policy keeps us from diluting the per-share impact of the comprehensive cash-productivity effort, thereby preserving its wealth-creating impact.

Cash-oriented managements should thus work as hard and resourcefully to limit the number of shares as they do in everything else that serves to enhance earnings per share—such as controlling costs and assets, building sales, reinvesting cash, and borrowing money.

By making acquisitions when our share prices are high, we pay out fewer shares for the same purchase price. Previously, when prices were low, we should have bought in the shares and kept them alive and available for just such an acquisition. So no newly issued shares need expand our capitalization now. We should also soft-pedal common stock in the securities package we offer sellers, or at least lean toward debentures convertible into common at prices far above the current market.

The minimum-capitalization "funnel" policy requires that shares issued publicly or in exchange for companies be timed so as to maximize equity creation in the form of ECO and ECA. This is when their prices provide the highest attainable premium over equity value, so that the fewest shares are relinquished for the equity formation achieved. The policies of equity formation and minimum capitalization are thus mutually reinforcing.

The crucial consideration is that the strategy of maximum cash productivity requires and implies the complementary strategy of minimum share capitalization. They are two sides of the same coin. We are maximizing earnings per share, always and everywhere, and one strategy is meaningless without the other.

The *ECO* and *LICO* strategies of public offerings and "leverage-in, cash-out" are best launched when we are well along the road from cash availability to cash productivity—notably when earnings per share and the price-earnings ratio are soaring. Both strategies are applicable to the acquired company if it was maintained as a separate entity, and especially if a public market in its stock has been preserved.

More likely the acquisition has been absorbed. Both strategies are then applied to the buying company, which has reaped the benefits of the initial Transaction ECA and the continuing Liquidity ECA of its new subsidiary. The buyer sells new shares at a substantial premium over equity value (ECO). And since it is heavily leveraged after fully utilizing the acquired company's borrowing capacity, LICO cash productivity assumes particular importance.

We might now conclude our discussion of acquisition strategy with some thoughts on the pratical realities of conducting an acquisition program.

PROFESSIONALIZING GROWTH BY ACQUISITION

A company's acquisition-merger activity can be random and hit-or-miss: we simply react to situations that wander in the president's door. Or it can be conducted systematically and professionally—either by the company's own highly trained acquisition staff or by outside professional acquisition counsel that *serves as* our staff.

The random method is by far the most common, and the results are usually what might be expected from amateurism. It is undesirable not because it is ineffective, which would be a blessing. But it is effective in a way that is downright harmful to the acquisitor company: it produces too many acquisitions that are "lemons" or disasters.

Soundly planned and executed acquisition programs consist of at least eight elements or phases. *All* eight phases must be included, without shortcuts:

Phase 1. Defining Our Corporate Objectives

An acquisition program must fit compactly into the company's overall framework of five-year-growth objectives. Hence we must first determine specifically and clearly just what they are. Chapter 19 on corporate planning will describe objective-setting procedures in detail.

Then we decide which goals can best be achieved by acquiring companies rather than by internal actions. One of our numberless objectives might be to develop a promising new product in our own research facilities. Should we acquire it outright by buying a company already in the field? Or, more broadly, should we acquire companies to help achieve specific sales or earnings targets, such as in consumer goods versus defense products or the Southwest versus the Northeast?

Phase 2. Planning the Acquisition Program to Achieve Specific Growth Objectives

Only against this background of well-conceived corporate objectives can we establish an acquisition program that will benefit us in terms of our long-range requirements. This involves setting acquisition goals, and the performance time schedules to guide us in measuring acquisition results against plan.

We have to measure acquisition candidates against precise *criteria*: what do we want in the way of product categories? minimum sales volume, earnings, and net worth? geographical location? management availability? and so forth, all geared to our company's objectives. Of course, selecting the criteria and the categories of companies to investigate must be tempered by *availability*. A very attractive category or industry might not have any suitable companies available at reasonable prices. So we should include some categories that are good second choices in terms of our acquisition interests, but in which there are likely to be reasonably priced candidates.

Phase 3. Searching for Promising Acquisition Candidates

We can now launch a systematic search for acquisition candidates that meet our specific criteria and relate to our corporate objectives. This involves locating desirable prospects *and* selling their management on the desirability of combining with us. We are in a seller's market for companies, and must act accordingly.

A brief *acquisition brochure* is essential. It describes our company, its people, our acquisition interests and requirements, and the benefits we can provide a prospective selling company. The brochure goes to prospective sellers, and also to intermediaries and professionals who know where and when companies are for sale.

This phase of the program is a very wide-ranging and intensive search among countless sources of acquisition candidates:

Professional referrals: law firms, accountants, commercial banks, management consultants, investment bankers and brokers, and all others who have client companies that may want to sell.
Subsidiaries of diversified corporations that might be divested.
Antitrust divestments of subsidiaries.
Trusts, estates and endowments that own companies and controlling interests.
Ads offering companies, which we follow.
Ads that we *place*.

We also prepare *lists* of the companies in an area, or industry and product line, in which we are interested. Their owners can be approached indirectly through established mutual contacts. This helps determine whether they might have a preliminary interest in merging with our (undisclosed) company if certain conditions and price were offered.

Phase 4. Screening and Researching Acquisition Candidates

From this type of wide-ranging search, we will normally get many more possible candidates than the number we have left as final choices after thorough screening and investigation. Screening now narrows down our field, and we can then thoroughly analyze and investigate those that come under final consideration.

Investigating involves gathering all pertinent financial, product, and other operating information on the candidate and its key people. We carefully analyze it to determine the earning power of the company, its basic or hard net asset value, and the maximum price we should pay for it. If this is in the same ballpark as the seller's asking price, we inspect the facilities, interview management, customers, competitors, banks, and other lenders, and so forth.

Phase 5. Reporting on Acceptable Candidates

In the course of this intensive three-step *search, screen* and *investigate* process, a few companies are located that meet our acquisition criteria and also bear up under intensive investigation. A detailed research report should then be prepared for management's consideration. It thoroughly analyzes the candidate and its earnings potential as a division or subsidiary of our company, and evaluates it within the stated price range.

Phase 6. Formulating the Most Beneficial Combination

Bearing in mind all tax and financial considerations on both sides of the proposed transaction, there is always one best way to structure a combination of two companies. This is necessarily a very creative time in the evolving acquisition. For instance, an owner might accept our offer price if the form of transaction substantially reduces his eventual estate taxes. But he will turn down the same price if a more usual transaction is proposed that does not give him this tax shelter.

Phase 7. Negotiating Advice and Assistance

The right person as an intermediary helps tremendously in negotiations. He increases the light and reduces the heat of emotion-charged meetings in which all the principals sometimes lose their perspective and a lot more. A skilled and objective third party assists in the crucial preliminary negotiation stages, when the basic structure of the proposed transaction is hammered out by the principals. He is the enabler during the delicate contract-signing stage and subsequently when various refinements are made. And he can be the oil on troubled waters during the final closing of the transaction, when personality factors may rise to the surface.

Phase 8. Financing the Acquisition

It is never too early in merger discussions for the buyer to provide for the permanent capital financing of the proposed transaction, usually through his investment banker. This is the long-term debt or equity capital, obtained privately or in a public offering, that we may need to finance all or part of the purchase price.

The full force of cash generation as it proceeds within and from the acquisition process has now been felt:

1. It probably began with the *bargain purchase* of a high-liquidity company—perhaps below equity value because of its inadequate leverage and CRE and numberless operating problems. In any case, it had a large cash potential from LICO (or low L/A), from low S/C and S/A ratios, and from R.

2. *Transaction ECA* materialized at the time of the acquisition.

3. *Liquidity ECA* was produced from $+S/C$ and $+S/A$, and from $+R$.

4. The *funnel effect* of minimum capitalization preserved the per-share impact of rising cash productivity. So share prices soared as rising earnings were capitalized by the rising price-earnings ratio.

5. *ECO and LICO* (stemming from $+L/A$) provided the final massive creation of equity and cash.

Acquisition cash productivity thus combines, as a strategy, all the others. And for this reason it is unsurpassed in force and effectiveness among the components of the overall strategy of cash.

This completes our examination, throughout Part Two, of the *external* sources of cash—leverage, equity, and acquisitions.

We now proceed to the *internal* strategies of sales cash and cost cash productivity, in Parts Three and Four. Sales cash is the functional link between the external and internal generation of cash, and is thus the most logical place to begin.

PART 3

GENERATING SALES CASH

CHAPTER 9

PRODUCING SALES CASH
AT THE CASH MARGIN

Sales volume is the initial source of external cash, on which depend the three external financing sources we have been discussing. Sales-generated cash flow is only a little trickle, to be sure, which eventually filters out of the company's huge cost structure. But it *is* the business from which leverage and equity and acquisition cash derive their existence. Without the continuing collection of customer receivables in amounts that more than pay for costs, there would be no business and no cash from any source.

SALES VOLUME (S) AND SALES CASH (Sc)

In this sense our most important strategy of all is the generation of external sales volume (S) and of internal sales cash (Sc). It is a dual strategy, or really two strategies in one, interdependent and inextricably related one to the other. We want both to increase the (external) dollar volume of sales to customers (S) *and* to increase the (internal) cash productivity of our existing dollar volume (Sc).

But our managerial focus in the strategy of cash is, always and everywhere, cash. This is the great energizer and moving force. So our focus is not on sales directly, but on the *sales cash* that it produces.

Sales cash (Sc) is the cash left over after deducting from sales all variable or volume costs (VC) that *fluctuate with* sales. When sales go up or down 10%, volume costs (VC) such as direct material and direct labor go up or down 10%. What remains is sales cash—the cash derived from sales. It pays for our fixed overhead, and what we have left is profit. Since only *cash* can pay for overhead or anything else, we multiply our profit-generating effectiveness simply by transferring our attention down the line from sales (S) to sales cash (Sc).

And by concentrating on the cash derived from sales (Sc), we *also* address ourselves to the indispensable task of expanding sales volume. This is why it is two strategies in one: when $+Sc$ is part of an effective total strategy of cash, we necessarily and directly produce dynamic sales growth $(+S)$.

Substituting Sc for S, we have $+Sc - C - A + L + D + E + R$. *All* these components of the strategy of cash are decisively sales producing, as we will see. They give us a crucial competitive marketing edge from such strengths as lower prices, better product performance and quality, a broader line of products, more maneuverability and reaction speed, and a more powerful sales and marketing effort.

For instance: $+Sc$ increases the cash productivity of our existing dollar volume. So it minimizes the upward pressure on our product prices while it helps finance the sales-development effort everywhere in the business—especially in Engineering, Manufacturing, and Sales. And $-C$ (or $-KC$, for constant costs, in the Sc analysis) also strengthens and sharpens our competitive cutting edge. It too alleviates the upward pressure on our price structure while contributing cash to sales development.

Joining $+Sc$ and $-C$ are $-A$, $+L$, and $+E$, to supply the developmental cash needed for $+R$: to create, make, and market the most desirable products at lowest cost. This cash finances the new-product-development programs and facilities, the low-cost manufacturing equipment, the most potent sales campaigns, and all the other building blocks of powerful sales expansion.

But perhaps most important to $+S$, a total strategy of cash provides the cash-oriented *motivational environment* on which sales expansion thrives. As we will discuss in Chapter 21, in a business where performance is measured solely by S/C and S/A throughout its length and breadth, *everyone* in his own way builds sales, not just the sales department.

So the present Part Three views sales volume as an extraordinarily productive *internal* source of cash (from $+Sc$), the increased productivity of which doubles back and increases the external sales volume itself $(+S)$. This is why it is two strategies in one: $+Sc$ generates cash from volume, but it also helps significantly to boost volume—which, in turn, provides additional sales cash.

A given volume will thus generate more or less cash and profits depending on our influence on *sales cash* (Sc)—again, the cash left over after deducting all volume costs (VC) that by definition vary directly with sales. With zero sales growth, in fact, a management that is sophisticated about sales cash will produce far more cash flow than one that aggressively expands volume without attending much to sales cash. Most managements probably do not attend much to sales cash. And there are quite a few that would be surprised to learn that there is such a thing.

The present chapter is, alas, both difficult and crucial to the entire sales-cash discussion that spans the next four chapters. It sets up the analytical framework, the rudimentary mathematics and formulas, and the terminology. Then Chapter 10 can talk about the profit-generating dynamics of sales cash, and Chapter 11 about sales cash decision-making to maximize profits. And in Chapter 12 we will discuss budgeting volume costs for maximum sales-cash impact, and methods of controlling sales-cash productivity.

SALES-CASH ANALYSIS AND BREAKEVEN VOLUME

To sum up: sales cash is the "net" sales that remains when we subtract from sales all variable or volume costs (VC) that fluctuate proportionately with it. It is therefore the cash contribution that sales makes to our fixed overhead or constant costs, or *capacity costs* (KC). Sales cash *pays for* capacity costs. And what is left over is our cash flow, which we will simply call profit (P).

Sales cash (Sc), not sales, is therefore our analytical focus: Sales less volume costs, or $S - VC$, pays the overhead and leaves a profit. Cash measured by *units* $(S - VC)$ must more than pay for costs measured by *time* (KC). In other words: Profit (P) is generated by selling the product (1) at a unit *price* (S) that exceeds volume costs (VC), thus generating unit sales cash (Sc); and (2) at a unit *volume* that more than pays for capacity costs (KC). For example:

1. Unit price (S)	$5
2. $-$ VC	-3
3. $=$ Sc	$2
4. %Sc (or $2 \div $5)	40%
5. Unit sales	50,000
6. Total sales	$250,000
7. $-$ VC	$-150,000$
8. Sc	$100,000
9. $-$ KC	$-100,000$
10. $=$ P	$ 0

Sales cash (Sc) is $2 a unit (line 3), and %Sc (or Sc/S) is 40% (line 4). Multiplying 50,000 units of sales (line 5) by the unit price of $5, and by VC of $3, gives us total sales of $250,000 and VC of $150,000 (lines 6 and 7).

But sales cash of $100,000 (line 8) was sufficient to pay only for the same amount of KC (line 9). So at 50,000 units of sales volume, the company broke even.

Sales-cash analysis thus requires an accurate and ironclad separation of volume costs (VC) that vary with sales, from constant or capacity costs (KC). We do this by volume budgeting, to be explained in Chapter 12, whereby VC's are *made* to behave like VC's. When sales are down 10%, the VC must automatically be reduced by 10%. Otherwise the manager is confronted with a budget variance that he must correct as one of the inescapable requirements of his position.

The following terms and relationships of sales cash must be clearly understood because they are the language of this and the next four chapters. To help our discussion, let us imagine a miniature *Sample Company* whose dimensions are noted at the right:

		Sample Company
S	Sales	$100,000
− VC	Volume costs (variable costs)	− 60,000
Sc	Sales cash (sales contribution to KC)	40,000
− KC	Capacity costs (constant or fixed costs)	− 30,000
P	Profit (cash flow)	$10,000

From these basic ingredients, we derive the following relationships that we will use throughout Part Three. To test any one of them, substitute the Sample Company dollar amounts for the formula letters in each case:

$$S - VC = Sc - KC = P:$$

S	$=$	$P + KC + VC;$	$Sc + VC;$	$\dfrac{Sc}{\%Sc}$
$VC =$		$S - Sc;$	$S - (P + KC)$	
$Sc =$		$S - VC;$	$KC + P$	
$KC =$		$Sc - P;$	$S - VC - P$	
P	$=$	$Sc - KC;$	$S - VC - KC;$	$\%Sc \times S - KC$

From these we develop the following indispensable definitions and formulas for analyzing sales cash (again, merely substitute Sample Company numbers to verify any of them):

$\%Sc = Sc/S$; breakeven volume $(BV) = KC/\%Sc$; cash margin (CM) $= S - BV$; $\%CM = CM/S$. That is, $\%CM = (S - BV)/S$, or the percentage by which sales exceeds the breakeven volume.

From $BV = KC/\%Sc$, we can derive alternative and very useful breakeven formulas, such as

$$BV = \frac{KC}{1 - (VC/S)}$$

$$= \frac{KC \times S}{KC + P}$$

$$= S - \frac{P}{\%Sc}$$

$$= \frac{KC}{(KC + P) \div S}$$

We can also derive many useful alternatives to $\%Sc$ (or Sc/S):

$$\%Sc = \frac{S - VC}{S}$$

$$= \frac{KC + P}{S}$$

$$= 1 - \frac{VC}{S}$$

$$= \frac{\text{delta } P}{\text{delta } S}$$

where delta means "a change in."

Breakeven volume (BV) is the all-important analytical result or output of which the *VC versus KC* classification is the input. BV is that amount of sales that, after subtracting volume costs (VC), provides only enough sales cash to *just* pay for our constant costs (KC). Nothing is left over for profit (P).

The level of BV depends on two things: (1) It depends on the *percentage of sales cash* generated by sales and available to pay for KC. It is symbolized by Sc/S (that is, $\%Sc$). (2) It depends on KC itself, an increase or decrease of which would naturally increase or decrease the amount of sales cash needed to break even.

So the breakeven formula is $BV = KC/\%Sc$, which is illustrated as follows:

	(000) 1	(000) 2
Sales (S)	$100	$100
Volume costs (VC)	−60	−60
Sales cash (Sc)	40	40
Constant costs (KC)	−40	−30
Profit (P)	$0	$10

In column 1 the breakeven volume is obviously $100,000. This produces $40,000 of sales cash, which is just enough to pay for KC of $40,000, and yield $0 profit. In column 2, KC is reduced to $30,000:

$$BV = \frac{KC}{\%Sc}$$

$$= \frac{\$30,000}{0.40} = \$75,000$$

Since VC, by definition, varies directly with sales, %Sc of 0.40 remains the same for any level of sales. The proof that $75,000 is the company's breakeven volume in column 2 is therefore: $75,000 × 40% = $30,000. This is the amount of sales cash that exactly pays for KC of $30,000, leaving a profit of $0. BV must therefore equal $75,000.

THE PROFIT IMPACT OF THE CASH MARGIN

Cash margin (CM) is our tool for analyzing sales cash and its impact on profits, of which BV analysis is a powerful component, but only a component. As sales rise above the no-profit breakeven volume (BV), the excess (S − BV) is the profit-generating portion of sales. This cash-productive component of sales, S − BV, is the cash margin.[1]

---

[1] It is often called the "margin of safety," which is descriptive as far as it goes. But it misses the real point by associating the CM concept with safety only, rather than with profit generation.

The *percentage* of profit-generating excess sales over BV is $(S-BV)/S$, or CM/S. It is thus $\%CM$. Using our previous illustration:

$$\%CM = \frac{S-BV}{S}$$

$$= \frac{\$100-\$75}{100}$$

$$= 25\%$$

It will be easier to work with these Sample Company numbers if we simply drop the last three zeros. Thus our *cash margin* is $S-BV$, or $\$100-\$75$, or $\$25$. Of the $\$100$ of sales, it is 25%: the cash-productive portion of sales, or CM, is 25% of total sales.

The crucial analytical importance of the cash margin is that it produces an amount of profit that is exactly determined and measured by $\%Sc$. In our illustration, the cash margin is $\$25$ and $\%Sc$ (or Sc/S) is 40%. Hence that amount of CM at that $\%Sc$ produces a profit of $\$25$ (0.40), or $\$10$.

In other words, profit (P) is determined by two factors: (1) the *quantity* of the cash margin $(S-BV)$ and (2) its *quality* or profitability $[(S-VC)/S$, or $\%Sc]$. *Profit is a function of the quality and the quality of our cash margin.*

The CM tool thus divides sales into two parts, described by $S = BV + CM$: (1) its BV, or *KC-absorbing*, portion $(KC/\%Sc)$ and (2) its CM, or surplus, or *profit-generating*, portion $(S-BV)$. That is,

S	=	KC-Absorbing	+	Profit-Generating	
	=	BV	+	CM	
	=	$\dfrac{KC}{\%Sc}$	+	$(S-BV)$	
	=	$\dfrac{\$30}{.40}$	+	($100–$75)	
	=	$75	+	$25	= $100.

Of our $\$100$ of sales, $\$75$ of BV does no more than absorb KC, leaving $\$25$ of CM to produce a *profit*. The precise amount of profit produced by CM is measured by $\%Sc$ of 0.40, or $\$10$.

Therefore, $P = CM \times \%Sc$ is the basic profit formula that dominates the analysis of sales cash and profits: Again, profit is the *amount* of the profit-generating surplus or CM portion of sales $(S-BV)$, multiplied by the *profitability* of that surplus ($\%Sc$, or Sc/S).[2]

It is also true that $\%CM$, or the degree to which sales exceed BV [that is, $(S-BV)/S$], precisely determines the profitability of sales cash (or P/Sc). In fact, $\%CM = P/Sc$:

$$\text{If } P = CM \times Sc/S, \qquad\qquad \$10 = \$25 \times 0.40$$

$$\text{then } CM = \frac{P}{Sc/S}, \qquad\qquad \$25 = \frac{\$10}{0.40}$$

$$\text{and } \frac{CM}{S} = \frac{P/(Sc/S)}{S}. \qquad \frac{\$25}{\$100} = \frac{\$10/0.40}{\$100}$$

$$\text{So } \%CM = \frac{P}{Sc}. \qquad\qquad 25\% = 25\%$$

The wider the cash margin in relation to sales ($\%CM$), the higher is the profitablity of sales cash (P/Sc): this is a stable, constant, and predictable relationship. And it is because profitability is thus precisely defined by the width of the cash margin, that CM rather than BV must be our analytical and strategic focus.

To illustrate, if $BV = KC/\%Sc = \$30/0.40 = \$75$:

	1	2	3	4
S	$75	$100	$125	$150
− VC (60%)	45	60	75	90
Sc (40%)	30	40	50	60
− KC	30	30	30	30
P	$ 0	$ 10	$ 20	$ 30
CM (or S − BV)	$ 0	$ 25	$ 50	$ 75
CM/S or P/Sc	0%	25%	40%	50%

[2]The arithmetic derivation of $P = CM \times \%Sc$ may be of interest:

Formula	Sample Company Arithmetic
$P = \%Sc \times S - KC$	$P = 0.40 \times \$100 - \$30$
$= \%Sc\left(S - \dfrac{KC}{\%Sc}\right)$	$= 0.40\left(100 - \dfrac{30}{0.40}\right)$
$= \%Sc(S - BV)$	$= 0.40 \times \$25 \qquad = \$10$
$= \%Sc \times CM.$	
$P = CM \times \%Sc$	$P = \$25 \times 0.40 \qquad = \$10$

As sales increase above BV of $75, %CM and P/Sc (bottom line) increase at an identical rate. In column 3, for example, with sales of $125, CM = $50; %CM = 50/125 or 40%; and P/Sc = 20/50 or 40%, also.

We are thus making a crucial distinction between %Sc and %CM:

1. *%Sc*, or (S–VC)/S, is the degree to which *sales generates sales cash* (*Sc*). As we will see, it is determined by the price per unit, VC per unit, and the product mix.

2. *%CM*, or *P/Sc*, is the degree to which *sales cash generates profits* (*P*). It is determined by BV (or KC/%Sc): sales cash generates profits to the extent of the KC dollars that it must first pay for.

Profit is thus the combined result of %Sc and %CM, which in turn are the result of the cash margin factors—price, VC, mix, and KC. Therefore, what we do to the CM factors directly affects profits via %Sc and %CM, whose product (we will soon see) is our profit margin. That is, profit margin = %Sc × %CM.

THE CASH MARGIN CHART: ANALYZING AND FORECASTING PROFITS

The previous example is graphically illustrated by Cash Margin (CM) Chart 1. It shows sales on the bottom horizontal axis, and costs and Sc on the vertical axis at the left. The KC line is drawn horizontally at $30 (that is, $30,000). A %Sc line is drawn diagonally upward from zero at the lower

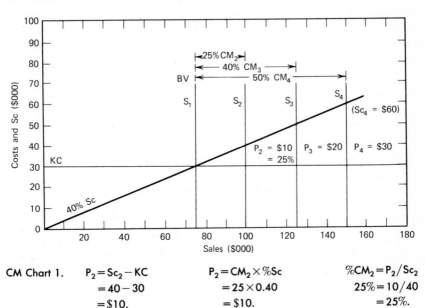

CM Chart 1.	$P_2 = Sc_2 - KC$	$P_2 = CM_2 \times \%Sc$	$\%CM_2 = P_2/Sc_2$
	$= 40 - 30$	$= 25 \times 0.40$	$25\% = 10/40$
	$= \$10.$	$= \$10.$	$= 25\%.$

left corner. So any point on the Sc line connects *that* sales level (bottom axis) with *that* Sc (left-hand axis).

BV is the vertical dashed line at the $75 point where Sc intersects with ("just pays for") KC. Sales (S) are the vertical solid lines, S_1 in this case corresponding with BV. So %CM at the top, with horizontal arrows, denotes the distance between BV and sales. Profit (P) on the vertical sales line is the excess of Sc (diagonal line) over the KC line.

KC is intersected by the 40% Sc line at $75 BV, as noted. At sales (S_1) of $75, that is, Sc at 40% equals $30 (column 1). It just pays for KC of $30, and profit is $0.

At sales (S_2) of $100 (column 2), Sc of 40% is $40. It therefore provides a profit over KC of $10 ($P_2$). The same holds true for S_3 and S_4, corresponding to columns 3 and 4, which yield profits of $20 and $30.

The cash margin for each level of sales is shown at the top of the chart. For instance, CM_2 results from S_2 of $100: it is ($100 - $75)/$100, or 25%. This corresponds to P_2/Sc of $10/0.40, or 25%.

Again, CM_4 is 50%, as is P_4/Sc_4 of $30/$60, or 50%. The extent to which sales exceeds the breakeven volume thus defines and measures the profitability of sales cash: $\%CM = P/Sc = 50\%$. And this also proves our formula, $P_4 = CM_4 \times \%Sc$: $30 = $75 \times 40\%$.

The cash margin chart was devised for use in this and the next several chapters—specifically as an analytical tool to visualize and demonstrate the profit formula $P = CM \times \%Sc$. It is so constructed as to direct our attention immediately to the two profit-creating forces, CM and %Sc. The CM chart is less concerned with the surface profit and breakeven picture than with the *below-the-surface* causes, quality, and potential for profits— as disclosed by the cash margin. It is therefore a more effective and versatile tool than conventional breakeven charts.

For instance, CM Chart 2 depicts Company 1 and Company 2 with identical profits of $10 each, shown as P_1 and P_2. But the $10 in each case was achieved in an entirely different way. And it was achieved with entirely different implications for the future quantity and safety (or quality) of profits.

Company 1 has a very low Sc_1 of 30%. But its KC_1 is also low, at $20. So BV_1 at the intersection is only $67. And CM_1 is a substantial 33%, or ($100 - $66.7)/$100.

On the other hand, Company 2 has a high 70% Sc_2. But because its KC_2 is also very high at $60, it has a lofty BV_2 of $86. Its CM is therefore only 14%, or ($100 - $86)/$100.

Company 1 thus earns the same $10 on sales of $100 as does Company

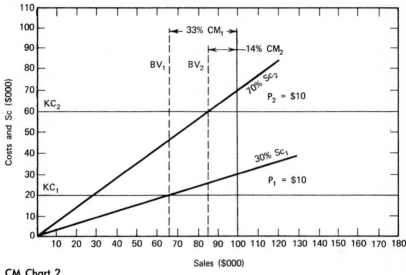

CM Chart 2

| | Profit | |
Sales	Company 1	Company 2
$80	$ 4	($4)
$120	$16	$24

2, but has a generous 33% CM rather than a thin 14% CM. Even if both companies had identical income statements and balance sheets, they would be quite different in terms of profit potential and quality.

Company 1's poor 30% Sc_1 gives it a relatively high cash-improvement potential from the reduction of excessive volume costs (VC). Company 2 has a high profit potential from the reduction of excessive KC_2. These are radically different cost-reduction approaches having entirely different cash-generating potentials, as we will see in Part Four.

And an identical change in sales volume will have entirely different profit implications. A sales increase to $120 would increase Company 1's profits to $16 ($Sc_1 - KC_1$). But because of Company 2's much higher KC_2 leverage, sales of $120 would generate profits of $24. Conversely, a decline in sales to $80 would reduce Company 1's profit from $10 to $4. But the highly leveraged Company 2 would incur a loss of $4.

The slope of %Sc and the level of KC in each case thus determine the location of BV and the width of the cash margin—that is, of S − BV, which is S − KC/%Sc. And this CM in turn determines the potential for profit, or the risk of loss, that confronts either company at various sales expectations.

The cash-margin approach is usually more effective in analyzing and forecasting profits than is conventional breakeven analysis. In the relationship $S = BV + CM$, the cash margin chart focuses on the dynamic profit-generating component CM. This swings widely and dynamically with sales, so a chart based on it gives us a better feel for the dynamics of cash and profits.

But the conventional breakeven chart is concerned mainly with the static and passive factor BV, which moves more slowly and grudgingly in response to changes in KC and in %Sc. KC hardly moves at all, by definition, and %Sc is influenced only gradually by changes in VC, prices, and mix. BV simply gives us a less effective grasp of the dynamics of profit than does CM.

CM focuses on the cash flow component of sales, $S - BV$. But BV focuses on the *loss* portion of sales, which pays for and absorbs KC. In other words, CM is dynamically cash oriented while BV is statically cost oriented. Therein, mostly, lies the advantage of the one over the other.

But above these considerations is the theoretical or conceptual superiority of CM. The cash margin chart is entirely rooted in the profit formula itself, $P = CM \times \%Sc$. So it is a formidable decision-making tool because it thereby compresses for us the *entire* profit picture—the causes, quantity, quality, and future of cash flow and profits. It tells us not only what the profit picture is, but *why*, in terms of its causal factors: a specific sales (1) *surplus* $(S - BV)$ and (2) *profitability* (%Sc) have been or will be attained. Our thinking and creativity about cash flow are thereby sharpened.

And further to the point, since $\%CM = P/Sc$, to concentrate on CM is to concentrate directly and specifically on corporate *profitability* as defined by P/Sc.

The CM chart and analysis, as we will see, is readily applicable to all types of sales cash situations requiring our decisions. It illuminates our present and prospective business environment in terms of the applicable cash margins that determine profits under different sales and cost circumstances. At a glance, we can tell under what conditions of (1) *profit* $(CM \times \%Sc)$, and (2) *safety and leverage* (%CM) we are now and will be operating.

CM also does a better job in describing and analyzing the behavior of the crucial CM factors—product volume, price, unit volume, VC, product mix, and KC—as they interact. These are the causal factors in the dynamics of sales cash, as we will see in the next chapter. From them, more than anything else, the CM chart derives its decision-making analytical value.

THE CRE LANGUAGE OF SALES CASH

Let us now translate the language of sales cash into the language of CRE, or cash return on equity, which is operating management's all-important preoccupation and test of performance.

CRE is *profit margin* multiplied by *turnover* (ignoring L/A, which is largely beyond operating management's control). We can use our Sample Company, whose BV is $30/0.40 or $75, and whose assets are $40,000. The following CRE picture emerges:

1. *Profit margin* $= \%CM \times \%Sc$. That is,

$$\frac{CM}{S} \times \frac{Sc}{S} = \frac{\$25}{\$100} \times \frac{\$40}{\$100}$$

$$= 25\% \times 40\% = 10\%$$

Since the profit was $10 on sales of $100, the profit margin was in fact 10%. By increasing *either* $\%CM$ or $\%Sc$, we increase our profit margin.

2. *Turnover* $= S/A$. That is,

$$\frac{\$100}{\$40} = 2.5 \times$$

3. *CRE* is therefore $10\% \times 2.5 = 25\%$. That is, $10/$40 (or profit/assets) is in fact 25%. By increasing *either* profit margin or turnover, we increase CRE.

In short, the CRE factors, in sales-cash language, are $\%CM$ and $\%Sc$ (profit margin), and S/A (turnover): an increase in any *one* factor increases CRE. We can therefore summarize CRE in the following sales cash language:

$$CRE = Profit\ margin \times turnover$$

$$CRE = \frac{CM}{S} \times \frac{Sc}{S} \times \frac{S}{A} = \frac{\$25}{\$100} \times \frac{\$40}{\$100} \times \frac{\$100}{\$40}$$

$$= \%CM \times \frac{Sc}{A} \qquad = 25\% \times \frac{\$40}{\$40} = 25\%$$

or

$$CRE = \frac{CM \times \%Sc}{A} \qquad = \frac{\$25 \times 0.40}{\$40} = \frac{\$10}{\$40} = 25\%$$

Since %CM equals P/Sc, we can also substitute as follows in %CM ×
Sc/A: CRE = (P/Sc) × (Sc/A), which means CRE = P/A.

To increase CRE, therefore, we must constantly strive to increase
(CM × %Sc)/A. This means increasing the *profit margin* through +%CM
and +%Sc. And it means minimizing the asset involvement or investment
required to generate that profit (−A). To increase %CM, we must widen
S − BV by increasing S or reducing BV—such reduction of BV coming
from − KC/ + %Sc. And to increase %Sc, we must also reduce VC.

This buildup of CRE is brought about, effectively and decisively,
through the adroit manipulation of the *cash margin factors*: They combine
to *increase sales* (number of products, unit volume, and price per unit);
reduce BV (+%Sc and − KC); and *increase %Sc* (VC and product mix).

The cash margin factors are so powerful and efficient a force in
generating CRE, in fact, that all of the next chapter is devoted to a study
of their behavior.

CHAPTER 10

THE PROFIT IMPACT OF SALES CASH

In the preceding chapter we developed seven cash-generating tools of analysis on which the extraordinary profit impact of sales cash depends:

1. Sales cash (Sc) is sales (S) less the variable costs (VC) associated with sales. Sc is crucial because it pays for fixed or capacity costs (KC), and what remains is profit (P). So $S - VC = Sc - KC = P$.

2. Our analytical focus is therefore not sales but sales cash: have we enough Sc to pay for KC? Or more to the point: given our %Sc (or Sc/S) and KC, at what sales level do we break even? Very simply, our breakeven volume (BV) is KC/%Sc.

3. But if BV merely absorbs KC, what about profit? This emerges from the *surplus* of sales over BV (or $S - BV$), which we call the cash margin (CM). Sales therefore consist of BV and CM, in the equation $S = BV + CM$. BV is the passive or KC-absorbing portion of sales; CM is the dynamic, *profit-generating* portion of sales.

4. Sales-cash analysis therefore necessarily focuses on the profit-generating *cash margin* ($S - BV$). CM's percentage of sales [$(S - BV)/S$, or %CM]—or the extent to which sales exceed BV—precisely determines the profitability of sales cash. That is, $\%CM = P/Sc$.

Around the crucial cash margin concept is constructed the CM chart, which helps to visualize the CM profit relationships, potentials, and risks. And the present chapter analyzes the impact of the "cash-margin factors" (notably S, VC, Sc, and KC) on the cash margin and, therefore, profit.

5. %Sc (or Sc/S) is the degree to which sales generates sales cash. %CM (or P/Sc) is the degree to which sales cash generates profit (P). So our profit margin is $\%CM \times \%Sc$.

6. Profit increases as we increase the *quantity* and *quality* of the cash margin. This we do by widening CM (or $S - BV$) at either end, and by increasing %Sc (or Sc/S), in the equation $P = CM \times \%Sc$.

7. Cash return on equity will therefore increase as we raise the numerator or lower the denominator of the equation, $CRE = (CM \times \%Sc)/A$. It is here that sales-cash analysis fits precisely into the general analytical framework of Pi—directed toward maximizing stockholders' wealth.

SALES-CASH BEHAVIOR AND THE CASH-MARGIN FACTORS

The cash-margin factors are the specific and total causal influence in our general equation $P = CM \times \%Sc$, whereby we generate profits. Their impact is on the determinative components of the equation, on $S - BV$ and $\%Sc$, through their *subcomponents*

$$S - \frac{KC}{\%Sc} \quad \text{and} \quad 1 - \frac{VC}{S}$$

The cash-margin factors thus generate profits through the subcomponents $+S$, $-KC$, $-VC$, and $+\%Sc$. There are six of these factors, some of which are themselves subcomponents. And they can be grouped according to the direction of their impact on the cash margin—toward either $+S$ or $-BV$. The cash-margin factors are the following:

Sales factors ($+S$)
1. Number of *products*.
2. *Unit volume* of each product.
3. *Price* per unit.

BV factors ($-KC$, $-VC$)
4. *VC* per unit.
5. *Mix*, or the product distribution of $\%Sc$.
6. *KC*.

The first three factors affect the cash margin mainly through the quantity of *sales*: our sales volume is the number of *products* multiplied by their *unit volume* multiplied by their *price*. They are largely independent of BV (affecting it only mildly through price).

And they are not affected *by* BV. None of the three BV factors, that is, influence the sales factors or sales volume. VC, product mix, and KC affect BV, in the CM chart, either by changing the slope of the $\%Sc$ line or by changing the level of the KC line. Both changes influence CM and profits directly, without affecting sales. We will see these relationships demonstrated shortly.

Because of their all-pervading influence in the profit equation, the CM factors constitute the entire foundation of sales-cash analysis. Table 4 shows what happens to the subcomponents of the profit equation, in response to the influence of the CM factors, when our company undergoes various short-run changes.

That is, it is in the short run that sales cash analysis performs its most valuable service. This is the time period within which factors like price, VC and KC are each assumed to have remained the same. Beyond the short-term period, these magnitudes tend to change. The breakeven analysis, therefore, loses its precision to the extent that the changes are incorrectly forecast. With this qualification in mind, let us look at Table 4.

Line 0. Our Sample Company again begins with sales of $100, VC of $60, and so forth. BV is KC/%Sc = $30/0.40, or $75. CM is $100 − $75, or $25. And %CM (CM/S, or P/Sc) is 25%.

Example 1: A sales increase (+S). Sales jump to $150 (column 1), BV remaining unchanged at $75 (column 6). This is because BV factors KC and %Sc are *not* affected by changes in sales. %Sc remains at 0.40 (column 4). That is, VC by definition continues at 60% of sales, rising to $90 (column 2).

Since P = CM × %Sc, a change (or "delta") in profit equals the change in CM × %Sc. But here the change in CM (or S − BV) is solely the change in S. So *delta P = delta S × %Sc*, or +$20 = +$50 × 0.40: the $20 increase in profits, from $10 to $30 (column 8) equals the $50 increase in sales × 40%Sc. We thus always know how much profit we will get from a sales increase if we know the %Sc.

And a sales increase does not affect BV, as noted, which remained at $75. So %CM doubled from $25/$100 or 25%, to $75/$150 or 50%, as did P/Sc (column 9).

Example 2a: Reducing VC. Our starting sales are again $100, as in line 0. But we have reduced VC (in column 2) to $50, from $60 in line 0. Everything else is the same. So %Sc, or S − VC/S, rises from 0.40 to 0.50 (column 4). It reduces BV (column 6) from $75 to $60 (or to $30/0.50).

So CM (or S − BV) goes up to $40 (column 7), and CM/S to 40% (column 9). On the larger CM *and* %Sc (or $40 × 0.50), profit doubles to $20 (column 8). That is, −VC boosts profit in two ways: by widening CM through −BV *and* by increasing %Sc.

Example 3a: Reducing KC. Here the only change from line 0 is a drop in KC (column 5) to $20, from $30. It reduces BV (column 6) to $50 (or $20/0.40), and widens CM. As in the −VC case (example 2a), profit doubled to $20. In contrast to −VC, however, the same $10 reduction lowers BV and widens CM more *sharply*.

Table 4 The Profit Impact of Sales Cash

		S 1	VC 2	Sc (1−2) 3	%Sc (3÷1) 4	KC 5	BV (5+4) 6	CM (1−6) 7	P (3−5) (7×4) 8	CM/S; P/Sc 9
	Line 0	$100	$60	$40	0.40	$30	$75	$25	$10	25%
+S:	Example 1	150	90	60	0.40	30	75	75	30	50
−VC:	Example 2a	100	50	50	0.50	30	60	40	20	40%
	2b	150	75	75	0.50	30	60	90	45	60
	2c	50	25	25	0.50	30	60	(10)	(5)	—
−KC:	Example 3a	100	60	40	0.40	20	50	50	20	50%
	3b	150	90	60	0.40	20	50	100	40	67
	3c	50	30	20	0.40	20	50	0	0	—

Examples 2b and 2c. Returning to the case of $-VC$, when we increase sales to $150 (example 2b), profit jumps to $45 (column 8). But if sales drop to $50 (example 2c), we have a loss of $5.

Examples 3b and 3c. But in the case of $-KC$, when sales increase to $150 (example 3b), profit rises only to *$40* (not to $45). And if sales drop to $50 (example 3c), we break even (rather than take a loss as in $-VC$).

We can see this CM behavior more clearly in CM Chart 3. Again, the CM chart has been designed around, and to express, the formula $P = CM \times \%Sc$, whose subcomponents are $S - KC/\%Sc$ and $1 - VC/S$.

We widen CM and increase P, therefore, in three ways: (1) move the sales line to the right ($+S$), which increases P at the diagonal Sc line; (2) move the BV line to the left ($-BV$) by lowering the KC line, which increases P on the vertical S line; (3) reduce BV by raising the slope of the Sc line ($-VC$ or $+\%Sc$), which also increases P on the vertical S line. The CM chart thereby expresses and fulfills the profit implications of our P equation, through its subcomponents.

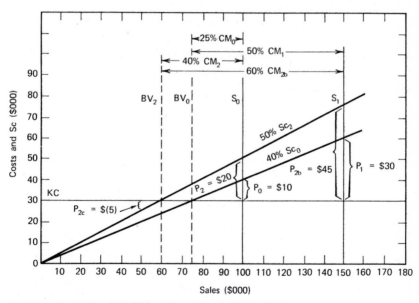

CM Chart 3.   At P_1, $\Delta S \times \%Sc = \Delta P$: $+50 \times 0.40 = +\$20$.

From line 0 of Table 4, S_0 is $100, and we generate 40% Sc_0. BV_0 of $75 is the point where Sc_0 intersects with (just pays for) KC. At the top, 25% CM_0 is $(S-BV)/S$ or $(\$100-\$75)/\$100$. And P_0 of $10 is the excess of Sc_0 over KC.

From example 1 (a sales increase): we move to S_1 of $150. On the same 40% Sc_0 line, P_1 jumps to $30 from $10. Nothing happens to BV, at $75, since nothing happened to the BV factors KC and %Sc. But at the top, we jump from 25% CM_0 to 50% CM_1 because of the increase in sales.

This huge CM_1 has created a sizable profit potential, especially from price increases or VC economies ($+$%Sc): the wider our %CM, the bigger the profit boost from a given increase in %Sc. We now also have a substantial cushion against loss.

From example 2a ($-VC$): we are back again at $100 of sales. $-VC$ raises the diagonal %Sc line up to 50% Sc_2. This reduces breakeven volume to BV_2 of $60, from BV_0 of $75. Profit therefore doubles to P_2 of $20, from P_0 of $10.

The cash margin widens from 25% CM_0 to 40%CM_2. So $P_2 = CM_2 \times 50\%$ Sc_2: of the higher $40 CM_2, 50% (not 40%) is P_2 of $20. A relatively modest increase in %Sc from 0.40 to 0.50 thus *doubles* our profit, for two reasons: it increases *CM* via $-BV$, and it improves the profit *return* on the higher CM from 0.40 to 0.50.

CM Chart 4 describes example 3a ($-KC$). KC drops $10, from KC_0 to KC_{3a}: it sharply reduces breakeven volume from BV_0 of $75 to BV_3 of $50. (This contrasts with $-VC$ in Chart 3, where the same $10 *VC* reduction lowered BV_2 only to $60.) Profit doubles from P_0 of $10 to P_3 of $20. *And* we double CM from 25% CM_0 to 50% CM_3 (it only rose to 40% CM_2 in the $-VC$ case).

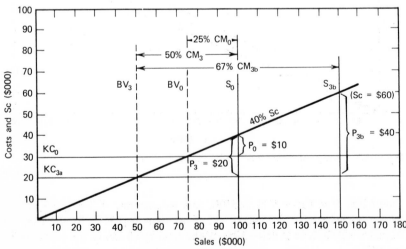

CM Chart 4.   At KC_{3a}, $BV = KC (1/\%Sc) = -10 (2.5) = -\$25$.

The $10 drop in KC reduces BV by $25 (or $75 − $50), because %Sc is 0.40. That is, BV = KC/%Sc. So − $10/0.40 = − $25.

The same $10 reduction in KC as in VC increases profits by the same $10, of course. But − KC results in a lower BV and a wider CM than does the same amount of − VC.

Moreover, back in Chart 3, *from example 2b (− VC)*, sales of $150 at 50% Sc_2 produce $45 P_{2b} and 60% CM_{2b}. *From example 2c*: if sales in Chart 3 were to plunge to $50, we would descend into a negative cash margin and a loss of $P_{2c} = ($5)$.

But in Chart 4, *from example 3b (− KC)*, an increase in sales to $150 produces P_{3b} of only $40 (rather than $45 P_{2b} as in − VC). But we wind up with 67% CM_{3b} (not 60% CM_{2b} as in the − VC case). *From example 3c*: should sales drop to $50 in Chart 4, we are at BV_3, where profit is $0. At least we are not losing money (as in − VC, where P_{2c} was − $5).

THE IMPACT OF SALES CASH ON BREAKEVEN VOLUME

There is a mathematically predictable relationship between this change in BV induced by a change in KC, and the change in KC. The relationship is defined by the reciprocal of %Sc. That is, delta BV = delta KC (1/%Sc). From example 3a:

$$\text{delta BV} = -\$10\left(\frac{1}{0.40}\right)$$

$$= -\$10 \ (2.5)$$

$$= -\$25$$

At 40%Sc, a $10 reduction in KC produces a $25 reduction in BV, from $75 to $50. But at 50%Sc, − KC of $10 would have produced − BV of $10 × 1/0.50, or only − $20.

Suppose that %Sc was 0.50, as in Chart 3. We reduce KC by $10, from $30 to $20. This reduces BV by $10 × 1/0.50 or $10 × 2, or $20. On the chart, at $30 KC and 50%$Sc_2$, BV = $60. But at $20 KC, BV is $40, a reduction in BV of $20.

Knowing the precise amount by which a change in KC produces a change in BV, and in CM, has obvious decision-making value. It tells us at what lower BV level our profits will begin, if we reduce constant costs by a stated amount. Or we can predict how much additional sales we will need to pay for a proposed increase in constant costs.

From this formula we can derive an equally useful relationship between

%Sc and the ratio of *BV to KC*, which is BV/KC = 1/%Sc:

$$(1) \quad BV = \frac{KC}{\%Sc} \qquad \$75 = \frac{\$30}{0.40}$$

$$(2) \quad BV = KC\left(\frac{1}{\%Sc}\right) \qquad \$75 = \$30\left(\frac{1}{0.40}\right)$$

$$(3) \quad \frac{BV}{KC} = \frac{1}{\%Sc} \qquad \frac{\$75}{\$30} = \frac{1}{0.40}$$

The relationship between BV and KC is thus defined by the reciprocal of %Sc. For instance:

%Sc	KC	BV (KC/%Sc)	1/%Sc or BV/KC
0.20	$30	$150	5.0×
0.30	30	100	3.3
0.40	30	75	2.5
0.50	30	60	2.0
0.60	30	50	1.7

The extent to which our breakeven sales exceed capacity costs (KC) is determined by 1/%Sc. At only 20% Sc, and KC of $30, we need sales of $150 to break even. This is an excessive BV/KC ratio of 5.0 times. But with a fat 60% Sc, we need only $50 of sales to break even on the same KC of $30. We enjoy a very low BV/KC ratio of *1.7 times*.

To drive BV downward toward KC, we must therefore widen (S − VC)/ S, or %Sc. In terms of the CM chart, it means increasing the *slope* of the %Sc line, which lowers BV. And the increase in %Sc which lowers the arithmetic values of 1/%Sc and BV/KC, increases CM correspondingly: as BV/KC declines, S − BV is expanding.

We can also predict the BV change induced by a change in VC. This is determined from the same basic equation, BV = KC/%Sc, or KC/[1 − (VC/S)]. Here we solve for VC. But this can best be shown illustratively later in the chapter rather than mathematically at this point: We will see that at low levels %Sc (that is, excessive VC), a given change in VC will produce a larger change in BV than if we are operating at high levels of %Sc.

GENERATING SALES CASH FROM PRODUCT MIX

Product mix is CM factor 5 in the BV category of our classification at the beginning of the chapter. Each of our products has a %Sc different from those of the others. Thus *mix* describes, in terms of %Sc, the distribution of a given quantity of sales among the company's products. The strategy objective is to maximize the weighted-average %Sc of all the products making up that quantity of sales. For any one product, $BV = KC/\%Sc$. So at a given level of KC, the company's total BV must vary with the weighted average of all the product %Sc's, or its product mix.

If the proportion of total sales accounted for by high-%Sc products increases relative to low-%Sc products, product mix has improved in terms of sales-cash productivity. The company's %Sc line will now slope upward at a steeper angle. BV is reduced (pushed to the left), and the cash margin is widened. Product mix *alone* affected profit. It did so independently of the total volume of sales and all the other CM factors, which we assume to have remained constant.

Table 5 is a very simplified sales mix schedule for a five-product company. Total sales of $10,000,000 at the right remains unchanged between our (1) original mix and (2) improved mix, as does the unit price and %Sc for each product. Nothing changes, in fact, but *unit sales* of the individual products.

Table 5 The Profit Impact of Sales Mix

	Products					
	T	U	V	W	X	Total
Unit price	$40	$30	$10	$13	$20	
1. *Original mix* (000)						
Unit sales	30	50	130	200	170	
Total sales	1200	1500	1300	2600	3400	$10,000
Sales cash (Sc)	700	900	500	1200	800	4,100
%Sc	58.3	60.0	38.5	46.1	23.5	41.0%
2. *Improved mix* (000)						
Unit sales	40	60	120	200	140	
Total sales	1600	1800	1200	2600	2800	$10,000
Sc	933	1080	462	1200	658	4,333
						43.3%
Sc increase (decrease)	233	180	(38)	0	(142)	$ 233

For example, product T now (as later) has a unit price of $40. Its unit sales are 30,000. This provides sales of $1,200,000, and generates $700,000 of sales cash. So %Sc is $700/$1,200, or 58.3%. The company's total sales cash of $4,100,000, at the right, provides 41% Sc. The %Sc's of the different products range from 60% for product U down to 23.5% for product X. And they remain the same for any level of product sales, by definition. So we persuade or threaten the sales department to boost unit sales of products T and U, whose Sc's are 58.3% and 60%, and to ease up on the less-profitable products.

They oblige by giving us the improved mix: volume of product T jumps from 30,000 to 40,000 units and of product U from 50,000 to 60,000 units, while products V and X decline. We wind up with exactly the same total sales of $10,000,000. But unit volume and sales cash increased in our high-%Sc products, and decreased in low-%Sc products. So total %Sc rose from 41% to 4,333/10,000, or 43.3%. And total Sc increased by $233,000.

Mix alone exerted an independent influence on BV, quite apart from the other CM factors. Let us assume that the company's KC is $4,000,000. With the original mix of product volume, BV was $4,000,000/41%, or $9,740,000. But the improved mix at 43.3% Sc sharply reduced our BV to $9,260,000.

CM Chart 5 demonstrates this independent influence that mix alone exerts on sales cash and profits. Chart 5*a* is the original mix of products. They are sequenced along the %Sc incline in the order of their individual %Sc's, from highest to lowest. We do the same in Chart 5*b* for the improved mix.

On the same $10,000,000 of sales volume, improved Chart 5*b* has a more steeply sloping 43.3% Sc line. This reflects the higher sales cash we now get from products U and T, as measured vertically on the left-hand axis. It more than offsets reduced sales cash from products V and X.

And on the same $4,000,000 of KC, the improved mix in Chart 5*b* gives us a lower BV, wider CM, and higher profit (Sc–KC) than does the original mix.

SUMMARY OF CASH-MARGIN STRATEGIES

We have already discussed some and alluded to other behavioral characteristics of the cash-margin factors. Let us now summarize these characteristics, so that we can use the factors in cash decision-making. This is best done by constructing a laboratory environment in which we allow one CM factor to vary while everything else remains constant. Then the observable effects within the environment can be attributed to the single variable.

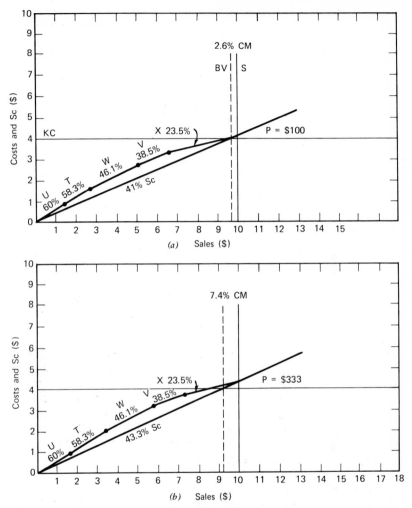

CM Chart 5. (a) Original mix; (b) improved mix.

In doing so, we must again remember that BV analysis is a decision-making and profit-forecasting tool applicable to the *short run*. It realistically assumes no change in each of the CM factors—in price, VC, mix, KC, and so forth—but only changes *between* the factors. It is immensely valuable and indeed indispensable in such short-term analysis, as we will see in the next chapter on Sc decision-making.

Table 6 is such a single-variable laboratory environment. It illustrates separately the behavior of (1) VC, (2) KC, and (3) S under controlled conditions in each case, all other factors being held constant. In the text, to

Table 6 Cash-Margin Productivity Strategies

	S 1	VC 2	Sc 3	%Sc 4	KC 5	BV 6	CM 7	P 8	CM/S P/Sc 9
1. VC Behavior									
	100	80	20	0.20[a]	30	150	(50)	(10)	—
		70	30	0.30		100	0	0	0
		60	40	0.40		75	25	10	25%
		50	50	0.50		60	40	20	40
		40	60	0.60		50	50	30	50
		30	70	0.70		43	57	40	57
		20	80	0.80		38	62	50	62
		10	90	0.90		33	67	60	67
2. KC Behavior									
	100	60	40	0.40[b]	40	100	0	0	0%
					30	75	25	10	25
					20	50	50	20	50
					10	25	75	30	75
					40	100	0	0	—
3. S Behavior									
	100	60	40	0.40[c]	20	50	50	20	50%
	90	54	36				40	16	44
	80	48	32				30	12	38
	70	42	28				20	8	29
	60	36	24				10	4	17
	100	60	40				50	20	50

[a] %Sc is also P/CM. BV/KC is also 1/%Sc.

[b] KC behavior at 60% Sc:	100	40	60	0.60	40	67	33	20	0.33
					30	50	50	30	0.50
					20	33	67	40	0.67
					10	17	83	50	0.83
[c] S behavior at 60% Sc:	100	40	60	0.60	20	33	67	40	0.67
	90	36	54				57	34	0.63
	80	32	48				47	28	0.59
	70	28	42				37	22	0.53

Table 6 (*Continued*)

Δ 10	Δ 11	BV/ VC 12	VC/ S 13	BV/ KC 14	ΔP 15	ΔCM 16	ΔP/ ΔCM 17
VC	BV						
—	—	187%	80%	500%	—	—	—
−12%	−33%	143	70	333	10	50	20%
−14	−25	125	60	250	10	25	40
−17	−20	120	50	200	10	15	67
−20	−17	125	40	167	10	10	100
−25	−14	143	30	143	10	7	143
−33	−12	190	20	127	10	5	200
−50	−13	330	10	110	10	5	200
KC	BV						
—	—			250%	—	—	
−25%	−25%			250	10	25	0.40
−33	−33			250	10	25	0.40
−50	−50			250	10	25	0.40
+300	+300			250	−30	−75	0.40
P	S	S(%Sc)					
—	—	—			—	—	
−4	−10	−4			−4	−10	0.40
−4	−10	−4			−4	−10	0.40
−4	−10	−4			−4	−10	0.40
−4	−10	−4			−4	−10	0.40
16	40	16			16	40	0.40
				167%	—	—	—
				167	10	17	0.60
				167	10	17	0.60
				167	10	17	0.60
P	S	S(%Sc)					
—	—	—			—	—	—
−6	−10	−6			−6	−10	0.60
−6	−10	−6			−6	−10	0.60
−6	−10	−6			−6	−10	0.60

make the illustration simpler and more manageable, we have again dropped the last three zeros of our Sample Company numbers.

1. *VC behavior.* Here sales are held constant at $100 (column 1) and KC at $30 (column 5). So a gradual reduction of VC from $80 downward (column 2), increases %Sc (column 4) and produces a decline in BV (column 6). This of course happens because the rise in %Sc reduces KC/%Sc. The decline in VC increases P directly (column 8). And via $-$BV it increases CM (column 7) and CM/S or P/Sc (column 9).

The decline in BV caused by $-$VC is defined by BV $=$ KC/[1$-$(VC/S)]. At high levels of VC/S (that is, low levels of %Sc at the top of the table) the same change in VC will produce a much larger change in BV, than at low levels. A drop in VC/S from 80% to 70% (column 13) corresponds to a 12% VC reduction (column 10), but causes a 33% decline in BV (column 11). But a decline in VC/S from 30% to 20%, or a reduction in VC of 33%,

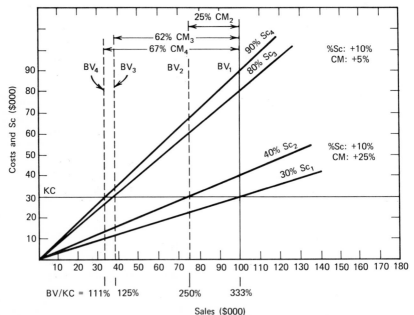

CM Chart 6.   At each level of %Sc, we can see that 1/%Sc $=$ BV/KC, as follows:

%Sc	1/%Sc	=	BV/KC
0.30	333%		100/30
0.40	250%		75/30
0.80	125%		38/30
0.90	111%		33/30

produces a decline in BV of only 12%.

This oblique VC effect on BV is shown graphically in CM Chart 6. The increase from 30% Sc_1 to 40% Sc_2 reduces BV from \$100 to \$75, and increases CM_2 from 0% to 25%. But the increase from 80% Sc_3 to 90% Sc_4 lowers BV and increases CM only slightly, from 62% CM_3 to 67% CM_4. Low-%Sc (that is, high-VC) companies and products thus have a higher cash-flow potential in terms of BV reduction from +%Sc, than do those enjoying a high %Sc.

BV/KC (column 14) is the reciprocal of %Sc (column 4), as we have noted. As %Sc rises, BV declines toward KC. It almost touches KC, at 110%, when Sc hits 90%. The company at this point enjoys its maximum cash margin and profitability (P/Sc), and protection against loss.

BV/VC (column 12) sheds further light on VC behavior and profit impact. As VC declines (column 2) from \$80 to \$50, BV/VC declines from 187% to 120%. But as VC continues to decline, to \$40 and below, there is an *increase* in BV/VC. This is because at the lower levels of VC (and higher Sc) there are smaller and smaller rates of decline in BV. It is another way of saying that at the highest VC levels, we get the biggest returns in the form of BV reductions. Diminishing returns from this source become evident at VC levels below \$50.

At progressively lower VC levels (while profits are rising correspondingly), CM/S and P/Sc (column 9) are increasing by smaller and smaller increments. This is shown precisely in columns 15, 16, and 17. Delta P is +\$10 for every corresponding reduction of VC. But delta CM (computed from column 7) experiences diminishing increments. So delta P/delta CM rises very sharply from 20% to 200%: the higher %Sc climbs, the bigger the change in profit that is associated with a given change in CM.

In CM Chart 7, for example, are two identical \$20 increases in CM (reductions in BV). One is caused by an increase from 20% Sc_1 to 25% Sc_2. The other results from a necessarily much larger increase from 50% Sc_3 to 98% Sc_4. The \$20 increase in CM at the lower %Sc level was associated with a profit increase of $P_2 = \$5$. But the same \$20 increase in CM at the higher %Sc level was associated with a profit increase of $P_4 = \$48$.

This is merely saying in reverse what we have already concluded: a change in %Sc at low levels will cause a much higher change in %CM than will the same change in %Sc at high levels.

2. *KC behavior*. Here everything remains the same except KC (column 5). It declines from \$40 to \$10, and goes back up to \$40. This produces an identical change in BV (column 6), since %Sc is constant. So the ratio BV/KC (column 14) remains constant at 250% for every level of KC. Given %Sc, therefore, delta KC = delta BV (columns 10 and 11).

If $P = CM \times \%Sc$, then $\%Sc = P/CM$. The change in P (column 8)

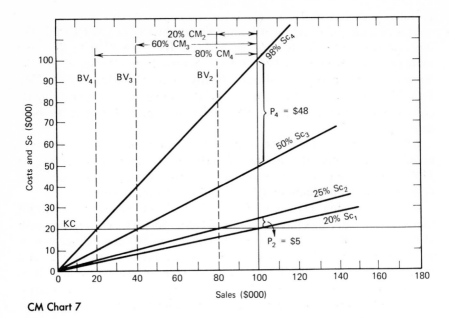

CM Chart 7

associated with the change in CM (column 7) is always determined by %Sc, which is 40% (column 4). So in columns 15, 16, and 17 we see that successive delta P's of $10 are 40% of delta CM's of $25. That is, %Sc = delta P/delta CM = $10/$25 = 40% (column 17).

Footnote b to the table on KC behavior shows the same situation except that Sc is 60%, not 40%. The identical relationships prevail throughout, and delta P/delta CM (column 17) is 60% (based on rounded numbers).

CM Chart 8 depicts a $10,000 reduction from KC_1 to KC_2, profit increasing from $P_1 = \$30$ to $P_2 = \$40$. Since delta KC = delta BV for any value of %Sc, the 33% reduction in KC ($20/$30) equals the 33% reduction in BV ($33/$50). At 60% Sc in this chart, the cash margin increased from 50% CM_1 to 67% CM_2. Had %Sc been lower, the same $10,000 reduction in KC would have produced a larger increase in %CM. And if %Sc had been higher, it would have produced a smaller increase in %CM.

3. *S behavior*. Here we have sales as the only variable, declining from $100. %Sc is constant at 0.40, KC at $20, and therefore BV is constant at $50. VC, by definition, fluctuates directly with sales. With BV constant at $50, the decline in CM (column 7) is of course identical with the decline in sales.

But %CM and P/Sc (column 9) decline at a more rapid rate than sales—from 50% down to 17%, while sales decline from $100 to $60. And their percentage increase is much larger—to 50% as sales return to $100. The cash margin and the profitability of sales cash are thus more volatile

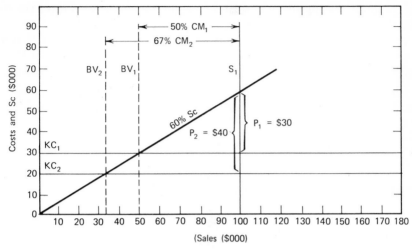

CM Chart 8. $\Delta KC = \Delta BV$: $-33\% = -33\%$ (i.e., $20/30 = 33/50$).

than sales. CM fluctuates more widely than sales for the purely arithmetical reason that it is smaller than sales by the amount of BV. %CM is therefore computed from a lower starting base.

Delta P = delta S $\times$ %Sc: the change in profit produced by a change in sales is always determined by %Sc, in this case 0.40 (columns 10, 11, and 12). As previously noted, this is because P = CM $\times$ %Sc, or delta P = delta CM $\times$ %Sc.[1] Since delta CM *is* delta S, we can substitute. So delta P/delta CM is 40% Sc (columns 15, 16, and 17).

Footnote c to the Table on S behavior shows the identical situation, but at %Sc of 0.60. All the relationships are the same. And delta P/delta S (columns 10 and 11), as well as delta P/delta CM (column 17), are 60%.

APPLYING PROFIT VOLUME (PV)

The profit volume (*PV*) point is a most useful modification of, or really tinkering with, the BV computation. It enables us to do three things all at once: establish a fixed *profit margin* target, determine what *sales volume*

---

[1]Delta P = delta CM $\times$ %Sc is true in the case of changes in KC and changes in S, in which %Sc is held *constant*. But it is *not* true in the case of changes in VC. Here a given percentage change produces *different* changes in BV and CM depending on the percentage of VC/S. At high levels of VC/S, as we have seen, the CM change is substantial; at low levels it is small. Specifically, the relationship between delta CM and delta P is determined by the level of VC/S in the equation BV = KC/[1 − (VC/S)]. Delta P = delta CM $\times$ %Sc is therefore true for changes in KC and S—where %Sc is constant—but not true for delta VC, where %Sc varies.

will produce that profit margin, and compute the *profit* we will realize at that target volume and profit margin.

To determine the PV for achieving a specific profit margin, (1) reduce %Sc in the BV equation KC/%Sc by *that* target margin, and solve for PV; (2) P will then be the original %Sc multiplied by the PV thus computed.

For example, if $BV = KC/\%Sc = \$30/0.40 = \$75$: (1) What *volume* produces a 10% profit (that is, 10% PV)? (2) What will be the dollar *profit* at that volume?

$$(1) \quad 10\% \ PV = \frac{KC}{\%Sc} - 0.10 = \frac{\$30}{0.30} = \$100,$$

which is the volume that produces a 10% profit.

$$(2) \quad P = \%Sc \times S - KC$$

$$= 0.40 \times 100 - 30 = \$10 \text{ profit.}$$

$$\text{Proof: } \frac{\$10}{\$100} = 10\%$$

What *volume* do we need to produce a 5% profit? What will be the *profit* at that sales volume?

$$5\% \ PV = \frac{\$30}{0.35} = \$85.7; \qquad P = 0.40 \times \$85.7 - 30 = \$4.3$$

$$\text{Proof: } \frac{\$4.3}{\$85.7} = 5\%$$

The profit volume device is also very useful as a margin of error: we substitute a low PV value for the internal BV computations. For example, internal decision-making that would normally be based on BV is based instead on a 2% PV: $BV = 30/0.40 = \$75$; but 2% $PV = 30/0.38 = \$79$. So everybody's internal decision-making is based on $BV = \$79$, which energizes the troops and keeps everyone on their toes (until they discover what we are up to).

Now that we have cataloged the behavior and profit impact of the cash margin factors, let us use them to make cash-generating decisions.

CHAPTER 11

SALES-CASH DECISION-MAKING TO MAXIMIZE PROFITS

Sales-cash decision-making focuses on the cash-margin (CM) factors, which together are the sole cause of profits. They are (1) product portfolio, (2) unit volume, and (3) price, which combine to produce the quantity of *sales*; and (4) variable costs (VC), (5) mix (%Sc), and (6) constant costs (KC), which have their direct and primary impact on the level of *breakeven volume* (BV).

We call them cash-margin factors because each one thus affects CM on one or the other side of $S - BV$. VC and mix are also the constituents of %Sc, which determines the quality or *profitability* of CM. So by determining both the quantity and quality of the cash margin, the six factors dominate our governing profit formula, $P = CM \times \%Sc$.

In the preceding chapter we recorded and analyzed the behavior of sales cash and the CM factors. Now let us *apply* them to the practical realities of business, where their decision-making role is so crucial to the production of cash. We have talked and will talk further about the BV factors—VC, KC, and %Sc (mix). But in this chapter we focus on profit decisions involving the three sales-related CM factors—products, units, and price. Let us call them CM1, CM2, and CM3.

PRODUCT PORTFOLIO DECISION-MAKING (CM1)

A company is no more or less than an integrated grouping of separately identifiable *products* (which are services). Each one is a product center, which is a profit center: the product's performance is measured by its sales less costs divided by assets $[(S - C)/A]$. Operating management's central focus is this product center—maximizing product profits as a return on product assets.

Our company is thus a *portfolio of product centers*. And our fundamental balance-sheet role is really that of investment manager of this product portfolio, whereby we seek to maximize the CRE of individual product-center components and of the total portfolio. All of our cash-generating analyses, techniques, programs, and strategies directed toward $+S/C$ and $+S/A$ *must* converge on the individual product centers. This is true in every managerial area—be it acquisitions, marketing, production, cost and asset control, new product development, or anything else.

Yet the product portfolio concept and strategy is specifically *customer* oriented: its purpose and direction are to be found in the clearly defined markets that our products serve. Everything we sell to a particular category of target customer should be grouped organizationally and managed within a *market center*—the unit that caters exclusively to that target customer category.

The market center is typically a company, subsidiary, or division that sells products or services to one customer market, through one distribution channel. It is continually and totally involved with the hopes, fears, and problems of *this* particular category of customer. So it knows his needs and business better than he does, and provides product-service solutions to those needs better and faster than do its competitors.

It is fair to summarize this as follows: *Customer service* is the foundation and total direction of a successful business. Products *are* customer services. They are not things we can feel, but rather the way a company gratifies its customers' needs, hopes, and dreams. A specific product is a specific category of customer gratification, nothing more or less.

To say that our company is organized around distinct product lines, each strong and independent in its own right, is to say that it is organized around separate categories of customer service and gratification. From product planning and design through manufacturing and marketing, the entire business must be totally directed toward the specific categories of customer gratification for which it is organized.

Management's job, then, is to maximize CRE of a product portfolio serving target customers within a unitary and homogeneous marketing framework, or market center. It highlights our first and perhaps most decisive cash-margin factor, the products in our portfolio. How do we know which to retain and which to replace? And what is the cash-generating basis for selecting the product replacement or addition to our line?

PRODUCT CONTRIBUTION TO CAPACITY COSTS (KC)

When deciding to add or drop a product, our consideration is *not* whether it will make or lose money on the conventional costing basis of full overhead absorption. This is the basis on which our published or outside income statement and balance sheet are constructed—for external reporting purposes and in accordance with generally accepted accounting principles.

The conventional unit cost of each product includes direct variable (VC) and fixed overhead (KC) costs associated specifically with the product. It also includes the product's share of all *indirect or general* company overhead (also KC). This is as it should be.

But adding or subtracting the product from our line will not in any way affect the indirect or general KC. So it is a mistake to factor this general KC into the decision process by adding it to unit costs. The crucial consideration is rather the product's impact on sales cash (Sc), which pays for KC and produces our profit: $Sc - KC = P$. Since KC is constant, by definition, adding or subtracting Sc *is* adding or subtracting the identical amount of P. General KC is therefore irrelevant as a decision variable in adding or dropping a product line.

KC is of course a legitimate cost to be charged against the product. The total income of all our products must pay for total general overhead, or our company will eventually go out of business. But in product decisions that in no way alter KC, it should be *ignored*. Dropping a product that is unprofitable on the basis of full absorption of all direct and indirect costs may not increase net income at all. It may *reduce* net income because its elimination reduces total Sc but leaves KC untouched. A smaller amount of Sc now must pay for the same amount of KC, so that profits are hurt for the company as a whole.

When deciding to add or drop a product, we must distinguish between two types of KC: direct KC, which *does* change, and indirect KC, which does not. The indirect or general KC is the cost of the company's overall capacity. It "keeps the doors open," whether or not we are making this product. But *direct KC* (DKC) is the overhead associated specifically with that product. DKC automatically terminates on the day the product is terminated. So it must be subtracted from the product's Sc, to give us the *direct cash* (Dc) that this product contributes to general KC and to profit. Our expression becomes $Dc - KC = P$.[1]

---

[1]This is merely saying that profit decisions must always deal with the variable and exclude the nonvariable. General and indirect KC is a *nonvariable* in most sales cash decisions; so it is excluded from consideration. Direct KC (DKC) is also normally a nonvariable in typical sales and product decisions, such as pricing, unit volume, adding more salesmen, and so forth. It is therefore lumped together with KC. We then deal with the variable amount of Sc available to pay for all that KC, both direct and general. But when an entire product will be added or subtracted, DKC becomes a *variable*. It will be entirely eliminated or added, as the case may be. So in this one type of product decision only, we suspend $Sc - KC = P$, and use $Sc - DKC = Dc - KC = P$. That is, we use $Dc - KC = P$.

THE CASH CONTRIBUTION OF LOSS PRODUCTS

Say that we make products X, Y, and Z. But Y is consistently unprofitable on our books and financial statements, based on conventional full absorption product costing. It is in fact losing money. Before we actually drop the line, someone computes the impact of each product on total Sc and Dc:

Product	X (000)	Y (000)	Z (000)	Total (000)
Sales	$400	$500	$600	$1500
VC	160	300	300	760
Sc	$240	$200	$300	$740
(%Sc)	(60%)	(40%)	(50%)	(49.3%)
DKC	60	75	70	205
Dc	180	125	230	535
(%Dc)	(45%)	(25%)	(38%)	
KC				−450
Profit				$ 85

It is quite true that product Y is losing money after being charged with its fair share of the $450,000 of general KC (lower right-hand column). This is the unhappy circumstance being broadcast in our conventional financial statements. But it is also true that eliminating product Y will not eliminate one penny of the $450,000 of general KC.

Even worse, it will eliminate $125,000 of product Y's direct cash (Dc) that now helps to *pay for* the $450,000 of general KC. Our company would go from a profit of $85,000 to a loss of $40,000. That is, after dropping product Y we will have total Dc of only $410,000 ($535,000 now, less product Y's $125,000) to pay for the $450,000 of KC.

Sales are $1,500,000. $BV = (KC + DKC)/\%Sc = \$655,000/49.3\% = \$1,325,000$. This provides a thin cash margin of $175,000 on which a profit of 49.3% Sc is generated, or $85,000.

CM Chart 9 describes the present situation: 49.3% Sc_1 intersects with $655,000 KC_1 at BV_1 of $1,325,000, to provide a 12% CM_1. P_1 is $85.

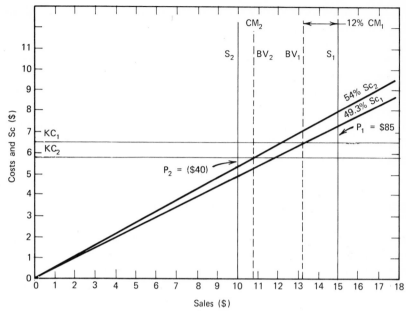

CM Chart 9

But with the elimination of loss product Y, the company consists of products X and Z, as follows:

Products X and Z	(000)	
Sales		$1000
VC		460
Sc		540
		(54%)
DKC	$130	
KC	450	
Total KC		580
Loss		$(40)

BV is now $580/0.54 = $1,075,000. On sales of $1,000,000, the company is losing ($75) CM × 0.54 = ($40).

Back on Chart 9, dropping product Y raised the slope of %Sc from 49.3% to 54% Sc_2. But KC dropped only moderately after product Y's DKC of $75 was eliminated. KC_2 continued to be dominated by the $450,000 of general KC, which was unaffected by the product elimination.

Remaining products X and Z generate insufficient sales cash to pay for KC_2, a negative CM_2 results, and $P_2 = (\$40)$.

We had better keep ailing product Y and try to cure it. Its abnormally low 25% Dc is an extraordinary cost-reduction opportunity, to trim excessive VC and DKC. At the same time we should concentrate much more selling effort in product X to improve the company's mix: it has a very profitable 45% Dc but the lowest product sales.

Depending on the success of these measures, and perhaps eventually in any event, we might replace product Y with a high-%Dc product that our customers really need and want to pay for.

ADDING PRODUCTS: THE CASH DECISION FACTORS

The opposite situation contemplates adding a product or service to our line. How do we determine if, or at what unit sales level, it will become profitable? Some new products add no additional KC (that is, DKC), contributing only Sc to pay for the general KC that will be there anyway. *Any* incremental sales cash from the new product will contribute to total company profits $(Sc - KC = P)$.

Suppose that we operate an imaginary household furnishings store that carries no appliances. Should we take on a popular television set line on a no-overhead basis? Our regular floor salesmen would sell to customers already in the store, from a floor model and catalog, and get a commission per unit sold. Delivery to the customer would be made directly by the distributor:

Price per set	$300
VC (our cost per set plus salesman's commission)	200
Sc	$100
%Sc	33.3%

Every set we sell adds $100 to store profits. It pays $100 toward the absorption of general overhead (KC) that would have to be paid for by the other products anyway, *without* the new TV line.

But what if the new line will cost us $1000 a month in additional direct KC such as fixed advertising and some clerical costs? The first ten sets we sell each month must pay for that DKC from their Sc of $100 per set:

$$BV = \frac{KC}{Sc} = \frac{\$1000}{\$100} = 10 \text{ sets to break even}$$

or

$$BV = \frac{KC}{\%Sc} = \frac{\$1000}{33.3\%} = \$3000 \ in \ sales \text{ to break even}$$

Every set we sell *over* ten contributes $100 to our total store profit.

In the same vein, let us return to our illustration of products X, Y, and Z. We have built up product X and Z volume and profitability, disposed of marginal product Y, and are considering the purchase of product W to replace it.

Table 7 is our present position (columns 1, 2, and 3) as to remaining products X and Z. In column 3: On total sales of $1,300,000, we are generating 61% Sc. Direct cash (Dc) of $620,000 pays for $510,000 of

Table 7 Product Contribution to Sales Cash

	Products			Product	Products XZW
	X (000) 1	Z (000) 2	Total (000) 3	W (000) 4	Total (000) 5
Sales	$600	$700	$1300	$350	$1650
VC	210	295	505	182	687
Sc	390	405	795	168	963
(%Sc)	(65%)	(58%)	(61%)	(48%)	(58%)
Direct KC	95	80	175	66	241
Dc	$295	$325	$620	$102	$722
(%Dc)	(49%)	(46%)	(48%)	(29%)	(44%)
Dc/Sc	(76%)	(80%)		(61%)	
KC[a]			510		510
Profit			$ 110		$ 212
(Profit margin)			(8.5%)		(12.8%)
Direct assets (DA)	$1260	$2950	$4210	$330	$4540
(Dc/DA)	23%	11%	14.7%	31%	15.9%

[a]BV: $\frac{685}{61\%} = \$1123$ $\frac{751}{58\%} = \$1295$

%CM: 13.6%   21.5%

general KC. Profit is therefore $110,000, or 8.5% of sales. We are a prosperous little company, in other words, but the product line is too limited.

Column 4: product W, if we buy it, will give us additional sales of only $350,000. And it generates a mere 48% Sc and 29% Dc, compared with our present 61% Sc and 48% Dc (column 3). But product W is one that our distributors could really use now, and it has excellent sales prospects. Our decision hinges on two questions: Will inclusion of relatively low-profit product W hurt our company's 8.5% profit margin? And even more important, how will it affect our return on equity?

Column 5: the inclusion of product W does in fact slightly reduce %Sc from 61% (column 3) to 58%, and %Dc from 48% to 44%. Yet it contributes $102,000 of Dc (column 4) toward the absorption of the same $510,000 of KC that we had in the first place.

So product W adds $102,000 of Dc to net income, which almost doubles from $110,000 to $212,000. Our profit margin jumps from 8.5% to 12.8%.

Even more intriguing is the *potential* of product W, whose DKC is much too high: Dc/Sc is only 61% (column 4) compared with the other products' 76% and 80%. But as product W's sales rise, DKC remaining constant by definition, its Dc/Sc should rise at a steeper rate. So product W will probably provide a much larger share of total profits than at present.

An even more important decision factor is the asset investment each product needs to generate its sales cash. These are their direct assets (DA) that are clearly associated with or allocable to the product, such as inventory, receivables, and machinery.

Product W's cash return on direct assets (Dc/DA) is $102/$330, or 31% (column 4). This compares with our present Dc/DA of 14.7% (column 3). We will thus increase the company's CRE performance by promoting sales of product W. Product decisions, of course, must never be based on profit margin only, unrelated to product assets. They are geared to profit margin multiplied by turnover, or *CRE*.

The crucial CRE test also requires that close and harsh scrutiny be given to product Z. It generates Dc of $325,000, or 46% of sales, which seems all right. But it needs direct assets in the enormous amount of $2,950,000, so that its Dc/DA is only 11%. Either its excessive assets should be trimmed without sacrificing Dc, or additional Dc should be generated from the same amount of assets. Or else the product should be dropped and replaced with one that provides a higher CRE.

Let us now plug product W into CM Chart 10. With original products X and Z we enjoyed a 61% Sc_1 on sales of $1,300,000 (at S_1). KC_1 of $685,000 (DKC of $175,000 + KC of $510,000) intersects with Sc_1 at BV_1 of $1,123,000, so that $P_1 = $110,000. It is a good profit, but our cash margin is scrawny at 14% CM_1.

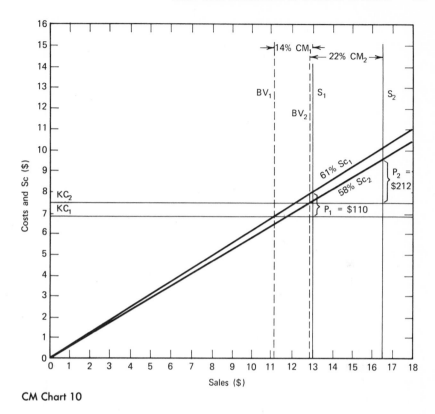

CM Chart 10

By adding product W, we drop to 58% Sc_2 and go up to KC_2 of $751,000, and BV_2 jumps to $1,295,000. But these setbacks are offset by product W's sales contribution: now at S_2 of $1,650,000, we have jumped from 14% CM_1 to 22% CM_2, and from $P_1 = 110,000$ to $P_2 = 212,000$. The new product has given us *both* additional profits and a generous cash margin, from which we derive additional earnings potential, safety, and maneuverability.

SALES-CASH DISTRIBUTION AS A SOURCE OF PROFITS

Time passes, and we want to analyze the market performance of products X, Y, and Z. This is the distribution of sales cash among products and territories, as shown in Table 8. The analysis helps us decide on specific marketing actions and corrective measures. For simplicity, we have assumed no change in product performance from Table 7.

Table 8 Sales-Cash Distribution as a Source of Profits

			Sales Territories				
		Jones: Eastern	% of Total	Smith: Midwest	% of Total	Davis: West	% of Total
	Totals	%Sc	3	4	5	6	7	8
	1	2						
Sales								
1. Product X	$600		$337		$192		$ 71	
2. Product Z	700		336		287		77	
3. Product W	350		178		94		78	
4.	$1650		$851		$573		$226	
Sales cash								
5. Product X	390	65%	$219	44%	$125	37%	$46	36%
6. Product Z	405	58	195	39	165	49	45	35
7. Product W	168	48	85	17	45	13	38	29
8.	$963	58%	$499		$335		$129	
9. (%Sc)			(59%)		(58%)		(57%)	
10. DKC[a]	135		109		19		7	
11. Dc	$828		$390		$316		$122	
12. (%Dc)			(46%)		(55%)		(54%)	
13. KC	616							
14. Profit	$212							

[a]Sales department KC.

Jones, Eastern District (column 3) produces the largest amount of sales cash, or $499,000 (line 8). And he has the most profitable mix of products, or 59% (line 9). Smith and Davis could benefit from his example.

But Jones spends far too much in DKC, at $109,000 (line 10) to achieve his profitable mix. His 46%Dc (line 12) is the lowest of the three territories. Proper corrective action would be evaluated by the extent to which he can reduce his DKC without sacrificing sales cash.

Davis's mix of only 57% Sc (line 9) suffers from the hefty 29% of his district's sales volume done in product W (column 8, line 7). Product W has only a 48% Sc (column 2, line 7). And he does only 36% of his volume in profitable product X (column 8, line 5), which has a 65% Sc (column 2, line 5).

A better emphasis in Davis's product sales would improve the mix and profits of his territory, quite apart from any improvement in sales volume. He could benefit from Jone's example, whose territory does 44% of its volume (column 4, line 5) in profitable product X and only 17% in product W.

It is true that we want to build the sales of W, a new and promising product. But it should be promoted in a balanced way along with other profitable products, rather than at their expense and to the detriment of present sales cash productivity.

UNIT VOLUME DECISION-MAKING (CM2)

Unit volume is the second cash-margin factor, and as crucial a decision area as product portfolio. It takes us from decisions about products themselves to those about *units* of product.

The profitability of a strategy to promote unit sales depends on the incremental VC and DKC associated with that strategy. We start by estimating the strategy's BV, or the sales level it will need to pay for its own direct KC (DKC). Then we forecast whether and to what extent the additional sales will exceed BV, and produce CM and an incremental profit. It is simply an application of $BV = KC/\%Sc$ and $P = CM \times \%Sc$.

Suppose that we market a product that has a 20% Sc. This is net of salesmen's commissions and variable expenses (VC) such as automobile mileage allowances. Now we must decide whether to hire an additional salesman who has suddenly come on the scene. He will incur DKC of $1800 a month in base salary, T&E, clerical service, and direct advertising support. *His* BV is therefore $1800/20\%$, or $9000 a month of sales.

We hire him in the expectation that he can produce sales of $25,000 a month. His cash margin $(S - BV)$ at that volume would be a substantial

$16,000, or 64%CM ($16/$25). And he would produce a profit of $16,000×20% Sc, or $3200 a month.

Even if it turns out that he can sell only $15,000 a month, he will still contribute $1200 a month to profits ($15,000−$9000 BV×20%). And it would be at a respectable 40% CM ($6/15), leaving us with a comfortable margin of error.

But we would probably not hire the additional man based on $15,000 of expected sales, if his DKC was likely to be as high as $2400 a month. His BV would then be a lofty $12,000 ($2400/20%). The thin $3000 CM (only 20% of sales), and a potential profit of only $600, would make the proposed hiring both unsafe and unpromising.

Another familiar instance of unit volume decision-making: the downtown department store that seeks increased sales by instituting free delivery and related services to its suburban customers. The store's average merchandise markup (%Sc) is 20%. A driver and truck will cost about 1% of sales in VC such as gas and repairs, reducing %Sc to 19%. And DKC such as salary and other fixed costs related to the truck should come to $2400 a month.

Free delivery service must boost sales by $12,600 a month to break even ($2400/19%). It is actually expected to produce an extra $20,000, which means the store gains $1400 a month of profit ($7400CM × 19%) at a comfortable 37% CM. The free service is instituted.

The acquisition and merger field is replete with opportunities for sales-cash decision-making involving unit volume considerations. The following imaginary situation is typical. We would like to acquire ailing competitor, Delta Corp. Its sales are $2,500,000, its %Sc is 39%, and it is losing $50,000 a year. We can easily manufacture Delta's products in our spacious plant at about our present %Sc, and distribute them through our regular sales dealerships.

Our sales are $5,000,000 a year and net income is $100,000. KC is $2,000,000 but will increase to $2,500,000 from higher manufacturing and sales DKC of the acquired products.

After we acquire Delta, what will be our %CM and profit?

Referring back to the original sales-cash formulas in Chapter 9, our present %Sc is computed as follows:

$$\%Sc = \frac{KC+P}{S} = \frac{\$2,000,000+\$100,000}{\$5,000,000} = 42\%$$

As noted, %Sc will not change after the acquisition. Our situation before and after is therefore as follows:

	Sales (000)	% Sc	Sc (000)	KC (000)	P (000)	BV (KC/%Sc) (000)	CM (S–BV) (000)	%CM (CM/S)
Now	$5000	42%	$2100	$2000	$100	$4750	$ 250	5%
Post-acquisition	7500	42	3150	2500	650	5950	1550	21

At 42% Sc, combined sales of $7,500,000 provide Sc of $3,150,000. KC increases only moderately. So profit jumps to $650,000, and %CM from a very thin 5% to 21%.

CM Chart 11 graphically compares pre-acquisition situation 1 with post-acquisition situation 2. At S_1 of $5,000,000 and KC_1 of $2,000,000, we have a thin 5% CM and P_1 of only $100,000. But the Delta merger gives us S_2 of $7,500,000 and only a modest rise to $2,500,000 KC_2. BV_2 is higher, but the much bigger S_2 volume widens the margin to 21% CM_2. Accordingly, profits jump to $650,000 P_2.

We have successfully completed the acquisition of Delta Corp., and now plan to increase our combined profits from $650,000 to $1,000,000 a year.

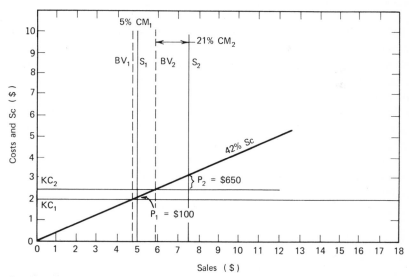

CM Chart 11

Since KC is $2,500,000, we will need $3,500,000 of sales cash $(P + KC = Sc)$.

Our strategy is to build sales by increasing the advertising of Delta Corp.'s neglected product line. Allowable advertising outlays, as a matter of policy, are always held at 5% of total budgeted VC. We should increase advertising, therefore, from its present $160,000 to an amount equal to 5% of the VC that we will incur when we have achieved the higher sales volume.

What is our sales requirement to produce $3,500,000 of Sc? And what is our allowable advertising costs (at 5% of anticipated VC) to achieve that Sc?

Since $S = Sc/\%Sc$ (Chapter 9, again), the sales required to achieve Sc of $3,500,000 with our 42% Sc, is $8,330,000.

Our allowable advertising expenditures to achieve this sales volume is 5% of VC. And VC is $100 - 0.42Sc = 0.58$. So $0.58VC \times \$8,330,000$ of required sales = $4,830,000 of VC. We can spend 5% of this on advertising, or $242,000, compared with our present advertising outlays of $160,000.

Of our total volume, $6,000,000 is contributed by product L, which accounts for 150,000 units at $40 a unit. It produces sales cash of $2,500,000 (%Sc of 0.417). We now want to strengthen our marketing position in the very competitive areas that we serve, while maintaining sales cash at $2,500,000. To do both, what are the various marketing options open to us in the form of increases and decreases in unit price and VC?

Table 9 ranks, from left to right, the desirability of all possible $\pm 10\%$ options available to us. For each, it gives the unit sales requirement that will provide our $2,500,000 Sc requirement. Column 1 is our present situation, with sales of 150,000 units and $6,000,000. The best option (column 2) is obviously a 10% price (Pr) increase and a 10% cost reduction $(+Pr - VC)$. It produces a sizable $23.03 of Sc per unit, or 52.3% Sc. So the requirement is only 108,000 units and sales of only $4,780,000, to provide the $2,500,000 of Sc (108,000 units $\times$ $23.03 Sc per unit).

As we move to the right, the options become less attractive. The last one that still gives some advantage over our present situation is $+Pr$, $+VC$ (column 5). It provides the same %Sc and total sales requiremment that we have now. But they are achieved with unit sales of only 136,000, compared with the present 150,000 unit requirement.

This is a kind of arithmetic doodling, to be sure, and somewhat removed from reality. But it does at least stretch our thinking to admit all possible marketing options, and in their order of preference. The exercise can be refined to reflect more closely the actual marketing price-cost environment. We would then have a rough but effective tool for determining our actual

Table 9 Cost-Price Strategies of Cash Generation: Sales of Product L Required to Produce $2,500,000 Sc at All Possible ±10% Variations in Price (Pr) and VC

	Present 1	+Pr −VC 2	+Pr 3	−VC 4	+Pr +VC 5	−Pr −VC 6	+VC 7	−Pr 8	−Pr +VC 9
Unit Pr	$40.00	$44.00	$44.00	$40.00	$44.00	$36.00	$40.00	$36.00	$36.00
VC	23.30	20.97	23.30	20.97	25.63	20.97	25.63	23.30	25.63
Sc	16.70	23.03	20.70	19.03	18.37	15.03	14.37	12.70	10.37
%Sc	41.7%	52.3%	47.0%	47.6%	41.7%	41.7%	35.9%	35.3%	28.8%
Unit Sales Requirement (000)[a]	150	108	121	131	136	166	174	197	241
USR index (%)	100	72	81	87	91	111	116	131	161
Total sales required (000)[b]	$6000	$4780	$5320	$5250	$6000	$6000	$6960	$7080	$8680

[a]$2500/unit Sc.
[b]$2500/%Sc, or units × price (that is, S=Sc/%Sc).

123

unit sales needed to maintain a target level of sales cash, at various realistic price and cost options.

PRICING STRATEGIES OF CASH GENERATION (CM3)

Price is the next CM factor to exert a powerful influence on sales volume and sales cash. We are of course continually faced with pricing decisions of one kind or another that are in their essence sales-cash decisions. They tend to group roughly into three camps. First, if we change our price to $X, what will be our sales cash and *profit*? Second, if we want our profit to be $Y, where must we set our *price*? And third, what is our sales requirement to maintain profits in the face of a change in market price?

These are important and usually urgent decisions. And they are all the more difficult because they must be made in recognition and within the framework of management's "power to price"—the degree to which we can in fact influence and control our pricing strategies. This of course depends on the degree of control we exercise in our marketplace. The power to price is a matter always in doubt and dispute, but the need to price effectively as best we can is always with us.

Table 9 on ±10% marketing options illustrated the kinds of creative arithmetic doodling we can pursue within the realities of our marketplace. It suggests pricing strategies that will provide a required profit, sales increases needed to offset a given price reduction, unit sales requirements under varying price conditions, and so forth. It is a table as readily applicable here as to the unit sales discussion where it is situated.

A pricing question that occurs more often than most, and falls in the third camp, is: By what amount will we have to increase sales to offset a price reduction that has been forced on us? This is the situation in Table 9, column 8, where the price had been lowered to $36 from $40 in column 1. A price reduction does not affect VC, which remained unchanged at $23.30. So Sc was reduced to $12.70, and %Sc to 35.3% (or $12.70/$36).

To maintain our required $2,500,000 of Sc, we now need to increase unit volume from 150,000 to 197,000, and to increase dollar volume from $6,000,000 to $7,080,000.

The formula is $S = Sc/\%Sc$. This is $2500/35.3\% = $7,080,000 of sales required. In units, it is $2500/12.70Sc = 197,000 units. We divide our desired Sc of $2,500,000 by the new %Sc of 35.3% (after the price reduction). It gives us the dollar sales that will produce that level of Sc at the new price. Or to get the higher unit sales required, we divide the $2,500,000 of required Sc by the reduced unit Sc of $12.70.

On the other hand, how do we estimate our profit at a proposed new price? The following simplified example is typical.

We manufacture a standard file cabinet that sells to retail outlets for $40 a unit. Our factory cost is $30, as follows: material, $10; direct labor, $5; and general overhead or KC, $15 (that is, applied at 300% of direct labor). Our company's general KC is about $100,000 a month.

We are now considering two orders. First, a national department store chain wants 1000 cabinets a month at a reduced price of $35 per cabinet. This business will require us to incur an additional $5000 a month in DKC. Second, we have a one-shot order for 5000 cabinets at $25 per cabinet.

Since the cost of making a cabinet is $30, whether to accept orders 1 and 2 narrows down to the BV and profit or loss to be expected on each piece of business:

	1	2
Unit price	$35	$25
− VC	15	15
Sc	$20	$10
%Sc	57%	40%
Unit volume	1,000	5,000
Total sales	$35,000	$125,000
VC	− 15,000	− 75,000
Sc	$20,000	$50,000
− DKC	− 5,000	
Dc	$15,000	

1. The order for 1000 cabinets a month at $35 each is only $5 over factory cost. But it provides additional profit of $15,000 a month. This is in the form of direct cash (Dc) which helps pay for the company's $100,000 of general KC. The $35 price less $15 of direct material and labor (VC) gives us an attractive 57% Sc.

On the additional $5000 of DKC, we break even with sales of only $8800 (5000/57%). At $35,000 of monthly sales, the order provides a huge $26,000 cash margin, or 75% CM. In units, we break even at $5000/$20 Sc, or at 250 units. Since 250 units at $20 pays for the $5,000 DKC, every unit over 250 adds $20 to the company's profit. We take the order.

2. The one-time order for 5000 cabinets at $25 each is priced $5 *below* factory cost. This would be unacceptable business if our plant were reasonably well loaded with production priced to cover all costs plus a target profit. It is true that *any* price over $15 of VC will add to P, less additional DKC. But it is also true that total KC of $100,000 a month must be paid for by total Sc if the company is to stay in business for the long pull.

But suppose we are hurting for business, and the $25 order will not really upset any existing customer relationships. The 5000 cabinets produce $10 of Sc apiece and are worth $50,000 in additional profit to us. Perhaps we should grab the business before somebody else does.

PRICING A TARGET PROFIT

If we are aiming for a particular profit, what *price* should we charge? The question is not as absurd as it may first appear to all those whose answer is: whatever price the market lets us charge, or whatever the traffic will bear. The decision process obviously must factor in the probable counterstrategies of our competitors to a price reduction, or customer resistance to an increase. This assumes that they even take notice of us. And it assumes that we cannot successfully camouflage the change with an actual or ostensible qualitative change in the product's performance, appearance, durability, or what not. But to the extent of our power to do so, as noted, we must constantly price and price effectively.

For example, our cabinet manufacturing business now does a monthly volume of 5000 units at a price of $40 each. VC has been held at $15 a unit, so we are generating $25 of sales cash, or $125,000 a month. We now decide to build monthly sales cash to $250,000. One way is to reduce the price and shoot for a 10% share of the market, which is 15,000 cabinets a month. But what price?

Sales cash target	$250,000
VC ($15 of standard DM and DL, 15,000 units)	+225,000
Sales needed (S = Sc + VC)	$475,000
Price (sales needed/15,000 units)	$31.75

Proof: $31.75 − $15VC = $16.75 Sc × 15,000 units = $250,000 Sc.

Actually, a market research study was the basis and support of the decision to work toward $250,000 of sales cash and 15,000 cabinets a month. It estimated the company's unit volume potential at prices ranging from $25 to $40, as follows:

Price	$25	$30	$35	$40
VC	15	15	15	15
Sc	10	15	20	25
		(000)		
Estimated unit volume	17	16	11	8
Sc	$170	$240	$220	$200

A price in the general area of $30 thus provided the largest sales cash potential, of $240,000. There was insufficient elasticity of demand at the low $25 price: the slight increase in sales to 17,000 units, from 16,000 at $30, hardly began to offset the sharp drop in Sc to $10. But the price was below factory cost of $30, so it was out of consideration anyway. At $35 and $40, the drop in estimated volume more than offset the increase in unit sales cash.

So much for the profit-generating dynamics of sales cash and the cash-margin factors—of products, units, and prices—from which our hard decisions must emerge every working day. Let us now back up a bit and see how the budgeting and control of volume costs (VC) help us to maximize sales cash.

CHAPTER 12

VOLUME BUDGETING
AND CONTROLLING SALES CASH

Sales-cash analysis is a remarkably versatile and powerful management tool. But its effectiveness, like that of any tool, depends on its precision and efficiency in the hands of the user. A precise and efficient system of budgeting and controlling sales cash gives us a powerful cash-generating tool indeed. Let us first look at budgeting, and then at controlling against budget.

THE VOLUME BUDGET AND SALES-CASH PRODUCTIVITY

Among the best statistical and accounting mechanisms for providing management with sales-cash data is the volume budget.[1] It should be used in conjunction with an effective internal system of direct standard costing, which dovetails and supplements the company's conventional full-absorption accounting system. We shall discuss both systems presently.

The volume budget systematically separates volume costs (VC) from total costs, whereby we can deal only with the sales cash (S − VC) of each product or service. So we can forecast and control cash for *any* level of sales that materializes: Unit costs now contain only volume costs, which fluctuate with sales and so are *fixed per unit* regardless of unit volume. We therefore *know* what our unit costs will be at any volume level. Unit costs do not now include fixed costs (KC), which *vary* per unit depending on the level of unit volume. That is, the more units by which a fixed quantity of KC is divided, the lower the KC per unit; and vice versa.

[1]Also known as a variable budget, and more popularly but less descriptively as a "flexible budget."

The conventional full-absorption accounting system does include (absorb) KC in unit costs. A variance in unit *volume* from our forecast will therefore cause a unit cost variance, only because KC per unit is now different from forecast. This was due to the volume variance alone, and not to any difference in the actual amount of KC incurred.

$P = \%Sc \times S - KC$ best explains the precision of sales-cash analysis, forecasting, and control. %Sc and KC are constant, and therefore *known*, for all levels of S. So we can easily forecast P, as well as BV and CM.

Take our Sample Company, for instance (000): S, $100; VC, $60; Sc, $40; KC, $30; and P, $10. $BV = \$30/0.40 = \$75$; and $CM = \$100 - \$75 = \$25$.

Now, if sales rise to $175, we have:

1. $P = \%Sc \times S - KC = 0.40 \times \$175 - \$30 = \$40$.
2. $BV = \$75$, which of course remains unchanged for all levels of sales.
3. $CM = \$175 - \$75 = \$100$.

The volume budget is thus a unique and formidable profit forecaster and controller because we know what %Sc and KC will be at any level of sales —the same as they are *now*.

Moreover, we budget *standard* costs, not actual costs. Applying readily available, predetermined standards makes the job of costing both easier and quicker. And it provides continuous guidelines against which we can promptly measure actual performance.

Suppose that our salesman's car has a standard VC per mile of $0.04. This is the variable expenses such as gasoline, oil, tires, and repairs, at the predetermined and measured standard, or *attainable good performance* (AGP). The car's standard direct KC such as depreciation, garage rental, and insurance is $60 a month.

We therefore know the car's standard monthly cost at any mileage level simply by applying the VC rate per mile of $0.04 to the actual mileage, and adding KC of $60. If it was driven 1700 miles in February, $VC = \$68$ and $DKC = \$60$. So the total standard or AGP cost of operating the car in February was $128. At 3100 miles, standard operating cost is $184. If the actual cost of driving 3100 miles was $205, the salesman has a negative variance for the month of $21. This is all we really mean by volume budgeting at standard cost.

Each of the company's departmental and other cost centers has a volume budget by months or weeks. It applies a standard *VC rate* to the cost center and each product flowing through it. This rate is a ratio whose denominator is the cost center's activity measurement, such as direct labor

(DL) hours. The VC rate for fuel might be $6/DL-hour. It means that, based on experience, the department's fuel costs should be around $6/ man-hour of its direct labor (the activity measurement).

A machine-paced center would probably be measured by machine-hours or dollars, stores or warehouse centers by the weight of goods handled, and so forth. The activity measurement gears the standard costing of that center to the company's sales volume, because it tends to fluctuate with sales.[2]

The VC rate, say $6/DL-hour, is applied to the actual activity of the center for that month, to determine its allowable or standard VC. It is the same procedure that was used for our salesman's car. The standard rate was $0.04/mile, miles being the activity measure. Each month the rate of $0.04 is applied to actual mileage: 1700 miles, in the example, gave us our standard or allowable VC of $68.

VOLUME BUDGETING THE COST CENTERS

For example, Production Department C's volume budget applies volume costs according to DL-hours and charges direct overhead at a standard KC per month:

	VC/DL-hour	DKC/month
Direct labor	$2.70	—
Indirect labor	0.90	$ 5,200
Supervision	—	17,600
Fringe benefits	0.30	3,400
Supplies, small tools, etc.	0.70	—
Electric power	1.10	—
Maintenance	0.30	3,800
	$6.00	$30,000

If the department clocked 2000 DL-hours, its total standard cost allow- ance would be $6×2000 DL-hours+$30,000=$42,000.

At 2000 DL-hours, the department's maintenance allowance (against which actual maintenance costs would be compared), is

[2]It does so, that is, after we adjust for inventory changes, which indicate the extent to which production is out of gear with sales.

VC ($0.30×2000 hours) $ 600
KC   3800
Maintenance allowance $4400

The foreman of Department C receives a cost allowance schedule each month, which he helped put together and which he believes in. It gives him his monthly allowance for each cost item, and for the entire center, at *any* level of production.

At the end of September, for instance, he receives October's production schedule for Department C. From his cost allowance schedule he predicts his department's costs at that planned level of production. Then, at the end of October: Based on the production volume actually attained, he computes his *actual* budget allowance from his cost allowance schedule and determines his cost variances.

This is illustrated in Table 10. His department produced 11,200 units in October, as shown in the lower left of the cost allowance schedule. So his allowable DL-hours, at the standard of 5 units/hour (or 1 unit=0.20 hours) is 2240 hours (column 2). At $6/hour, his variable cost allowance is therefore $13,440 (column 3).

So his departmental total cost (TC) allowance, including $30,000 of KC, is $43,440 (column 4). Since actual departmental costs were $44,100, he incurred a negative variance of $660. His costs per unit are shown in columns 5 to 7. It actually cost him $3.94 to make each unit, compared with his allowance of $3.88 (column 7). His negative variance was therefore $0.06 a unit.

Volume-budget variance control everywhere in the business thus forces VCs to behave as VCs, whereby we move from cost forecasting to "cost forcing." Unless VC negative variances are prevented, budgetarily, what we thought were VCs turn out actually to be KCs. This increases both Sc and BV, and we have more cost leverage up and down than we bargained for. That is, a given increase in sales will now yield more profit, and a drop in sales will cut profit more sharply, because %Sc and BV are higher (recalling Chart 2 in Chapter 9). Our control over profit has been undermined, perhaps dangerously, to the extent of the inflexibility in VC (excess of KC).

CONTROLLING SALES-CASH PRODUCTIVITY

Sales cash should be reported and controlled in terms of the cash-margin factors that produce it. First, the most revealing Sc reports are constructed

Table 10 Sales Cash and Production Scheduling: Cost Allowance Schedule, W. C. Smith, Production Department C

| | | | | | Cost/Unit | |
Units Produced 1	DL-hours (1 unit = 0.20 hours) 2	VC ($6/hour) 3	TC Standard Allowance [(3) + $30,000] 4	VC [(3)÷(1)] 5	KC [$30,000÷(1)] 6	TC [(4)÷(1)] 7
8,000	1600	$ 9,600	$39,600	$1.20	$3.75	$4.95
12,000	2400	14,400	44,400	1.20	2.50	3.70
16,000	3200	19,200	49,200	1.20	1.87	3.07
24,000	4800	28,800	58,800	1.20	1.25	2.45
October actual, 11,200 units:						
Allowance	2240	13,440	43,440	1.20	2.68	3.88
Actual			44,100			3.94
Variance			($ 660)			($0.06)

around and broken down to the individual *products*, which are always management's central focus.

Unit volume generates the primal inflow of cash. So it is the appropriate starting point at the top of the report's product columns. But unit volume is one-dimensional; by itself it is unrelated to sales cash and profit.

Price is the cash-margin factor that constitutes a second dimension to unit volume. VC is the third. That is, units × price − VC = sales cash. Since price has about the same impact on sales cash as does VC, we must control both factors very closely. In fact, our actual control focus is the *net* price variance between what we charge our customers and what we are charged by our suppliers.

Volume costs (VC), mainly the direct standard costs of manufacturing the product, are the center of gravity of Sc control reporting. Variance control of the other CM factors revolves around and depends on VC control.

To illustrate one of many ways of reporting and controlling sales cash, let us conjure up an imaginary two-product (labeled G and K) company. It simply buys precut steel and components and fabricates them into heavy equipment and machinery.

Each product's standard manufacturing cost per unit, such as for product G shown in Table 11, was developed from carefully engineered specifications as to material and labor-machine input. They were prepared by the industrial engineering department in cooperation with the foreman of each cost center through which the product passes.

Table 11 is the direct standard cost of manufacturing 100 units of product G. It is sequenced in the order that production flows through the plant: from the receipt of raw and semifabricated steel and other materials, through shearing, pressing, welding, assembling, painting, inspection, and packing.

A *code number* identifies each item of material. The *quantity needed* at each work center is derived from the product's manufacturing specification (not shown). It is the standard amount of material required per 100 units, net of allowable spoilage or loss. And for each conversion operation, it is the standard DL-hours or machine-hours needed, net of allowable downtime. The *cost rate* is the standard dollar amount per piece or per hour.

The *cost per 100 units* is therefore the quantity needed multiplied by the cost rate. To make 100 units of product G, on the top line, we thus need 8 pieces of 11-D steel at a standard cost of $160/piece, or $1,280. Shearing, or cost center 1, requires 120 machine-hours at standard. This is at a cost rate of $3/hour, totaling $360.

As we go down Table 11 through the various manufacturing operations, each cost center is subtotaled as to cost per 100 units. Finally we come

Table 11 Sales Cash and Production Costing. Direct Standard Manufacturing Cost: 100 Units[a] (Product G)

	Code Number	Quantity Needed	Cost Rate	Cost/100 Units		
				Material	Labor, etc. (Conversion)	Total
Steel	11-D	8	$160	$1280		$1280
Steel	14-D	6	220	1320		1320
Shearing—center 1		120[b]	3		360	360
Subtotal				$2600	$ 360	$2960
Material	9-R	26	47.70	1240		1240
Pressing—center 2		360[b]	3.55		280	1280
Subtotal				$3840	$1640	$5480
Material	116-L	5	62	310		310
Welding—center 3		210[c]	2.50		520	520
Subtotal				$4150	$2160	$6310
Material	5-W	20	12.50	250		250
Material	17-W	8	91.20	730		730
Component	RX3	100	16.00	1600		1600
Assembling—center 4		200[c]	3.25		650	650

Subtotal				$6730	$2810	$ 9540
Material	8-R	26	47.70	1240		1240
Material	10-R	108	6.57	710		710
Painting—center 5		210[b]	4.50		940	940
Subtotal				$8680	$3750	$12,430
Inspection—center 6		29[c]	3.80		110	110
Subtotal				$8680	$3860	$12,540
Material	3-P	100	3.20	320		320
Packing—center 7		52[c]	2.70		140	140
Total direct standard cost, 100 units				$9000	$4000	$13,000
Standard cost/unit				$ 90	$ 40	$ 130

[a] Figures are rounded.
[b] Machine-hours.
[c] DL-hours.

down to the total direct standard cost to manufacture 100 units: material of $9000 and conversion of $4000, or a total cost of $13,000. The cost of 1 unit is therefore $90 of material and $40 of conversion, or $130.

Product G's nonmanufacturing direct volume costs—derived from the volume budgets of the nonmanufacturing cost centers—total $35/unit. And its price per unit is $300. So we can now make the following sales cash calculation for the standard Sc/unit of product G:

Price		$300
Direct costs		
Manufacturing	$130	
Other	35	165
Sales cash (Sc)		$135/unit

Product K was also costed at standard, in the same way.

Table 12 is therefore a standard operating plan for the two products, covering the 9 months ended September 30.

It forecasts G and K's unit volume for the period at 9000 and 8600 (line 1). At those prices and VCs, the company's sales cash should total $2,850,000 (line 8) on sales of $7,000,000 (line 6). It means an average %Sc for both products of 40.7% (line 9). Against this overall plan, actual sales cash and sales mix will later be compared.[3]

As we move forward through this 9-month segment of production time, whose sales-cash generation we seek to monitor, reports are received on the crucial focuses of cash-margin control: net price variance; material variance; conversion variance; and direct cost variance for all the other cost centers. And we get a comprehensive report on total sales-cash variance.

REPORTING NET PRICE VARIANCES

Table 13 shows actual unit sales valued at *standard* price compared with actual sales at *actual* price, the difference being the sales price variance. We sold 11,000 units of product G (line 1) at a price that created dollar sales of $3,350,000 (line 4)—not $3,300,000 (line 3), which would have

---

[3]To simplify these illustrations, we use only year-to-date controls, and ignore the usual monthly and weekly budget control points.

Table 12 The Profit Forecast (9 Months Ended September 30)

	G	K	Total
1. Unit volume	9000	8600	
2. Unit price	$ 300	$ 500	
3. Unit VC[a]	165	310	
4. Unit Sc	$ 135	$ 190	
5. (%Sc)	(45%)	(38%)	
6. Total sales (000)	$2700	$4300	$7000
7. Total VC (000)	1485	2665	4150
8. Total Sc (000)	$1215	$1635	$2850
9. (%Sc)			(40.7%)

[a] Direct standard cost.

Table 13 Sales-Cash Generation and Net Price Variance

	G	K	Total
1. *Unit* sales, actual	11,000	7200	
2. Unit price, standard	$ 300	$ 500	
3. Total sales at *standard* price (000)	$3,300	$3600	$6900
4. Total sales at *actual* price (000)	3,350	3620	6970
5. Sales price variance (000)	$ 50	$ 20	$ 70
6. Materials purchase price at *standard* (000)	$ 990	$1220	$2210
7. Materials purchase price at actual (000)	1,050	1220	2270
8. Purchase price variance (000)	($ 60)	$ 0	($ 60)
9. Net price variance (000)	($ 10)	$ 20	$ 10

resulted if they had been sold at the standard price of $300. It was a price increase of about 1.5% that accounted for this positive sales price variance of $50,000 (line 5). Product K was also sold at slightly higher prices than standard, causing a favorable sales price variance of $20,000 (line 5).

Next, the purchase price variance (line 8) is the difference between the cost of materials at standard and their actual cost. Standard materials purchase price (line 6) is the cost per unit (from the product's standard manufacturing cost, as in Table 11) multiplied by the number of units sold. Product G's standard material cost per unit was $90, and we sold 11,000 units. So material purchase price at standard (line 6) is $990,000. But material to manufacture product G actually cost $1,050,000 (line 7), causing a negative purchase price variance of $60,000 (line 8).

Since product G had a positive sales price variance of $50,000 and a negative purchase price variance of $60,000, its *net price variance* (line 9) was ($10,000). Product K's standard material cost per unit was $170 (not shown), so the standard cost of 7200 units was $1,220,000 (line 6). Since this was the actual outlay for K's materials (line 7), it had no purchase price variance to offset its positive $20,000 sales price variance.

The company's *total* net price variance for both products therefore was a positive $10,000 (line 9). Price increases on unit sales totaling $70,000 more than offset $60,000 of cost increases for materials.

The principle of the *single variable* thus underlies all control reporting of sales cash. Only the factor under analysis is allowed to vary, everything else remaining constant, as in the net price variance report. Actual unit sales of both products were very different from plan (Table 12), which called for 9000 units of product G and 8600 units of product K. But the report held unit sales constant, ignoring the huge variances. It did so by multiplying the *same* actual unit sales by the standard price, and then by the actual price.

Price was thus the single variable that produced the sales price variance. And purchase price was the single variable that caused the purchase price variance. We shall see this single-variable principle of analysis at work throughout control reporting.

MATERIAL AND CONVERSION VARIANCES

In the same way we isolate and deal with material *usage* as a single variable. This is shown in Table 14. For the actual unit volume attained, it compares the actual material used with the standard or allowable usage. The usage variance is valued at *standard* cost to eliminate price variances,

Table 14 Sales Cash Generation and Material Variance (9 Months Ended September 30)

	Code Number	Usage (pieces) Standard	Usage (pieces) Actual	Usage Variance (pieces)	At Standard Cost	Variance ($)
Product G: 11000 units						
1. Steel	11-D	880	883	(3)	$160	$ (480)
2. Steel	14-D	660	661	(1)	220	(220)
3. Material	9-R	2,860	2,854	6	47.70	286
4. Material	116-L	550	557	(7)	62	(434)
5. Material	5-W	2,200	2,208	(8)	12.50	(100)
6. Material	17-W	880	878	2	91.20	182
7. Component	RX3	11,000	11,000	0	16	0
8. Material	8-R	2,860	2,884	(24)	47.70	(1145)
9. Material	10-R	11,880	11,872	8	6.57	53
10. Material	3-P	11,000	11,134	(134)	3.20	(429)
11. Total material variance, product G						$(2287)

Table 14 (*Continued*)

Product K: 7200 units

	Code Number	Usage (pieces) Standard	Actual	Usage Variance (pieces)	At Standard Cost	Variance ($)
12. Plastic	3-H	140	142	(2)	119	$ (238)
13. Steel	11-D	960	960	0	160	0
14. Material	116-L	840	844	(4)	62	(248)
15. Material	8-R	3110	3144	(34)	47.70	(1622)
16. Material	5-W	2380	2374	6	12.50	75
17. Material	9-R	2940	2947	(7)	47.70	(334)
18. Component	RX3	7200	7190	10	16	160
19. Component	RX9	180	180	0	211	0
20. Material	3-P	7200	7221	(21)	3.20	(67)
21. Total material variance, product K						$(2274)
22. Total material variance (−Sc)						$(4561)

Material Summary	Code Number		Variance ($)	% of Total
1. Steel	11-D		$ (480)	(10.5%)
2. Steel	14-D		(220)	(4.8)
3. Material	9-R	$286		
4.		(334)	(48)	(1.0)
5. Material	116-L	(434)		
6.		(248)	(682)	(15.0)
7. Material	5-W	(100)		
8.		75		
9. Material	17-W		(25)	(0.5)
10. Component	RX-3		182	4.1
11. Material	8-R	(1145)	160	3.5
12.		(1622)	(2767)	(60.7)
13. Material	10-R		53	1.2
14. Material	3-P	(429)		
15.		(67)	(496)	(10.9)
16. Plastic	3-H		(238)	(5.3)
17. Total material variance			$(4561)	(100.0%)

and thus isolate material usage as the single variable. The information comes from the products' standard manufacturing cost sheet (such as Table 11).

Product G's actual unit volume was 11,000, so type 11-D steel (line 1) had a standard usage of 880 pieces. That is, to manufacture 100 units we need 8 pieces at standard (from Table 11). For 11,000 units, we need *880 pieces* at standard $(11,000 \div 100 = 110 \times 8 = 880)$.

But the actual usage was 883 pieces, so the usage variance was a negative 3 pieces. Valued at the standard cost per piece of $160 (Table 11, cost rate), the usage variance for 11-D steel in product G is ($480).

And so on down the table for all the material inputs, to arrive at a total material variance for product G (line 11) of ($2,287). And product K's total material variance, at 7200 units sold (line 21), is ($2,274). So the company's total material variance, which directly reduces sales cash (line 22), is ($4,561).

A *material summary* of variances gives us a usage breakdown by type of material, regardless of the products in which it is used. For instance, the material variance report shows material 8-R with a negative usage variance in both products of $1,145 and $1,622, respectively (lines 8 and 15). They are noticeable but not really disturbing when examined within the overall product context of material variance.

But in the material summary a large total negative variance of $2,767 pops out at us for the single material 8-R (line 12). It is more than 60% of the total material variance (line 17) of ($4,561), and is clearly an urgent problem. We would also not delay going after the 116-L variance (line 6) of ($682), which is almost hidden in the conventional material variance report. Both types of variance must be reported to the responsible foreman weekly and daily, to give him a precise and meaningful basis for prompt correction.

Table 15 gives us the direct costs incurred by labor and machinery to convert material into finished equipment. The volume budget of each cost center supplies the standard and actual costs of all conversion work as well as the variance between the two.

In footnote *a*, for instance, the Welding Department (center 3) had standard costs of $110,000 and actual costs of $112,000, so the variance was ($2000) (line 13). This is summarized, as are those of the other cost centers, at the top in the main conversion variance table. The right-hand column shows total conversion costs, at standard, of $980,000 (line 1). Actual conversion costs for all centers totaled $993,000 (line 2). So the total conversion variance for the company (line 3) is ($13,000).

We next compute the *product* conversion variances by cost centers. For instance, product G's total conversion cost variance (line 4) is ($6,000).

Table 15 Sales-Cash Generation and Conversion Variance (000)

	Cost Center							Total Conversion Costs
	1	2	3[a]	4	5	6	7	
1. Standard	120	260	110	140	220	40	90	980[b]
2. Actual	124	266	112	141	215	41	94	993
3. Variance	(4)	(6)	(2)	(1)	5	(1)	(4)	($13)
4. Product G	(2)	(1)	5	(3)	(4)	2	(3)	(6)[c]
5. Product K	(2)	(5)	(7)	2	9	(3)	(1)	(7)
6.								($13)

[a]Welding—Center 3, direct costs year to date:

	Standard Costs	Actual Costs	Variance
7. Labor	$ 60	$ 60	$ 0
8. Fringe benefits	13	14	(1)
9. Fuel and electricity	9	10	(1)
10. Repairs	11	13	(2)
11. Supplies	13	14	(1)
12. Scrap and rework	4	1	3
13.	$110	$112	$(2)

[b]Conversion costs: product G—$40/unit × 11,000 units = $440
product K—75/unit × 7,200 units = 540
$980

[c]11,000 units × $40/unit (standard conversion cost) = $440
446 actual
($ 6) variance

This is its standard conversion cost of $440,000 (11,000 units multiplied by $40 of conversion cost per unit) *less* its actual conversion costs, which (we assume) are $446,000.

Again, variances must be communicated immediately to the responsible supervisor for correction. This kind of pinpoint costing—in grid form by cost centers and by products—provides a meticulous and tight grasp of the particular cost environment under review, and greatly facilitates variance correction.

Nonmanufacturing cost centers are also controlled in terms of correctable variances, of course, as illustrated in Table 16. It shows summary cost and variance results for the company's sales branch office system, or cost

Table 16 Cost Center Profitability: Cost Center 9 (OOO)

	Branch Office					Total Branch Direct Costs
	1	2	3[a]	4	5	
1. Standard	42	59	56	70	53	$ 280
2. Actual	45	62	51	79	55	292
3. Variance	(3)	(3)	5	(9)	(2)	$(12)
4. Product G	(1)	2	2	(3)	(2)	(2)
5. Product K	(2)	(5)	3	(6)	0	(10)
6.						$(12)

[a]Branch office 3, direct costs year to date:

	Standard Costs	Actual Costs	Variance
7. Commissions	$14	$14	$0
8. Bonuses	11	11	0
9. Temporary sales help	9	4	5
10. Temporary clerical help	4	3	1
11. Fringe benefits	11	12	(1)
12. Miscellaneous	7	7	0
13.	$56	$51	$5

center 9. The figures come up from the volume budgets of each subcenter, as illustrated by branch office 3 (footnote *a*). Standard costs of the branch were $56,000 and actual costs were $51,000; hence there was a positive variance of $5000 (line 13). These are direct costs incurred in behalf of specific products, so the report also gives branch variances by products. Their total of ($12,000) on line 6 agrees with the total of the branch variances (line 3).

THE SALES-CASH VARIANCE CONTROL

These and many other varieties of sales cash reporting flow into the comprehensive *sales cash summary* (Table 17). One of many possible types, it isolates sales cash itself as the single variable and analyzes its variance in terms of the two component causes. They are the *quantity* of sales (sales variance) and the *quality* of sales (mix variance).

The first section of Table 17 repeats the essential information of the original profit forecast, or standard operating plan (Table 12), which is our basis of comparison with actual results.

Product G's actual sales of $3,300,000 were much better than plan (line 8 vs. line 4). But K's $3,600,000 were well below the plan's $4,300,000. Total company sales of $6,900,000 were therefore slightly under plan's $7,000,000.

Total sales mix improved, however, with %Sc of 41.3% (line 10) instead of the planned 40.7% (line 6). Despite the below-standard sales performance, therefore, actual sales cash (line 9) of $2,853,000 was slightly *above* the planned $2,850,000 (line 5). This is because successful product G has a higher %Sc, at 45%, than laggard K's 38% (line 10).

As shown farther down in the *Sc variance* section, product G's positive sales variance over plan (line 12) of $600,000 produced a positive Sc variance (line 11) of $270,000 (or $1,485,000 – $1,215,000). But product K's larger negative variance of $700,000 reduced Sc by only $267,000, because it has a lower %Sc than does product G. Despite the company's total sales variance of ($100,000), therefore, its sales cash was $3000 ahead of plan. This was due solely to the improvement in total average %Sc, or sales *mix*.

"Mix variance" above plan was therefore $103,000 (line 13), in the total column: sales were $100,000 below plan, but Sc was $3000 above plan. So there must have been a $103,000 improvement in mix (from +%Sc) to account for the favorable Sc variance *not* caused by the sales variance.

Mix variance is thus equal to the sales cash variance minus the sales variance (000):

Mix variance		=	Sc variance	−	Sales variance
Product G	($330)	=	$270	−	$600
Product K	433	=	(267)	−	(700)
Company	$103	=	$ 3	−	($100)

Finally, the table summarizes all the component variances that directly affect the amount of sales cash generated, as reported in the preceding control tables. The company's sales-cash reporting system has now come about full circle. And management has a tight and responsive "feel" of this critically important sector of the total cash-generating mechanism.

Table 17 The Sales Cash Summary (9 Months Ended September 30)

	G	K	Total
Plan			
1. Unit volume	9,000	8600	
2. Unit Price[a]	$ 300	$ 500	
3. Unit Sc	135	190	
4. Total sales (000)	$2,700	$4300	$7000
5. Total Sc (000)	1,215	1635	2850
6. (%Sc)	(45%)	(38%)	(40.7%)
Actual			
7. Unit volume	11,000	7200	
8. Total sales[a] (000)	$3,300	$3600	$6900
9. Total Sc (000)	1,485	1368	2853
10. (%Sc)	(45%)	(38%)	(41.3%)
11. Sc variance (000)	$ 270	($ 267)	$ 3
12. Sales variance (000)	600	(700)	(100)
13. Mix variance (000)	(330)	433	103
Summary of variances (000)			
Net price	($ 10)	$ 20	$ 10
Direct material	(2.3)	(2.3)	(4.6)
Conversion	(6)	(7)	(13)
Cost center 8	4	(1)	3
Cost center 9	(2)	(10)	(12)
Cost center 10			
Etc.			

[a] Standard price.

With an effective system of sales-cash budgeting and control, the comprehensive strategy of cash is armed with a formidable weapon. We have a precise fix on our breakeven volume, and on the cash-margin surplus of sales from which profits flow.

Increasing this margin in relation to sales increases the profitability of sales cash, in $CM/S = P/Sc$. Increasing its absolute quantity and quality increases the absolute amount of profit, in $P = CM \times \%Sc$.

And increasing $(CM \times \%Sc)/A$ provides the total impact that sales cash makes on CRE, within the all-inclusive cash-generating framework of Pi.

Thus armed, the strategy of cash can harness the six cash-margin factors —which together are the sole cause of profits—in precise and rewarding profit decisions: concerning products, unit volume, price, VC, mix, and KC. The cash-margin chart greatly facilitates this decision-making process.

Few weapons in our cash-generating arsenal are the equals of sales-cash productivity. Yet one of them is important enough at least to involve us for the next four chapters. This is the strategy of *cost cash*.

PART 4

GENERATING COST CASH

CHAPTER 13

THE COSTING FRAMEWORK
FOR GENERATING CASH

Cost control ($-$C) is the single most important continuing source of cash available to the well-run company. This is the firm that has already squeezed the liquidity out of excess assets ($-$A), is adequately leveraged ($+$L), and has an efficient mechanism for the generation and control of sales cash ($+$Sc). There is nothing such a management can do that would have a stronger impact on cash productivity than maintaining an effective cost control and reduction capability. For this well-run company, in fact, cash improvement *means* cost control and reduction. We shall use the terms interchangeably.

The relative cash-generating impact of cost reduction can be seen arithmetically: product R has %Sc (or sales cash/sales) of 0.40, and a 30% cash return on its direct assets. What is the pretax cash-generating impact of a $100,000 cost reduction, compared with the same amount of sales increase or asset reduction?

	% Impact on Cash	Annual Cash Return
$-$C	100%	$100,000
$+$S	40	40,000
$-$A	30	30,000

The $100,000 cost reduction provides a 100%, dollar-for dollar improvement in cash flow. The same increase in sales produces $40,000 of cash flow, equal to its 40% Sc. And a $100,000 reduction in assets, releasing that amount of cash for reinvestment, provides $30,000 of cash—from the product's 30% return on direct assets.

This is an arithmetic and not necessarily a pragmatic comparison of cash-improvement alternatives. Yet a $100,000 cost reduction may be no more difficult to achieve—and in many cases is more easily achieved—than the same amount of sales increase or asset reduction. With costs as with nothing else, a penny saved is a penny earned.

THE "SEVEN C'S" OF COST CONTROL

We might first summarize so deadly serious a subject in an almost lighthearted way—though quite realistically—in terms of the seven C's of cost control:

1. *Collection* of costs: We need a simple, flexible, and inexpensive cost accounting system that *pinpoints* product unit costs in meticulous detail, promptly and accurately. Let us call it pinpoint costing.

2. *Classification* of costs: However sharply we pinpoint cost collection, we still must organize and classify the raw data into the most meaningful categories—as to origin and cause, location, behavioral type, person responsible, and so forth. Costs so organized can then be analyzed imaginatively and creatively.

3. *Comparison* of costs: Properly collected and classified costs are meaningless apart from their correctible variances. They must be immediately comparable with predetermined engineered standards and budget allowances that reflect "attainable good performance."

4. *Communication* of costs and variances: We must promptly transmit all variances to the cost-responsible man, to whom they are meaningful and controllable. Our cost control system should therefore be one of unitary responsibility, in which every cost is the responsibility of *one* man.

5. *Correction* of variances: The man who is thus unitarily responsible for the cost variance gets it back to standard in an organized and controlled way.

6. *Consciousness* of costs and cash: Cost consciousness is cash consciousness for virtually all operating people. It is a total awareness of and eager receptiveness to cost savings opportunities everywhere they can be found. The company's motivational environment is a reward-penalty system geared to each man's sales/cost ratios.

7. *Creativity* toward costs and cash: Above and beyond cash consciousness is cash creativity—everyone initiating cash-generating cost reduction proposals and projects. This happy condition is sustained by an organized cash improvement capability that involves the entire company.

GENERATING COST CASH

Cost cash is that portion of the company's available cash that we reinvest in cost expenditures, as opposed to noncost expenditures such as the purchase of assets or the retirement of debt. It is simply the $+C$ among four possible reinvestments of cash to which the sources of cash can be applied:

Sources of Cash	Reinvestment of Cash
$S - C - A + L + D + E + R$	$+C + A - L - E$

We *generate* cost cash by reducing the amount of cash reinvested in cost expenditures while maintaining the same level of sales. Or we generate it by increasing the level of sales without increasing the cash reinvestment in cost expenditures. Cost cash is thus produced by $+S/C$, whether through an increase in the numerator or a decrease in the denominator.

The sources of cash are directed to the four applications of cash in accordance with payback or cash-return criteria, our objective being always to maximize CRE. Which of the $+C + A - L - E$ applications will produce the highest percentage cash return? Costs must therefore compete with the other investment outlets for a given quantity of investable cash, and payback alone determines the competitive order of priority. It follows that every cost expenditure—no matter how trivial or how difficult to evaluate in terms of payback—must derive its justification solely from cash-return considerations, just as do the other three applications of cash.[1]

The generation of cost cash is thus a *payback* concept and strategy, as it is a *relative* strategy—to sales. As noted, we seek to minimize the dollar of cost input per dollar of existing or potential sales, and to maximize the dollar of sales per dollar of cost input. Either way, it is a cost reduction effort. Both ideas—of cost payback and of relativity—are worth pondering because they apply forcefully in many unlikely corners of the strategy of cash. A marketing program or a research effort, for instance, is in its final

---

[1]Whether our investment of cash has been in C or in A is a tangible and pragmatic question, not a conventional or bookkeeping one. Cash invested in A has given us possession of a salable asset such as a building or machine. It is defined as A to the extent and in the dollar amount that it is actually marketable for cash. The cash has been invested in C if it does not give us title to a salable asset. Conventional accounting might capitalize various research and development costs. for instance, and put them on the balance sheet as intangible assets. But our tangible and pragmatic distinction between costs and assets would classify them as costs, because they are not salable assets.

effect a cost reduction program if it serves to extract sales from costs and increase S/C.

In its broadest context, the production of cost cash is really the $-BV$ side of $+CM$, which of course is widened either by $+S$ or $-BV$: the cash margin is widened by an increase in sales or a reduction in breakeven volume. And $-BV = -KC/+\%Sc$. We reduce BV either by reducing constant costs (KC) or by reducing variable costs (VC)—that is, increasing %Sc, which is $(S-VC)/S$. Our choice of cost reduction strategies is guided, to a considerable extent, by the particular cost category we are attacking within the general breakeven equation.

DIRECT STANDARD COSTING

As we suggested in Chapter 12, our costing framework for generating cash will derive considerable benefit from an accounting system of direct standard costing (or a practical equivalent). This gears into and functions in close parallel with the volume budget, which separates volume costs and thus generates indispensable sales-cash data. In so doing, direct costing and volume budgeting are extremely useful in the control and reduction of costs.

For external reporting purposes, however, we must still depend on conventional full-absorption procedures applied in accordance with generally accepted accounting principles. Since direct costing and full-absorption costing give us different profit and inventory results, the distinction between the two systems is important to our understanding and application of cost reduction procedures.

Table 18 illustrates in a simplistic way the difference between them. It is based on the following assumptions about product L:

Produced	10,000 units
Sold	−8,000 units
Inventoried	2,000 units
Price	$20/unit
Direct standard cost (VC)	$10/unit
Manufacturing overhead (KC)	$20,000

Under direct costing (left-hand column): sales (line 1) are $160,000, or 8000 units sold multiplied by the $20 price. Cost of goods sold (line 4) is $80,000, or 8000 units multiplied by direct costs (VC) of $10 per unit. The difference is sales cash (line 5) of $80,000. This pays for total manufacturing and other overhead (line 9) of $27,000, to provide a profit (line 10) of $53,000. It is simply $S - VC = Sc - KC = P$.

Table 18   The Profit Impact of the Costing System

	Direct Costing			Full-Absorption Costing		
1. Sales	8000 units sold × $20 price		$160	8000 units sold × $20 price		$160
2. VC (direct costs)	8000 × $10 VC	$80		8000 × $10 VC	$80	
3. KC				8000 × $2 KC ($20,000 KC/10,000 units produced)	16	
4. Cost of goods sold			80			96
5. Sales cash						
6. Gross profit			$ 80			$64
7. Manufacturing		$20				
8. Engineering		2			2	
9. S, G and A		5	27		5	7
10. Profit			$ 53			$57
Inventory:						
11. Raw material		$ 20			$20	
12. Finished	2000 into inventory at $10 VC	20		2000 units into inventory at $12 ($10 VC + $2 KC)	24	
13. Other assets			100			100
14. Total assets			$140			$144
15. Liabilities			50			50
16. Equity			$ 90			$94

155

Down a bit further is the balance sheet. Since we inventoried 2000 units (assumptions, above) valued at $10 of direct cost (VC), $20,000 of finished units are added to inventory (line 12). *No* overhead goes into inventory under direct costing. The entire $27,000 of overhead had already been charged directly against earnings (line 9).

Under full-absorption costing: sales (line 1) are the same $160,000. But cost of goods sold (line 4) is $96,000—higher than the $80,000 under direct costing by $16,000 of overhead. This overhead was charged to sales at the rate of 8000 units sold multiplied by $2 per unit. That is, under absorption procedure, the $2 OH rate is the $20,000 of total manufacturing overhead divided by 10,000 units produced (our initial assumptions). So cost of goods was charged with 8000 units sold multiplied by $*12* per unit ($10 of VC as under direct costing, plus $2 of KC), or $96,000.

Full absorption thus gives us a gross profit (line 6) of $64,000. From this we deduct the remaining $7000 of *non*manufacturing overhead (line 9), leaving a profit (line 10) of $57,000. This exceeds the $53,000 direct costing profit by $4000: only $16,000 of manufacturing overhead was deducted from sales under full absorption (line 3), but the entire $20,000 was deducted under direct costing (line 7).

The $4000 of undeducted overhead, in full absorption, was instead capitalized into inventory. This is seen further down in the balance sheet. The 2000 unsold units went into inventory at $*12* per unit, or $10 of VC *plus* $*2 of overhead*, adding $24,000 to finished goods (line 12). (Under direct costing, the 2000 units were inventoried at only $10 of VC, or $20,000.)

So, to the extent that full-absorption accounting capitalizes overhead into inventory rather than charging it to cost of goods sold, (1) it inflates profits over the direct costing method (which charges *all* the overhead to cost of goods sold), and (2) it inflates inventory.

Our true profit is what we earn by making and selling products, not by changes in inventory. So if we do not receive direct-costing types of profit reports, we must adjust full-absorption profits by *reversing* the change in the KC component of inventory—which change is the distortion of profits associated with inventory changes.

In our simplistic example, we reduce profit by $4000: the 2000 units we inventoried included $2 per unit of KC, which should have been expensed. Conversely, reductions in the KC component of inventory—and heavy expensing of the KC—artificially reduce profits, so we make an upward adjustment.

We look at absorption accounting in closer detail in Chapter 22. For now it is sufficient that we keep in mind the very general differences between the two procedures. They will influence our thinking about and approach to cost reduction.

THE APPLICATION OF PINPOINT COSTING

Cost control and reduction are in the cost *detail*—in the meticulous pinpointing of cost origin, cause, location, responsible individual, time of incurrence, and so forth. The more detailed and precise our cost reporting, the tighter is our control of the cost environment.

A good lead paragraph in our morning newspaper precisely describes the reported event by means of "five W's and an H." Borrowing from the journalist's format, our cost reporting should pinpoint at a glance *when, where, what, who, why,* and *how.* For instance:

1. *When*: April 19–26
2. *Where*: Chicago sales office (cost center 11).
3. *What*: Product G's magazine space advertising costs per inquiry, versus standard: that is, *this* product. *Magazine,* not TV or other advertising. *Space,* not classified or other type of magazine advertising. *Per-inquiry* unit costs, not absolute costs. And actual versus *standard* unit costs:

Standard	$9.70 per inquiry
Actual ($22,000/2100 inquiries)	10.50
Variance	($0.80) per inquiry

4. *Who*: D.W. Robbens, V. P., Chicago sales office: responsible for the incurrence and correction of the ($0.80) variance.
5. *Why; How*: Robbens promptly submits up the line a cash variance report (CVR) that explains precisely the origin and cause of the variance, how it will be corrected, and when. His plan details advertising cost reductions that will not undermine the inquiry inflow, or ways to achieve more inquiries from his present advertising dollar.

Pinpoint costing requires that *every* identifiable expense category be subjected to unit costing against an AGP standard. The unit cost denominator (such as inquiries received) measures the intended *result* of the cost, as noted. We must so pinpoint cost reporting that the precise *cause* of the variance can be promptly located and identified. And pinpointing is of course done within the costing framework of individual products, which are always our central focus as managers.

The unit cost standards must be carefully engineered, with the help of the cost center's supervisor, to reflect attainable good performance (AGP) in the foreseeable future. Pinpointed unit standards tell us exactly what we can reasonably expect in (1) *quantity,* or units; (2) *cost,* or dollars; (3) *time,* or hours; and (4) *quality,* such as rejects, rework, or returns.

The heart of pinpoint costing is the *cash contribution ratio* (S/C and

S/A), as we shall see. We divide the broad CCRs (such as sales/ manufacturing costs), as finely and in as minute detail as possible, in the form of detailed backup ratios down through the organization.

This should be done for both cost centers (S/C) and asset centers (S/A). *Cost centers* are broken down into (1) *position* cost centers, showing the cost CCRs (company sales/$ of cost) for which each manager is responsible; (2) *product* cost centers, detailing the cost CCRs (product sales/$) associated with each product; and (3) *region-customer* cost centers, giving the cost CCRs associated with each sales territory (territory sales/$). Each cost item gives the *name* of the responsible man.

And for the *asset centers*, the identical CCR calculations are made for positions, products, and sales territories, resulting in sales/$ of assets for each center.

Every item in the cost centers and asset centers is then divided into all its subcomponent cash contribution ratios, down to the smallest possible breakdown of measurable costs and assets. Every identifiable cost and asset in the company, however small, is the denominator of a cash contribution ratio that is closely followed by the responsible supervisor, from accounting period to accounting period. He controls his costs and assets by monitoring the *slope* of the ratios, and their *variance* from the plan ratio.

The monthly cost ratios (S/C) are based on *12-month total* costs, to eliminate seasonality. And they should be *charted*, to reveal dramatically the problem and opportunity areas within which we can initiate corrective cash-generating actions.

Our entire focus is strategy. Strategy concerns itself with *what* must be done and especially *why*; *where* it must be done in our organization; and *when*. Then tactics can deal with *who* is to do it, and especially *how*. The forecasted cost and asset CCRs—S/C and S/A throughout the company —give us the strategic *what*, *why*, *where*, and *when* of our potential problems and opportunities. Then the tactical expert (who)—a man far more qualified in the pinpointed area than we are (how)—can produce a maximum beneficial impact in that area.

Asking the right strategic questions is 75% of the job of running any business. The CCR cash-generating principle goes a long way toward pinpointing those strategic questions, in response to which the correct tactical solutions can be implemented.

THE COST CONTROL CATEGORIES: LOCATION, FLOW, AND INPUT

Pinpoint costing for the control and reduction of costs, in our accounting system, should be in terms of three superimposed or overlapping cost control categories—by means of which the pinpoints are defined. It is a three-dimensional definition of each pinpointed cost: in terms of its precise *location* in the business process; in terms of its evolution or *flow* from incurrence to eventual disposition; and in terms of its *input* category, such as material or labor.

The three together give us a complete and indeed exhaustive definition of the costing pinpoints, on which a maximum-impact cost control program can be constructed. The following illustrates each definitional category:

1. *Cost location.* We first locate or charge a cost to its own "standing order" account, derived from the company's dual classification system of functional and natural cost categories. The functional classification is by cost center, such as *163, Welding Department.* The natural classification is by type of expense, such as *3.9.1, Fuel.* So costing for fuel consumed by the Welding Department is to standing order 163/3.9.1.

But we then must intensify our cost pinpointing within that standing order: such as subclassifying the cost of different types of fuel for different types of welding operations, and for the different products flowing through Welding. Up to the point of diminishing returns from our Accounting expenses, we thus cut up and precisely define all the cost locations—until they are truly pinpointed.

2. *Cost flow* through the accounts. Every cost is incurred, converted, and disposed of. This is the flow or *dynamics* of cost identification, supplementing its location or statics, as follows:

Incurrence of costs: a cost commitment is made at a precise place and time by a one-headed person who did something, like punch a time clock or write a purchase order. He is the cost control "pressure point." Properly pinpointed, here is where we can usually make our biggest cost savings and exercise the most telling control. It is where the first-line supervisor becomes the critical factor in our total cost control effort.

Conversion or transformation of costs: once incurred, costs should be further pinpointed in the accounting system as they flow through and are transformed by the various processing and service operations. They are converted repeatedly, for instance, as they are charged to and transferred from successive accounts in the production process—from raw material to work-in-process to finished goods, and out the shipping door. Pinpoint costing of value added (that is, costs added) in manufacture can provide us with remarkable control, and savings. The same principle is fully applicable in a nonmanufacturing service business, of course.

Disposition of costs: when we sell the product, finally, we cost our shipments from the product cost records. Costs flow from finished inventory to cost of goods sold and are finally disposed of. Tight (pinpointed) variance analysis here can have important backward and forward cash implications, revealing cost excesses in the earlier production stages and potential excesses in the later distribution stages.

3. *Cost input*. Having pinpointed our costs in terms of static location and dynamic flow, we must precisely classify them as to input category. Material, labor, overhead, and the nonmanufacturing inputs, after all, are what costing is all about.

Material control: This is usually our largest dollar cost item and most fruitful cost pressure point. Pinpoint costing should be applied at least to four successive stages in the material input sequence: *design and engineering* of the product, where material specifications mostly originate; *purchasing*, whose material saving potentials are endless; *raw material inventory*, for savings from stores requisition and control, perpetual inventory procedures, and so forth; and *production*, for pinpoint reporting of material quantities in process, spoilage and losses, and the like.

Labor is the second major cost input category, next to material, whose control subdivisions it tends to parallel closely or overlap. The most effective pinpointing areas, and pressure points for minimizing labor cost input, are usually product design and engineering; industrial engineering (IE); and production and inventory control (Princo).

The *cost system* itself also helps define the costing pinpoints, through which costs are controlled and reduced. The type of cost accounting system depends on the nature and type of business. It also hinges on the degree of simplicity we want, and on the price we are willing to pay for the information we will get from the system. As we move from standardized, large-volume, multiple-product costing, other cost accounting mechanisms are called for. For instance, a *process* cost system for a one-product, large-volume business—such as oil refining or cement manufacturing—is totally unlike *job order* costing for large-unit products made to customer specifications.

RESPONSIBILITY COST REPORTING

Responsibility reporting is really costing our organization chart in accordance with the position relationships in the chain of command. It helps us to further define and refine the costing categories. Yet it is a complex term for a simple principle that is implicit in *all* good costing methods: pinpoint cost variances are useless without a two-legged, human corrector of those variances—to whom everyone points until he corrects them. This man has a precisely defined organizational relationship in terms of which his costs are recorded and his variances systematically corrected.

It is what we call unitary responsibility, whereby *every* cost incurred within the company is the responsibility of *one man* only. And no cost can have no one directly and solely responsible for it, or more than one person responsible for it.

Responsibility reporting is a costing principle that focuses intensively on the first-line supervisor, who is the man responsible for the original incurrence of most of our costs. From him the costing mechanism builds upward, climbing the tiers and levels of authority and responsibility. Each level is a precisely defined costing category within the organizational hierarchy of interconnected costing categories.

In responsibility reporting, costing and budgeting thus dovetail precisely with the organization chart and the chain of command. Delineation of organizational responsibility and authority up and down the line conforms exactly to the delineation and definition of costing categories. This is as it should be.

The management team at each organizational level prescribes and monitors the costing system and responsibilities of the level just below it. Each manager down to the first-line supervisor has his own cost report covering the team of men for which he is solely responsible and accountable. It includes all costs over which he has control, and does not include any cost over which he has no control.

But there is nothing in all of this, as we have said, that is not implied in and is not a basic feature of any effective cost accounting and reporting system.

We have now explored important segments of the costing and accounting framework within which, and by means of which, management exercises effective control over cost expenditures. Our discussion was built on the procedures developed in the previous sales-cash chapter, whereby we control the cash margin factors—products, units, price, VC, and %Sc (control of KC, the sixth CM factor, is left to Chapter 16 on capacity costs).

Let us now make the long leap from cost control to cost *reduction*, which is the dimension of cash creativity.

CHAPTER 14

CASH CREATIVITY AND PROFITS

Cash creativity is the link between cost control and cost reduction. It takes us from the control of costs against standards to the tightening up and toughening of the standards.

To the bulk of our operating people, who have nothing to do with exotic cash sources like $+L$, cash creativity means *cost* creativity: initiating cost reduction ideas and projects that generate cash from every corner of the business. And it means implementing the ideas in an organized and comprehensive way—promptly, productively, and permanently.

These cash (cost) improvements must be reflected immediately in leaner standards and budget allowances, thus freezing the cash benefits permanently into the operations to which they apply. Projects do not simply provide temporary improvements that are later lost. The higher overall level of cash productivity and efficiency then serves as the new starting point—the cost structure on which next year's budget will be established and toward which further cost reduction efforts will be directed.

The objective of cash creativity and improvement is to maximize S/C (and S/A, which in this context *is* S/C) everywhere in the business and by everyone in the business. It is to maximize the ratios of sales to costs (and sales to assets). For just about everyone, again—except for the few in top management, sales, and finance, who are also directly concerned with $+L$, $+E$, $+D$, and $+S$—cash creativity *means* $-C$. And the surest way to maximize S/C through cash creativity is by forging a cash-creative corporate environment.

ACHIEVING THE CASH-CREATIVE ENVIRONMENT

To maximize cash productivity from cost reduction, we must lift the company's total population upward progressively through three separate target levels of attainment.

First, as we have discussed, is the bottom level of *cash responsibility*—the solid accounting foundation of precise cost reporting and control. It is characterized mainly by the pinpoint and unitary assignment of every cost to a particular person, who is solely responsible for its incurrence and correction back to standard.

Second, we move up to the level of *cash consciousness*. This is a constant awareness of the existence and reality of such an animal as cost cash— which is cash dollars, or savings opportunities, masquerading as costs. That is, costs are cash potentials everywhere we look. We can pinpoint costs all we want, and still never become conscious of their cash-generating potency. The average company has not reached this second plateau.

The highest level of attainment is *cash creativity*: a relentless and even remorseless searching out and implementing of cost-reducing improvements, everywhere by everyone. It is an attainment level of extraordinary cash productivity and growth, and a vital ingredient in the comprehensive strategy of cash.

Upon the solid foundation of cash responsibility and cash consciousness, we thus construct a corporate environment that motivates, organizes, implements, and controls cash creativity, as follows:

1. *Motivating* cash creativity. We build an importance-conferring motivational environment geared to the CCRs (the S/C and S/A ratios), in which every employee will soon come to *demand* three things: help and guidance in personally achieving creativity in cost reduction; implementation of his cost-reduction proposals and the achievement of their intended savings; and that everyone around him also be very creative as to cost savings.

2. *Organizing* and coordinating cash creativity. This is spearheaded by a permanent cash-improvement (CI) capability, which emerges in response to the intense and general demand for guidance in creating and implementing cost-reduction proposals.

3. *Implementing* cash creativity through various core strategies of cost reduction.

4. *Controlling* cash improvement results by assuring that cost reduction projects are proposed; that they are profitably implemented; and that their intended long-term savings are realized.

The remainder of this and the subsequent chapters of Part Four will examine each of these four avenues to the establishment of a cash-creative corporate environment.

MOTIVATING CASH CREATIVITY

Our reasoning about cash motivation should follow a logical track much like the following:

1. The most powerful motivational environment by far has proved to be, time and time again, one whose reward system gratifies each man's *craving for importance*. It responds to his primeval need for status, recognition, security, a feeling of personal worth and accomplishment, and a sense of belonging.

2. *Promotion* to higher status and salary positions is by far the most powerful gratification of a man's desire for importance.

3. *Contribution* to cash productivity—to corporate wealth—is the only possible basis for promotion and importance-gratification consistent with the definition and meaning of the business enterprise.

4. *Cost reduction* and control is by far the most lucrative long-term or continuing source of cash productivity and corporate wealth, and for most employees the only exposure to cash-generating opportunities.

Cost reduction thus becomes the company's motivational anchor. The glory, prestige, promotions, salary increases, and bonuses now go to the *cost-reducing* manager or employee, simply because he is by far the most significant contributor to cash and profits. The more he personally contributes to cash, the more important he is to the company. So we confer a corresponding degree of importance on him, with status-conferring promotions, to sustain and enhance the system's motivational force.

In a cash-directed motivational system, each man can know how bright his future is in the company by answering the question: How strong a contribution am I personally making to cash productivity through my cost reduction efforts?

The *cash contribution ratios* (CCRs), as we have seen, are the S/C and S/A computations that apply to a man's own area of supervision or work, and to those for whose performance he is personally responsible. They are the most accurate, most objective, and fairest measurment of each man's contribution to cash productivity, or CRE, because they *define* CRE. An increase in a man's CCRs benefits CRE, and vice versa. There are other measurements, as we shall see, but they merely supplement and support the CCRs.

Each function and department of the company, down to the smallest identifiable unit, has its own CCRs for which it is exclusively responsible. Manufacturing might be measured by such ratios as sales/material costs; sales/direct labor; sales/indirect labor; sales/manufacturing inventory;

and many others. These are now our motivational anchor, on which performance recognition is based.

For example, Jones and Smith each head a department whose costs have necessarily increased during the last five years of substantial company growth:

	Company Sales	Jones, Dept. A		Smith, Dept. B		S/C Index (Year 1 = 100)	
						Jones Dept.	Smith Dept.
	Sales	Costs	CCR	Costs	CCR	A	B
Year	(million)	(000)	(2÷3)	(000)	(2÷5)		
1	2	3	4	5	6	7	8
1	$3	$32	93.7×	$24	125.0×	100	100
2	4	42	95.2	33	121.2	102	97
3	5	53	94.3	46	108.7	101	87
4	6	62	96.8	61	98.4	103	79
5	7	71	98.6	69	101.4	105	81

Jones's costs moved up from $32,000 to $71,000 (column 3), while Smith's rose from $24,000 to $69,000 (column 5). At first glance, this cost behavior seems normal.

But Jone's costs were controlled in relation to sales, as reflected in the five-year rise of his CCR (or S/C) from 93.7 to 98.6 (column 4). Smith's costs increased at a faster pace than sales: his CCRs *declined* from 125.0 to 101.4 (column 6).

This unfavorable comparison of Smith versus Jones is spelled out more clearly in the S/C index (columns 7 and 8), in which year 1's CCR of each department is 100. To calculate each subsequent year's index, its CCR is divided by that of the base year.

Jones's cash index thus rises to 105, but Smith's declines to 81. Jones is controlling costs and generating cash, for which he should be rewarded promptly, generously, and publicly. Smith has failed in his single most important responsibility, the control of his costs. He is in trouble in a motivational environment that has its entire basis in cash productivity.

Rewards flow from the *improvement* of a man's cost standards and budget allowances, so that there is an increase in his CCRs. He is not rewarded simply for operating within the existing standards and allowances, while his CCRs remain steady or even decline. That is, he is powerfully motivated in a cash-oriented promotion system to seek out and implement cost reductions, constantly and aggressively—so as to reduce his dollar budget allowances and increase his CCRs.

The transition from a conventional to a cash-motivated corporate environment is spearheaded and greatly facilitated by this exclusive reliance on +S/C measurement. But the transition must nevertheless go through three stages. First, we *overcome resistance to change*. This stage can be shortened materially by concentrating, early in the transition, on the second stage—*building acceptance of change*. And third, we create a *demand for change*.

Building acceptance of change, in stage 2, means general acceptance of the cash-motivation principle. Promotion is now based on cost-reduction creativity rather than primarily on seniority, politics, being on time, working Saturdays, "doing one's job," and all the rest. Acceptance of change is a delicate plant that grows only in a carefully tended garden. Everyone must be fully informed about the transition in advance, to forestall groundless fears and insecurity pangs. We must get opinions and use suggestions; maintain clear channels for feedback and static; and, above all, win everyone's full participation in working out details and the mechanics of the transition.

ORGANIZING CASH CREATIVITY: THE CI CAPABILITY

Having built acceptance of a cash-motivational environment in which everyone benefits, we move swiftly and emphatically to *stage 3*. Here a powerful *demand* for change is stimulated by the exclusive reliance on +S/C evaluation of everyone. Cash evaluation is dramatized and becomes deeply ingrained as an organizational way of life. A man's promotability or demotability and even his continued employment with the company are now based solely on the performance of his CCRs.

It gives rise to a compelling demand for organizational help and guidance to improve that performance. Such help might well take the form of a permanent cash-improvement capability, centering on a CI *Committee*. This sees to it that people doing their daily work or supervision *also* generate substantial cost-reduction cash—by originating and implementing ideas that save the company money.

That is, in the supercharged cash-maximizing, cost-reducing motivational environment, a cash-improvement capability is necessarily installed by acclamation—as a *service* to supervisors and employees whose status and financial rewards flow from +S/C and from nothing else.

The Cash Improvement (CI) Committee adds a new dimension to standard two-dimensional business activity. With it we have three dimensions: (1) *performing* the work; (2) *supervising* the performance of work; and (3) *generating cash* by actively reducing the cost of performing and supervising work. The CI Committee is concerned exclusively with the cash-generating third dimension, or $-C$. It is a unique force. Companies everywhere get by fairly well with only the first two dimensions, having no organized capability for generating incremental cash from S/C.

The CI Committee sustains—is indeed the organizational *expression* of—total cost consciousness and cash creativity as a vital and permanent state of mind of everyone in his daily work. Total consciousness means *all* employees multiplied by *all* operations multiplied by *all* working hours. The Committee is thus never a separate function, or a "program" of cost reduction (crash or otherwise). It is not something imposed on the existing two-dimensional organization of work and supervision. Cost reduction as expressed and coordinated by the CI Committee is a conscious and continuing *by-product* of everyone's daily supervisory and operating performance.

By its very nature, therefore, the CI Committee intimately involves everybody. It is a total living organism. But its brain and vital organs are necessarily the most cost-sensitive and cost-influential supervisors at all levels in the company. Its hard-core membership includes, for a start, all top managers, particularly the president; a CI coordinator, who reports to the president; and, in rotating fashion, the heads of such critical functions as purchasing, product engineering, industrial engineering, and production. It especially includes, as required, first-line supervisors and department heads, who spend the company's money or know exactly how and where it is spent. But depending on the problems needing solution, the Committee enlists the talents and knowledge of any cost-influential key man who can be helpful.

The CI capability—as expressed organizationally by the Committee—has five jobs:

1. To nourish *cost consciousness and creativity* throughout the company.
2. To involve supervisors in setting challenging *cost-reduction* targets or quotas of dollar-saving proposals.
3. To encourage and coordinate the *inflow of projects* and proposals from every area and level.
4. *To evaluate projects*.
5. *To improve standards* and allowances to reflect and make permanent the cash benefits realized from the projects.

The CI capability works. It does so because it is composed of cash-motivated men who will benefit directly from its success or suffer directly from its failure. All five of its jobs or objectives produce $+S/C$, so it is an indispensable *service* to them.

The cash improvement capability takes a companywide, interfunctional, coordinative approach to cost reduction and cash improvement. Thus it functions best through interacting committees, with the CI Committee at the center, like the hub of a wheel. A multiple-committee structure leading out of this hub engages the broad *participation* of knowledgeable and effective supervisors, in both the origination of ideas and their implementation. Especially in the initial stages, also, committees provide a confidence factor stemming from safety-in-numbers, which a more individualized approach lacks. And they provide a forum and organizational mechanism that facilitates the *line's* performance of its cost responsibilities. They never replace the line or do its work.

A vigorous cash improvement capability has a full-time *CI coordinator*, preferably a vice president reporting to the president. He is chairman of the top-level CI Committee, whose (rotating) membership he determines. And he sits in on all meetings of subcommittees and task forces formed to tackle special cost problems and areas. His job is to tie together, day to day, the firm's comprehensive cost-reduction effort involving many committees and participants. He is a thoroughly professional cost-reduction specialist by training and long experience. And he is an excellent catalyst who works well with and brings out the best in line people.

The CI Committee should meet weekly for 2 hours, for instance. It must start promptly and adjourn on time. Members hear reports on open projects and on new ones, given by the responsible man. Later they receive from the secretary a typed *minutes-agenda* that summarizes the meeting, and itemizes the agreed-upon agenda (mainly the projects) for next week's meeting.

The Committee is a *line* function. It is the line organization reducing *its* costs, in an all-embracing and coordinative way—generating cost-reduction projects and implementing projects. It is the grouping together of line managers (with appropriate staff support) to help those down the line identify the highest-potential problem areas and set cost-reduction objectives and quotas. And it counsels them on the best cost-reduction approaches and techniques.

From these men down the line, it receives written cost-reduction project proposals. Each proposal is assigned, for investigation and follow-up, to the Committee member who represents that particular line area or function. He evaluates it for potential savings (net of installation costs). And if acceptable, he delegates it to the appropriate supervisor in his area for implementation.

If it is a purchasing cost-reduction project, for instance, the purchasing member of the Committee delegates it to one of the key men in his department for implementation. Thereafter, he follows the man's progress, and reports periodically to the Committee. He keeps on top of the project from its inception to the final realization of dollar savings.

The Committee members receive outside cost control training, course work, and seminars. They are, after all, the focal point of cost-reduction activity throughout the company. And they set the example and the pace for cost-reduction training of men down the line.

TOTAL CASH MOBILIZATION

Companywide participation is the essence of the CI capability and cash creativity. The Committee is only the hub of the wheel, whose spokes lead out to every corner of the organization and keep things spinning. It is successful if each person in the company contributes knowledge of his own job to the cash-creating effort as a whole. But this will happen only if planning, implementation, and control of cost reduction travels *upward* from the lowest supervisory and hourly ranks.

CI Teams are one example of the kind of organizational improvization that might occur at the rim of the wheel whose spokes converge on the CI Committee hub. They are temporary *task forces* to whom the CI Committee delegates responsibility for a specific problem department, cost category, or product line. The task force consists of perhaps three cost-sensitive key men from that problem category, such as the foreman of the department and a man from industrial engineering and production control (Princo). The CI Team is a *line* unit, again, all action toward cost control being a line responsibility. It originates, investigates, implements, and follows up cost reduction projects and proposals in its problem area, and reports to the CI Committee.

A *Departmental Committee* is a regular operating department with cost problems. Once a month it constitutes itself a committee, with the foreman or supervisor as chairman. Meeting on a fixed date and time, after hours and on an overtime basis, the men of the department generate cost reduction projects and proposals.

Its foreman *must* be trained to run a meeting well—on schedule, with a secretary providing minutes-agenda, and so forth. An atmosphere and spirit of achievement, with a clearly defined system of recognition and rewards, can produce extraordinary dollar results. At least one valuable by-product is the radiating climate of cost creativity that flows from its efforts, to surrounding departments and areas in the company.

Projects go to the CI Committee for approval and come back for implementation. Or there might be an intermediate filtering process, whereby projects first go to a *CI Screening Group*. This is made up of perhaps 10 rotating members who are the best performers on the Departmental Committees. The Screening Group meets monthly on an overtime basis to sift the projects generated by the Departmental Committees. And it passes up to the CI Committee those that are potentially the most lucrative.

THE DECISIVE ROLE OF FIRST-LINE SUPERVISION

The first-line supervisor is the frontline of cost reduction. He must loom large on task forces and subcommittees and on the top CI Committee. This is the management man, albeit on the lowest rung, with whom upper management and the CI Committee necessarily maintain the closest liaison. He is the one on whom cost-reduction training is primarily concentrated. And, properly trained and motivated, he is the one we can depend on primarily for project origination, evaluation, and implementation. That is, he is closest of anyone in management to the point of cost incurrence—usually supervising more than 75% of all operating costs. Having come up from the ranks, he knows the jobs and the men doing the jobs in his area.

And he is crucial because he is pivotal, a kind of localized center around which cash creativity revolves. That is, he can make or break cost reduction. Much depends on the *way* he is regarded by upper management and is involved in the effort. He will achieve extraordinary cost-reduction mileage if he identifies with management and the company's cash-improvement objectives. But he must have confidence in the organizational paths through which his ideas will reach the points of evaluation and implementation. And he must be personally inspired by the system of rewards granted for superior cash-generating performance.

Above all, he needs prompt and effective cost data that are meaningful to him and that he can control—comprehensive *pinpoint* reporting on every man multiplied by every operation multiplied by every hour. This is not just to control costs against his volume budget allowances, as vital as that is. The real savings are in his relentless *improvement* in standards and allowances. He needs to know that every piece of material R needing rework in the production line costs his department \$5/unit; that for each man-hour below budget on his direct labor payroll, his department earns \$9/unit; and so forth.

Training in cost-reduction techniques is essential to the supervisor's success. An effective program must start with the company's training *needs*, and the goals to be reached: the type of technique to be communicated, to whom, how intensively, and so forth. Only then can we decide on the best combination of lecture and/or film, demonstration, and discussion that will fill these needs.

After-hour sessions work well, following a light dinner. Two hours a week for about 25 weeks is a typical allotment of training time, with one week a year devoted to refresher and update courses. The CI Coordinator as the training coordinator brings in consultants and ad hoc training managers with strong track records. He also invites the best outside lecturers and discussion leaders who are known quantities; specialists from vendor companies; experts from local trade or secondary schools and universities; and many others. It is usually easier to find outside talent than to use it effectively in conducting training sessions. But effective sessions are the crucial ingredient of the training program.

The subjects should be taught in an order of priority based on need or urgency, and on the amount of potential savings to be derived from alternative subjects. The list of training courses is of course endless: work simplification; flow process charts and diagrams; value analysis; operations research; brainstorming techniques; IE; purchasing methods; and on and on.

If a *Cost Reduction Manual* also results from the training effort, so much the better. Distributed to everyone, it consists of all the training notes (boiled down for ready reference) on the best techniques, methods, and strategies of cost reduction. How the manual is put together and used is one way to *test* the effectiveness of the training program—which must be done regularly in any event.

MAXIMIZING CASH IMPROVEMENT

We stimulate and bring forth a higher dollar value of cash-improvement projects if we "communicate, activate, and reward":

1. *Communicate* to everyone the cost priority areas where the biggest cash benefits can be derived. These are areas of low or downward-sloping S/C and S/A performance ratios—that is, of excessive costs and assets, from which the largest number of projects either are *needed* or are *available*.

And if everyone is kept closely informed about the details of his *company's* operating progress and problems, he fits his job into the company as a whole. He is motivated more productively and creatively because he identifies with the firm's hopes and dreams. Such communication increases the dollar value of project submissions, quite apart from increasing the level of employee gratification, enthusiasm, and productivity.

Companywide communication helps to make cash improvement and cost reduction a way of life. It must utilize all forms and techniques of transmitting information, not the least of which are charts and graphic displays with personal rather than abstract messages. These translate cost reduction potentials and progress—his own and the company's—into dollars of wages, hours, units, and other earthy expressions that are tangible and meaningful to him.

2. *Activate* all sources of cash-improvement proposals. Outside the company, they originate from the systematic study of trade and technical publications; suppliers' purchasing ideas; competitors' techniques; consultants; and so on.

Inside the company, the really fruitful and continuing sources of proposals are supervisory, professional, and other key employees. A powerful magnetic force for drawing out projects from this elite group is the Committee itself. It is the direct and completely reliable liaison between lower management and professional people, on the one hand, and top management on the other. The supervisor or professional *knows* his proposal will get prompt and fair evaluation by his boss, whose own superior must review it and send it up the line to the CI Committee (and to the president).

3. *Reward* and recognition. There must be a permanent "contest" flavor and ambiance permeating the cash-improvement environment. A trip to Portugal or a convertible automobile for first prize, cash awards for second and third prizes, and so forth, recognize and reward the best project generators. This reinforces an already powerful competitive drive to create projects and dollar savings, especially when accompanied by publicity; hoopla; testimonial dinners; membership on status-conferring committees; and all the rest.

But this simply takes us back again full circle to the wisdom of a cash-creative motivational environment that confers *importance* on its cash-creative people. Prizes and hoopla notwithstanding, *they* are the people who get promoted to positions of ever-higher status and salary.

CONTROLLING COST-REDUCTION PROJECTS

Controlling cash creativity is therefore an indispensable ingredient of the cost-reduction program. The CI Committee must precisely record and publicize to all participants both the *project inflow* and the *realized savings* from the projects. This is the dollar amount of projects submitted by each department, compared with that department's project quota. And it is the dollar savings being derived from each project, compared with the savings originally forecast in the project proposal.

Department R, for instance, has an annual project quota valued at $63,000 of cost savings. Its monthly report might show that to date it has submitted projects totaling $12,200 of estimated annual savings, or 19% of its quota. Of these, $9400 worth of savings have been installed, or 15%.

Cost-reduction reports must also show annual savings by *cost element*, such as by material items or labor categories; by *type of saving*, such as material cost-reduction, method improvement, or product redesign; by *committee*; and so forth.

Such control reports on every aspect of the program should be dramatized and depicted in chart form, in a manner that is meaningful even in the lowest employee ranks. The essence of cash creativity is the sense of involvement and participation, enthusiasm, accomplishment, and competitive spirit that it fosters and on which it depends for its success. Effective project control reporting is a crucial requirement to that success.

We have been journeying upward from cash responsibility to cash consciousness to *cash creativity*, and profoundly transforming the life of our company. If we powerfully motivate and effectively organize the broad base of our employees, as we have seen, the journey will succeed.

But it is a journey through a *cash system*, which defines the corporation and within which certain core concepts and strategies of cost reduction are decisive. Having motivated and organized cash creativity, that is, we are ready to implement.

Chapter 15 therefore examines cost reduction within its companywide cash system context, where it bears fruit.

REDUCING COSTS IN THE CASH SYSTEM ENVIRONMENT

A company that is effectively motivated and organized to achieve cost reduction, achieves the incremental cash productivity through specific core strategies. These strategies do not work in a vacuum, nor do they work in a mechanistic environment in which things are made to happen by simple cause-and-effect. Rather, cost reduction or any business strategy occurs within a living organism (or system) which is the corporation. Here everything affects and is affected by everything else.

Cost reduction must therefore combine two parallel but interdependent approaches. One is concerned with the core strategies operating within the corporate cash system. The other is concerned with the cash system itself. We must at the same time solve (1) *individual cost* excesses wherever they are found and (2) the overall *cash system* imbalances that produce or aggravate cost excesses. Neither approach is effective or enduring without the other. Pursued together, the cash-improvement impact is likely to be substantial and permanent.

THE BUSINESS AS A CASH SYSTEM

Cash system solutions to cost excesses are implied by our central definition of the corporation as a cash machine or system. Upon this definition is predicated the entire strategy of cash. If the company is in fact a cash system, then cash system solutions must be the most realistic and effective ones. This approach is a radical departure from conventional cost-reduction thinking, to be sure, but it is no less valid for its uniqueness.

It is an approach that treats an ailing patient who is suffering from cost abnormalities. Three things are involved in this quasi-medical frame of reference. First, we think of our business patient as a *cash system*, just as a physician thinks in terms of the human system. Next, we diagnose its cost maladies in terms of *time-cost imbalances* in the system. And finally, we cure the cost excesses with *system solutions* rather than ad hoc or localized solutions. Let us discuss each step.

Our underlying theme of these many chapters—the Ariadne's Thread guiding us through the maze—is of course the cash system concept, by means of which the corporation is most realistically defined and most effectively managed. The system generates and reinvests cash, which it recirculates at maximum attainable velocity to produce maximum profits and growth. Analytically and pragmatically, the business is seen as a *totality* of organically interrelated and interacting cash contribution ratios. S/C and S/A, on which is superimposed L/A, thus combine to maximize cash and CRE in every corner, nook, and cranny of our company.

In generating cash comprehensively in this way, the business fulfills the essential behavioral requirements of a living creature. It is a fully effective organic entity, a cash-generating and cash-absorbing total system that is *alive*. It has a head, brain, nervous system, body, and muscle, as does any other creature. And cash itself is the lifeblood of the living business firm. It generates and absorbs and recirculates cash pulsatively, in a similar manner and for a similar purpose and result as does the living organism with its circulatory system.

Going further, we can characterize and manage our business on any one of three levels of comprehension. It can be viewed *mechanistically*, as a machine whose individual parts and components function together in accordance with the physical properties of cause and effect. The functioning company is thus inert and dead, behaviorally, rather than alive and partaking of the behavioral properties of a living organism. The mechanistic level of management is the lowest and least effective, and yet quite prevalent. Its shortcomings are illustrated by the financier who buys and sells companies as he would inanimate apartment buildings. Suddenly he discovers that warm-blooded people are not working hard or happily any more, and profits are plunging.

More realistically, up one notch, we can view and manage the firm *sociologically*. It is as a group-behavior phenomenon of people who think, feel, hope, and fear, and who interact and are group-motivated. But we are still treating each department and person as a self-contained behavioral entity. Department A and Department B are viewed sociologically as dynamic groupings of people. But there remains a mechanistic (or simplistic cause-and-effect) undertone in the way the comprehensive human interrelationships are viewed and the way they are managed. Most companies are managed this way, nevertheless, and usually with satisfactory results.

Or we can manage *existentially*,[1] at the highest behavioral level. The company (and each subsection of people) is not only analogous to but in a practical sense *is* a living creature. It thinks, feels, behaves, acts, and reacts in accordance with a self-sustaining and creative life force. Each part is intimately involved functionally, and mutually interactive, with every other part of the total being. It is a cash system perspective and approach to cost reduction and to its obverse, cash improvement. This existential view of business management is implicit in the strategy of cash.

TIME-COST IMBALANCES: THE SYSTEM'S PATHOLOGY

The existential view of the business as a living creature sees it occupying four dimensions. Three dimensions are *spatial*, whereby it occupies a cubic area of land and air.The fourth dimension is *time*, or duration. Three-dimensional spatial existence is imaginary. There obviously must be a fourth, or time, dimension to confer existence on anything.

Not only the existence, however, but the essence and meaning of an entity are defined by this fourth dimension. The reality of anything is not what it is at any point in time, as a static phenomenon. It is what it reveals of itself *over time*, as a *dynamic* phenomenon. Our meaning in the world is not what we are but what we are doing—not being but becoming.

Time is in this sense the sovereign "causal" influence on us all, and on the living corporation. (Actually, time only *measures* change rather than causes it, but the phenomenon and the effect are the same.) Time's measurable impact is on everything that occurs from one accounting period to the next, on all business inputs and outputs. And especially, and most importantly for cash generation within the corporate cash system, its impact is on *costs*.

That is, costs are a function of time and vary with it.The least-cost system, all else being equal, is the one with the shortest elapsed time between input of raw material into the plant and receipt of cash from the customer. Anything that adds *time* to the least-cost condition, adds *costs*. Time must be paid for; time is money. Whatever adds cost or asset time—extra man-hours, machine-hours, plant-hours, inventory-hours, receivables-hours—slows down the velocity of cash circulation in the cash system. It raises costs and lowers S/C or S/A, and thereby decreases cash return on equity.

We can call this malady *time-cost imbalance*. Any illness we treat, human or corporate, manifests itself by a malfunctioning or underfunctioning of the system. Here the illness is a time-associated reduction of the system's

[1]From existence, or life.

cash velocity and profits, caused by time-cost imbalances. Too much time (money) is being spent at one or more locations in an otherwise perfectly balanced corporate cash system. So the system to that extent suffers from time-cost imbalances. And CRE suffers, because time (velocity) is inversely related to CRE. The more of one, the less of the other.

These imbalances usually originate not in the business functions themselves, but in the elapsed time consumed *between* functions and cost centers. They occur in the functional spaces, or gaps, that breach an otherwise perfectly continuous business flow or process. They are the time-cost buildups caused by the *delays*, waste, downtime, interference with work, and confusions that occur *between* the normally well-run functional cost centers.

The well-managed company has gotten effective control over the material and labor costs of individual operations, at individual work points. It does a good job with individual costs incurred in its selling and distribution system. And the same is probably true elsewhere in its business. It is controlling, that is, the cost of the functional *parts* or components of the system.

But the system's total elapsed *time*—its cash cycle between receipt of material and collection of receivables—is nevertheless too long and costly. We are being robbed blind in the time *gaps*, or cracks and crevices, between operations. And it shows up as wasted man-hours, machine-hours, inventory-hours, and every other kind of hour.

These interjacent time-cost imbalances are total *systems* imbalances and are caused by an overall systems malfunctioning. Suppose that our Welding Department's labor costs suddenly shoot up above budget allowance. The cause is almost certainly not the skilled welders. Nor is it even to be found anywhere in the well-run Welding Department. Welding is a symptom, not a cause—a distinction that is fundamental to the systems analysis of time-cost imbalances. A *systems* imbalance increased the department's ratio of waiting-to-working time. It might have been the failure of units to arrive in the welding area on time, the arrival of defective units, a power failure down the line, or whatever.

And the same system imbalance also helped pile up work-in-process inventory in and around Welding, reducing turnover and further undermining profits and CRE. The costly inventory glut was produced by an interjacent time-cost imbalance that became apparent in Welding. It was produced by a system time-cost imbalance of as yet undetermined origin, of which Welding was merely a symptom and effect. A rash on my chest is a symptom or effect that is almost certainly unrelated to the affected area of the chest itself. It has a deep-seated systems cause originating elsewhere in my body.

Cash system time-cost imbalances are thus cost-producing *time* overruns.

They are caused by a malfunctioning at some point or points in the sequential movement or *distribution* of things or people or paperwork through the cash system. Something or someone did not arrive in the right (scheduled) place at the right time or in the right condition. This could be inventory, tooling, machine parts, information, work orders, people, drawings, forklift trucks, or almost anything or anyone. They were needed for the efficient functioning of the work point in question, *and* for the least-cost functioning of the total cash system.

The systems imbalance was probably caused either by an error in flow *scheduling*, somewhere in the system, or by a performance variance against a sound flow schedule. It might have been something on the order of a shipment forecast that was wrong in relation to actual shipment requirements; too early or late scheduling of raw material purchase orders; or poor production scheduling. Or else it was a failure to conform to an accurate schedule—whether of customer shipments, raw material deliveries, the in-plant movement of work, or something else.

Either way, a systems *maldistribution* of people or things has radiated time-cost imbalances in many directions and with varying impacts. But the individual or local disturbances, like the Welding Department cost overruns and inventory glut, must be treated as symptoms of the maldistribution—not as causes. Nothing we do to the Welding Department itself will really cure the Welding cost and inventory problem.[2]

This may come as a shock or even as sacrilege to the multitude of well-meaning cost cutters who will instinctively set upon the adverse Welding variances with an axe. Under conventional cost reduction procedures, the corrective solutions are always sought primarily in the area suffering from the negative budget variances. The axe will certainly correct the dollar variances. But it will have corrected a symptom only, and it will have corrected it only temporarily. Worst of all, the axe will surely generate *further* systems imbalances. These radiate outward from the now somewhat debilitated Welding area, in the form of systems maldistributions and cost overruns in *other* cost centers.

We must look rather to a systems solution. In our living business organism, like an animal or plant, every function affects and is affected by every other function. All costs are related to and are affected by all other costs, in a multilateral and interactive way. In our existential perspective, cost excesses anywhere in the business are malignancies that are symptoms of an imbalance and malaise of the corporate body as a whole.

[2]Inventory imbalances originate in or somewhere between the sales plan and production schedule, on the one hand, and shipment variances from plan on the other. The cause of the inventory glut is rarely to be found in the inventory, but in the distribution sequence and flow scheduling before and after the point where the glut is evident.

For our doctor to treat a localized malady with ad hoc medicine is to treat a symptom and not a cause, which is usually worthless if not dangerous to the patient. It is dangerous because he is thereby neglecting to treat the deep-seated physiological or even psychological imbalance of the patient's system, which is the *cause* of the symptom.

CURING SYSTEMS IMBALANCES AND COST EXCESSES

As corporate doctors, we thus treat systems causes with total systems remedies, and do not treat local and surface symptoms with ad hoc and temporary remedies. Cost control and reduction (cost cash productivity) are the production of sales cash per dollar of cost cash expended, whether through $+S/C$ or $-C/S$. To be worthy of the name, cost control must have a *permanent* impact on S/C, not one that later causes either $-S$ or $+C$ in the same area or elsewhere. We can slash advertising costs and find later that we have torpedoed sales volume, or slash maintenance only to boost capital spending requirements inordinately later on. By treating symptoms, we create systems imbalances in other directions *and* other time periods. But if we attack the systems imbalance directly, we *cure* the cause and the symptom without generating new imbalances.

Curing cost excesses in cash system terms is like tackling any problem: it must be *defined, analyzed, and solved.* Here we can only touch briefly on the broad strategy considerations, leaving the specialized tactical solutions to management's best judgement in its own specialized circumstances.

1. *Defining* the cost problem within its broad systems context is our first and most important job. It is usually done best in terms of the company-wide scheduling and *distribution* flow of men, materials, information, conveyances, and the numberless other factors that make up a dynamic system. We thus define the cost problem in terms of, and thereby locate it within, its broad *time* framework or sequence. This sequence begins with the sales forecast itself, and carries through all the subordinate scheduling and distribution sequences that respond to and flow from the sales fore-cast.

2. *Analyzing* the cost problem within its now precisely defined and located systems setting is an exploration into *causes* and their systems interrelationships. We study exhaustively, and get a solid fix on, all the proximate—and the remote but influential—contributing systems causes of the problem. Then we can accurately weigh and *rank* the alternative probable causes, and evaluate the functional systems interrelationships among these alternative causes.

3. *Solving* the cost problem now becomes a matter of choosing the maximum-impact cause or causes from among the ranked alternatives. We have explored backwards in *time* and into the system, causally, to locate the best place in which to tackle our local symptomatic problem and correct it. To produce the systems solution, we then direct our cure of the system's imbalance at that pressure point in the comprehensive distributive sequence where it has the strongest impact on the localized cost symptom.

In this way we have addressed ourselves not to any isolated cost problem, but to the *profitability* of the entire business. This is the real meaning of cost reduction within the cash system context.

SOLVING COST EXCESSES: THE CORE STRATEGIES

We can now take up the second of the two parallel but interdependent approaches to cost reduction, of which the cash system was the first. The second approach bears down on the individual costs themselves, by means of various core strategies.

These strategies are pursued most fruitfully within the context of the cash system, which provides both a conceptual and a very practical framework. Within it, our Cash Improvement Committee and the totally mobilized cost reduction effort establishes and achieves cost reduction objectives. In the remainder of the chapter we look at a few of the more important core concepts and strategies, as illustrations of the full range of possibilities.

By far the strongest impact from a cost-reduction effort comes from the rifle, not the shotgun. We attack the relatively small number of cost items that will provide the largest proportion of dollar savings. This core strategy is the "20–80" principle, more fully discussed in a later chapter. It assumes that 20% of the cost items or categories produce 80% of the total available cost savings. The rule-of-thumb is adapted from Pareto's Law of Maldistribution, which says roughly that in all human and natural situations a small proportion of inputs provides the largest proportion of the output.

The term "20–80" is an ideal to shoot for. An 80% cost-reduction payback is certainly attainable in the least-efficient companies. But in the typical business it may be a bit of an exaggeration, though not by much and not always. Yet the principle of a lopsided or skewed payback is quite true and demonstrably so, no matter what the situation or the company.

The most useful application of "20–80" to cost reduction is in the fixing of priorities and potentials among alternative cost problems. Which costs do we attack first, as being the most cash-productive?

BC CASH AVAILABILITY: FIXING PRIORITIES AND POTENTIALS

BC cash availability is a technique that helps us determine which costs are excessive in comparison with those of our best competitors (BC). It thereby establishes the order of priority in which to tackle individual cost categories, so as to achieve a 20–80 response.

This procedure is illustrated in Table 19. Our company has total costs (and sales) of $6 million. They are subdivided among the major cost categories in the dollar amounts and percentages of sales shown in columns 2 and 3.

BC% of sales (column 4) is the standard or target percentage of sales for each cost. It is based on the average performance of our best competitors (BC) and is arrived at by at least two approximations:

1. *Best component performance (BCP)*. This is the best ratio-to-sales of that cost item *ever* achieved by *any* operating component or unit in our own company. Together the BCP ratios for all our costs present a composite S/C picture of a company at a more efficient level of performance than it has ever actually achieved. But we *have* achieved these efficiency levels with respect to each component cost, so it is not an unreasonable standard. What man has done, man can do.

Direct labor/sales, for instance, is now 20% (column 3). Three years ago Department 16 achieved 19.4%, the best performance ever for any unit of the company. So our direct labor BCP is 19.4%.

2. *Best Competitor (BC)*. This is the average cost/sales ratio (for that cost item) of our highest-CRE industry competitors. Their DL/sales ratio, on the average, may be above or below our BCP ratio of 19.4%. In any event, using the two ratios as reference points, we establish the *BC% of sales* (column 4). So "BC" can mean either best component or best competitor, or something in between.

These BC percentages are then applied to our $6,000,000 of sales to give us, for each cost, the *BC dollars allowed* (column 5). Direct labor at 19.6% BC is $1,176,000. Subtracting this BC allowance from the actual amount of the cost (column 2) gives *BC cash available* (column 6). This is the cash we would release from the cost item if we were operating as efficiently as our best competitors.

The *Cash-improvement (CI) potential* (column 7) is simply the BC cash available (column 6) divided by the present amount of the cost (column 2). If we operated at the BC level of $1,176,000 for direct labor (column 5), we would have $24,000 of BC cash available ($1,200,000 now less $1,176,000). So $24,000 would be an improvement over $1,200,000, of *2%*.

Table 19 Setting Cash-Improvement Priorities

Cost Categories	Amount (000)	% of Sales ($6 million)	BC% of Sales	BC$'s Allowed [$6 mil × (4)] (000)	BC Cash Available [(2)−(5)] (000)	CI Potential [(6)÷(2)]	CI Factor [(3)×(7)]
	2	3	4	5	6	7	8
VC							
Direct labor	$1200	20.0%	19.60%	$ 1176	$ 24	2%	0.40%
Purchased materials	1600	26.7	26.40	1584	16	1	0.267
Supplies and utilities	300	5.0	4.60	276	24	8	0.40
Variable sales costs	200	3.3	3.26	196	4	2	0.066
Total VC	$3300	55.0%		$ 3232	$ 68	2.06%	1.13%
KC							
Indirect labor	$ 800	13.3%	12.30%	$ 738	$ 62	8%	1.064%
Maintenance	200	3.3	3.16	190	10	5	0.165
Fixed charges	300	5.0	4.98	299	1	0.5	0.025
Selling expenses	400	6.7	6.06	364	36	9	0.603
G and A	300	5.0	4.79	287	13	4	0.20
Payback costs	400	6.7	6.33	380	20	5	0.335
Optional costs	300	5.0	4.30	258	42	14	0.70
Total KC	$2700	45.0%		$ 2516	$184	6.81%	3.06%
Total costs	$6000	100.0%		$ 5748	$252		

CI Priority	CI Factor	BC Cash Available (000)	Cumulative (000)	% of Total BC Cash Available
I. Indirect labor	1.064%	$ 62	$ 62	24.6%
Optional costs	0.70	42	104	41.3
Selling expenses (fixed)	0.603	36	140	55.5
II. Direct labor	0.40%	$ 24	$164	
Supplies and utilities	0.40	24	188	
Payback costs	0.335	20	208	
Purchased materials	0.267	16	224	88.9
G and A	0.20	13		
Maintenance	0.165	10		
Variable sales costs	0.066	4		
Fixed charges	0.025	1		
Total		$252		

The *CI factor* (column 8) is the importance of each cost to the cost-reduction program: its percent of sales (column 3) multiplied by its CI potential (column 7). Direct labor is 20% of sales (column 3) and has a 2% CI potential (column 7), so its CI factor is 0.40 (column 8). Purchased materials are 26.7% of sales; since they have only a 1% CI potential, their CI factor of 0.267 is far below DL. But whereas supplies and utilities are a very low 5% of total sales, their CI potential is 8%. So this tiny category of cost reduction is as important as direct labor, with a CI factor of *0.40*.

"Twenty-eighty" priority (opportunity) is now clearly demonstrated for the CI Committee and for everyone in the company. Our potential for cash improvement is very high in total KC, for instance, with BC cash available (column 6) of $184,000 compared with only $68,000 in total VC. The CI factor for KC is 3.06% (column 8), compared with only 1.13% for VC.

CI priority (lower half of the table) is now established simply by ranking the CI factors (column 8). We could have ranked the costs by BC cash available (column 6) and come up with the same order of priority. But the CI factor gives us a better feel of the cost-reduction potentials available, as a percentage of sales, apart from the *level* of sales.

The CI Committee now directs everyone's attention and cash creativity to priority I, consisting of indirect labor, optional costs, and selling expenses. The three items together account for 55.5% of the company's potential cost savings. The positions and cost areas represented on the Committee are now strongly influenced by the nature of the priority I cost items. Everyone converges on—and relentlessly hammers away at— indirect labor, optional costs, and fixed selling expenses. Only then do we go to priority II, if cash priorities (opportunities) have not changed by then.

Priority is influenced secondarily, of course, by the cost and time input needed to generate particular savings, and when and for how long we will enjoy them. This has to do with rate of return, and is examined thoroughly in Chapter 18.

CASH PRODUCTIVITY FROM SALES/EXPENSES

Sales/expense productivity—which my earthier management colleagues abbreviated to S/EX productivity almost from the day I introduced the concept—is what we are really trying to maximize in the comprehensive cost-reduction effort. It is simply to maximize the sales volume generated by each dollar of costs and expenses (S/C).

We can, in fact, give the benefit of the doubt to my ingenious abbreviating associates: S/EX productivity creates and sustains the dynamic growth pattern of a well-managed company, just as the sex drive and productivity creates and sustains the growth pattern of the family, species, race, nation, and society in general. S/EX productivity is the most vital force in building a business, because it is the basis and meaning of the entire cost control effort. This effort is the main source of cash generation, which in turn is the most powerful weapon available to build the business.

Though theoretically unassailable, the S/EX productivity concept is difficult to apply to *individual* cost situations. Suppose we want to do a sales productivity analysis of all the component costs making up our priority I categories. That is, we want to know how much sales are produced by each cost item. The costs with the least sales productivity would then get first priority in the cost-reduction effort.

But how do we determine the amount of sales produced by the Machinery Maintenance Department, for instance, which costs the company $67,000 a year? We do not know. Even negatively, we do not know. That is, we do not know how much sales we will *lose* if we eliminated the machinery maintenance outlay, or any portion of it.

All we really know is the department's breakeven volume. The profit center against which machinery maintenance is charged has a 45% Sc, or sales cash/sales. So the $67,000 of fixed maintenance costs require $149,000 of sales to break even ($67,000/45%). But we cannot relate machinery maintenance to a specific quantity of sales volume, BV or otherwise.

Nor is it helpful to apply the sales/expense concept to incremental maintenance expenditures. Would an additional maintenance man be justified at a salary of $10,000 a year? That is, because of him, will the company produce at least $22,000 of additional sales volume ($10,000/45%)? No one knows.

So we fall back on the more objective *BC* measurement of the power of individual costs to produce sales:

	Amount	% of Sales ($6 million)	BC%	BC $'s Allowed $(0.992 \times \$6$ million)	BC Available $[(1)-(4)]$	CI Potential $[(1) \div (5)]$
	1	2	3	4	5	6
Machinery maintenance	$67,000	1.12%	0.992%	$59,500	$7,500	11.2%

We have an extraordinary 11.2% cash-improvement (CI) potential in machinery maintenance. In this way, we go through the back door and test every expense of the business for its contribution to sales productivity. It is not done directly, but in terms of the sales productivity of that expense category in the BC company. Our final answer is *both* theoretically sound, in terms of sales/expense productivity, and pragmatically sound in the mechanical or arithmetical way it was arrived at.

THE PRODUCT FOCUS OF CASH CREATIVITY

Product cost reduction, as a core concept, is based on the obvious but oft-forgot truth that a business is the sum of its component products (and services). By focusing cost control and reduction on the individual product, we are at bedrock and the ultimate reality of our business. We have geared our cost efforts to the actual and definable *components* of that business.

Product committees, for instance, can be very profitable.They consist of men involved directly with the product in such areas as production, engineering, and purchasing. Meeting weekly for 2 hours, they take one product at a time and thoroughly explore its cost-savings opportunities. All necessary product information is on hand at the meeting, including cost data and estimates, engineering drawings, and the cost of purchased parts. The product is dismantled and completely picked apart, compared with competitive products, brainstormed, and ideas about it turned inside out.

Starting with a cost-reduction dollar objective for that product, the committee tries to achieve it by looking for parts substitutions, eliminations, combinations, and whatever else creative imagination and energy can bring to bear on its input costs. It also looks into savings in assembly, finishing, shipping, and distribution. Or it might study re-engineering possibilities, or the desirability of pruning a low-return product from the line.

Promising ideas go into the minutes of the meeting. They are assigned to a committee member, who investigates them and reports back to the following week's meeting for action. Accepted ideas are costed for dollar savings, and submitted to the CI Committee.

Often the biggest product cost reduction mileage comes from trimming direct standard unit costs, or manufacturing VC. The product approach assumes that we have good standard costs for direct material and direct labor. Again, "good" means engineered standards based on attainable good performance (AGP) over the forseeable future. For the typical high-unit-volume product, even a 1 cent reduction in the Manufacturing Specification's standard allowances for material, labor, spoilage, or downtime can produce substantial cash increases. This is the planning stage where effective control of direct unit costs is best achieved, rather than after low-efficiency plans have already been launched.

To reduce the product's direct *material* costs, we should usually break the cost categories into their component classifications—direct material, indirect material, expensed versus depreciated materials, maintenance materials, capital expenditure materials, and so forth. Then we can deal with each material category separately, tightening up standards, finding better supply sources and better ways to handle them, and so forth. And purchasing must be completely professionalized, of course, since it is almost certainly our biggest dollar outlay.

For product cost control in the areas of *labor and machinery*, industrial engineering (IE) is the predominant capability. Its tasks are endless: work measurement and standards (time and motion study); job evaluation; work simplification and methods improvement; labor control reporting; plant layout; expenditures for equipment and plant; systems and procedures; Princo; and many others. IE's larger purpose is to design and install organically integrated *systems* of men, materials, and machines—to produce products at maximum profit.

Function costing is a core concept more than a strategy.[3] It is a cost-reduction orientation or approach rather than a method, since it uses all available cost-reduction methods to implement the approach. The function costing approach looks at the product as a *service* or function performed for a target customer. A product, like anything else, is not what it is but what it *does*.

Typically, the function costing group is really a task force assigned to a particular product, and consists of people from engineering, manufacturing, purchasing, or other pertinent capabilities, *and* a value engineering specialist.

Once we have identified the product's function or service, we rethink its entire manufacturing and distribution process—to provide that *function* at least cost. It does not necessarily mean that we try to make that product at less cost. The function may require an entirely new product, or perhaps a service rather than a product. The function is at stage center, not the product as such.

In other words, we are in business to perform a specific group of functions for a clearly defined target customer, and to do them at least cost and maximum profit. How much of the direct material, direct labor, and overhead content of the product or service can be trimmed without impairing its function?

This gets the function costing (value analysis) group into alternative manufacturing methods, materials, product features, performance specifi-

---

[3]It can also be called "service costing", and is known more popularly but much less descriptively as value analysis, or value engineering.

cations, appearance and aesthetic requirements, suppliers, and so on, in numberless directions. Each element of product cost is challenged from a *function* point of view, and the cost is reduced or eliminated if there is no impairment of function.

When pursued within the conceptual and pragmatic framework of the cash system, these and many other core strategies take on an entirely new dimension of cash productivity.

This is certainly true of capacity costs, which we have not yet mentioned. The control and reduction of KC is in fact of such cash-generating importance as to justify its own chapter, to which we now turn.

CHAPTER 16

CAPACITY COSTS
AND CASH GENERATION

It is a rare company that does not have in its constant costs a solid cash-generating opportunity. Excessive KC abounds in even the best-run firms, but not for lack of the means to stamp it out. It abounds because it is largely invisible. While the best companies hone their managerial tools to razor sharpness and apply them flawlessly everywhere, constant costs seem to pile up unchecked and unnoticed.

KC'S DEFINITIONAL VISIBILITY

KC tends to evaporate when it is made visible. A bad approach is to wait for volume to slump, when constant costs become painfully or dangerously visible. A good approach is to *define* KC into recognizable form. Once we know what the animal is that stands ready to devour us, and the precise definition of its physical and behavioral characteristics, we can deal with it. This means defining the total animal, and also its components.

We fight an octopus differently from an elephant (I assume, having had no usable experience with either animal). But KC partakes of the characteristics of both the octopus and the elephant. So we had better make a quick definitional distinction between them and do battle accordingly, before we get either constricted or stomped, as the case may be.

The definitional approach to KC not only puts the animal into recognizable form, where it is most vulnerable, but determines our choice of weapon. Each of the categories of KC, as defined according to cause and behavior, requires its own cost-reduction assumptions and its own strategies. The best approach for one may be wrong for another.

We have already defined capacity costs as constant costs (and a function of time) that provide the resource capability to create, make, and market our product. They must therefore consist of irreducible *fixed* costs, deferrable *payback* costs, and optional *staff* costs. Let us define these parts of the KC animal into recognizable cash-generating form.

REDUCING FIXED OR CADRE KC

Fixed KC are irreducible going-concern costs, the pure standby expense of being ready to produce. Yet as a group they are reducible definitionally, as we shall see.

They would not be affected, for instance, by a 50% reduction in sales volume that will last 6 to 12 months. So we could also call them disaster or storm cellar costs.They represent our minimum structural and functional capacity of plant, machines, and men without which we can no longer consider ourselves as being in business.

They are really *cadre* costs, in the military sense. In simpler times the cadre was the bare-bones skeleton of officers and key enlisted men, with their barracks and minimal equipment and supplies. It was maintained in peacetime as a potential nucleus of leadership and training. Around it a fully manned and effective wartime unit of raw recruits could be quickly formed.

The corporate cadre, for which fixed KC is incurred, is defined more subjectively. And its actual dimensions depend on the operating and cyclical characteristics of our business. But in general it will probably include: management down through the first-line supervisors of the departments; minimum maintenance crews and supplies for plant and equipment; irreplaceable skilled and professional people; and the untouchable costs of royalties and licenses, property taxes, casualty insurance, and interest and amortization of debt.

The cadre definition is not academic, but the basis of a lucrative cost reduction strategy. That is, we precisely and *narrowly* define our irreducible fixed or cadre costs. Then everything else that was in the fixed-cost category will have been ipso facto reclassified as variable overhead and other variable costs (VC). They will now be forced to decline with reductions in volume, exerting a corresponding cash-generating and profit impact.

CONTROLLING CONSTANT OVERHEAD

For any level of sales, however, this variable overhead is in effect constant overhead. If volume never does go into a slump, it does not either. Then the lucrative distinction between cadre and variable overhead is not a source of cost savings. For a given level of sales, therefore, we still want to *minimize* overhead and breakeven volume, and maximize profits.

This we do with all the core strategies and tools of cash creativity at our disposal, as we have been discussing. Overhead represents an especially important cost-reduction opportunity where it is a high percentage of the product's cost input. And overhead is a high percentage in companies whose direct labor input is much higher than material input. Job shops that manufacture to customer specification are an extreme example of labor-weighted operations, so their overhead tends to be heavy.

Overhead is low, on the other hand, where cost input is mostly purchased material and components for assembly, rather than direct labor. Equipment manufacturers with the lowest direct labor usually have the lowest overhead, which therefore tends to rank low in their cost-reduction priorities.

Indirect labor is by far the largest component of overhead. Products with the heaviest direct labor and overhead therefore usually have the heaviest indirect labor input. This indirect labor is concentrated typically in the actual processing departments, though service and support departments may take a sizable share.

One of the best ways to control and reduce overhead, or really indirect labor, is with prompt and detailed reporting of *head counts* and the associated dollar costs. These reports go to the responsible supervisor, in the form of variances from budget. They should be imaginative and revealing analyses—especially of trends and ratios illustrated with charts or graphs—that inspire him to take prompt corrective action.

One of many possible ways to control manpower variances, and thereby largely control KC, is illustrated by Table 20. Our Sales Department has four divisions: Sales Administration, Field Sales Force, Advertising, and Warehousing. The *Field Sales Force* has three branch office cost centers—in Massachusetts, Rhode Island, and Connecticut.

Table 20 starts with the control reporting for the Sales Department as a whole. *The KC Variance Report* gives budget and actual dollars, and variances, for the four Sales Department functions. We have a total Sales Department variance to date, on line 5, of ($2900).

The *Constant Personnel Report* head count tells us that the Sales Department is now 2 people over budget (September, line 6). Its budget column calls for 21 employees.

The culprit is obviously the Field Sales Force: on *line 2* of the KC Variance Report, it accounts for ($2600) out of the total Sales Department variance of ($2900). And it is 1 man over budget in the Constant Personnel Report (11 against 10), accounting for half the 2-man total variance (line 6).

So we must look for the cause of our problem largely in the detail of the *Field Sales Force* KC and head count reports, shown just below those of the Sales Department. Its KC Variance Report covers the three branch offices: This gives the branch detail of the Sales Department KC Report, whose budget, actual, and variance for the Field Sales Force (line 2) is $104,200, $106,800, and ($2600).

From the Field Sales Force's KC Variance, we now see that the Connecticut branch office is the culprit (line 9), with a whopping $2700 negative variance. This and the other two branch office totals are each fed by a detailed variance report submitted up the line by the branch manager. So we look into the one for *Connecticut*.

Connecticut's KC Variance Report now tells us that four variances caused the problem: secretaries ($800), clerical ($800), fringes ($500), and utilities and taxes ($700). We cannot really do anything about utilities and taxes, and fringes are a dependent variable of secretaries and clerical. So the main cause and solution of the ($2900) Sales Department variance (line 5) has been pinpointed to excessive personnel costs in the Connecticut branch office.

Just what this personnel overage means in terms of people, which is our control *factor*, is spelled out in the Field Sales Force's Constant Personnel Report (lines 7 to 9). Though Connecticut's budget allowance is 3 people (line 9), it has had 4 and even 5 on its payroll.

Connecticut's Constant Personnel Report gives the detail of the Connecticut head count. Pinpoint costing has finally tracked the variance down to a *second* clerk-bookkeeper hired in March, which caused a 1 person negative variance (line 15).

If this tiny branch office really needs a second clerk-bookkeeper, we have one kind of problem. But if she is a close relative of the branch vice president or an attractive nonrelative, we have another kind of problem.

CONTROLLING PAYBACK KC

We should define payback costs as those we incur for programs and projects undertaken for a definite number of years, to earn a specific rate of return (payback). Projects (expensed or capitalized) may include everything from major advertising campaigns and product development programs, to reconstructing the leaky roof on plant 3.

We could also call them project, program, capital, or even deferrable costs. But by whatever name, as a source of cost reduction they can be virtually ignored *by definition*. That is, a project is approved on the basis of

Table 20 Capacity Costs and Cash Control (9 Months Ended September 30)

	KC Variance (000)			Constant Personnel									
	Budget	Actual	Variance	Budget	J	F	M	A	My	J	Jy	A	S
Sales Department													
1. Sales Administration	$ 19.7	$ 19.9	($0.2)	4	4	4	4	4	4	4	4	4	4
2. Field Sales Force	104.2	106.8	(2.6)	10	10	10	11	11	12	12	11	11	11
3. Advertising	63.8	63.4	0.4	3	3	3	4	4	3	3	3	3	3
4. Warehousing	15.6	16.1	(0.5)	4	4	4	5	5	5	5	5	5	5
5.	$203.3	$206.2	($2.9)	21	21	21	24	24	24	24	23	23	23
6.				Variance	0	0	(3)	(3)	(3)	(3)	(2)	(2)	(2)
Field Sales Force													
7. Massachusetts	$ 38.4	$ 38.1	$ 0.3	4	4	4	4	4	4	4	4	4	4
8. Rhode Island	29.2	29.4	(0.2)	3	3	3	3	3	3	3	3	3	3
9. Connecticut	36.6	39.3	(2.7)	3	3	3	4	4	5	5	4	4	4
10.	$104.2	$106.8	($2.6)	10	10	10	11	11	12	12	11	11	11
11.				Variance	0	0	(1)	(1)	(2)	(2)	(1)	(1)	(1)

Connecticut Branch

12. Branch manager	$10.6	$10.6	$0.0	1	1	1	1	1	1	1
13. Salesman	8.4	8.3	0.1	1	1	1	1	1	1	1
14. Secretaries	4.4	5.2	(0.8)			2	2	2	1	1
15. Clerk-bookkeepers	4.5	5.3	(0.8)			2	2	2	2	2
16. Fringes	3.1	3.6	(0.5)							
17. Depreciation	1.8	1.8	0.0							
18. Utilities and taxes	3.8	4.5	(0.7)							
19.	$36.6	$39.3	($2.7)							
20.	Variance		3	3	3	4	4	5	4	4
			0	0	(1)	(1)	(1)	(2)	(1)	(1)

a stiff percentage cutoff return on the investment, against which its forecasted return is tested. Proposed projects that fail this test are rejected, so that payback costs are those incurred only for the most profitable projects. Any reduction in payback costs (other than from purging inefficiences) will therefore reduce future earnings substantially.

To treat them as deferrable costs, as a way to bolster this year's poor earnings and kid our public stockholders, therefore does injury to the business: it delays or perhaps torpedoes future project earnings.

Our definitional approach to KC thus "defines" payback costs out of the cost-reduction area ($-$C) and into the reinvestment area ($+$R). In chapter 18 we shall deal exhaustively with their cash-generating potentials.

For the purposes of this chapter, however, it is necessary to see how payback KC is *controlled*. This must be done in two stages. We control payback *expenditures* against budgeted expenditures. And we control its *cash flow return* against the forecast for which the project expenditures were originally approved.

Table 21 is a two-part control device that does just that. 1. *Payback expenditures* illustrates the control of actual against budgeted expenditures. The annual budget (column 2) itemizes all the approved and activated project requests that were previously submitted up the line. The rest of the report flows from or controls the detailed monthly expenditure estimates included in each request.

Columns 3 through 8 detail the actual versus budgeted expenditures for the current month and for the year to date. Manufacturing project 12-26, for instance, should have used up $140,000 to date, according to budget (column 6). But project expenditures have actually been $165,000 (column 7). So, in column 8, the variance is ($25,000). This type of variance may be more illusory than real, or might actually be beneficial if the more rapid expenditures were themselves beneficial. An explanation is called for, in any event.

More important is column 9's remaining budget balance of $25,000. It is the $190,000 budgeted (column 2), less $165,000 spent to date (column 7). This $25,000 compares with the actual balance still needed to finish the project—of $40,000 (column 10). That is, the original estimate of $190,000 was too low: it allows us an additional $25,000, but we still need $40,000 to complete project 12-26.

We now see that total expenditures on project 12-26 will probably be $205,000 (column 11), or the $165,000 spent so far (column 7) plus the $40,000 balance still required for this project (column 10). We will thus be over budget by $15,000 (column 12), the difference between the original budget appropriation of $190,000 and the total required expenditure of $205,000.

Project 12-31, on the other hand, will cost only $50,000 (column 11), compared with budget of $60,000 (column 2). So $10,000 will remain unspent (column 12).

For all Manufacturing, $380,000 of projects were budgeted (column 2), against which total expenditures probably will be $390,000 (column 11), putting us $10,000 over budget. But the total company will be only $15,000 (column 12) over its total project authorization of $1,220,000 (column 2).

2. *Payback cash flow* shows us the output of which the foregoing payback expenditures were the input. It controls each project's payback cash flow against the annual amounts estimated in the original project request. Manufacturing project 1-48 has just completed its sixth year of life (column 2), having earned $43,000 (column 4) against an original forecast for the year of $37,000 (column 3). So it has a positive variance for the year of $6000.

Cumulatively, from the time the project was inaugurated, it has earned $117,000 (column 7) against a cumulative forecast of $126,000 (column 6). So its variance for the six years is ($9000).

As shown in the backup information for project 1-48, in footnote *a*, it has an estimated life of 11 years. Earnings should reach their peak of $42,000 in the seventh year. The cumulative section of the payback cash flow table, and its backup tables, usually have more decision-making validity than the current year's variances. Cumulating tends to smooth out extraordinary years and helps us to evaluate the success or failure of the total project.

REDUCING OPTIONAL KC

Optional KC is our advisory and service staff overhead. It is defined as optional only in the sense that these services are also available entirely or substantially on the outside. Staff is our legal department or general counsel, insurance people, personnel men or executive recruiters, advertising department, public relations group, and all the rest. The dividing line between optional staff and mandatory staff (such as the controller's department) boils down to the practical and immediate availability of that capability on the outside. It would hardly be practical for us to seek outside controllership or chief executive assistance whenever we needed it.

To define a particular staff department or individual as optional means only that we do not *have to* consult him or seek his services. We might not do so in any event if his office were not just down the hall from us. Or we could simply go to an outside firm that provides the identical capability.

Our staff specialists may or may not provide a high return on their

Table 21 Controlling Project Outlay and Cash Return (000)

1. Payback Expenditures (September 30)

Mfg. Project	Budget	Expenditures						Budget Balance to Spend	Actual Balance Needed	Forecast	
		This Month			Year to Date					Total Expenditure	Under (Over)
		Budget	Actual	Variance	Budget	Actual	Variance	[(2) − (7)]		[(7) + (10)]	[(2) − (11)]
1	2	3	4	5	6	7	8	9	10	11	12
12–26	$190	$15	$19	($ 4)	$140	$165	($25)	$ 25	$ 40	$ 205	($15)
12–31	60	5	0	5	45	30	15	30	20	50	10
12–48	20	3	3	0	15	17	(2)	3	3	20	0
12–56	110	10	22	(12)	90	110	(20)	0	5	115	(5)
Total	$380	$ 33	$ 44	($11)	$290	$322	($32)	$ 58	$ 68	$ 390	($10)
R & D											
16–14											
16–19											
Etc.											
Total	$1220	$130	$145	($15)	$ 950	$ 970	($ 20)	$250	$265	$1235	($15)

2. Payback Cash Flow

Manufacturing Project	Payback Year	This Year			Cumulative		
1	2	Forecast 3	Actual 4	Variance 5	Forecast 6	Actual 7	Variance 8
1–9	11	$14	$12	($2)	$ 59	$ 58	($1)
1–48[a]	6	37	43	6	126	117	(9)
2–16	4	10	9	(1)	36	32	(4)
3–11	4	17	19	2	165	171	6
Total		$78	$83	$5	$386	$378	($8)

Table 21 (*Continued*)

*Manufacturing project 1-48 (total cost, $210,000; DCF return, 96%):

Payback Year	This Year			Cumulative		
	Forecast	Actual	Variance	Forecast	Actual	Variance
1	$11	$12	1	$11	$12	1
2	11	13	2	22	25	3
3	16	11	(5)	38	36	(2)
4	22	19	(3)	60	55	(5)
5	29	19	(10)	89	74	(15)
6	37	43	6	126	117	(9)
7	42			168		
8	36			204		
9	21			225		
10	9			234		
11	3			237		

198

overhead-cost dollars. But we must *know* whether these dollars are profitable, just as we must with all the other dollars spent in the business. There are at least two ways of making staff overhead demonstrably profitable. One is to eliminate it entirely under a "no-staff" policy, whereby it is replaced as needed with highly visible outside-staff and consulting expenses. The other is to turn it all into a "staff profit center". Both methods work well, in the cash-generating sense, because they are sound exercises in definitional visibility. They define staff services in hard profit-center terms, where they are plainly (and sometimes embarassingly) visible.

• The *no-staff* policy is one of hiring only outside advisory and service specialists, with no full-time in-house staff. It eliminates fixed staff overhead and reduces BV, by converting KC to *VC* which is bought only when needed. It also provides the most up-to-date and able specialist available— and one who has multiple-company experience, rather than one who happens to be working for us.

Our management people are now forced to learn *what* the problems are and to define them specifically. The clearly defined problem is then presented to the best available outside specialist for solution. He is *never* brought in to tell us what is wrong.

The consultant reports to the manager who has retained him, and the relationship is like that of manager and professional subordinate. Together they plan the project objectives and target date; organize people to best achieve the objectives; motivate progress; and control results according to the original project plan. The manager evaluates his consultant's performance in a memo that goes into the central company file, which serves as a guide for all managers in the selection of the best outside assistance.

The consulting fee is charged to the manager's own budget and affects his S/C performance. So he will be scrupulous in deciding *if*, *who*, at what *fee*, and for how *long* the specialist will be retained: KC tends to evaporate when it is made visible.

The *staff profit center* policy is an alternative way to make staff overhead visible. All advisory and service people are combined organizationally into a staff profit center, headed by a VP with full profit responsibility. Each staff specialty, such as advertising or insurance, is a profit subcenter. The staff VP *must* make a profit on the total staff profit center. And each specialty subcenter *must* make a profit.

The staff subcenter bills the user of its advice or service on a fully costed basis: the fee includes its variable costs, salaries, office space, an overhead rate high enough to absorb idle time, and profit. However sacred or tradition-bound the service, it is dropped if there is no profit.

A $1200 legal fee billed to Sales Branch D is income to the Legal Department profit subcenter—perhaps much-needed income in terms of the department's survival. And the $1200 is a cost to the sales branch, which it had to weigh carefully against possible adverse budget variances and S/C performance.

The branch manager is completely free to choose staff help from inside or outside the company. So he uses the inside staff service *only* (1) if it is *competitive* in cost with outside service; (2) if it *excels* professionally and is of significant help to him; (3) *when* essential; and (4) to the *extent*, in terms of duration and cost, that the service is really needed. Actually, a charge for staff service should be made to the lowest responsibility level (such as to the branch *salesman's* budget) where it is in fact used and the cost actually incurred. The user (salesman) must justify this billing to his boss (branch manager) before the fact.

Both the "no-staff" and the "staff profit center" principles can be applied to many forms of overhead that have always been thought of as mandatory and nondiscretionary. We define the function as optional, upon careful consideration, and confer profit-center status on it. Then it bills its users directly and justifies its existence by the profit it makes, lest it be replaced with a comparable outside but occasional service.

Either way, overhead has been made visible under a definitional spotlight where excessive KC tends to evaporate.

This concludes our inquiry throughout Part Four into the production and control of cost cash.

It was an inquiry that formulated the costing framework and concepts in Chapter 13, and the conditions for cash creativity in Chapter 14. From this foundation we could trace the implementation of cost reduction in cash system terms (in Chapter 15) and the reduction of capacity costs in the present chapter.

We can now move logically into the production of *asset cash*—where the fruits of cost control are employed, but which is an entirely separate battleground in the strategy of cash.

PART 5

ASSET SOURCES OF CASH

CHAPTER 17

GENERATING ASSET CASH

Assets are a prolific source of cash because they exert both quantitative and qualitative impacts that are mutually reinforcing. That is, we generate asset cash in two ways: (1) negatively, by controlling the *quantity* of assets in relation to sales ($+S/A$), and (2) positively, by increasing the *quality* or profitability of assets ($+R$). We shall discuss them in that order in this and the next chapter.

But let us first recall how asset cash productivity fits into our overall liquidity framework, which we constructed in Part One to comprehend and apply the strategy of cash. This framework divides roughly into two equity-creating segments, one internal and the other external. The internal segment is cash return on equity (CRE), and the external one is equity created by public offerings and acquisitions (ECO and ECA). Percentage increase of equity (Pi) must therefore describe the essence and dynamics of the liquidity framework, which is summarized by the expression Pi $= CRE \times ECA \times ECO$.

Its strategy implications are, first, that $CRE = (S/C \times S/A \times L/A)(R)$. We maximize cash productivity as follows:

1. Generate *sales* cash ($+S$ and $+Sc$).
2. Generate *cost* cash ($-C$). Together items 1 and 2 provide operating cash flow.
3. Generate *leverage* cash ($+L/A$), based on this operating cash flow.
4. Generate *asset* cash ($+S/A$) by minimizing the diversion of cash to nonproductive asset expansion. This is the quantitative side of the asset productivity coin ($-A$).
5. Generate *reinvestment* cash ($+R$) by channeling the cash derived from $S/C \times S/A \times L/A$ into maximum-profitability assets. This is the qualitative side of the asset productivity coin ($+S$), in the ratio S/A: we increase the sales productivity and profitability of our existing quantum of assets.

203

So we maximize the cash from $+S$, $-C$, and $+L$; and minimize the amount of it absorbed nonproductively by assets $(-A)$. The balance we invest at maximum cash return in $+R$, and thereby maximize CRE.

The second strategy implication of the Pi expression is ECA and ECO. These external strategies of equity formation, from acquisitions and public offerings, supplement internal CRE to yield Pi. Hence $Pi = CRE \times ECA \times ECO$.

We will thus concern ourselves in this chapter with item 4: generating cash from assets by minimizing their quantity in relation to sales. To the extent that we contain our assets, as noted, they do not divert or drain the investable cash coming from operations, leverage, and equity formation. The cash now flows into maximum-return investments $(+R)$, and we maximize CRE.

ASSET CASH MACROPRODUCTIVITY

We approach the generation of asset cash from two directions. The companywide *macroproductive* strategy minimizes *total* assets in relation to total sales, or the rate of asset growth in relation to sales growth. More actual and potential cash is thereby generated from cash flow and leverage than is absorbed by asset expansion. Macroproductivity is thus concerned with the influence exerted on total cash generation by the causal sequence: sales to assets to leverage to cash.

Microproductivity of assets, on the other hand, is the generation of cash from *individual* asset items. These are slow receivables; heavy inventories; underutilized fixed and miscellaneous assets; and low-profit subsidiaries, divisions, and product lines; to name the most obvious. Microproductivity is concerned with the turnover of individual assets, described by their S/A ratios. In cash terms, it is the liquidity velocity of total assets—the productivity and speed with which cash is recirculated within the existing quantity of corporate assets. It will be discussed later in the chapter, because it involves a substantially different set of problems than does macroproductivity. And they are susceptible of different varieties of cash-generating solutions.

The extraordinary phenomenon of asset macroproductivity can be seen in Table 22. It consists of two parallel examples in which assets are the single variable. That is, *Example A* and *Example B* are identical except in the behavior of assets (line 7). In Example B they grow at the same rate as sales (line 1). But in Example A they grow less rapidly. This causes an explosive cash effect, as we shall see, that provides much more liquidity than the asset savings themselves. Asset cash productivity is thus really an *asset cash multiplier*.

Table 22 Maximizing Asset Cash Productivity

	Example A			Example B		
	Year 1	Year 3	Year 5	Year 1	Year 3	Year 5
1. Sales (S) (000)	5000	7000	9000	5000	7000	9000
2. Costs (C)[a] (000)	4700	6580	8460	4700	6650	8650
3. S/C	1.064	1.064	1.064	1.064	1.053	1.040
4. Cost Cash Index	100	100	100	100	99	98
5. Cash flow [(1)−(2)] (000)	300	420	540	300	350	350
6. Retained earnings [50% of (5)] (000)	150	210	270	150	175	175
7. Assets (A) (000)	5150	5540	6050	5150	7000	9000
8. S/A	0.97	1.26	1.49	0.97	1.00	1.00
9. Asset Cash Index	100	130	154	100	103	103
10. Debt (L) (000)	2000	2000	2000	2000	3525	5175
11. L/A	0.39	0.36	0.33	0.39	0.50	0.57
12. Leverage Cash Index	100	92	85	100	128	146
13. Cash productivity factor [(3)×(8)×(11)]	0.40	0.48	0.52	0.40	0.53	0.59
14. Equity (E) (000)	3150	3540	4050	3150	3475	3825
15. Debt/equity	0.63	0.56	0.49	0.63	1.01	1.35
16. Debt capacity [(5) ÷ 15%] (000)	2000	2800	3600	2000	2330	2330
17. Leverage cash availability [(16)−(10)]	0	800	1600	0	(1195)	(2845)
18. Debt/sales [(10)÷(1)](L/S)	0.40	0.29	0.22	0.40	0.50	0.57
19. CRE [(5)÷(14)]	9.5	11.9	13.3	9.5	10.1	9.2

[a] Cash costs, including taxes,

In *year 1* of both examples, we are in exactly the same position with respect to every factor as we go down the columns. The horses at the starting gate are indistinguishable from each other. And in both examples, sales (line 1) increase over the five years from $5,000,000 to $9,000,000. Now let us look at each example, and then compare them.

Example A. Costs (line 2) remain at the same percentage of sales during the five years, so that sales/costs (line 3) is constant at 1.064. The Cost Cash Index (line 4) is the percentage that the S/C ratio each year (line 3) is of the base year 1, or a constant 100%. Cash flow (line 5) is the difference between sales and costs. And retained earnings (line 6) are assumed to be 50% of cash flow.

Assets (line 7) are crucial, as noted, because they are the single variable.

They start at $5,150,000 in year 1 (after giving effect to retained earnings). Management each year is able to hold the growth of assets to the retained earnings increment, so that assets increase during the five-year period to $6,050,000.

Since sales grow at a more rapid rate, sales/assets (line 8) rises from 0.97 to 1.49 in year 5. The Asset Cash Index (line 9), or the percentage that each year's S/A ratio is of year 1's 0.97, moves up correspondingly to 154%.

The company started with $2,000,000 of debt (line 10). But we do not need to borrow as sales volume soars, because assets are increasing more slowly. That is, external financing of assets to supplement retained earnings is unnecessary. Leverage/assets (line 11) in fact declines moderately from 0.39 to 0.33, reducing the Leverage Cash Index (line 12) to 85. Again, this is the percentage that each year's L/A ratio (line 11) is of year 1's 0.39.

The *cash productivity factor* (line 13) summarizes the various cash impacts on cash return on equity (refer to Chapter 3 for the rationale of CPF). Our comprehensive cash-generating formula is $CPF = S/C \times S/A \times L/A$. So each year we multiply S/C by S/A by L/A (lines 3, 8, and 11) to get the CPF. In year 3, for instance, $1.064 \times 1.26 \times 0.36$ is the CPF of 0.48.

But S/C is constant at 1.064 for the five years (line 3). And L/A is declining a bit (line 11). So the five-year increase in CPF from 0.40 to 0.52 can only be due to the increase in S/A (line 8), which rose from 0.97 to 1.49. Management demonstrated a remarkable ability to control assets in relation to expanding sales volume.

Equity (line 14) rises with each increment in retained earnings (line 6). So with debt constant at $2,000,000 (line 10), debt/equity declines from 63 to 49% (line 15). The company's capacity to incur debt is substantial by almost any test, especially that of cash flow (line 5). It is management's policy never to increase debt above the amount whose cash flow is 15%. This is how it has computed debt capacity (line 16) each year. It also decrees that debt should not exceed 40% of sales, where the ratio stands in year 1, and declines to 22% (line 18).

Because of the tight asset control, which held debt to $2,000,000, cash flow debt capacity (line 16) has risen substantially above actual debt—to $3,600,000 in year 5. The company thus can generate, at reasonable rates and terms, additional cash from leverage (line 17) of up to $1,600,000.

Example B is an entirely different matter. The *only* change from Example A is management's inability or disinclination to control assets (line 7). They move up from $5,150,000 to $9,000,000 in year 5, not to $6,050, 000 as in Example A. Yet this growth is no more than the growth rate of sales. So S/A remains at 1.00 (line 8), and the *Asset Cash Index* (line 9) at around 100%.

But debt (line 10) increases substantially to $5,175,000, to finance the buildup in assets to $9,000,000. That is, equity (line 14) increases somewhat less than in Example A, because soaring interest and asset costs have reduced the rate of accumulation of retained earnings. Even more so than in Example A, therefore, the overwhelming weight of financing new assets must come from leverage—or the arithmetic difference between burgeoning assets and virtually stationary equity.

In years 2 to 5, specifically, $3,175,000 had to be added to debt (line 10) in order to finance an increase in assets of $3,850,000 (the difference being $675,000 of accumulated retained earnings).[1] While assets (line 7) increased by 3850/5150 or 75%, debt increased by 3175/2000, or 159%. L/A (line 11) shot up from 0.39 to 0.57, and the Leverage Cash Index (line 12) to 146%.

Example B's profit margin was therefore narrower than that of Example A. This came partly from higher asset-carrying costs, such as storage, insurance, maintenance, security, and loss and spoilage. But it came especially from soaring interest costs, whose adverse effect on the profit margin is suggested by the steep rise in debt/sales from 0.40 to 0.57 (line 18). The amount of interest rose sharply with the amount of debt. But so too did the *rate* of interest. It increased to reflect the higher credit risk to which lenders are now exposed, as prudent or safe debt limits are exceeded. So the interest burden climbed more steeply than the debt burden.

Example B's profit margin therefore narrows a bit—from 6% in year 1 to about 4%—to reflect the accelerating rise in asset and interest costs: S/C (line 3) declines from 1.064 to 1.040, and the Cost Cash Index (line 4) recedes to 98%. That is, cash flow (line 5) rises, but only to $350,000.

The cash productivity factor (line 13) again summarizes the influence of the three cash contribution ratios. It rises to 0.59 (vs. 0.52 in Example A). S/C and S/A (lines 3 and 8) are virtually constant or declining, so that the upward impetus to CPF is provided entirely by L/A (line 11). In Example A, S/C and L/A were constant or declining, and the upward impetus was provided by S/A (line 8), entirely and forcefully.

In terms of Example B's Cash Indexes, cost cash (line 4) declines a bit to 98, and asset cash (line 9) is virtually stationary at 103. But leverage cash (line 12), as noted, jumps to 146.

Thus while Example A's Leverage Cash Index (line 12) declined to 85, that of Example B jumped to 146. And while Example A's Asset Cash Index (line 9) rose to 154, Example B's remained level. The rise in Example B's Leverage Index was as unhealthy and potentially dangerous as the rise in Example A's Asset Index was healthy and potentially profitable. The difference was asset control, and nothing else.

[1]Depreciation cash (cash flow less retained earnings) was assumed to have merely replaced depreciating assets. It thus only offset normal attrition, rather than contribute to the net addition of assets—which was done with retained earnings.

Example B's debt/equity ratio (line 15) climbed to 1.35..Debt/sales (line 18) jumped above managment's 40% danger point, to 57%. And its CRE (line 19) of 9.2% is lower than Example A's 13.3%, because of the pressure of soaring interest and asset costs on the profit margin.

Part of Example B's problem is the lower debt capacity (line 16), caused by lower cash flow (line 5). The other part is the shear weight of its debt burden. Debt may be judged excessive against management's 15% cash flow standard to the extent that it exceeds debt capacity, or by the amount of debt in excess of capacity (line 17). By year 5 the excess reached an untenable $2,845,000. Somewhere along the line, the debt load might have torpedoed sales growth or even corporate solvency.

THE ASSET CASH MULTIPLIER

Example A's effective control of assets by year 5 provided a potential $1,600,000 of *additional cash from leverage* (line 17), or leverage cash availability (the + L component of liquidity). It is the excess of debt capacity (line 16) over debt (line 10). But Example B's failure to control assets, under otherwise identical conditions, created *debt in excess of capacity* (line 17) of $2,845,000. Between Example A and Example B, therefore (on line 17), liquidity was reduced by a total of $4,445,000. It was reduced *solely* by Example B's assets (line 7) in year 5 being $2,950,000 higher than those of Example A ($9,000,000 less $6,050,000).

In other words, the control of Example A's assets versus those of Example B in the amount of $2,950,000 *produced* liquidity (which is effective cash) of $4,445,000. It was the amount by which assets produced cash—negatively, to be sure, but spendable and reinvestable cash nevertheless.

This is summarized as follows, abstracted from year 5 of Examples A and B:

	Example B (000) 1	Example A (000) 2	Example B − Example A (000) 3
7. Assets	$9000	$6050	$2950
16. Debt capacity	2330	3600	(1270)
10. Debt	5175	2000	3175
17. Leverage cash availability [(16) − (10)]	($2845)	$1600	$4445

Asset cash multiplier [(17) ÷ (7)]: 4445/2950 = 151%

In column 3, Example A's additional cash availability versus that of Example B is $4,445,000 (line 17). This is its $3,175,000 smaller amount of debt (line 10), plus $1,270,000 of higher debt capacity (line 16). The $4,445,000 of leverage cash availability was the effect, of which $2,950,000 of asset control (line 7) was the cause. In this sense, $+S/A$ asset control *creates* cash availability, which availability is financed and converted into spendable cash by leverage $(+L)$.

An *asset cash multiplier* thus describes Example A versus Example B. It measures the extent to which Example A's asset control of $2,950,000 (line 7) is converted into cash availability of $4,445,000 (line 17). It is $4445/2950 = 151\%$. Asset cash thus multiplies, in short, because asset control not only controls our borrowing requirement but expands our (cash flow) capacity to borrow.

THE RATIONALE OF ASSET CASH PRODUCTIVITY

Assets are a *major* source of cash productivity, and yet are often ignored, misunderstood, or not even recognized. They do not require, for their impact, the simplistic and deliberately exaggerated laboratory conditions of this illustration. The necessary conditions are everywhere to be found in the typical company.

This impact derives from the fact that S/A is largely an independent or causal variable, which primarily determines the dependent variable L/A. And S/A and L/A have an important impact on S/C, or the profit margin, usually through L/S (to a greater or lesser extent). The causal tendency is roughly as follows:

$-A$: $+S/A = -L/A = -L/S = +S/C$ (or $+P$),   as in Example A

$+A$: $-S/A = +L/A = +L/S = -S/C$ (or $-P$),   as in Example B

So the independent variable S/A has a considerable impact on S/C, which is the most unstable and dependent variable of all. Yet CRE, the all-important measurement of corporate success, depends on S/C more than on anything else. In the CRE ratio cash flow/equity, cash flow is a fragile dependent variable; equity is a relatively fixed quantity. Asset control thus tends to be a crucial influence on CRE because it is the predominant moving force behind leverage, and both together materially affect costs and therefore operating cash generation. And it is volatile operating cash, not stodgy equity, that really swings the CRE ratio.

The *rationale* of asset cash productivity can be seen in Examples A and B, in terms of $S/C \times S/A \times L/A$ and L/S:

	S/A		L/A		L/S	S/C
Example B						
Year 1	5000/5150	0.97	2000/5150	0.39	0.40	1.064
Year 5	9000/9000	1.00	5175/9000	0.57	0.57	1.040
Example A						
Year 1	5000/5150	0.97	2000/5150	0.39	0.40	1.064
Year 5	9000/6050	1.49	2000/6050	0.33	0.22	1.064
Example A						
vs. Example B,						
Year 5		+0.49		−0.24	−0.35	+0.024

Example A's asset productivity versus that of Example B was +0.49; it *generated* liquidity in the form of L/A (−0.24), L/S (−0.35), and S/C (+0.024).

We can therefore come to the following strategy conclusions—the implications of asset productivity for the general strategy of cash:

1. Asset growth (−S/A) *absorbs* liquidity from +L/A and +L/S, and from −S/C (Example B): it uses up our available borrowing power and cash.

2. Asset control (+S/A) *produces* usable liquidity from −L/A and −L/S, and from +S/C (Example A). It does so negatively, by not using up borrowing power and cash, and positively by augmenting our borrowing power.

3. To the extent of the asset control (+S/A), liquidity (cash) that otherwise would have been invested in A to produce that incremental amount of S, is *not* invested in A. So it is free to be invested elsewhere to produce *additional* sales and profits. Asset control thus creates *asset cash* in the form of free and uncommitted liquidity.

4. CRE thus benefits from asset control in two ways. First, the more profitable sales produce a higher cash flow, which is now a higher percentage of A (that is, +CRE). This was seen in Example A, compared with B. Second, the cash that was not invested in A is free to be invested elsewhere to produce additional sales and profits (that is, +CRE).

For instance, in Table 23 we use Example A's available liquidity to borrow (line 1) at easy rates and terms up to but not above our debt capacity (from line 16 of Table 22). This finances a higher level of assets (line 3) to produce additional sales (line 6). They are more *profitable* sales than those of Example B because (1) they flow from generally more profitable assets, chosen more selectively, and (2) they benefit from a low and declining debt/sales ratio (line 12). So S/C (line 7) remains at least constant at 1.064.

In year 5, cash flow (line 9) on the higher sales jumps to $700,000, from Table 22's $540,000 in Example A and $350,000 in Example B. And CRE (line 11) moves up to 17.3%, from Table 22's 13.3% in Example A.

CPF (line 10) now benefits from the benign and *balanced* generation of cash from all sources, and rises sharply to *0.74*, from Example A's 0.52 and Example B's 0.59.

Available liquidity (L/A) has now been employed benignly, to exert the full impact of asset cash productivity on CRE.

Table 23 Generating Profits from Asset Cash (Example A)

	Year 3	Year 5
1. Debt (L), at capacity	2800	3600
2. Equity[a]	3540	4050
3. Assets (A) [(1)+(2)]	6340	7650
4. L/A [(1)÷(3)]	0.44	0.47
5. S/A (from Table 22)	1.26	1.49
6. Sales (S) [(3)×(5)]	7970	11,400
7. S/C (from Table 22)	1.064	1.064
8. Costs [(6)÷(7)]	7480	10,700
9. Cash flow [(6)−(8)]	490	700
10. CPF [(4)×(5)×(7)]	0.59	0.74
11. CRE [(9)÷(2)]	13.9	17.3
12. L/S [(1)÷(6)]	0.35	0.32

[a]Minor upward adjustment for additional retained earnings was not made.

ASSET GRAVEYARDS AND THE P & L OBSESSION

Assets are so often the undoing of otherwise well-run companies because they pile up disproportionate costs to carry and finance them. We saw how this reduces the profit margin and debt capacity in the face of soaring debt —and, ominously, debt/sales. Assets alone have put the reduced debt capacity and higher borrowing requirements on collision course.

Two remedies for all this havoc were probably either too little or too late, which so often happens, and we assumed as much in Example B: (1) the new cash flow for which the burgeoning assets were acquired and (2) new equity financing to supplement the burgeoning debt.

Managements that muddle into asset-related financial strain always seem to be obsessed with the income statement and oblivious to the balance sheet. Their premise is that earnings per share can be maximized without regard to the circumstances of corporate liquidity. But this P&L obsession *must* defeat the earnings-per-share objective.

We can easily distinguish three levels of cash sophistication in this regard. The lowest level usually, and the middle level not infrequently, leads to some form of asset-liquidity problem or calamity—possibly to the asset graveyard, where the company is laid to rest.

The lower depths of the P&L monomania is a single-minded and possibly simple-minded preoccupation with raising sales volume, and nothing else. Unbelievably, these managements pursue sales without regard either to the amount of costs they incur to achieve those sales, or the amount of debt they incur to finance the required assets. Their attention is riveted on one part of the income statement, sales ($+S$), to the exclusion of the rest of it ($+C$). So they certainly have no interest in the balance sheet ($+A$) and ($+L$), even the existence of which may not be a matter of common knowledge around much of their front office.

These companies are everywhere. They actually survive amazingly well when times are good; Government contracts are fat, or whatever their temporary good fortune. But the sales-happy firm is an accurate leading indicator of general business conditions—almost invariably the first category of company to run into financial difficulties.

The next higher order of cash sophistication—characteristic of many more if not most companies today—is an intelligent preoccupation with the *entire* P&L statement (S and C), but nothing else. Intensive planning and effort are directed equally to increasing sales and controlling costs. The balance sheet *as such* does not actively influence management's decision-making, except where it clearly affects the income statement—such as a dramatic increase in interest charges. They usually achieve consistent year-to-year improvements in earnings per share, often for long periods of time. And everybody is happy including the stockholders, which makes everybody twice as happy.

But eventually, and perhaps inevitably, the profit margin begins to decline while business is good and sales are soaring. Margins continue to narrow, and profits themselves may begin to drop off. The budget is trimmed everywhere and the axe swings. This helps for a time. But sooner or later, and frequently much too soon, the profit squeeze is on again.

There is another great hue and cry to get the volume up even *more* and cut costs to the bone.

Nobody really looks at the balance sheet because nobody seriously thinks about the balance sheet, either for the source of the problem or its solution. But the balance sheet is what is strangling the company. Assets and debt have mushroomed in response to sales growth, and both are severely out of proportion to equity. Turnover ratios for virtually all the assets have dropped precipitously, and current liquidity may be the next casualty.

The crux of the problem is that a constant S/A, not even a declining one, is potentially dangerous—as in Example B. But the P&L-oriented management does not see the incipient liquidity crisis, or rationalizes it away with heady profit forecasts.

A quick peek at the balance sheet and some sixth grade arithmetic, at almost any point in its sales (and asset) growth orgy, would have sobered everyone up. It reveals that liabilities (and fixed charges) must increase at a higher rate than do sales and assets. Again, this is because equity is a rather fixed quantity, either by ignorance or design. So all the financing of assets (sales) must come from the small liability section of the balance sheet. The crucial debt/sales ratio *must* increase, and eventually to dangerous heights.

The highest level of cash sophistication therefore, again, seems to be one that is centered on the balance sheet. Here are displayed the income-producing asset and leverage resources, and stockholders' equity (itself a resource). And it records the retained-earnings inflow generated by these resources and added to the equity as a percentage return (CRE).

Such a management is riveted to the balance sheet, as the investment manager of its assets and liabilities. It will maximize the productivity of its assets by maximizing sales and minimizing costs ($+S/C$), just as does the P&L-oriented management. But it is a P&L effort that is consciously subservient and contributory to the balance-sheet grand strategy—of maximizing its liquidity velocity, which is the strategy of cash. The P&L effort is now only *two* strategies ($+S$ and $-C$) of the entire liquidity-maximizing bag of tricks, in which are contained all *seven* SCALDER sources of cash.

ASSET MICROPRODUCTIVITY

Now we focus on the many current and fixed asset items from which cash can be released by increasing their turnover (sales/assets). But for the most part we can simply insert the word "asset" in place of "cost" throughout the cost reduction chapters of Part Four, and have a highly effective battle plan for asset reduction.

This is because assets *are* costs and costs are assets. Both measure the expenditure of dollars. Assets are merely cost expenditures that have temporarily retained a tangible, salable value. So when we organize and motivate cost reduction, we are at the same time organizing and motivating asset reduction. Nothing new is required.

To illustrate, let us pick a few highlights of the cost chapters, and insert the word asset for cost. The "seven C's" of asset control (from Chapter 13) first come to mind, as a useful summary:

1. *Collection* and recording of all asset items in *pinpoint* detail.
2. *Classifying* the detailed assets so as to best analyze them, especially according to the *man* responsible for each one.
3. *Comparison* of every asset CCR (or S/A) with its standard CCR, down to the minutest detail.
4. *Communication* of asset detail and variances to the man responsible, promptly and meaningfully.
5. *Correction* of S/A variances by that man.
6. *Consciousness* of assets as an absorber of cash and a lucrative source of cash productivity.
7. *Creativity* as to asset cash generation, by everyone, within the highly motivated and organized framework of the CI capability.

Pinpoint "asseting" (which is not a word, but will have to do as the counterpart of costing): asset reports from the man responsible must precisely describe the asset variance in terms of when, where, what, who, why and how. And assets should be pinpointed and controlled in terms of *asset control categories*, which are based on the circumstance that gave rise to the asset (and its variance): *location* within the business or production process, such as its standing order (torches, Welding Department); *flow* of assets from the time of its purchase through its final disposition; and *input* category in the production process—the asset outlay is controllable at the point of material input, labor input, or overhead input.

Responsibility asseting corresponds to responsibility reporting or costing: *every* asset category, however minute, is the responsibility of one man only, who monitors and *corrects* its S/A variances against standard or BC. His budget might be charged monthly, at the company's average cost of capital, for the assets he supervises. If our cost of capital is 8%, and the sales manager supervises $250,000 of assets, his budget is charged $20,000 a year. When he reduces his assets, he reduces the cost penalty on his performance.

Asset cash creativity is (1) motivated by a promotion and reward system geared solely to each man's $+S/A$ and $+S/C$ performance; and (2) organized within a CI capability consisting of the CI Committee, coordinator, Teams, and mobilization of first-line supervision.

The cash system environment for asset control is a least-*time* system, from raw material input when cash is committed, to the collection of customer receivables (cash received). The shorter the time cycle, the lower the costs and the fewer the *assets* required in relation to sales—that is, asset *turnover* is maximized (S/A). Creating a least-time asset system involves three steps:

First, we determine our company's *true cycle*, which can be approximated roughly by turnover: \$5,000,000 sales/2,000,000 equity is 2.5 times a year. Our business thus turns over every 4.8 months, or 146 days.

Second, we determine the *asset waiting times* at each stage of our true cycle, during which our *cash* is committed. How long does our cash have to wait (be frozen) in raw material, goods-in-process, finished goods, receivables? For each asset, we divide 365 days by its turnover ratio to get the number of days our cash is frozen into it. For instance, $365 \div$ sales/ receivables. Or, $365 \div$ cost of goods sold/finished inventory. This turnover computation gives us the waiting days for each asset at each cash commitment stage of the production process.

Finally, we *shorten* the asset waiting times, concentrating first on those in which our cash is committed for the longest time compared with industry or best competitor (BC) norms.

The *core strategies* of asset reduction dovetail those of cost reduction: 20–80 ordering of priorities; BC cash availability calculations, centering on S/A; providing a *product* focus to asset reduction; and all the rest. Product committees and function costing (value analysis) groups minimize the asset requirements for, and involvement in, each product.

Particularly, a *product portfolio analysis* at regular intervals can substantially reduce assets and increase CRE. In every company's portfolio of products, 20% are maximum-CRE that can be assumed to produce 80% of the profits, and tie up the smallest dollar amount of its capital. These are the winners. Then there are the loser products, that generate a much smaller proportion of the profits and tie up the largest amount of the company's assets.

The best product portfolio policy is one of *backing the winners*— concentrating all our corporate strength and resources on the present and potential maximum-CRE products. It means we must unhesitatingly and even ruthlessly *liquidate the losers*. This is without exception, other than the rare instance of a loser that provides significant sales support to a high-CRE product.

Cash thus released from the pruning of losers must be directed into the highest-return investment projects of the winning products. And it should be channeled into research and development or the outside acquisition of very-high-return new products. Few if any asset policies are more productive of cash and CRE than this one—of ruthlessly converting lowest-return product losers into cash with which to back the winners.

Assets are thus a powerful generator of liquidity, cash, and profits. Uncontrolled, they waste liquidity and hurt profits by absorbing debt capacity that could be otherwise productively employed. This is malignant growth, on which constraints are eventually imposed by a soaring debt/sales ratio that squeezes profits.

Controlled in relation to sales $(+S/A)$, assets *produce* liquidity in the form of unused and enhanced borrowing power $(-L/A$ and $-L/S)$ and of cash flow $(+S/C)$. It is the portion of the company's liquidity that *would* have been absorbed by higher assets (to produce our present level of sales), but *was not* absorbed because we controlled assets in relation to those sales $(+S/A)$. The free liquidity now buys *additional* sales-supporting assets to attain entirely new levels of cash productivity.

This is all we mean by asset cash productivity, whose independent role is indeed a formidable one in the total strategy of cash.

But having squeezed the liquidity out of assets—overall (macro) and from the cash velocity of individual assets (micro)—we must reinvest it productively or little is gained. *Reinvestment* $(+R)$, therefore, will now take us from the quantity side of the asset coin to its quality side—from generating cash by controlling assets, to generating maximum *return* on assets. They are mutually reinforcing strategies that exert a cumulative impact within the company's overall mechanism of liquidity.

CHAPTER 18

GENERATING REINVESTMENT CASH

When we direct cash into either cost or capital outlays for a stated return over a stated period of time, a reinvestment source of cash has been created. And when we direct our total stream of cash into maximum-return investments, we are maximizing reinvestment cash productivity ($+R$). By maximizing both the production and the investment return of that total stream of cash, therefore, we maximize the company's CRE.

To the extent that our cost or capital outlays create highly productive assets—and our total return on assets thereby improves—the strategy of asset *control* is not undermined but supported. They are complementary asset strategies.

Reinvestment cash productivity in fact strongly reinforces asset cash productivity, and is strongly reinforced by it. When we increase the quality or profitability of our total assets, we can more effectively limit their quantity in relation to sales. That is, upgrading asset payback either helps us reduce or itself reduces the quantity of assets needed to produce a given volume of sales ($+S/A$).

Conversely, as we saw, by controlling the quantity of assets, we supply the liquidity needed to make cash-generating reinvestments ($+R$). Limiting asset quantity thus finances the improvement of their quality. On both sides of the coin, therefore, the combined cash impact of the reinvestment and asset strategies—thus interacting and reinforcing each other—can be powerful indeed.

Accordingly, let us look at reinvestment cash productivity in its role as the culminating source of cash within the SCALDER liquidity process.

DISCOUNTING CASH FLOW FOR MAXIMUM RETURN

It follows that our search for the highest-return projects must be systematic and relentless. So it falls squarely within the province of the cash-improvement capability, as delineated in Chapter 14 on cash creativity. We

217

sensitize *all* our people to cash-producing investment opportunities—to recognize them and to initiate project proposals. This is an inescapable requirement of each supervisor's position, on which he is evaluated in terms of S/C and S/A performance measurements within the company's cash-creative motivational environment.

Then we select the most lucrative projects from among all the competing alternatives presented up the line for approval. But to do this successfully, we need a simple and accurate yardstick for distinguishing among projects on the basis of their potential contribution to CRE. This yardstick is the project's *discounted cash flow*.

We will probably choose an investment that promises a 50% annual return over one that promises only 40%. But maybe not. We cannot be sure about anything until we have *time-discounted* the cash returns of each project: cash flow of $10,000 to be received next year will be valued more highly than $10,000 to be received five years from now. This is because the money received next year will be promptly reinvested to produce a cash return, which we cannot do with the more distant cash.

The extent to which we would weight next year's $10,000 over the more distant $10,000 depends on our reinvestment rate of return. The higher the rate, the more valuable to us is the early cash compared with the later cash. So we discount the later cash more severely than if the rate were lower, because we lose more by not having it now. The present value to us of the future cash is thus reduced (discounted) to the extent that our current return is increased, and the time when we will receive the cash is moved forward.

Suppose that we sell a customer some machinery worth $100,000, payable to us in one year and evidenced by a $110,000 note (that is, with 10% interest added). In time-discounting terms: at 10% interest, the *present value* of $110,000 due in one year is $100,000. In project evaluation terms: cash flow of $110,000 due in one year has been discounted back, at 10%, to $100,000.

If the return were only 5%, cash flow of $105,000 due in one year is discounted back to a present value of $100,000. That is, the $100,000 invested at 5% will be worth $105,000 at the end of one year.

The easiest way to make present value computations is not to make the computations at all, but to use the present-value table found in almost any financial reference book. As we move along the top of the table from left to right, its columns are headed by interest rates ranging from 1 to 90%. Moving downward at the left are the years from 1 to 50.

So in our 10% example above, we go to the 10% column and move one line down (to year 1) and get the present value of $1 due in one year. This shows a present value factor of $0.91. The $110,000 due in one year times

0.91 gives us a present value of $100,000. It is the present value of $110,000 due in one year, discounted at 10%.

If the $100,000 sale of machinery had been for a *two*-year note at 10%, $121,000 would be due from our customer:

Present value	$100,000
Interest at 10%, year 1	10,000
Due in one year	$110,000
Interest at 10%, year 2	11,000
Due in two years	$121,000

The present value of $121,000 due in two years, discounted at 10%, is $100,000. In the 10% column of the present-value table, two lines down to the second year, we see a PV factor of 0.83: $121,000 times 0.83 is $100,000 of present value.

If the 10% interest (or discount) rate increases, the present value of future money decreases: We are being penalized more severely by not having our money for reinvestment now, than we would be if the interest rate were less. And the farther ahead in time the future sum of money is to be received, as we have seen, the lower is its present value to us. At 20%, the present value of $121,000 due in two years is not $100,000 but $83,000. The present value of $121,000 at 20% due in *10 years* is only $19,400, the sum that will grow in 10 years (at 20% compound interest) to $121,000.

Now let us apply this important idea of cash-flow discounting to the business of selecting the most lucrative projects.

EVALUATING INVESTMENT CASH RETURN

The annual cash flow of a project—such as the labor savings from a machine—consists of a portion that is *principal* repayment on the original investment, and a portion that is the *return* on the investment. Over the project's economic life, therefore, its total cash flow should fully repay the original investment *and* provide the stipulated rate of return on the investment.

This duality tells us how to compute the rate of return on a proposed project: we discount (to present value) the total expected cash flow over its life by that interest rate which reduces the cash flow to the amount of the original investment. The interest rate must then represent the *return* on that investment.

Let us illustrate this with Table 24. Machines A and B each cost $15,000, and each provides $22,500 of total cash flow savings over five years (columns 1 and 2). But the annual amounts of cash flow are distributed differently. Machine A's (column 1) are weighted toward the early years, and machine B's (column 2) are spread evenly among the five years. In each case, the *return* on the machine is the discount rate that reduces $22,500 of total cash flow down to a present value of $15,000 (the original investment). It would therefore be the return provided by $7500 of income ($22,500−$15,000).

Through some trial and error in the present-value table (footnote *a*), we find that approximately *18%* discounts to $15,000 the $22,500 of total cash received from machine A over five years. So 18% is the annual *return* on the machine: The $22,500 gives us an 18% annual compounded return (from $7500 of income) *and* repays our original investment of $15,000.

The specific procedure is as follows: Machine A's cash flow each year (column 1) is discounted by the present-value factors in the 18% column (footnote *a*), to give us the discounted cash flows each year shown in column 3. They total $15,110 for the five years (column 3). That is, for year 1, $6,500 of cash flow (column 1) multiplied by PV of 0.85 equals $5,525 (column 3). For year 2, $5,500 of cash flow multiplied by 0.72 is $3,960 (column 3). And so on for each of the five years.

But if we discount machine A's cash flows (column 1) by the factors in the PV table's *20%* column, they total only $14,440 (column 4). So 18% is the closest we come to the $15,000 cost of machine A. By interpolating, we can find that the interest rate that discounts machine A's cash flow exactly to $15,000, is *18.2%*. But investment projects are based on rough long-term forecasts of cash flow. So nailing down the rate to decimal precision tends to mislead by implying a degree of accuracy that does not exist.

Machine B also cost $15,000 and provides the same total cash-flow savings of $22,500 (column 2), But it is a steady annual cash flow, as noted, unlike that for machine A (column 1). Discounting its savings each year at 15% (column 5) gives a total discounted cash flow of $15,120. But at 16% (column 6) it is only $14,715. So we use 15% as its rate of return.

Machine A is the more lucrative investment because it provides an 18% return, from the same $22,500, compared with machine B's 15%. These rates equate the present value of future cash flows, totaling $22,500, with the present investment outlay of $15,000. Going *forward* in time, $15,000 invested in machine A at 18.2% (compounded annually) will produce $22,500 of cash flow. Of this, $15,000 will be the repayment of the original investment, and the balance of $7500 will be income *on* the investment.

This is illustrated in columns 7 to 10, in the discount computation for

Table 24 Forecasting Investment Cash Return

	Cash flow		Present Value[a]				Machine A			
	Machine A	Machine B	Machine A		Machine B			Cash Flow [from (1)]	Income [18.2% of (1)]	Repayment of Principal [(8) − (9)]
			18%	20%	15%	16%	Investment			
Year	1	2	3	4	5	6	7	8	9	10
1	$6,500	$4,500	$5,525	$5,395	$3,915	$3,870	$15,000	$6,500	$2730	$3,770
2	5,500	4,500	3,960	3,795	3,420	3,330	11,230	5,500	2040	3,460
3	4,500	4,500	2,745	2,610	2,970	2,880	7,770	4,500	1410	3,090
4	3,000	4,500	1,560	1,440	2,565	2,475	4,680	3,000	850	2,150
5	3,000	4,500	1,320	1,200	2,250	2,160	2,530	3,000	470	2,530
							$ 0			
	$22,500	$22,500	$15,110	$14,440	$15,120	$14,715		$22,500	$7500	$15,000

[a]Excerpt from present-value table:

Year	Machine A		Machine B	
	18%	20%	15%	16%
1	0.85	0.83	0.87	0.86
2	0.72	0.69	0.76	0.74
3	0.61	0.58	0.66	0.64
4	0.52	0.48	0.57	0.55
5	0.44	0.40	0.50	0.48

machine A. In year 1 the investment is $15,000 (column 7), from which cash flow is forecast at $6500 (column 8, taken from column 1). At 18.2% of the $15,000 starting balance, cash income is $2730 (column 9). So the remainder of the $6500 must be principal repayment of $3770 (column 10).

In year 2 the $15,000 investment is now reduced by this $3770 principal repayment, to $11,230 (column 7). On this balance, cash income at 18.2% is $2040 (column 9). Subtracting $2040 from $5500 of cash flow (column 8) gives the principal repayment portion of $3460 (column 10).

And so forth to the end of machine A's five-year life, when the investment is reduced to zero (column 7). Cash flow then totals $22,500 (column 8). Cash income at 18.2% of each year's investment balance totals $7500 (column 9). And we have been paid back our original investment of $15,000 (column 10).

THE NET CASH IMPACT OF ALTERNATIVE PROJECTS

We must, in this way, investigate and weigh each project in terms of its potential *net cash impact*. This is not its accrual basis cash flow, but the difference between *all* the cash it actually receives and disburses.

Our sights are thus on the project's expected receivables collections, not on its sales. On cash receipts from nonoperating items that do not affect income in the conventional accounting sense. On cash payments, even though they do not affect current earnings but those of earlier or later accounting periods. And we ignore depreciation and other noncash charges against project assets.[1] The increased corporate taxes caused by the project earnings (computed conventionally) are of course treated as a cash disbursement of the project.

In the project's earlier years, the net cash impact (of total cash receipts and disbursements) tends to be *lower* than its accrual-basis profits. This is because large startup payments for inventory and other assets penalize cash but not earnings. And its cash collections lag the rising sales volume from which accrual earnings are computed. But in the project's declining years, net cash impact tends to *exceed* accrual-basis profits: assets liquidate (build up cash) rapidly, and cash collections of receivables exceed the declining sales volume.

In this way, we are analyzing unmistakable and spendable dollars of project cash—not guessing about accrual "cash" whose amount depends so much on our accounting premises and judgments. And these hard dollars

---

[1]The discount rate we applied to the proposed project, in any event, has already provided for the full repayment of our original investment. The rate is after annual principal repayments that reduce the investment to zero.

of net cash impact are both easier to forecast and amenable to *time discounting*. "Earnings" cannot realistically be so discounted. They are an accrual-basis estimate of the increment in value between two accounting periods, not necessarily spendable or even liquid.

Yet time-discounting alternative streams of future cash is the crucial concept and tool of the entire capital productivity program, whereby we maximize reinvestment cash. It lets us compare alternative projects easily and accurately, as with machines A and B. They both produced the same $22,500 of cash, but it was distributed differently over the five years. In discounting their streams of cash, machine A's 18% prevailed over machine B's 15%.

Suppose that machine A's cash flow is reversed, with the lower amounts now occurring in the early years and the high ones in the later years. The high but distant cash flows in years 4 and 5 would now be more drastically discounted, and the project's five-year rate of return would drop from 18 to *13%*. Machine B at 15% would now be the more attractive investment alternative (everything else being equal).

And time discounting of net cash impact simplifies comparison of projects having different time periods. It downgrades the anticipated return and therefore tends to eliminate projects with very distant paybacks: The far-off cash flows are discounted more severely than those nearby, which is itself a safety measure against accepting long-term uncertainties. The project must show a higher rate of return than its identical near-term counterpart before the time-discounting yardstick will accept it.

Our investment decision-making is thus immeasurably simplified and sharpened by the time discounting of net cash impact. By reducing the complexities of project "earnings" to hard dollars—and the complex factors affecting project comparisons to a single figure of present value—it narrows down the choice among countless alternatives to the one with the highest percentage return.

CAPITAL COSTS AND PAYBACK

To maximize cash return on equity (CRE), we must accept and implement the highest-return project proposals and reject low-return proposals. Otherwise we pile up costly, low-productivity assets and excessive debt that nullify asset cash productivity and scuttle CRE. But what payback percentage is the *cutoff* between those we accept and those we reject?

Before answering so crucial a question, we should determine the *cost* to our company of the capital that flows into the various investment projects. Just as we cannot price our products profitably until we know their cost, we cannot target a return on our capital until we know *its* cost.

Not that the cost of capital determines the cutoff percentage, any more than the cost of the product determines its price. Both are determined externally, by our *competitors*. The cutoff percentage is set for us by the rates of return now enjoyed by our best competitors (BC). And our prices are largely set by them, either directly or indirectly. But costs have enough influence on price, and more than enough on profits, for us to know exactly what they are. We must know what our products and our capital cost us now, in today's market, or we will not long flourish as a profitable competitor among competitors.

Looking at our balance sheet, at the left are assets that produce the earnings. At the right are liabilities of debt and equity that paid for the assets and incur capital costs. The asset earnings on the left must be favorably related to the liability costs at the right. But it is not feasible to relate the cash return on any one asset to the cost of the cash going into that asset. We must therefore estimate the cost of our *total* capital structure that supplied all the investable cash. And we want to know its cost *now*, or its present opportunity cost. A good approximation is the cost of our capital, as interest and earnings per share, if we were to issue the same debt and equity securities under today's market conditions.

To do this we compute the weighted-average, after-tax opportunity cost of our capital structure, as in Table 25. Our annual cost of each security after taxes (column 3) is simply the coupon rate or share earnings (column 1) multiplied by the book value or number of shares (column 2). The cost of debt securities is reduced by 50% to give effect to the tax deductibility of interest.

Total current market value of our capital structure is $3,400,000 (column 4). Column 5 is each issue's percentage of that total market value, or its relative importance in the capital structure. And the percentage cost of capital (column 6) is the market yield, or the opportunity cost to us of each issue: it is the cost of capital (column 3) divided by the current market value (column 4).

By multiplying each security's percent of market value (column 5) by its percent cost of capital (column 6), we get its *weighted-average cost* (column 7). For instance, the preferred stock and the common stock both cost us 5% of their market value (column 6). But the preferred constitutes only 5.9% of the capital structure (column 5), and the common stock is 65.9%. So the weighted-average cost of the preferred (column 7) is only 0.29%, but the cost of the common is an overwhelming 3.30%.

Our company's weighted-average net opportunity cost of capital is therefore the total of the percentage costs in column 7, or *3.95%*. The bulk of this cost of capital is accounted for by the common stock (column 8),

Table 25 Computing the Cost of Capital

Source of Capital 1	Book Value or Shares (000) 2	Cost of Capital (after Taxes) (000) 3	Market Value (Net of Financing Costs) (000) 4	% of Market Value 5	% Cost of Capital [(3)÷(4)] 6	Weighted Average Cost [(5)×(6)] 7	% Total Average Cost 8
Accounts payable[a]	$400	$ 0	$400	11.8%	0%	0.0%	0.0%
6% note payable	$100	3	100	2.9	3	0.09	2.3
4.6% debenture	$400	9	460	13.5	2	0.27	6.8
5% preferred stock	2 shares	10	200	5.9	5	0.29	7.3
Common stock ($1.12/share)	100 shares	112	2240	65.9	5	3.30	83.5
Total		$134	$3400	100.0%		3.95%	100.0%

[a]All trade discounts are taken.

which is 83.5%. The typical company's opportunity cost of capital thus tends to fluctuate inversely with the price of the common stock: the cost falls as the price increases in anticipation of improved earnings, and increases as the stock declines.

LOCATING THE CUTOFF RATE OF RETURN

Few decisions influence CRE as strongly as the one that sets our cutoff rate of return for proposed investment projects. Proposals offering discounted returns below the cutoff are not considered at all. Projects are therefore chosen for implementation only from among those that rank above the cutoff, starting at the highest percentages of the ranking continuum. We cream off the top and move downward as far as our budgeted capital takes us, perhaps as far as the cutoff return but never below it.

If blessed with more capital than acceptable projects, we direct it to outside investments that rank above our cutoff—such as to the acquisition of other companies. Our reinvestment program thus functions along a ranking continuum of investments that is not confined to our own business.

The ranking continuum is not only return-related, but *risk*-related. Riskier projects rank below safer ones offering the same return. At the top are the highest returns and least risk. And as we descend, both returns and risks become less and less favorable in relation to those available outside the company. But since comparable external investments tend to be more risky—only because they are external—the ranking continuum confers a moderate *internal* bias on the reinvestment of capital.

Where, then, along the continuum do we locate our cutoff? It must be high enough to compensate us for the extraordinary risks to which such long-term and essentially irreversible project decisions expose our capital. This certainly would be much higher than our present CRE, which is the far safer return we get today—and on our *total* equity investment (in both safe *and* risky assets).

And it must be high enough to eliminate the competitive risk of *not* making such payback investments—of not keeping up with our best competitors (BC) and their rates of return. Survival of the fittest demands that we be among the fit: *they* determine our cutoff rate of return, lest we eventually be trampled on. So it certainly can be no less than the cash return on equity of our best competitors—if not more, to rival the higher long-term project returns they need to earn that CRE.

Besides, the average CRE of our best competitors is our *external opportunity rate of return*. It is a proxy of, or is in fact, what we could get from the best external investments (of equivalent risk to that of the internal projects under consideration). Our cutoff rate for internal projects must be *at least* the external opportunity rate, or we are behaving irresponsibly toward our stockholders. We are undertaking investments in our own company with capital that could earn more in equivalent-risk investments elsewhere. Management never has any business discounting cash flow from proposed internal projects at rates of return below those available externally.

Our internal cutoff should stand somewhere between this external (best-competitor) opportunity rate of return and the higher percentages demanded by the extraordinary risk-reward dimensions of such projects. But this depends on each company's particular risk environment for investments. So we might simply add to the opportunity rate of return a safety factor, preferably our opportunity cost of capital, and apply them jointly in the following general rather than specific rule of thumb:

Our cutoff rate of return, below which reinvestment projects are unacceptable, is the external opportunity rate of return (average CRE of our best competitors) plus our opportunity cost of capital.

Suppose that the following describes our situation over a period of years:

Year	Cost of Capital 1	CRE 2	BC (Opportunity) Rate 3	Cutoff Rate [(1)+(3)] 4
1	5%	12%	20%	25%
2	10	12	20	30
3	5	15	20	25
4	5	15	25	30
5	10	17	25	35

In year 1 our cost of capital is 5% and the BC opportunity rate is 20%; so we place our cutoff at 25%. In year 2 a major slump in the market for our securities doubles our cost of capital to 10%, raising our cutoff to 30%. The soaring market in year 3 *lowers* our cost of capital and our cutoff. But in year 4, an increase in BC rates of return lifts our cutoff to 30%. And another market drop the following year raises it further to 35%.

Our cutoff thus logically responds to the combined pressure of two external opportunity yardsticks, the cost of and return on investment capital. Some of the behavioral implications of this are illustrated in the following ranking continuum:

Rate of Return 1	Cost (000) 2	Income (000) 3	Cumulative Cost (000) 4	Cumulative Income (000) 5	Cumulative Return [(4)÷(5)] 6
Over 100%	$ 40	$ 40	$ 40	$ 40	100%
100–76	110	82	150	122	81
75–51	430	215	580	337	58
50–26	640	160	1220	497	41
25–16	980	147	2200	644	29
15–10	1150	115	3350	759	23

For each rate-of-return bracket (column 1) it gives the estimated investment cost (column 2) and income (column 3) of all projects submitted. Only $40,000 worth of recommended projects (column 2) will return 100% or more. But the 100%–76% range includes $110,000 of projects (column 2), whose estimated income (column 3) totals $82,000. And so forth.

Columns 4 to 6 cumulate downward our project costs, income, and rates of return. Down to a 51% cutoff, for example, $580,000 of projects (column

4) have been submitted whose total income is $337,000 (column 5). Their cumulative rate of return is 58%. If the cutoff rate drops to 26%—because the external cost or return of capital drops—we can consider projects totaling $1,220,000 with incomes of $497,000 (columns 4 and 5).

At the 26% cutoff, the cumulative rate of return (column 6) is 41%. That is, the cutoff being the rate *below which* a project is unacceptable, the cumulative return of all the accepted projects will be higher.

The cost of external capital is also a rough indicator of its availability, which at the extremes can affect our cutoff more decisively than its cost. When capital becomes very expensive, it may also become scarce; when it is very cheap, it is probably also abundant. Our cutoff might be 26%, based on opportunity cost and opportunity (BC) return. But if our inability to finance externally limits our total fundable projects to $580,000 (column 4), the cutoff has in fact been boosted to 51%. Our project income (column 5) drops from $497,000 at 26% to $337,000 at 51%, though our cumulative return (column 6) rises from 41 to 58%.

But under less-than-extreme conditions, when capital availability accommodates our actual cutoff, we have in this yardstick a potent ally of CRE. If the cutoff fully recognizes both our cost of capital and our best competitors' rates of return, it helps a good deal to keep us sharply competitive and growing rapidly. *And* it helps shield balance-sheet liquidity from the drain of excessive assets and debt.

PAYBACK AND RISK

In the ranking of proposals, of course, the decisive test is always the project's impact on the earning capacity and risk exposure of the business *as a whole*. A project ranked low on its own merits might take precedence over those with the highest returns: it is strategically indispensable in the comprehensive systems context within which we manage the business. So that which ranked low on a project basis ranked extremely high on a *systems* basis. It takes precedence because it addresses itself directly and more forcefully to total company profits.

This means that *every* proposal must be subjected to rigorous cash-flow discounting, in comparison with all the alternatives. *No* proposal can ever be so "urgent," strategic, prestigious, routine, hallowed, sacrosanct, or economically unpredictable as to escape rate-of-return evaluation and comparison. Besides, *any* return applied to a proposal is better than none. At least it forced us to explore and analyze the project deeper down and into mustier corners than we would have done otherwise.

And we must consider *all* the competing alternatives to a project. The alternative to buying machine A might not be machine B at all, but an entirely different unit or device. Or it might be renting a machine; doing the work manually; buying rather than machining the product components; or subcontracting out the work. Then we discount all the alternative cash flows, and the one with the highest return should get the most favorable consideration.

The single most important alternate consideration, always, is to do *nothing*. What exactly happens to cash flow if none of the alternatives are implemented? What happens to *CRE*? The difference between doing nothing and implementing the most favorable alternative gives us the clearest picture of what we will really get out of this investment.

The do-nothing exercise also forces us to look for ways of eating our cake and having it: of getting the same cash return by pursuing the project's directions, but not the project, or without any cash investment in it. This increases our payback percentage to infinity, and reduces our risk to zero. It is done time and time again.

As for project risk and uncertainty, we have already discussed *time* risk. The discounted-cash-flow computation helps protect us against the hazards of distant paybacks, by reducing the project's present value the farther out the cash stream extends.

Project risk is inherent in the project itself, apart from the remoteness of time. A 10-year undertaking may have a high probability of going sour by the third or fourth year. It if does not, however, it will pay us an extraordinarily high return over its total life. How it would rank with lesser risks that pay lesser returns may be largely a subjective matter that only management can sort out and resolve. Perhaps all we can say is that the higher the risk of a project, the lower it *must* rank on the continuum.

Or we might have two continuums. The quantitative one we have been discussing ranks the *amount* of return. Then a qualitative continuum would rank the *value* or quality of the income return—as to risk, dependability, volatility, durability, and so forth. Our final ranking of each project would then be a creative blending of the quantitative and qualitative sequences.

Another possibility is to divide up the project's anticipated percentage return, say 25%, into its various risk components. First is the riskless segment, or the yield available from AAA bonds. This might be 7%. The remainder of the return above the riskless portion is the *risk premium*, amounting to 18%. Then we divide the risk premium itself into two sections: one is the return from the project's normal business risks; the other is from its extrordinary and abnormal risks. So the 18% risk premium might be divided into 12% normal, and 6% abnormal and excessive. Projects having the largest *abnormal risk* sections of their risk premium rank lower than those with the same return whose risk premium consists mainly of a normal business risk component.

Perhaps we can even construct a *Profit Reliability Index*. This would measure the dependability of each of the many cost and income factors that entered into our forecast of the project's cash flow. We simply rate, on a scale from 5 to 1, the reliability of our forecast of each cost and income item in the project. This would also include the extent to which each item was investigated, ranging from thorough to casual.

Then we add up the profit reliability ratings of the cost and income items, to get the index. The higher the Profit Reliability Index, the less risk is likely to be associated with that project. The lower the rating, the less reliable and the riskier is the projected cash flow.

Then *risk-return* guidelines can be communicated down to the ranks of people from which project recommendations originate. It can be merely a scale that gives the acceptable rate of return for each risk level of the Profit Reliability Index. The higher the rating on the Reliability Index, and the safety associated with the project, the lower would be the required rates of return. In this way proposals are prescreened in the first instance, where they originate. It weeds out shaky projects whose cash-flow potentials are insufficient for the degree of risk disclosed by the index.

Reinvestment can thus be seen as the climactic event in the comprehensive liquidity process. A truly productive investment capability encourages a steady inflow of lucrative project proposals; weighs and compares them by time-discounting their potential cash impacts; bases its cutoff percentage on the external opportunity cost and return of capital; and implements projects high up on the ranking continuum before it pours much money into those near the cutoff.

Such an investment capability helps maximize liquidity velocity while it maximizes cash payback: it minimizes the elapsed *time* between reinvesting the cash inflow (from receivables and debt) and the payback of cash from the investment projects. And by maximizing the individual cash *returns*, it maximizes the company's total discounted return flow of cash per dollar of equity. In time-discounting terms, reinvestment has contributed heavily to maximizing the "present value" of the firm.

The liquidity velocity—or cash recirculation—ring defined by $+S$ $-C$ $-A$ $+L$ $+D$ $+E$, and $+R$, is thereby closed. And to the extent that cash was maximized at each stage, we have maximized CRE and Pi.

PART 6

IMPLEMENTING THE STRATEGY
OF MAXIMUM CASH PRODUCTIVITY

CHAPTER 19

PLANNING MAXIMUM CASH PRODUCTIVITY

The strategy of cash says only this: To maximize the company's profits, maximize liquidity and the equity potential for creating liquidity. We create and maintain, that is, a liquidity environment of maximum cash productivity and equity expansion. The company will then necessarily achieve its maximum compounded rate of earnings growth while preserving an invulnerable balance-sheet position.

Part One developed the basic *Pi framework* of liquidity and profit maximizing. And Parts Two through Five explored the seven external and internal *cash-generating strategies* that logically emerge from the liquidity concept: leverage, equity, acquisitions, sales, costs, assets, and reinvestment.

Parts Six and Seven will therefore apply the specific managerial *implementing strategies* that produce the liquidity environment from which maximum profits necessarily flow. Though uniquely cash-generating in form and substance, these strategies have nevertheless been grouped into the familiar management categories to simplify our examination of them: planning, organizing, coordinating, motivating, and controlling.

We devote this chapter to *planning* maximum cash productivity, which is mainly the construction of a companywide Cash Productivity Plan. Subsequent chapters will each discuss ways to implement the Plan, around which revolves all business activity at every level. So the chapter after this is on *organizing* everyone to best implement the Plan. Then the next one is on *motivating* our people to generate cash-productivity results in accordance with the Plan—in an atmosphere of cash consciousness and creativity that has become a corporate way of life. And finally, all of Part Seven is devoted to *controlling* cash-productivity results against the Plan.

Only by maximizing cash from all seven sources, as we have seen, does management maximize earnings per share and thereby stockholders' wealth. So our only job is to maximize cash productivity. Anything else we do with our time is unrelated to earnings per share and stockholders'

233

wealth, and is therefore outside the scope and function of management.

It must follow that management's only job, as manager of the balance sheet, is to create and accomplish the Cash Productivity Plan. First, we cause a Plan to be constructed whereby a specific quantity of cash flow and equity will be achieved in five years (or whatever the time span). Second, we achieve on schedule *that* Plan level of cash flow and equity— by organizing and coordinating people, motivating them, and controlling their cash-productivity results, all in accordance with Plan.

THE CASH PRODUCTIVITY PLAN: CRE VERSUS ECO AND ECA

By organizing the entire business around a specific five-year Cash Productivity Plan, management invokes and puts to work the Pi expression:

$$CRE = \left(\frac{S}{C} \times \frac{S}{A} \times \frac{L}{A} \right)(R)$$

$$Pi = CRE \times ECO \times ECA$$

We plan and implement the Pi grand strategy in two segments: *the Cash Productivity Plan* maximizes cash return on equity (CRE). And the *Cash Productivity Worksheet* (or the Worksheet), a semi-autonomous branch of the Plan, provides for equity formation in the shape of ECO and ECA. It was described in Chapter 5, and is illustrated there on page 36 in Table 1.

This dual treatment is needed because we are dealing with two separate planning realities: CRE is amenable to fairly accurate planning and control within the framework of a fixed five-year Cash Productivity Plan. But external equity formation is not. We cannot be sure whether, when, or in what amounts we will complete major acquisitions or public offerings within the five-year planning framework. Depending on many conditions of which not the least is the level of stock prices, we might conclude several of these transactions or conceivably none.

So we use a fixed Cash Productivity Plan to achieve maximum CRE over the five years. And we supplement it with the Worksheet, which introduces more volatile and less predictable equity-formation events into the planning process. The Cash Productivity Plan should of course make provision and allowances for the minimum probable dollar amounts of acquisitions and public offerings during the five years. It is modified only if these minimum ECA and ECO targets are *exceeded* by an amount sufficient to require a Plan revision in midcourse.

The Cash Productivity Plan is the center around which all corporate activity revolves and from which, in fact, the activity derives its meaning and purpose. By maximizing CRE through $S/C \times S/A \times L/A$ (R), it achieves the predetermined cash flow and equity by the fifth or target year, called TY5. It does so by increasing the cash contribution ratios S/C, S/A, and L/A everywhere in the business, sufficiently to generate that quantity of target cash flow.

And by incorporating the equity-formation impacts of the Worksheet, the Plan gives expression to the highest potential growth rate of which the company is capable.

THE CASH PLANNING SEQUENCE

The Cash Productivity Plan may be constructed in the following sequence of steps:

1. Delineate our *planning environment* in terms of the BC industry ratios. From these we can gauge our own cash-generating potentials, comparing our present performance with the industry's.

2. Decide on the *Pi percentage* growth rate that we will achieve and maintain. It is a decision on the equity level to be reached in the target year (TY5), and the cumulative cash flow we will generate during the five years to provide that equity.

3. Compute the *Cash Productivity Guide* (or Pi Frame) and the supporting Guide financial statements for the five years.

4. Organize to construct the *Cash Productivity Plan*, with everyone's participation.

5. Construct a *market grid* that expresses the company's maximum-impact marketing direction. And prepare *resource plans* that provide each function with the cost and asset dollars to support that maximum-impact direction.

6. Construct the *financial plan*: break down to the smallest functional units our cost and asset budgets, against which performance will be measured.

7. Construct the *interim and base years' Plans*, going backward in time in more and more detail.

Let us now look at each of these planning steps.

DELINEATING OUR PLANNING ENVIRONMENT

To formulate a realistic and challenging Cash Productivity Plan, we must *know* the cash planning environment in which our company functions.

Through diligent research, we can map this environment in terms of the performance of our most efficient and successful competitors (BC, or best-competitor companies).

These are the ones with the highest cash returns on equity, as we have seen. So they must have the highest cash contribution ratios (CCRs), or S/C and S/A, which are the operating components of CRE. And they must therefore have the highest S/C and S/A *backup* ratios, at all organizational levels and in all corners of the business.

We conduct these *BC studies* in order to benefit from a continuous and detailed inflow of information on all aspects of our highest-CRE competitors. A company that does not relate its cash-generating performance in every functional area to that of its most successful competitors, is in a sense dying without realizing it. Its higher-CRE adversaries will eventually kill it off or buy it off.

Business is a game of war. And the corporation is an army whose minimum standard of comparison must be its most formidable and efficient enemy. The company must be no worse than its best enemies to win its wars—or perhaps only to survive—within the markets all are fighting for.

Our minimum performance standard is always and only our best competitors in the industry. How our particular cost and asset ratios are generating cash in relation to our best competitors, is the basis for the most important actions we can take as a management.

There is an amazing abundance and variety of comparative industry and company financial ratios, published and unpublished, obvious and not so obvious. In addition to the well-known published ratios by Dun & Bradstreet and many others, we have those from the company's industry association, Government agencies, and innumerable other sources. And our banker or accountant can usually supply them from his ample files of companies like ours, anonymously, without divulging their names.

When we have clearly delineated our planning environment in terms of BC performance ratios, we can conduct an analysis of our total corporate liquidity—our *BC cash availability*. As we have seen, this tells us the *amount* of cash we are capable of generating if we operated as efficiently as the BC companies. It is a very comprehensive and detailed ratio analysis that compares *costs* in every corner of our business with total sales volume. And it compares *assets* throughout the company with sales volume. Then we compare all our sales/cost and sales/asset ratios with the same or corresponding ratios of the BC companies.

The best-competitor (BC) cash availability analysis thus identifies the specific areas where our costs and assets are too high in relation to sales, compared with the most efficient companies in our industry. In these areas, substantial cost and asset cash can be generated, because other companies have already done so.

Our sole objective in this entire procedure is to *identify* CCR problems, which are opportunities. They are cash-producing opportunities. In the arena of cash productivity, it is worth repeating, a problem correctly identified is a problem three-quarters solved.

The following is an oversimplified example of a best-competitor (BC) cash-availability calculation that covers the entire company, rather than the cost and asset details in each and every corner of it:

	Present Cash Investment (000) 1	Ratio to Sales ($3,500,000) 2	BC Ratio to Sales 3	BC $'s Required [Sales ×(3)] (000) 4	BC Cash Available [(1)−(4)] (000) 5
Costs	$3400	97.1%	93.6%	$3276	$124/year
Receivables	1200	34.3	26.6	931	269
Inventory	820	23.4	20.2	707	113
Fixed assets	450	12.9	13.7	479	(29)
Total BC cash available					$ 477

Column 1 lists our present cash investments in costs and assets, and column 2 their ratio to sales of $3,500,000. Column 3 gives the corresponding BC ratios, taken from industry statistical sources. The better-managed companies had total costs of 93.6% of sales, inventory of 20.2%, and so forth.

BC dollars required (column 4): The company would need a lower cash investment to generate its present level of sales, if it were run as efficiently as its best competitors. Here sales of $3,500,000 are multiplied by each of the BC ratios (column 3).

The amount of *BC cash available* to the company (column 5) is the difference between the dollars required under BC conditions (column 4) and the present investment (column 1). A total of $477,000 of BC cash could thus be made available (before taxes) for profitable reinvestment in the company.

The overall cash-generating capability of our company is thus staked out, but in much finer detail, and the potential BC magnitudes determined. To the realization of this capability the planning process can now effectively address itself.

Here the "20–80" principle again comes into play. We introduce into the planning mechanism, for correction or solution, only the highest-priority cost and asset problems. They are the worst problems, in comparison with BC and industry experience, or are the most readily solvable. The poorest planning attempts to correct *all* the problems, big and little, with equal energy. In maximum-impact fashion, instead, we go after the biggest fish first and leave the lower-priority levels for later years' Plans.

The Plan is therefore constructed to deal specifically with the "20–80" areas. The expression is of course figurative, not literal. One such area's input-output ratio might be 15–85, another's 25–75, and so forth. So we plan with reference to the 20% of our products that cause 80% of our cost and asset excesses; the 20% of our customers that cause 80% of our receivable excesses and slowness; the 20% of our cost items that represent 80% of the corporate fat; the 20% of our inventory items that cause 80% of our inventory slowness; the 20% of our suppliers that cause 80% of our purchase cost excesses and delivery problems; and so forth. The "20–80" strategy helps assure us of a maximum-cash-impact Plan.

So far we have done three important things: (1) delineated our *planning environment* of best competitor companies (BC ratios); (2) determined our BC *cash availability*, or operating efficiency within that environment; and (3) determined which *"20–80" areas* of cost and asset excesses should be given top priority in the planning process. The objective of the five-year Cash Productivity Plan is to generate the total quantity of cash that we are capable of releasing (BC cash availability) if we became as efficient as our best competitors.[1]

ESTABLISHING THE PI GROWTH RATE

The Pi rate of equity growth is management's undeviating focus, as we have seen, because it is the essence and purpose of business activity. We can make no more crucial decision than the rate of Pi, our percentage growth of equity, and we have no more crucial responsibility than to achieve it. But this we can do only by means of a Cash Productivity Plan that is the institutionalized expression of that rate, and to the achievement of which everyone is fully committed.

The Cash Productivity Guide (Table 26) is the comprehensive expression of Pi and the CCRs, on which we build the Cash Productivity Plan. The

---

[1]And if a management is already the most efficient in its industry, the Plan should be geared to the performance of the most efficient companies in the country, or in the world. But so worthy a management probably would not be reading *The Strategy of Cash* anyway.

Table 26 Applying the Cash Productivity Guide (Pi Frame) ($000)

Line	Base Year 1	Year 2	Year 3	Year 4	Target Year 5	Year-End TY5[b]
1. Equity (E)[a] ($+15\%$/year)	1000	1150	1,322	1,521	1,749	2,010
2. Cash flow ($+15\%$/year)	250	287	330	380	437	502
3. Cumulative cash flow	250	537	867	1,247	1,684	1,684
4. Cash flow/sales (from BC)	5.7%	5.7%	5.8%	5.9%	5.9%	6.0%
5. Sales (S) [(2)÷(4)]	4386	5035	5,690	6,441	7,407	8,367
6. Cumulative sales	4386	9421	15,111	21,552	28,959	28,959
7. Costs (C) [(5)−(2)]	4136	4748	5,360	6,061	6,970	
8. Cumulative costs	4136	8884	14,244	20,305	27,275	27,275
9. S/C [(5)÷(7)]	1.060	1.060	1.062	1.063	1.063	
10. Cost Cash Index	100.0	100.0	100.2	100.3	100.3	
11. S/A (from BC)	2.50	2.50	2.55	2.60	2.60	2.65
12. Asset Cash Index	100	100	102	104	104	
13. Assets (A) [(5)÷(11)][a]	1754	2014	2,231	2,477	2,849	3,157
14. Debt (L) [(13)−(1)][a]	754	864	909	956	1,100	1,147
15. L/A	0.430	0.429	0.407	0.386	0.386	
16. Leverage Cash Index	100.0	99.8	94.6	89.8	89.8	
17. Cash productivity factor (CPF)	1.139	1.137	1.102	1.067	1.067	
18. Net CPF [(9)×(11)]	2.65	2.65	2.71	2.76	2.76	
19. CRE: cash flow/equity	25%	25%	25%	25%	25%	
20. Cash flow/assets	14.2%	14.2%	14.8%	15.3%	15.3%	15.9%
21. Sales/equity	4.39	4.39	4.30	4.23	4.23	4.16
22. Debt/equity	75%	75%	69%	63%	63%	
23. Debt/sales	17%	17%	16%	15%	15%	
24. Cash flow debt capacity (20%)	1250	1435	1,650	1,900	2,185	

[a]January 1.
[b]Five-year cash summary:

1. Earnings (+E)	$1010	
2. Depreciation (−A)	+674	
2. Cash flow	1684	
14. Debt (+L)	+393	
Cash provided	$2077	
13. Asset depreciation (−A)	$674	
13. Net asset formation (+A)	1403	
Cash applied	$2077	

Guide, or Pi Frame, is the CCR structure that houses the fixed Pi growth rate, in terms of S/C, S/A, and L/A annual targets over the five years. It is the essential arithmetic skeleton of ratios, that is, calculated from our Pi percentage.

Then the Plan fills in the flesh-and-blood details of human, physical, technological, financial, and other resources, on which its achievement depends. It directs our company, *at the Pi rate*, toward its predetermined fifth year (TY5) level of cash flow and equity.

So the first thing we do is decide on the constant five-year Pi rate on which to base the Guide, which is the outline of the Plan. Each company and industry is different, and there are no rules of thumb. But the growth rate of our best competitors—particularly the rate needed to absorb our BC cash availability and operate as efficiently as they do—is at least one useful decision factor. If their average Pi rate is 18% a year and we have been experiencing 11%, it may be reasonable to construct our Plan on Pi = 15%.

THE CASH PRODUCTIVITY GUIDE (PI FRAME)

The Guide illustrated in Table 26 sets our five-year corporate sights at *Pi = 15%*. External equity formation is ignored, for simplicity, so that Pi is the rate at which equity increases because of retained earnings. It is a modest target, as we will see, which nevertheless doubles the size of our company.

Line 1. Base year 1's equity of $1,000,000 is the amount we will have on January 1 of next year, when the Plan begins. From this we compute annual 15% Pi increments over the five years, until we reach year-end target year 5 (TY5) equity of *$2,010,000.* Achieving this 15% compounded Pi growth rate and the TY5 equity is the entire meaning and purpose of the Cash Productivity Plan—and therefore of the company itself.

Line 2. Reaching $2,010,000 of TY5 equity requires corresponding cash flow increments of 15% a year, beginning with base year 1's $250,000. So we are actually programming a constant 25% CRE for each of the five years (on line 19).

Line 3. The Guide thus targets total cumulative cash flow, by the end of TY5, of *$1,684,000.* After depreciation, it produces the target equity (computed in terms of retained earnings). We assume that depreciation cash merely replenishes wasting assets, and does not contribute to the buildup of assets. It is held neutral, analytically.

Now we construct the bulk of the Guide, specifying *how* $2,010,000 of equity and $1,684,000 of cash flow are to be achieved. This is best done by planning backwards in time, starting with TY5. It reverses everyday experience and the normal inclination to plan forward.

First we *"photograph"* our company as it will look, in all respects and in detail, at the end of TY5. We bring that year to life, depicting it clearly and precisely as to the amount and composition of sales, costs, assets, debt, and equity. And then we do the same for each earlier year, one by one, back to base year 1.

The first thing to put into TY5's photograph is the sales level needed to produce its cash flow of $437,000 (line 2). Sales volume is not an objective, but a *means* of achieving the Plan's cash flow and equity objectives. Determining the sales requirement is crucial, however, because it determines in turn the amount of costs, assets, and debt we will need to produce it.

Line 4. We compute TY5 sales by applying to the $437,000 of TY5 cash flow an appropriate *cash flow / sales* percentage: It is 5.9%, which is based on BC performance and compares with our 5.7% at present (base year 1). We will have five years to improve our sales profitability very slightly.

Line 5. Achieving 5.9% will mean TY5 sales of 437/5.9, or $7,407,000. With that margin, in other words, sales of $7,407,000 will be needed to produce TY5 cash flow of $437,000.

We can buttress this sales estimate with our industry's BC turnover ratios of *sales / equity*. They help forecast the sales we could achieve with TY5 equity of $1,749,000 (line 1.) We find that $7,407,000/$1,749,000, or a turnover of 4.24×, is about in line with above-average industry experience. So we are inclined to stay with TY5 sales of $7,407,000.

Line 6. After computing sales for the four earlier years, we cumulate them annually and arrive at *total* five-year volume of $28,959,000.

Line 8. Now we subtract cash flow (line 2) from sales (line 5) to get *costs* each year (line 7) and cumulatively, totaling $27,275,000 in TY5.

Line 13. Assets required to generate this volume are derived from the various BC turnover ratios of sales/assets (S/A). Sales (line 5) each year are divided by the S/A ratio (line 11), to give us assets. Those for year-end TY5 are $3,157,000, and are based on a sixth-year S/A turnover ratio of 2.65.

Line 14. Finally, debt is simply assets (line 13) less equity (line 1). We will require $1,147,000 by the end of TY5.

To summarize TY5: Building our *equity* (line 1) at 15% a year to

$2,010,000 requires $1,684,000 of cumulative *cash flow* (line 3). This in turn requires that we generate total *sales* (line 6) of $28,959,000 at a *cost* input (line 8) of no more than $27,275,000. And to do this we will need *assets* (line 13) of $3,157,000 by the end of TY5, which will be financed with *debt* (line 14) of $1,147,000.

When all the years of the Guide are thus computed, we structure the TY5 and earlier years' Guide statements to provide us with tighter planning detail. Table 27 shows only two of them, the income statement and balance sheet for TY5. They are constructed mainly from the amounts already included in TY5 of the Guide. At the far left are numbers showing the logical sequence of steps to assemble each statement, starting with step 1.

Figures not available from the Guide are based on industry BC ratios and data, in much the same way as the Guide numbers themselves were derived. Gross profit of $2,222,000, for instance, is computed at BC industry experience of 30% of sales. And subtracting gross profit from sales gives us cost of shipments of $5,185,000 (Income Statement, steps 5 and 6).

Analytical ratios are then spread below the TY5 statements—as are the broader ratios underneath the Guide itself (lines 20 to 23). They reveal, year by year, the Plan's CRE and liquidity impact. We will refrain from commenting on them here because virtually all of Part Seven is devoted to ratio analysis.

Table 27 Profit Planning and the Guide Statements

Sequence of Steps	Income Statement (000)	TY 5
2.	Sales	$7407
6.	Cost of shipments	5185
5.	Gross profit	2222
8.	Operating expenses	1698
7.	Operating profit	524
7.	Other income (expenses)	—
4.	Pretax net income	524
3.	Taxes	262
1.	Net income	262
1.	Depreciation	175
1.	Cash flow	$ 437

Table 27 (*Continued*)

Sequence of Steps	Balance Sheet (000)	TY 5
7.	Cash and receivables	$420
7.	Inventory	680
4.	Current assets	1100
6.	Fixed assets	1250
7.	Miscellaneous assets	807
2.	Total assets	$3157
5.	Current liabilities	$ 647
5.	Long term debt	500
3.	Total liabilities	1147
1.	Equity	2010
2.	Total liabilities and equity	$3157

Analytical Ratios

Sales/working capital	16.4
Sales/receivables	18.5
Sales/inventory	11.9
Sales/fixed assets	5.9
Current liabilities/current assets	0.59
Receivables/working capital	0.88
Inventory/working capital	1.5
Fixed assets/equity	0.62
Miscellaneous assets/equity	0.40
Current liabilities/equity	0.32
Long term debt/working capital	1.11
Cash flow/total debt charges	2.6

The income statements, balance sheets, and all pertinent ratios are then assembled for the four earlier Plan years back to base zero (the start of year 1).

Finally, for TY5 and each earlier year we contruct the remainder of the Guide statements that are fully described and applied in Chapters 22 and 23:

> Net cash impact
> Cash velocity
> Working capital velocity
> Liquidity velocity

The various Guide statements and their accompanying ratios become the basis of subsequent *performance control* against Plan—by the prevention of variances—as Part Seven will demonstrate.

Now let us see what kind of Guide Plan we are coming up with in Table 26:

Line 10. The Cost Cash Index over the five years increases slightly to 100.3%, reflecting the planned improvement in S/C (line 9).

Line 11. And we plan for an S/A increase from 2.50 to 2.60, and finally to 2.65 (beyond TY5).

Line 13. So assets, or sales divided by S/A, do not increase at quite the rate as sales. The Asset Cash Index therefore rises to 104% in TY5.

Line 16. Since the Guide thus intends to keep assets under tight control, L/A falls (line 15), and the Leverage Cash Index declines to 89.8% by TY5.

Line 17. The cash productivity factor, or total cash impact of $S/C \times S/A \times L/A$ (lines 9, 11, and 15), declines moderately from 1.139 to 1.067. That is, *net CPF* (line 18), or $S/C \times S/A$, increases from 2.65 to 2.76, reflecting cash productivity from cost and asset control. But it is not sufficient to offset the decline in L/A (line 15).

Lines 22 to 24 give further testimony to the underutilization of debt: debt/equity and debt/sales decline. And cash flow debt capacity (cash flow to be no less than 20% of debt) is quite high in relation to debt (line 14).

The cash summary (footnote *b*) wraps up the five years: funds of $2,077,000 were provided by $1,010,000 of retained earnings (line 1), $674,000 of depreciation (for a total of $1,684,000 of cash flow), plus the $393,000 increase in debt (line 14). All $2,077,000 was applied to the replacement of deteriorating assets ($674,000) plus the net increase in assets of $1,403,000 (line 13).

This is not an especially ambitious Guide, even though the company is about twice as large at the end. Management might indeed utilize debt more aggressively, and shoot for a more challenging Pi target than 15%.

ORGANIZING TO CONSTRUCT THE CASH PRODUCTIVITY PLAN

When the Guide and its supporting statements are completed, we launch the main planning effort. It involves everyone, and it locks into the Guide's externally derived BC standards and numerical targets. What others are *now* doing, we can certainly do in five years if we set our minds to it. Merely by operating our company as efficiently as our above-average competitors, as in the illustration, we will grow rapidly and profitably without straining the balance sheet.

Constructing an achievable Plan based on the Guide, and accomplishing it on schedule, *both* require the total mobilization of our people and resources. The Cash Productivity Plan is the heart of everything a company does, which is to maximize cash productivity. The quality of the Plan will benefit tremendously from this broad collective experience, as will its implementation. Total participation is the indispensable requirement for enthusiastic acceptance and implementation of the Plan by all employees.

If management's sole function is to maximize cash productivity, whereby it maximizes Pi, its sole function is to preside over the formulation and implementation of the Cash Productivity Plan. Top management is thus really a Cash Productivity Committee that meets regularly and frequently for this purpose alone. It plans, organizes, coordinates, motivates, and controls, but only with respect to the preparation of the Plan and the implementation of the Plan. Management has no function or reality outside the scope of the Cash Productivity Plan.

Each supervisor explains to his men the quantities and ratios of the Guide, and the objectives of the Plan, stressing the portions applicable to their own area. The Cash Productivity Committee disseminates the planning *Time Schedule* for the company as a whole, and separate schedules for each function (Manufacturing, Sales, etc.). From each function, in accordance with the Schedule, the Committee will receive Cost Plans and Asset Plans.

A schedule details all the work to be done, under column headings from left to right: Item; Responsibility of; Reviewed by; On Due Date of; Directed to; On Due Date of. Down the columns, the due dates give a running account of progress toward the Plan's completion. Everyone receives the schedule for his area, which dramatizes the broad base of participation in constructing the Plan. And it provides clear communication among all participants, encouraging cooperation and mutual understanding.

Every employee is thus deeply involved in *planning* cash productivity. He is *organized* and coordinated solely to implement the Plan, and he is motivated solely in terms of its most effective implementation. The progress of everyone is therefore *controlled* and evaluated solely in terms of the Cash Productivity Plan.

DETERMINING OUR MAXIMUM-IMPACT DIRECTION

Business is a condition of defensive-offensive warfare. The Cash Productivity Plan is our blueprint of military strategy to gain major strategic objectives. This it must do by the shrewd and flexible employment of the company's most powerful resources. The Plan carefully considers the company's strengths and weaknesses, and the competition's strengths and weaknesses. It exploits our strengths and shores up our weaknesses, while attacking the competition at its weakest point.

Thus, to construct a truly effective Plan, we must decide on our own unique, maximum-impact direction as a company. What business are we in? More specifically and fruitfully, what market do we supply? Who is our target customer? And what *service* can we best provide him?

And above all, what is the nature of our *competition* that also supplies our service and is therefore in our business, no matter how different from us he may seem. The nation's railroads discovered too late that they were in the business of transportation, not running trains; that their target customer was therefore a much different breed of cat than they thought he was; and that they competed directly with other companies in the *transportation* business, not merely (if at all) with other railroads. Instead of adapting its unique and prodigious transportation advantages to shifting customer transportation needs, the industry went steadily downhill under the tattered banner of "railroading."

What is our business? The single right answer is one that exploits our strengths and avoids our weaknesses. To lead from strength, we must know our strengths. Then every service and product (which is really a service) that comes within our definition of the business, now or in the future, *is* our business. It is a legitimate application of our resources to the extent that it serves our CRE objectives.

The *unitary marketing* concept summarizes these market-impact planning considerations. Our profit center (company) is built around a specific group of services performed for a specific target customer. This   defines precisely what business we are in. It is *our* corner of the market—the most promising homogeneous customer market for *us*. We recruit and organize to serve that market *best; know* it better than anyone else; stay with it day and night until we are the strongest and most profitable in that market; and *keep* ahead of everyone else.

In other words, our company gratifies customer desires—markets valuable ideas and services, not products as such. It sells the fulfillment of hopes and dreams, which are ever shifting. So it must be closely and constantly tuned in to these shifts. We must know what our customer wants and dreams of now, next year, five years from now, and be the dream merchant who delivers.

It requires all-out *market specialization*, whereby we become far more expert in our segment of the market than any single competitor. And we constantly press our advantage derived from that specialization and knowledge.

And it means achieving *marketing superiority*—perfecting the techniques that make us the most effective marketer of our services (products) in our market. These are the disciplines of market research, product engineering, distribution, advertising, and everything else that contributes to our marketing impact on the target customer.

Because unitary marketing is thus built on tight market specialization and marketing superiority within that speciality, it implies *systems marketing*. We supply the *total* integrated service to our customer. Suppose that we manufacture man-operated factory power sweepers. To grow, in accordance with unitary marketing, we redefine our business as providing cost-reducing maintenance technology to industrial customers. Every product and service that does this profitably is our business. We are now in the business of selling our customer a factory maintenance system: supplying *all* his cost-reducing maintenance requirements in an integrated manner.

Finally, unitary marketing depends for maximum profitability on a *unitary manufacturing* capability. We must be a low-cost producer in our industry, which was the subject matter and concern of Part Four. But unitary manufacturing is an approach to costs that is implied by an approach to marketing, for both of which the common denominator is "unitary."

A unitary manufacturing system helps to achieve lowest cost by building the entire product line around a relatively narrow core of production know-how and capability. The product line can be broadened out almost without limit, within the framework of unitary *marketing*, while staying within the narrow confines of unitary *manufacturing*.

A unitary manufacturing capability provides all the cost advantages of interchangeable parts and components, interchangeable labor, single-purpose plants, long machine runs, and so forth. The large number of related products serving the unitary market provides the volume that generates the manufacturing economies. The longer each product line is extended, the greater our efficiency of interchangeability and large scale.

A determination of our maximum-impact direction involves not just the quantity but the quality of sales volume. This is its durability, depression-resistance, growth potential, and profitability. It would be pointless if not a bit suicidal to achieve a targeted quantity of cash flow by reaching out indiscriminately for poor-quality sales. These are derived, for example, from customers in declining industries, poor credit risks, "fluff" markets that tend to collapse at the first sign of general business deterioration, low-profit products, and so forth.

Once we know our maximum-impact direction, we can quantify it by constructing a *market grid* for target year 5 (or TY5). This assigns both percentages-of-total and dollar amounts of TY5 sales volume ($7,407,000) to each of our present and future products, which are listed vertically at the left margin of the grid.

It does this according to the company's geographical sales territories or marketing areas, which are the column headings across the top. Further down, it also gives the geographical sales breakdowns by type of *customer*, or customer category.

The TY5 market grid, or product mix, is a vitally important combined effort of the key functions of the company, such as Marketing, International Sales, New Product Development, and Manufacturing. As finally conceived, it must be the best expression of our maximum-impact direction.

We now have a Cash Productivity *Guide*. We know our *maximum-impact direction* for the achievement of the targeted quantity and quality of sales needed to produce the targeted cash flow and equity. We have a target-year *market grid* that gives quantified expression to our maximum-impact direction, in terms of product and customer sales distribution by marketing territories. And by now we have genuine and enduring companywide participation in the entire planning and implementing process.

PREPARING THE FUNCTIONAL RESOURCE PLANS

The five-year Cash Productivity Plan embraces all areas of company activity and integrates their *resource plans*. These describe the cost and asset structures that each function will need if we are to achieve our sales targets It is organization and facilities planning: determinining the amount, type, and timing of future requirements for physical facilities, manpower, management, capital, and all the rest.

Resource plans are received from all functions—Marketing, New Product Development, Manufacturing, Personnel, Accounting and Finance, and so forth. They detail what will be needed in the way of costs and assets to create, make, and market the products and provide the targeted sales volume. The following very brief comments are merely suggestive of their scope and content.

The Marketing Plan is spearheaded by intensive and continuing market research. It provides insights into our present and future customers, and into our competition that is courting the same group of customers. We maximize marketing impact by moving against our competitors' weaknesses, as we have seen, not by hitting their strengths head-on. The underlying objective of the Marketing Plan is to know what our customers and market, our competition, and our industry and product technology will look like and feel like throughout the next five years. The plan makes certain that we respond accordingly, with maximum impact.

Our own maximum-impact advantage should of course be built solidly into the Marketing Plan. We must lead from a position of strength, whether it is the recognized quality of our products, breadth and aggressiveness of our sales organization, effectiveness of our customer service units, small size and maneuverability, or whatever.

The New Product Development (NPD) Plan is really part of the Marketing Plan, even though it is usually the creature of a separate Engineering capability. Only a small percentage of new product ideas come to fruition as successful products. The NPD Plan supports that function's product development intentions. It does this with realistic assessments of (1) our technical, productive, and engineering capabilities needed to create and manufacture them and (2) our marketing capabilities to sell them.

And it backs its proposals with well-documented projections of trends that are most likely to have an impact on our future products. The plan appraises projects currently under way to determine how they fit the market research and technological forecasts for our industry. If our percentage of NPD dollars-to-sales is higher than the industry average, but our new-product profitability has been low, the NPD Plan must provide for an improvement in the situation.

NPD planning defines the specific new product goals in the light of Cash Productivity Plan objectives. And it determines precisely how many dollars, what personnel and facilities, and what time schedule will apply to each project.

The Manufacturing Plan analyzes this function's present and future position as to plant and equipment, manpower, location, production know-how, and all the other resources it needs to ship the Cash Productivity Plan's targeted sales volume at the targeted profit.

Indispensable to these and all the other resource plans is the provision of adequate and effective *managerial resources*, which is the crucial resource for all the others. A strong management can bring in and mobilize the other resources—financial, human, physical, technological, intangible, and anything else needed to make a profit. But the other resources are useless without management. Each resource plan evaluates its present organization and personnel. With reference to the Plan objectives and the supporting objectives, it determines what organization and managerial talents it will need in *each* of the five years,

THE FINANCIAL PLAN

Once the many functional resource plans have been submitted and approved, we can put together the Cash Productivity Plan. This is the comprehensive document that provides the detailed sales, cost, and asset numbers for every organizational unit over the five-year period. But the Plan is actually two things in one. First, it is the *financial plan* of the company and its subdivisions, which quantifies all the resource plans numerically in dollars. Against these numbers, the performance of each function is thereafter measured and evaluated. Second, it is the supporting *resource plans*, which give life and substance to the Financial Plan within the quantitative boundry lines of the Guide.

The Financial Plan is prepared by the financial officer, during the preparation of all the resource plans (when he also puts together the resource plan for his finance function). He supplies cost figures to the functional planners. And he assures that cost reduction (S/C) and asset control (S/A) is programmed into the various functional plans to conform to the dictates of the Guide.

Each function thus winds up with its cost (or operating) plan and its asset (or capital) plan, for every one of the five years. Together, *all* the function plans each year must mesh with the Cash Productivity Guide for that year: the combined Cost Plans must stay within the cost limitations of the Guide income statement, and the combined Asset Plans must remain within the asset limitations of the balance sheet.

The resulting Cash Productivity Plan thus reflects the year-to-year improvement of S/C and S/A calculated in the Guide—and the consequent buildup of cash productivity, which is what the entire exercise is all about.

The Cost Plans and Asset Plans are therefore a measure of the creative intelligence and simple business effectiveness of the men who constructed them: it is their all-important job to keep resource requirements to a minimum. They must know precisely *what* resources of costs and assets are to be acquired, in what *quantity* and *quality*, and at what *time* and *place*. It is this creative and practical intelligence about productive resources, and little else, that generates corportate cash within the framework of the Plan.

When the Financial Plan is completed, it is converted into graphic *charts* —as are the supporting functional plans—year-by-year and month-by-month. A picture is worth a thousand words and ten thousand numbers. The plan is a mass of numbers, which the charts bring to life and dramatize. Copies of the Chart Book are given to *all* management and key people. It is updated monthly, with performance posted against objectives for all the company's operations.

THE INTERIM AND BASE-YEAR PLANS

Most of the planning effort centers on TY5. Realization of $2,010,000 of equity and $1,684,000 of total (cumulative) cash flow, in our example, is the climactic effect toward which all our energies for five years will have been directed.

Once the TY5 Plan has been completed, therefore, it is easy to structure the four *interim years'* plans. They are done in progressively tighter and finer detail for each earlier year, starting with year 4. But otherwise the procedure is roughly the same as for TY5. *Each year's* Plan contains and expresses the cost and asset resource plans for each function, which must conform to that year's Guide: the equity and cash flow designated by the Guide is the output of each year's Plan—its reason for being.

The base-year Plan (year 1) is also similar in format except that the detail is *monthly* rather than annual: monthly income statements and balance sheets, monthly cost plans and asset plans, and so forth.

And year 1's format is much more heavily influenced than are later years' by considerations of sales cash and breakeven analysis, explored in Part Three. These are strictly short-term tools, and indispensable ones in profit planning. In the base year, unlike later years, we can closely estimate KC, prices, VC, and the other cash-margin factors. So we use them, as in the following illustration derived from the Cash Productivity Guide:

Guide	Base Year 1 (000)		
Line 2	P (cash flow)		$ 250
Add	KC (constant costs)		
	Fixed costs	$1000	
	Project costs	500	1500
	Sales cash required (Sc)		$1750
Add	VC (60% of sales)		2636
Line 5	Sales required		$4386
	BV (1500/40% Sc)		− 3750
	CM (cash margin)		$ 636

To provide $250,000 of cash flow (line 2), we add $1,500,000 of fixed and project KC to give us the sales cash (Sc) requirement of $1,750,000. We also get the Sc requirement from sales (line 5) less volume costs (VC being 60% of sales).

Since everything else is either fixed or given, project costs are the flexible "swing" factor that we adjust to provide the Sc requirement. This also keeps costs within the Guide requirement (line 7) of $4,136,000. Year 1 results in BV of $3,750,000, or a cash margin of $636,000 (14.5% of sales).

Subsequent Plan years can also benefit from breakeven analysis, but with diminishing precision and reliability as we go forward.

Each year's Plan is thus, in essence, the company's cash contribution ratios brought to life: cost cash $(+S/C)$, asset cash $(+S/A)$, and leverage cash $(+L/A)$, which combine to generate CRE. And it pinpoints the *backup* ratios for each category of CCR, detailing them down to the smallest units and subsections of the company. They tell us how S/C and S/A will behave each year for each position, department, sales area, and product line.

As the company and all of us move forward in time, variances against the Plan CCRs are recorded and corrected accordingly. This is the CRE *control* function, which we will examine closely in Part Seven.

VISUALIZING AND ACTUALIZING TARGET YEAR 5

Planning must be done in large and stable time chunks, typically five years. The Guide Plan is *fixed* and unchanging over its time-span: it is *made* to happen, in its comprehensive Guide outlines, no matter what it takes. This means there is never any tinkering with the five-year equity and cumulative cash-flow objectives—with Pi and CRE—or with the cumulative sales objective on which they depend. They are the immovable strategy ends toward which ever-shifting tactical means are directed.

Only a major structural change originating in the Worksheet—from public offerings and acquisitions (ECO or ECA)—could alter the overall dimensions of the Plan. This would come from an occasional mammoth acquisition or public offering that *overshot* the minimum level of ECA and ECO already provided for in the Plan itself.

And after the restructuring, the new Plan is again immovable and unchanging in its overall Pi dimensions. As long as management and the stockholders are happy with the Pi growth rate, this is the *only* Cash Productivity Plan that the entire organization lives with and works toward as an all-consuming activity.

A fixed five-year Plan has one enormous advantage over the one-year type—or those that are tinkered with at the first sign that they may take some unusual effort to be achieved. It energizes the entire organization. Everyone has participated in the construction of a momentous Plan that they believe in. Its fifth-year goals have been "photographed" for them both in companywide terms and in terms of their own operating unit. They can *visualize*, enthusiastically and meaningfully, their company and their own operation (and especially themselves and their associates) in the *fifth year*.

A tremendous group force, determination and energy is released by this visualization and belief in the attainment of the Plan. It is, after all, achievable because the better companies in our own or related industries have *already* achieved these performance levels (BC ratios).

But a Plan that is tinkered with from time to time dilutes and must ultimately destroy this enormous group-psychological staying power. This is so not only because the visualized goal keeps changing for them, but because it undermines their respect for the Plan and its goal—if not for the planning process itself.

The five-year type of Plan is also in a much more realistic time frame. It corresponds with and is geared to the tempo of basic corporate directions, technology, and industry and economic trends. To make a structural change in the Plan within the five-year period, to say nothing of annual changes, means that we are shifting gears and direction much too quickly. The company is scattering its energies rather than moving with the inexorable tide in its own affairs and taking full advantage of it. And it is scattering its planning energies: the fixed Plan saves everyone's time, because a new five-year plan is not structured until the fourth year of the present one.

But we always return to its central advantage: a fixed TY5 target will be *made* to happen much more readily than if it were tinkered with in the interim. What we are planning and controlling are *cumulative* magnitudes to be achieved during the five years. In Table 26, we are working toward *total* cash flow of $1,684,000 over the five years. This is accomplished by achieving *total* sales of $28,959,000 without incurring any higher total costs than $27,275,000. We thus control progress toward $2,010,000 of TY5 equity, on a cumulative basis. This is done in terms of *results-to-date*, from the base zero start of the Plan on January 1 of year 1 to whatever control point along the five-year span we now happen to be located.

At the end of year 2, for instance, the Plan requires total cumulative sales (line 6) of $9,421,000, and cumulative costs (line 8) of $8,884,000. Say that we are now at the close of year 2 and find that cumulative sales are in fact around $9,421,000, but costs are in excess of the allowed $8,884,000. We know that in year 3 this cost overage must be compensated for by reducing actual *three-year* cumulative costs below the $14,244,000 permitted by the Plan, or we must boost sales above its cumulative three-year-target.

By means of this type of compensating reaction to leads and lags in the achievement of the Plan—cumulatively—the likelihood of achieving the *five-year* Plan totals is very high.

QUALITIES OF AN ACHIEVABLE PLAN

Preparation of the Cash Productivity Plan is the most important effort a management can launch, because all corporate decisions and actions flow from and are interpreted against the existing Plan. An effective Plan is in this sense one of the most valuable assets we possess—probably our most potent tool for building the business. The essential requirement is that it be a document in which all have faith. Its goals have to be reached for, but can be attained through intelligent hard work that will be appropriately rewarded.

There should be inherent flexibility *within* our fixed Guide Plan in order to maintain the integrity of its fixed overall targets. We have noted that it already provides for a reasonable infusion of ECO and ECA, only a surfeit of which would occasion an alteration in the basic Plan.

It should also designate any crucial *pivotal* factors that have an overwhelming influence on the company's success or failure during the five-year Plan period. These might be a major customer defection; the opening of a huge new market we have been trying to develop; the loss of a key employee who controls a third of our sales; the loss (or gain) of a major raw material source of supply; or whatever.

The Plan should program alternative courses of action with respect to these main areas of risk exposure and opportunity, so that we know exactly what to do if and when they affect us. The reed that bends with the wind does not crack: the Plan that has inner flexibility and turnaround room does not require structural adjustments to its overall Guide dimensions.

The planning process must be kept very *simple*, of course, with a minimum of paperwork and short, easy-to-understand formats. In this way, and if it is a fixed five-year Plan, it will take very little of everyone's time. To help keep it simple, it should also be *unitary*—one should plan for his own area of activity only. And he controls results unitarily, against the part of the Plan applicable only to his area.

Communication of the Cash Productivity Plan to every employee, especially the part applying only to him, goes to the heart of its implementation. If he understands its relation to his own work, and his work's relation to the entire company's work, the Plan will have its strongest possible impact as a practical tool for corporate growth. And communication must flow *upward* as well. Everyone then has a deeper feeling of participation in the Plan, and management also gets the indispensable feedback against which to test the Plan's reasonableness and workability.

Apart from everything else, planning and the management of a business within a planned structure benefits everyone on a day-to-day basis. It helps us tremendously to delegate authority and responsibility; to communicate; to make decisions; and to enlist active and effective participation in everything that goes on.

A well-constructed Cash Productivity Plan is probably our single most valuable corporate asset. Emerging from a sound assessment of our BC industry environment, it is both the expression of and the blueprint for achieving our predetermined rate of growth. It therefore expresses and achieves $Pi = CRE \times ECO \times ECA$.

Progress toward the company's maximum-impact direction gathers momentum as the Plan mobilizes our strongest resources in support of that direction. And broad participation in both constructing and implementing the Plan, more than anything else, assures us of its fulfillment.

But the Plan alone is nothing unless the company is effectively organized to accomplish it. So we will talk next about how to organize ourselves in terms of, and solely for the achievement of, a maximum-impact Plan.

CHAPTER 20

ORGANIZING AND COORDINATING CASH PRODUCTIVITY

We organize our company to achieve the Cash Productivity Plan, and for no other reason. The effectiveness of the organizational structure, companywide and at all levels, is measured solely by its effectiveness in achieving the Plan's cash-productivity objectives.

The completed Plan actually forms a four-level hierarchy of objectives. At the top is the *Pi objective* itself, which is the Plan objective, directed toward the achievement of a predetermined five-year rate of equity growth. This involves generating the cumulative five-year quantity of cash flow, resulting in the targeted fifth-year level of equity.

Just below are the *line objectives* for new product development, manufacturing, and marketing. They directly achieve the Plan objective by creating, making, and marketing the products (or services). On the next level in the hierarchy are the *resource objectives*. These provide manpower, money, materials, facilities, and whatever else we need to accomplish the "create, make, and market" line objectives—by which we achieve the Plan objective. And finally there are the *staff objectives*, which provide advisory and service assistance in achieving line and resource objectives.

Because the Plan objective is expressed in terms of Pi and CRE, this four-level hierarchy of objectives is—everywhere in the company—an expression of $+S/C$ and $+S/A$. That is, to the extent that the hierarchy of objectives generates cash by improving the ratios everywhere, it directly serves the Pi objective. So our organizational pattern and structure, everywhere and at every level, must provide maximum support in achieving cash productivity objectives whose $+S/C$ and $+S/A$ impacts converge on the Plan objective. Our organization may in fact be *defined* as an objective-achieving framework, focusing on Pi.

So we must first talk about structuring cash-productivity $(-C+S-A)$

objectives before we can talk about structuring an organization to house objective-achieving activity.

STRUCTURING CASH-PRODUCTIVITY OBJECTIVES

In combat, to direct total striking power narrowly on a single strategic objective is the best guaranty of achieving the objective. The parallel strategy in business is to mobilize an entire corporation in terms of cash productivity (or CSA) objectives, and thus direct its total striking power narrowly on one strategic objective: the Plan's equity target five years ahead.

We structure downward through all levels a system of CSA objectives. At each level they mesh with and support the objectives up the line, and all of them converge narrowly on the Plan objective. Such a cash-productivity objectives program provides a tremendous impact in building a company. *Every* employee pursues about 10 high-priority CSA objectives, which combine throughout the company to produce massive cash-generating results over and above the routine day-to-day work. And routine work is all that ever happens without a cash-productivity objectives program.

Communicating the completed Cash Productivity Plan launches the objective-setting process throughout the company. The Plan filters down the line as far as possible to every responsible person in the organization. In cooperation with his immediate supervisor, each man then establishes objectives in his own area of work that support the objectives up the line.

The Plan is not merely communicated. Each supervisor in fact brings his subordinates *up to* his level. They are asked to share responsibility equally with him in achieving the objectives of their unit in support of the comprehensive Plan objectives. The men identify strongly with the responsibilities of the higher level, because of the higher prestige. And they are therefore much more solidly committed to the plans that emerge.

The *subordinate* is the active ingredient and the supervisor is the passive ingredient in a dynamic system of cash-productivity objectives. At the objective-setting session between the two, which we will call a *CSA Review* meeting, the objectives established are those of the *employee*. He knows and fully understands by now the requirements of the Plan as they relate to his area. So the help he needs is largely mechanical: to set his objectives in definite terms; be certain they are the most important objectives; not be too ambitious; be sure they are compatible with the overall Plan objectives; and see that they are written so as to meet the various criteria of effectiveness.

The typical first session begins with the supervisor and employee jointly reaching agreement on the crucial elements of the employee's position, against the background of the existing Cash Productivity Plan. The employee summarizes this understanding in a Position Guide, as we will see.

Then he sets his own CSA objectives, to support his supervisor's and higher echelon objectives. Each one provides a specific cash-generating impact in one or more of the categories, − C, + S, and − A. Both men also agree on realistic target dates for achieving each objective, extending out six months or more. And the longer the duration, the more numerous are the interim review dates that they schedule.

The "20–80" rule is the basis of selecting objectives. He must concentrate objective-setting on the *20%* of all possible CSA projects in his area that produce *80%* of the cash-productivity results: on the 20% of the possible *cost-reduction* projects that will produce 80% of the cost-reduction cash; on the 20% of the *asset reduction* projects that will produce 80% of the asset reduction cash; and on the 20% of the *sales development* projects that will produce 80% of the sales cash.

So in the objective-setting meeting, the man and his supervisor decide on about 10 objectives of top priority. And the man formulates specific plans to achieve them: planning subtargets; organizing people to achieve the objectives; coordinating with other objectives and personnel; motivating people; and controlling performance toward the objectives, versus his plan.

CHARACTERISTICS OF CASH-EFFECTIVE OBJECTIVES

Each objective is the responsibility of one man only. *He* chose it, and is fully convinced of its importance. He knows he can achieve it in the time and within the cost and asset limitations agreed upon. And he wants to be judged in terms of it. Otherwise, in the evaluation session with his boss, his reasons for not completing an imposed objective may be the same ones he gave when he first resisted it.

The objective spells out *what* the man will do but not how to do it. He knows the "how" because he knows his own area best. So he is held accountable for the ends, not the means. The objective-setting environment thereby also develops strong managers and leaders, not followers.

Each cash productivity (CSA) objective is in writing, in language clear and unmistakable to both men. It states precisely *what* will be accomplished, at what *quality* level, *when*, and at what *cost* and *asset* outlay. Objectives are thus in quantitative terms only—in units, pounds, yards of spoilage, and so forth.

The objective must of course be an attainable challenge for the man. It should be resilient and *adaptable* to shifting operating conditions as time passes. Adaptability is enhanced by subdividing the objective into its subcomponents. Each subobjective has an interim completion date, on the basis of which interim progress can be readily measured and objectives modified.

The objective should also be appropriate to the man's authority and responsibility. And it should conform to the objectives of other men in his area and interrelated areas, so they are pulling together and not apart.

But the essence of an effective objective is its *cash-productive* impact: $+S/C$ or $-C/S$, or else $+S/A$ or $-A/S$. Each of the man's 10 objectives is maximum-priority in reducing costs or assets, so that his area's CCRs will increase substantially as a result.

The comprehensive objective-setting process throughout the organization is thus a *cash-generating* process. It emerges and grows from the *bottom* levels upward, as an exercise in total participation. Objectives and the plans for achieving them are talked back and forth, and modified where necessary. What emerges is a harmonious working balance among them, up and down and sideways, organizationally.

And such an objective-setting process also results in a blending of individual and company objectives, so that progress in one is automatically progress in the other. It is a fusion, or interaction, of goals.

This interaction releases tremendous additional energy and enthusiasm, because the whole is now more than the sum of its parts. The company has again been dealt with existentially, as a living system made up of living and dynamic people. It is a powerful cash-generating organism for everyone's benefit because of the *identity* of personal and corporate goals, hopes, and dreams. The corporate dream is to accomplish a challenging five-year Cash Productivity Plan. It is fulfilled as it becomes everybody's dream, intimately and personally.

FORMATS FOR ADMINISTERING OBJECTIVES

Figure 1 shows one possible type of format for establishing and monitoring objectives. At the top, *Result* provides space for writing the objective (the desired result) quantitatively, and very specifically and clearly, so that it is precisely understood and measurable. *Responsibility of* is the subordinate's name. And *CSA Plan* is the main cash-generating impact of this objective, either $+S$, $-C$, or $-A$.

In the *Dates* column, the last line is the *Completion Date* of the objective. *Subtargets* and their *Interim Review Dates* are filled in as shown. *B, O, or A*

RESULT: _____

_____

_____

_____

_____

RESPONSIBILITY OF _____CSA Plan _____

Lead Time _____ Days

DATES   SubTargets and Interim Review Dates (B, O, or A)

_____ _____

_____ _____
_____ _____
_____ _____
_____ _____
_____ _____

_____ Completion Date

Coordinate with:	(1) $ Gain	(2) $ Loss	(3) CSA Earnings ($-C=100\%$ $+S=20\%$ $-A=20\%$)	(4) CSA Earnings/ Investment (%)
_____	$-C$ $20	$+C$ $50\times2	$20	$26/110=
_____	$+S$ 30	$-S$	6	23.6%
_____	$-A$	$+A$ 10		

Results accomplished (enumerate specifically, using measurement data):

_____

_____
_____
_____
_____

CSA Performance (check one)

Below Plan (B) ☐
On Plan (O)   ☐
Above Plan (A) ☐

Comments on any special factors
affecting achievement of results:

_____
_____
_____
_____

Final estimate, CSA Earnings/Investment _____ %

Professional development objective: Completion Date:

_____   _____

_____   _____

Figure 1

mean below, on, or above plan: at the time of each interim review, the man thus rates his performance status. *Coordinate with*, at the lower left, are the men whose objectives mesh with this one, and with whom he should therefore maintain liaison.

The four columns at the bottom are the guts of the objective. Here it is evaluated as to cash productivity potential, and ranked with other possible objectives that might be pursued. Every objective promises a *dollar gain* (column 1) from $-C$, $+S$, or $-A$. And it will cause some *dollar loss* (column 2) in the form of the additional costs incurred by the objective $(+C)$, or higher assets $(+A)$, or possibly even reduced sales volume $(-S)$.

$ *Loss* (column 2). This objective is a product engineering effort that will cost $(+C)$ $50,000 for two years, and will require $10,000 of additional equipment $(+A)$.

The $ *Gain* (column 1) is a cost reduction $(-C)$ of $20,000 a year and additional product sales of $30,000 a year. The engineering will not only reduce costs, that is, but will also improve the design and therefore its customer acceptance.

CSA Earnings (column 3). The $20,000 of cost reduction $(-C)$ flows into cash earnings at 100%, because $1 of cost reduction produces $1 of additional pretax cash. Sales increase $(+S)$ of $30,000 produces additional cash at the 20% Sc contribution to overhead, or $6000 a year. Had the project caused a reduction of assets, cash from $-A$ would be computed at the 20% return on investment that the company experiences overall.

CSA Earnings / Investment (column 4). CSA cash of $26,000, or $20,000 from costs and $6000 from sales (column 3), is divided by the total investment of $110,000. From column 2, this investment is $50,000 of costs for two years, or $100,000, plus $10,000 of additional assets. It results in CSA Earnings/Investment of 23.6%.

Whether this return (and the objective) is acceptable depends on the company's reinvestment cutoff percentage and other project-screening criteria we discussed in Chapter 18 on reinvestment cash. The computation is only the man's first-approximation estimate, in any event. It lacks the time-discounting and tax-impact sophistication that we will have to apply to it before the objective is finally approved or rejected.

On Side 2 are *Results accomplished*. Here the man describes very specifically the results he accomplished while pursuing the objective. He uses the same quantitative measurement data that are already incorporated in the wording of the objective (*Result*, top of front side). This later forms one of the bases of his overall performance evaluation.

He then checks whether his *CSA Performance* was below, on, or above Plan, and comments on any special factors affecting his achievements against Plan. Finally, he computes actual *CSA Earnings / Investment*, against the original estimate of 23.6%. And at the bottom, he notes any new *Professional development* objective that may have grown out of his work, such as additional reading or course work.

INTERIM CASH PRODUCTIVITY REVIEWS

Progress toward each objective is analyzed at regular interim review meetings, as noted, usually every three months. Between these meetings, the man has received performance *measurement data* promptly and meaningfully on the progress of each objective. Frequent reporting and accounting assistance enables him to take corrective action at the first sign of a performance variance.

The subordinate as the active member of the meeting reviews his progress with his supervisor, whose role *must* be that of a coach and understanding counselor. He is there only as a resource person, to listen, answer questions if asked, and provide whatever guidance the man requests.

The employee's evaluation of his own progress is invariably harsher than if it had been made by his supervisor. It must be done solely in the precise quantitative and measurable terms in which he wrote the objective in the first place. Otherwise the self-appraisal deteriorates into vague generalities and becomes worthless.

If performance above or below an interim objective is expected to vary by more than a fixed percentage, he hands his supervisor a *Cash Variance Report* (CVR). This *anticipates* problems with respect to a particular objective, and is a concise analysis in three sections:

1. The exact *origin and nature* of the anticipated problem.

2. The employee's *best solution* (quickest, least expensive, least disruptive, most permanent, etc.).

3. (*a*) The *date* when his variance will be corrected, objective completed, and so on; (*b*) The *condition* that will exist in his area when the variance is corrected.

The cash variance report (CVR) *prevents* fires, rather than waits to put them out. It closes the circle for the subordinate in his active role of planning, organizing, coordinating, motivating, and controlling. That is, the CVR takes the process from the control stage, where a variance is indicated, back again to the planning stage. He plans specific corrective action in the CVR to accomplish the objective on schedule, or perhaps to modify it.

Senior management (above the man's supervisor) controls objectives by *exception*. We review only the CVR's on those that will *not* be reached by their target dates. This helps avoid the strangulating mass of detail in which a poorly run objectives program can immerse us.

Managing by cash-productivity objectives is an extraordinarily effective way to build a company, and to build people. It turns the decision-making process upside down by transferring authority as far down the line as possible, to where the work is *done*. That is where objectives must be set, to support the higher objectives. And that is where we place accountability for achieving objectives, and where we reward the achievement.

That is, authority is decision-making power. The extent of one's authority is the extent to which he can make decisions without asking his boss about them. An organization managed by objectives is infused *at all levels* with decision-making authority, responsibility, and accountability. Nothing builds the company *and* future managers more powerfully than this.

Such an environment dramatizes the basic distinction between decision-making, where the work is done, and decision *management* at the higher levels. The manager is a decision manager: he makes certain the right decision emerges from the right man at the right time. He *never* makes the decision for the man, in the counseling session or anywhere else. In such an environment, down in the ranks of the decision-makers, are the outstanding future managers developed.

Managing a decision into being, rather than trying to make it oneself, also results in a more realistic and much sounder decision. It is made by the functional *specialist* who is down in the actual decision area. And he will implement the decision readily and enthusiastically, because it is his and not the boss's.

The secret of decision management is really the proficiency we develop in (1) asking the most sensitive and pointed *questions* of our subordinate, in his own vocabulary and terminology; (2) *listening* to him skillfully; and (3) *evaluating* his decisions within our higher and therefore broader managerial perspective.

ORGANIZING TO ACHIEVE THE CASH PRODUCTIVITY PLAN

The company organizes to maximize cash productivity—to accomplish the Cash Productivity Plan. So the organization, everywhere and at all levels, derives its structural and functional characteristics from the scheme of CSA *objectives* that emerges from—and responds to and supports—the Plan.

But the first organizational decision, even before the Plan is completed, is the one top management makes about the overall or general structure of the company. It concerns the structure as it will evolve over the five years of the Plan. The best organization will best achieve the four-tiered hierarchy of objectives—Plan, line, resource, and staff. This is the only area of Plan preparation that cannot be delegated to lower levels—where some units may be less important, or not even needed, in the emerging organization.

What major organizational capabilities will the company require to achieve the new Cash Productivity Plan? Do we still need the functional unit, Manufacturing? If so, what should its main organizational segments now be? Or would the Plan be better served if we replaced Manufacturing with a capability that simply bought our products for resale? How will our organization in year 5 differ from year 4, or 3? And so forth.

Our comprehensive organizational structure having been determined, and the Plan communicated, each component *unit* then redefines or modifies its central purpose with respect to the Plan's achievement. The unit has a specific role or mission, distinguishable from all the others, that will be fulfilled as the Plan is fulfilled. This is an intensive and fresh rethinking of the unit's purpose by its own people, who alone have the job of achieving their section of the Plan.

Only when this is done, and done precisely, can they determine the *work* of their group—its routine and its higher cash-generating activities. These activities are needed to achieve their unit's central purpose in support of the Plan, and to achieve their own CSA objectives within the unit.

Then they conduct a *work sequence* analysis of each activity and subactivity, to determine exactly who is to do what and when with respect to each one. The Accounting Department, for instance, may have a Work Sequence for running accounts payable, another for payrolling, another for budget administration, and so on. Every person who is connected directly or indirectly with the activity, in this unit and elsewhere, meets together around a blackboard—with four columns labeled as follows:

Work   Positions Needed (Who)   Actions Needed (What)   When

They fill in the columns in the sequence in which the work is to be performed, detailing what each position does and when. Each group member receives a copy of the completed Work Sequence, and mulls it over for a week or so until the group meets again to finalize it. The Sequence must be kept simple and uncluttered, of course. "When in doubt, leave it out:" if the step is really needed, somebody will yell loud enough later to put it back in.

The Work Sequence governs all the continuing and recurring activities and subactivities for which this unit is responsible throughout the life of the Plan. As such, it is unique and indispensable.

CHARTING THE ORGANIZATIONAL STRUCTURE

Organization charting now responds to the objective-setting and work-sequencing pattern that is emerging throughout the company in support of the Plan. Each unit sends up the line its organization chart, which depicts the positions involved; the lateral relationships among positions; and the vertical relationships between its group of positions (team) and those above and below.

Each chart shows the relationships affecting a *team* of men at a particular organizational level, whose objectives extend out as far as five years. So the team must construct a fifth-year organization chart of the structure and staffing needed at that time. And it makes charts in tighter detail for each of the earlier interim years, and one for the present year. The charts trace the staffing changes to be required as that unit progresses forward within the five-year planning framework.

All the charts are sent up for approval and inclusion in the company-wide organization chart, found at the beginning of the Organization Manual. The companywide chart is of course the thoroughly familiar network of interlocking teams, each consisting of the supervisor and the subordinate men reporting to him. Every subordinate heads another inter-locking team, consisting of himself and the men on the next level below, who report to him.

For the entire company, every manager therefore belongs to two teams: the one below for which he is the "coach," to use the overworked but completely descriptive term, and the one on his own level in which he is a team member.

Each team *must* be administratively self-contained and inviolable. It will lose effectiveness or even be destroyed if the inviolability is questioned. The inviolability proceeds upward and downward: (1) each man reports to his supervisor, and to no one else; and (2) the supervisor must never even *appear* to make decisions below the level of his own team, with respect to somebody reporting to one of his subordinates. It would immediately undermine the subordinate's authority and the respect of his men for that authority. Nothing destroys the morale and effectiveness of a team faster than a meddling superior's shortcutting of the chain of command.

The team must therefore be inviolable externally, from the destructive incursions of the mindless or meddling boss's boss. But it also must remain inviolable *internally*, as to the things the supervisor must do himself and never delegate. He, and no one else, organizes and staffs his team. He alone trains his men; keeps them posted (with measurement data) on their progress toward objectives; evaluates their results; and rewards or penalizes their performance.

Each interlocking team of supervisor and men is thus inviolable from the outside, and from within. And, as in an orchestra, each man is a specialist and sticks to his specialty. But he knows the other specialties, as the professional musician knows several instruments. When necessary, he can shift over or double up with another member. In fact, the ideal organizational team is very much like a superb, completely professional, and immensely versatile orchestra.

Or it can be likened to a crack hockey team: its players have an intimate knowledge of and deep respect for the best rules and practises of the game. Each man trains incessantly until he is an expert and the team is thoroughly professional. The coach (supervisor) is indeed their coach, helpful in the breadth of his experience and perspective. The team and its members have high standards of performance, knowing that even *one* below-standard player can lose a game. They have a common objective; intimate knowledge of their adversaries (competitors); and so forth. No matter how far we carry the winning-hockey-team analogy, we are precisely describing the winning corporate team.

As to the span of control, or the maximum number of men that a supervisor can coach, he should of course supervise no more men than there is time for—time *they* need to achieve their objectives. So we increase the span of control and reduce supervisory overhead by shrinking this supervisory *time* requirement: recruiting better men and better supervisors; training them well; giving them the most effective and up-to-date policy and procedure guides; administering the best objective-setting program; providing prompt and effective measurement data; and so forth.

RECRUITING CASH-MOTIVATED PEOPLE

The best Cash Productivity Plan cannot be implemented without an effective organizational structure. But the best organization can do little without effective people in the key positions. There are not many self-evident principles of business management. But surely ranking high among them is the dictum that we must recruit the *best available* man for the position, either internally or from the outside. Either way, in this sense, effective business management is a talent hunt.

If he is not available from within, let us not compound an inexcusable personnel-development felony by recruiting from within anyway. We must go outside the company, buy the best possible *track record*, and necessarily pay well for it. The exceptional overpriced man is the only really safe bargain around.

The track record of the best available man is his long history of outstanding cash-productive (CSA) results in a similar position, but with a company that outperforms ours (best competitor). He is successful there by definition, and probably happy, so we will have to headhunt. And we will offer him more than just a higher salary: he wants a piece of the action, and to achieve *glory* along with wealth if he succeeds.

Only the man's future boss can recruit and hire him, as we have noted. If it were done *above* the boss's level, or even if it just looked that way, an effective relationship between the two men will have been precluded before it began. The new man is being told that the organization does not have the confidence in his prospective boss to give him carte blanche in hiring his own people.

So his boss-to-be must master the art of recruiting the best man, because his success as a manager depends so heavily on it. This involves correctly evaluating: (1) the man's *résumé*; (2) *tests* that are professionally administered; (3) *references* covering his complete work history and education; and (4) *interviews* that are fully prepared beforehand. Here we do the asking and *listening*, and when he is gone we immediately make a written summary of the interview and our impressions and conclusions.

Recruiting can be much more effective if we first prepare an ideal *Position Guide* and a *Standard of Performance* related to it. The best available man will best fit this Position Guide, promising to fulfill its responsibilities and achieve its objectives better than other candidates.

Before receiving applications, also, we should prepare a *Position Specification*. It details precisely the requirements of the best-qualified man: his experience; schooling; aptitude; personality; contacts; types of references; and so forth. The Position Specification, together with the Position Guide and its Standard, provide a picture of our best available candidate that is detailed, accurate, and complete. And they are valuable screening tools for those who are helping us locate candidates for the position. But mostly, since they were prepared before we even met the candidate, they help us evaluate him objectively.

POSITION GUIDES FOR ORGANIZATIONAL CLARITY

Cash-productivity *objectives* are now being formulated in response to the Plan. Implementing *activities* are being sequenced. And we have structured, and recruited for, a maximum-efficiency *organization* to house these objectives and activities. Now we must clearly define the position responsibilities, authority, and standards of performance of each salaried employee in the organization. This is best done with the *Position Guide* and *Standard of Performance*, one possible style of which is shown below.

The Position Guide (Figure 2) is written by the man himself. After describing the purpose (objective) and scope of his position, he particularizes *quantitatively* each of his responsibilities—the 10 or so jobs for which he is paid a salary. These are the crucial $-C$, $+S$, and $-A$ elements of his position. He lists them in "20–80" priority order, with the responsibility of highest cash-generating impact described first.

At the right he notes his degree of authority, as 1, 2, or 3: (1) He performs this responsibility without telling anyone; (2) he does this but must then tell his supervisor; or (3) he performs this only after receiving his supervisor's permission.

In the *Standard of Performance* (Figure 3), for each responsibility he describes exactly the conditions that will exist when satisfactory performance has been attained. These are *measurable* conditions, described in terms of quantity, quality, costs, assets, and time. And the description corresponds to the quantitative wording of the responsibility, for which it is the standard of performance. On each quarterly review date, as we will see, he evaluates his Actual Performance of those responsibilities against the conditions enumerated in the Standards—just as he rates his progress toward each of his CSA objectives.

Responsibilities are not objectives, of course. They are the actual structure and substance of the position for which the man is paid a salary. The CSA objectives *emerge from* the man's position responsibilities. They transform the position from a routine company-running function to a dynamic cash-producing and company-*building* function. Position responsibilities *run* the company; objective achievement *builds* the company.

POSITION GUIDE _____ _____
                      (Position Description)   (Name)

Purpose (objective)
and scope of position:_____

_____

MY RESPONSIBILITY ("20-80": $-C, +S, -A$):   AUTHORITY*
                                                       (1, 2, or 3)

1)	
2)	
3)	
4)	
5)	
6)	
7)	
8)	

*(1) No notification; (2) O. K., but post supervisor; (3) Do only with permission.

Figure 2

Both must be done well and rewarded. The former is rewarded with continued employment at a salary, the latter with _promotions_ to higher-salary and higher-status positions.

The Position Guide performs an indispensable service: it clarifies each man's responsibilities in achieving his unit's objectives, as distinguished from everyone else's responsibilities. It powerfully boosts morale; prevents overlapping of work, or gaps in the work; and greatly helps coordination within and among the operating units of the company.

MY STANDARD OF PERFORMANCE

Satisfactory performance has been attained with respect to this responsibility when the following conditions exist in my area (quantity, quality, cost, assets, time):

1)

2)

3)

4)

5)

6)

7)

8)

MY ACTUAL PERFORMANCE

[Excellent (3); Very Good (2); Good (1); Poor (0)]

Quarter (19__)

1 2 3 4

Figure 3

EFFECTIVE POLICIES AND PROCEDURES

Formulating and updating *policy decisions* and *procedures* is the final organizational task needed to implement the Plan. Policy decisions supply everyone with standing answers to repetitive questions, and standing solutions to recurring problems. They are thus an enormous simplifier and time-saver. And they keep the peace among operating units whose functional dividing lines may not always be too clear. Approved policy decisions are corporate law, to be strictly complied with by everyone, in both letter and spirit.

Each manager is responsible for promptly recommending up the line new policies, and policy modifications, relating to the activities in his jurisdiction. Figure 4 shows a useful format for policy decisions. Its most important feature is probably the *Next review date*. This should never be longer than 12 months forward, so that the policy remains up to date.

Procedures also greatly facilitate the organization process and help to keep it simple. Policy Decisions and Position Guides describe *what* to do. Procedures describe *how* to do it. They detail the most effective way to do a job—the best practice of the moment. So they eliminate a tremendous amount of time that would otherwise be devoted to discovering and proving out the best way, over and over again. Since a Procedure is a standing decision with respect to routine work, it must be reviewed and revised frequently lest it discourage initiative and innovation. For writing up Procedures, we can use the *Policy* format and simply change "policy" to "procedure."

All of these organizational mechanisms and tools are now compressed into a convenient *Organization Manual*, which is distributed to everyone. It is divided into sections for each functional unit of the company—Manufacturing, Sales, Engineering, and so forth. And each such section is divided into its organizational subcomponents, properly index-tabbed for ready reference. A section contains: (1) a statement of the *purpose* of that unit, in achieving the Plan; (2) its *Organization Chart*; (3) *Position Guides* and *Standards of Performance* for each man; and (4) *Policy Decisions* and *Procedures* applicable to the unit.

The business has now been structured to maximize cash. No other consideration influenced the organizational pattern and framework, nor was any other needed. Such an organization focuses total corporate striking power narrowly on the single strategic objective, Pi.

This massive striking power is every employee *times ten*—or the explo-

POLICY DECISION

Subject: _____ Date _____

_____ Replaces _____

_____ Approved by _____

_____ Next review date _____

Objective or purpose (why):

_____

_____

_____

Responsibility (who):

_____

Policy (what, where, when):

1.

2.

3.

4.

5.

Figure 4

sive cash productivity of a company mobilized totally in terms of "20–80" CSA objectives.

An organizational network of interlocking and inviolate teams—into which only cash-motivated people have been recruited—houses and facilitates the achievement of $-C+S-A$. So the organization is an objective-achieving framework wherein $+S/C$ and $+S/A$ at all levels converge on the Plan's Pi and equity target.

But even the most brilliantly conceived organization will be frustrated if an effective *motivational* substance has not been introduced. This is the subject of our next chapter.

CHAPTER 21

MOTIVATING CASH PRODUCTIVITY

Our people will labor and persevere for the Cash Productivity Plan to the extent that they *participated* in its construction, so that it is their own; *visualize* its achievement, because they believe in it; and personally *identify* with its goals, whereby they attain their own goals. This is the substance of motivation, which is the ultimate generator of cash.

THE SUBSTANCE OF MOTIVATION

Participation in the construction of the Plan gives a man a personal stake in its achievement. So too does his participation in its objective-setting and organizational implementation. To the extent that the Plan and the means to its implementation are his own, so that a piece of himself is cemented into it, he will work hard to achieve it—much harder than if the same Plan were handed down from above.

And he will work harder still for the Plan if he believes in and can *visualize* the achievement of its fifth-year objectives. These objectives for the company and his own unit were "photographed" vividly in the Plan. He now sees them clearly, precisely, and constantly. He sees a more important company, and himself as more important in that company.

When every person thus maintains a fully-developed and fixed mental picture of the target year *as being already achieved*, we have set free the extraordinary power of the subconscious mind—as a *group* phenomenon. It surfaces as an irresistable force in the achievement of Plan objectives.

The subconscious mind is highly receptive and easily convinced of whatever is suggested to it, especially if done repetitively. Simple, repetitive affirmations and suggestions evoking a mental picture of the fifth-year objectives, powerfully activate the corporate subconscious. It enhances tremendously the visualization of and *belief in* the attainment of those objectives.

274

No opportunity should therefore be lost in dramatizing the fifth-year mental picture, by whatever means, especially in an emotional and exciting way: posters, photographs, slogans, pep meetings, and everything and anything that will serve to picture the goals vividly and dramatically. To see is to believe; and belief is the mightiest force of all.

But motivation must go one step further—beyond participation and visualization, to a personal *identification* with these group goals. Each man identifies with them so intimately and profoundly that they become his own. His generalized desire for their attainment has become a personal and therefore an intense desire. It is here specifically that visualization—to activate the corporate subconscious and strengthen belief in the achievement of objectives—will release irresistible motivational energies.

This personal identification with corporate goals, which triggers the motivational process, is rooted in every man's *craving for importance*.[1] He sees himself in the fifth-year company as a much more important person, in a specific way that is deeply meaningful to him and that he profoundly desires.

He can visualize clearly for himself in the fifth-year realization of Plan objectives: the recognition and esteem of associates and superiors; career accomplishment; personal dignity; a gratifying sense of belonging; financial and occupational security; and everything else that in one way or another comes simply from being more important.

But this importance attaches to him entirely because of his higher fifth-year *position* in the company—notably from the status intangibles and symbolism of the position. It is here, precisely, that he makes the crucial identifying connection between the company's and his *own* elevated fifth-year importance. Here, in the promotion process, is the engine of the motivational system.

To be more important, in a way that is crucial to him and that is there for all to see, he will contribute everything he has—and a lot extra he never thought he had—to achieving the Cash Productivity Plan. In its fulfillment are his own very real dreams fulfilled.

When all have thus participated, visualized, and identified, a motivational force of unparalleled cash-generating impact has been set free.

THE CASH CONTRIBUTION RATIO AS PERFORMANCE GAUGE

So motivated, each man will insist that his own contribution to the Plan be measured fairly, accurately, and promptly. And he will want to be recognized accordingly, in a manner that enhances his importance within and to the corporation.

[1]Which we first touched upon in Chapter 14 on cash creativity.

We have seen that the measure of a man's contribution to the Cash Productivity Plan, on which alone his rewards are based, can only be the *cash contribution ratios* (CCRs) that apply to his area of responsibility. These are his S/C and S/A ratios. There simply is no other basis for measuring his performance, because they measure the only contribution he is ever asked to make: to contribute, in his own unit, to the achievement of the Plan's Pi objective.

But except for a very few in the company who are also concerned with L/A, ECO, and ECA, everyone's operating objective is $+ CRE$.[2] And his contribution to it is measurable in terms of the CCRs, $+S/C$ and $+S/A$. These are in effect the components of CRE, profit margin multiplied by turnover.

So CRE = CCRs: the company's growth, defined by cash return on equity, is determined solely by the sum of all the cash contribution ratios (CCRs) throughout the organization and at every level.

The CCRs, as we have seen, are the *company's* sales divided by the *man's* costs and assets. We can express them as 12-month totals, to eliminate seasonality. Each month, 12-month sales are divided by the particular 12-month cost or by the present book value of the particular asset. This gives us the cost or asset CCR for that month.

CRE will be favorably affected to the extent that the overall ratios sales/costs and sales/assets increase. So the same is obviously true for the sales/cost and sales/asset ratios (CCRs) of *each function* of the company: Sales, Manufacturing, Engineering, Accounting, and so forth. It must therefore also be true for each subcomponent unit and department, as far down the line as we can realistically apply CCR ratios.

Thus, CRE = sales/costs × sales/assets *everywhere* in the company: $CRE = CCRs$. Since rewards or penalties are based exclusively on each man's contribution to Plan CRE, they must necessarily be based solely on the performance of his CCRs.

The CCRs will vary according to the type of business. For the typical manufacturing company, the overall ratios, which are then subdivided for the subfunctions down the line, might include the following:

Manufacturing. Sales/material costs; sales/labor costs; sales/overhead; sales/manufacturing costs; sales/manufacturing inventory; sales/manufacturing machinery; sales/plant; and so forth.

---

[2]This recalls our general Pi expression:

$$CRE = (S/C \times S/A \times L/A)(R);$$

$$Pi = CRE \times ECO \times ECA.$$

Engineering. Sales/engineering costs; sales/engineering assets; and so forth.

Sales Department. Sales/Sales Department costs; sales/finished and parts inventory; and so forth.

Accounting Department. Sales/Accounting costs; sales/receivables; sales/administrative costs; sales/prepayments; sales/office equipment; and so forth.

Here the Accounting function polices administrative costs and office equipment puchases throughout the company. So these CCRs are part of its own performance yardstick.

The same companywide sales volume is the numerator of all the CCRs, because all functions and employees contribute equally to sales. The sole purpose of *every* function and employee is to sell the company's products to the company's customers. They do this from the design stage where the product is created; through manufacture at the lowest cost, highest quality, and best delivery; to the final sale.

The Sales Department could not make the final sale if the product had been designed poorly or too expensively, or if it were manufactured at excessive cost or below-standard quality. Sales volume is a *company* effort: nobody's impact on sales can be greater or less than anyone else's.

So everyone's *measurable* contribution to cash productivity and CRE is his cost and asset *denominators*. As company sales rise, he contributes to the growth of CRE if he controls his costs and assets, so that his CCRs rise. If sales are steady, he contributes to the growth of CRE by reducing costs and assets, thereby increasing his CCRs. But if his CCR line is declining, under any circumstances, he has failed to control his costs or assets in relation to sales volume. To that extent he is undermining the company's cash productivity and cash return on equity.

The CRE contribution and performance of each function, which is the *only* long-term performance we are ever concerned with, is therefore measured in general by the following:

1. *Slope* of each CCR line. If rising, the CCR tends to make a contribution to the growth of CRE. If steady, its cash contribution is neutral in terms of corporate growth. And if declining, costs or assets are moving unfavorably against sales, thereby reducing cash contribution.

2. *Variance* in relation to the Planned CCR for that cost or asset item. Regardless of slope, an actual CCR higher than the corresponding Planned CCR means the function is making a higher cash contribution than originally planned. Conversely for below-Plan CCRs.

3. *BC comparison.* This was already included in item 2, at the Planning

stage, to the extent that the Planned CCRs were established with reference
to those of the best competitor (BC) companies. Nevertheless, a continuing
comparison of actual CCRs with the BCs is a useful double check. They
are compared as to slope and level, to the extent that BC data are available
(which usually are to a remarkable extent). How does the head of each of
our functions and departments compare, in CCR performance, with his
opposite number in above-average competitor companies?

Down to the tiniest organizational unit, therefore, the slope and level of
the CCRs relate each man's cost and asset *outflows* of cash to the
company's cash *inflows* from sales. This is all we are interested in or can
possibly be interested in, given the fundamental CRE direction of the
company to which the CCRs are the sole operating contributors.

A CCR should not be interpreted in an absolutistic way, of course, but
relatively and with reference to its own peculiar circumstances. Sometimes
a temporarily declining CCR means new assets or costs were incurred that
will eventually provide disproportionately large sales and cash improvements. Or a level CCR could mean that the maximum possible sales
volume (relative to BC) is already being generated by that asset or cost
category. And so forth. But in general, and in the typical situation, up is
good (cash-generating) and down is bad (cash-absorbing).

Performance evaluation in terms of cash productivity must also be
directed to positions that simply do not lend themselves to measurement
solely in terms of CCRs, if at all. So we need to use supplemental
measurements and evaluations. These *estimate* the man's cash contribution
and his probable impact on the CCRs of his unit. A first and obvious
approximation to his CCR impact is the extent to which he has set
challenging *CSA* objectives and achieved them. These objectives produce
cash in the form of $-C$, $+S$, and $-A$, as we saw, and thereby contribute
to his unit's CCRs.

A strong second approximation to the CCR is his performance of the
responsibilities (which have a high "20–80" priority order of cash-
generating impact) enumerated in his *Position Guide*, and on which he
evaluates himself in his *Standards of Performance*.

EVALUATING AND REWARDING CASH PRODUCTIVITY

Performance evaluation *must* be automatic, and might well be conducted
in a manner such as the following. On a fixed day, such as the first Friday
of each quarter, every employee has a 45-minute *CSA Review* meeting with
his supervisor. He previously completed and now submits an *Evaluation
Package* containing his (1) Standard of Performance, (2) CSA Objectives

Report, and (3) Cash Productivity Appraisal.

The CSA Review is a coaching and counseling session, as already noted in Chapter 20. Both men should be fully prepared and in agreement as to the topics of discussion, which center on problem objectives and areas in the three reports. The man does most of the talking and the supervisor *listens*. It is an opportunity to counsel and help him, not judge him: what is wrong, not who is at fault. This is the meeting, as we saw, at which the man also recommends new objectives and projects for the coming period.

The CSA Review is also an *evaluation* session. This is one of the most important responsibilities of every supervisor, and one for the performance of which he himself is strictly evaluated. He must promptly recommend either rewards or penalties based on each man's cash contribution, as determined objectively from the three reports. Failure to reward outstanding performance undermines morale and destroys performance. But a recommendation to reward a man should *never* be acceptable unless fully supported by performance measurements of the type set forth in these reports.

The first component of the Evaluation Package is the *Standard of Performance*, which we have discussed. The man rates his actual performance of each responsibility described in his Position Guide, from excellent (3) to poor (0). He had originally worded each responsibility in a specific and measurable way as to performance quantity, quality, costs, assets, and time. So there should now be no ambiguity and fuzziness about his actual performance.

The *CSA Objectives Report* tells us which objective formats the man has completed. For each objective, it provides the CSA dollar contribution $(-C, +S,$ or $-A)$. And it gives the man's total cash contribution from all completed objectives.

Finally, the *Cash Productivity Appraisal* is the man's summary of his performance. (1) He evaluates his CSA results, as disclosed by his CSA Objectives Report and his Standard of Performance. (2) Then he rates the performance of *each* of his CCRs, from excellent to poor. They are rated as to *slope* during the three months under review; *variance* above or below Plan; and how they compare with the corresponding *BC* companies' CCRs (which data was supplied to him beforehand).

And (3) finally, he comments on his methods for getting things done. This is a basis for determining the benefit (or harm) caused by the means he employs to achieve his cash-productivity ends. He may achieve all his objectives on target, but cause more disruption and ill-feeling in and around his area than it is worth. If so, this type of question at least raises the red flag for him. He is alerted to management's concern about means as well as ends.

The *supervisor* makes his evaluations and recommendations at the end of the Cash Productivity Appraisal, including actions to be taken with respect to the man's performance or assignment.

PROMOTION AS THE ENGINE OF THE MOTIVATIONAL SYSTEM

Each man's cash-contributing performance is evaluated regularly and objectively in this way, to determine his *importance* to CRE and therefore to the organization. It now remains for us to recognize that importance. Again recalling our earlier conclusion: By far the most effective way, and really the only way, to recognize a man is by *promoting* him to a position of higher importance. It gratifies the all-powerful craving for importance by publicly making explicit the *fact* of enhanced importance.

Promotion and the prospect of promotion, with all its status and financial accoutrements, therefore exerts the profoundest motivational impact. All at once a man is given overt recognition, an exhilarating sense of accomplishment, and a feeling of professional and personal development. Promotion is the reward he prizes much more highly than any other, including the accompanying salary increase by itself.

The larger office, deeper carpet, or fancier dining room gratifies his craving for importance directly, measurably, and for all to see. No other motivational energizer in the company's arsenal has anything like its clout and effectiveness, nor is there even a close second worthy of consideration.

It follows that promotions should proceed up the ladder within precisely graded and defined position *titles*. They must be consistent throughout the company, and recognized for what they actually are. An Assistant Department Head in one part of the organization is on the same salary and status level as one anywhere else.

The more positions we have and the finer the differentiation in grades, the more flexibility we have in promoting people. A moderate or average promotion moves a man up one grade, but a really important one can jump him two or more grades. And the more position gradations or levels we have, the less likely we are to exhaust the promotion possibilities for a good man.

Each position category must provide a level of salary, responsibility, prestige, and status that is higher than the position below it. And they must be commensurate with the cash-productivity contribution *inherent* in that position. That is, the position has been *rated* as to its cash-producing importance or impact within the organization, apart from the capabilities of the man who happens to occupy that positon. And the salary and status accoutrements are geared to its cash-productivity importance. This clear-cut delineation of pecking order is essential for motivational effectiveness.

A promotion is a move up to a higher *status* position. Increased salary is just one of many status symbols associated with the higher position, such as bigger office, company car, and special dining room. For the man, the money value of his salary is secondary to its role as an indication of his *ranking* among his fellows.

So the precise evaluation of positions and administration of salaries are crucial in enabling the man to judge what the company thinks of him as a cash contributor—of his *importance* to the firm in relation to others. That is, the precise evaluation of positions creates *confidence* in the validity of the system that determines a man's salary and, above all, status.

To maximize the motivational impact from promotion based on cash-productivity results, we must attract men to the company who thrive in this kind of environment. The qualified applicant understands clearly that either he will be promoted at the end of the first year or his employment will probably be terminated. It has the dual effect of helping to attract the entrepreneurial self-starters we want, and of keeping out the deadwood.

The promotion concept also requires that early in a man's career he be reviewed with special care, and weeded out if he is one who somehow got recruited by mistake. This meshes with a sanely administered "up or out" policy applicable throughout a man's career, which he wants and under which he thrives. We must at all cost maintain an environment in which good CSA performers are promoted promptly. The best men quit wherever nonperformers obstruct the promotion lines.

A promotion type of incentive system therefore also demands room at the top, to maintain the upward mobility of position occupants at all levels. Retirement at full pension should be mandatory at age 65 and optional at age 60. Pension income can be sweetened with deferred compensation, earned during the man's employment, for above-average cash contribution.

CUMULATING PROMOTIONAL INCENTIVES

The promotion structure motivates best when it is a hierarchy of *compounded incentives*. As one goes up the ladder, the incentives increase cumulatively. Each higher status level not only provides *more* of what the lower levels have—such as salary—but also new *kinds* of incentives. This means that the value of a man's total incentive package grows in a somewhat geometrical fashion, rather than arithmetically, as he climbs the ladder. He is getting more dollars and status from each type of incentive, but he is also enjoying more *types*.

For example, suppose that promotions in our company proceed upward through the following position *categories* (each containing many possible gradations or levels):

Hourly positions

Salary positions

Bonus positions: upper level Salary positions that also provide stock bonus compensation based on one's cash contribution

Officer positions: upper level Bonus positions

Stock option positions: upper level officer positions that *also* provide stock options.

The cumulative impact might perhaps be something like the following:

1. The *higher salary and status* of each higher position provides the underlying motivational substance.

2. The *necessity* of being promoted, or the fear of not being promoted, is an entirely separate (negative) reinforcement of the incentive to get promoted—in line with the policy of "up or out."

3. *Bonus positions*. Promotion into these higher Salary-level positions *also* provides stock bonus compensation. The man can now participate in the annual *Bonus Pool*, whose size increases geometrically with increases in the company's cash return on equity. For instance, if CRE is 10% this year, the stock deposited in the Bonus Pool (at market price or equity per share) amounts to 4% of cash flow. If cash flow next year increases to 12% of equity, the Bonus Pool will increase to 6% of cash flow. And so forth. Each higher percentage of CRE thus calls for a donation to the Bonus Pool of a higher *percentage* of the higher cash flow.

The Pool is thus based on the *return* that can be generated with the company's (stockholders') equity. But the stockholders' investment in the company is subject to much higher risks than if the same dollars were in high-quality bonds or mortgages—at 9%, for instance. To compensate for their equity risk, a much higher net return than 9% is required.

So the CRE floor, below which there is no Bonus contribution, must be the external *safe* return available to stockholders. If salaried management and other Bonus personnel can produce no more than a 9% net return on equity, they are not compensating stockholders for the much higher equity risk. They are not performing their jobs or earning their salaries very well —to say nothing of being entitled to bonuses. But to the extent that management provides stockholders with a net return of *more* than 9%, in this case, they provide risk compensation for which they in turn merit additional (Bonus) compensation.

4. The *lower limit* of Bonus positions varies each year with the *amount* of the Bonus Pool, thus providing a further compounding of incentives. If CRE is high this year and the Bonus Pool is correspondingly large, Bonus participation extends to lower salary levels than it did last year. If the Pool gets smaller, higher and higher salary levels are deprived of Bonus participation. This is a separate and independent incentive to make the Pool large, so that *our* position level will participate in it this year.

5. *Participation* of each man in the Bonus Pool is determined solely by his own CSA contribution to the size of the Pool, which further compounds his cash-productivity incentive. That is, his CSA results contribute both to the *size* of the Pool and to his percentage *share* of that Pool. So his percentage share is based on the degree to which he contributed to the size of the Pool, through $-C$, $+S$, and $-A$.

6. Bonus payments tend to be a *higher percentage* of a man's salary at the higher positions than at lower ones. This is because higher positions have been rated as, and inherently are, higher cash contributors to the company than are lower positions. It further compounds the incentive to get promoted to the higher Bonus positions, where a man's organizational capacity to earn substantial Bonuses is increased relative to the size of his salary.

7. *Common stock* bonuses, as opposed to cash payments, give a further compounding thrust to the promotion incentive. By conferring ownership and partnership status on the recipient, stock provides a motivational influence that is independent because it is inherent in the *form* of payment and nothing else. And it also provides him with potential additional compensation in the form of dividend income and capital gains.

8. *Installment payments* of the Bonus, over many subsequent months or years, is a further (negative) incentive. The man will perform well and keep his job, lest he be denied substantial amounts of Bonus stock that he has not "earned out."

9. The top-level *Stock option* positions provide this coveted incentive in addition to all the other forms of compensation. Higher market prices (or book value in the case of a private company) reflect increased cash flow to which the man contributed, and it is an additional compounding of the promotion incentive. The amount and value of options granted to a man each year is determined, as are Bonus payments, by the amount of his CSA contribution to *CRE*.

Publicity must underline the incentive program, to maximize its importance-conferring impact. Every employee is instructed in and is repeatedly reminded of the entire incentive package. Down to the lowest salary levels, employees have copies of the Bonus Plan and the Stock Option Plan. And they are told each month the size of the accumulating Bonus Pool, whether or not they share in it. Names of Bonus and option participants are publicized. And all promotions are promptly and liberally recognized in the company and public press and other media, and by recognition dinners, awards, and the like. Publicity thus makes the program of compounded incentives a truly powerful motivational influence throughout the company, from the lowest hourly levels to the very top.

We have *planned* cash productivity. We have *organized* and *coordinated* our people to implement the Plan. And they are now powerfully *motivated* to achieve its five-year cash and equity targets. We are implementing the strategy of cash, that is, and roaring ahead toward the challenging objective of Pi.

But unless we carefully *control* cash results against Plan, failure of greater or lesser severity will be an ever-present threat. Inadequate cash control has been the ruin of many an otherwise superbly managed company.

So crucial a subject is it, in fact, that all of Part Seven will now be devoted to the control of cash productivity results.

PART 7

SAFEGUARDING CASH PRODUCTIVITY: CONTROLLING RESULTS AGAINST PLAN

CHAPTER 22

THE MECHANICS OF CASH
AND LIQUIDITY CONTROL

To achieve our Pi rate of corporate growth, the strategy of cash needs an effective mechanism to control results against the Cash Productivity Plan. Otherwise the best organizational and motivational structure erected to achieve that Plan will eventually prove useless.

Without proper controls, results may fall short of expectations. We learn too late that we have provided too much physical, financial, personnel, and other resources, to the detriment of profits. Or we may exceed expectations without anyone paying enough attention, and now find we have fewer resources than we need.

Worse yet, and more typical, we may discover that we are ahead of expectations in some areas and behind in others. Since all corporate areas are functionally interdependent, chaos reigns supreme and profits are hurt while the different sections of the business are put back in gear.

So this final Part Seven looks at the ways of forecasting cash variances against Plan, analyzing the forecasted variances, and preventing them from actually happening. In this and the next chapter we examine the various financial statements, and those of cash and liquidity velocity, that are periodically forecast against the corresponding Plan statements. And in the final three chapters we will analyze the forecasted statements for cash and CRE impact, whereby variances can best be prevented and the strategy of cash kept solidly on track.

QUANTITATIVE CONTROLS: FINANCIAL VERSUS NONFINANCIAL

Results are controlled *quantitatively*. They are precisely measurable against, and can be unambiguously interpreted in terms of, their corresponding objectives. So-called nonquantitative "controls" are a contradiction in terms. These are on-the-spot surprise visits, operation review meetings, and many other ways to keep tabs on what is going on. They are crucial management tools supplementary to the control process. But they are not a part of it, and management would regard them as such only at its peril.

Quantitative controls are financial and nonfinancial: *Financial controls* are expressed in the accounting language of our various financial statements as dollars of cash (sales, costs, assets, and liabilities). *Nonfinancial* controls relate to all objectives that are expressed in numbers of anything besides dollars of cash: numbers of transactions, errors, customer bad debts, units produced, and so forth.

If we are a well-run investment brokerage firm, for instance, we use many types of nonfinancial controls. To forecast the earnings impact on our financial statements of each *customer*, we monitor the ratio of his small (unprofitable) transactions with our firm to his total transactions. We forecast each *salesman's* profit value to our business with such quantitative but nonfinancial ratios as his transactions/customer, slow-paying trades/total trades, unprofitable trades/total trades, and so forth. And we anticipate the impact of the "back office" on our financial statements with error ratios broken down by departments and individuals; effectiveness ratios, such as failure to deliver securities/failure to receive; and many others.

These nonfinancial controls are really the province of the *objectives* process throughout the organization, as discussed in Chapter 20. The objective format is written quantitatively, of course, so that subsequent results can be measured accurately and unambiguously. Sooner or later, these nonfinancial quantitative results are reflected in financial results. But control must be explicit and unremitting in both areas.

NONQUANTITATIVE "CONTROLS": EYEBALL-TO-EYEBALL

Financial controls and quantitative nonfinancial controls (objectives) must be supplemented with the *personal encounter* type of nonquantitative "control." They are not controls, as we have said, because they are not quantitative and therefore cannot generate measurable variances. But they give us the crucial eyeball-to-eyeball verification (or lack of verification) of the validity and effectiveness of our formalized information inflow, of which the control mechanism is a vital component.

Suppose that our president now and then makes unannounced and unaccompanied visits, each time to a different department. He chats with the men on the floor or the people in the office. The resulting information breakthrough is a marvel to behold. The boss just popped in all by himself and is talking with some of the men, which is a morale booster apart from anything else. Soon they open up to him and he receives, along with the gripes and irrelevancies, a flood of extremely valuable grassroots information. And he gets a feel of what is actually going on behind all those quantitative reports he receives upstairs.

The president obviously must never undercut the immediate supervisor of these men by making spot decisions or commitments to them, especially if the gripes are legitimate. Back in his office later on, he simply asks the same questions of his own immediate subordinate, who (needless to say) telegraphs them down to the supervisor of the men on the floor. By the time the answers and corrective solutions come back to the president, things have tightened up considerably down in that area. And they have probably tightened up in many of the surrounding areas if not the entire company as it becomes known that the head man makes unscheduled and unattended visits with the hourly people and lower office staffs.

Informal personal encounters such as this have endless possibilities as a device to supplement the formal control mechanism. *Meetings* of all kinds, for instance, can either be very effective control supplements or largely a waste of time. The difference often boils down to something as simple as a *minutes-agenda*. It is the minutes of this meeting and the agenda of the next meeting, that are distributed soon after adjournment. Then everyone knows what he must be prepared to discuss at the next meeting, which usually proves to be productive for that reason alone. And everyone remembers and uses the information and decisions generated in this meeting.

Policy adherence meetings, conducted regularly by the head man and his team, are a very useful informal control procedure. The meeting draws out and evaluates the facts as to deviations from existing policies. It initiates corrective measures or calls for a beneficial modification (or even elimination) of the policy.

Policies and procedures, after all, are existing *decisions* that apply to recurring situations: the same decision does not have to be made every time that situation is faced by anyone. So they are "control" devices against which performance is measured, just like any other control device. The policy must be *enforced*, via the adherence meeting, or scrapped and replaced with something more appropriate. There can never be a middle ground or gray area in performance control, or the control system itself will inevitably collapse.

THE THREE TIERS OF CASH CONTROL: FORECAST, ANALYZE, PREVENT

Yet control is *not* a matter of measuring and evaluating performance against objectives, however peculiar a statement this may first appear to be. A control system that precisely measures performance against objectives and Plan, promptly and faithfully, is a poor control system. It tells us promptly and faithfully where a fire has broken out, so we can with marvelous efficiency dash over and extinguish it. Countless managements, hurting for a better control mechanism, work long and hard toward this type of system as an ideal to be achieved. And companies that have achieved it consider themselves lucky to have gone as far as possible in the control process.

The essence of effective control, on the contrary, is anticipating and *preventing* fires—rather than receiving prompt information about one that has broken out. There are indeed *three tiers* or levels along which the control process moves simultaneously.

First, we regularly *forecast* the Plan's financial statements and nonfinancial objectives, whereby variances are anticipated. Second, we *analyze* and evaluate the CRE impact of the forecasted variances, by means of ratio and trend computations. And third, we *prevent* the anticipated variances from occurring, with exception-control tools such as cash variance reports (CVRs).

These CVR tools preventively solve adverse cumulative variances from base 0 of the Plan to the forecast target. That is, a CVR initiates preventive solutions and releases counteracting forces in time to offset and "correct" a forecasted variance from Plan.

As we noted, therefore, the chapters of the present Part Seven are organized and sequenced in terms of these three tiers of control: *forecasting* variances, *analyzing* variances, and *preventing* variances.

FORECASTING CASH VARIANCES

Anticipating *nonfinancial* quantitative variances, in the objective formats, was discussed in Chapter 20 on organization—especially the use of CVRs during quarterly review meetings between the man and his supervisor. Anticipating *financial* variances is the parallel activity of forecasting the company's various financial statements each month—such as by months for the next 12 months and by quarters for the following year. Each month's revised forecast of the financial statements *anticipates variances* against the corresponding statements contained in the Cash Productivity Plan.

This distinction between *plan* and *forecast* is fundamental to the control process. The Plan is fixed and unchanging as to the cumulative results to be achieved by each organizational segment to which it applies, measured from base 0 at the start of year 1. By the end of year 5, we will have achieved the Plan's total five-year requirements as to sales, cash flow, and the other operating magnitudes. We will have thereby achieved the fifth-year target *equity*, which is absolutely fixed and final—as are the cumulative five-year operating magnitudes that produce it. At any interim point in time, we *know* from the Plan what our cumulative performance from base 0 must be.

The Plan, after all, is achievable (BC) performance based on what comparable companies in our industry are *now* doing. And it was constructed with the full participation and concurrence of those responsible for its achievement. We therefore regularly *forecast* actual results against the fixed and achievable results called for in the Plan: we *anticipate variances* against Plan, and initiate counteracting solutions to prevent them from occurring. The sole purpose of forecasts is to keep us on Plan.

We have already examined the control of sales cash, mainly in Chapter 12, for the specific purpose of short-term breakeven analysis. Now let us look at control as a comprehensive process that locks total cash productivity into the long-term Plan. We do this, as noted, by regularly forecasting all of our financial results, and comparing them with those called for in the Plan.

Our sample Cash Productivity Plan in Chapter 19 included seven such financial statements, some of which were merely listed there by name. Forecasting cash variances, the first tier of our control system, might therefore involve predicting these seven interconnected statements against the corresponding Plan statements for that period of time. They are:

1. *Functional Forecasts*, or the budget for each function of the company (Manufacturing, Sales, Engineering, and so forth).

2. *Statement of Net Cash Impact* (NCI), a modified Statement of Cash Receipts and Disbursements. And *Statement of Cash Velocity*, which merely transposes the NCI Statement into a flow of funds sequence of cash productivity and reinvestment.

3. *Income Statement*.

4. *Balance Sheet*.

5. *Liquidity Analysis* of the balance sheet, showing changes in the composition and liquidity of working capital, and its sources and uses.

6. *Working Capital Velocity*, or the production and reinvestment of working capital.

7. *Liquidity Velocity*, or *cash* productivity and reinvestment.

We regularly forecast each of these statements, but in finer detail, against that period's corresponding Plan statement (which was necessarily phrased in much more general terms).

Let us look at each one, using an oversimplified illustration. Our mythical little company is fashioned around operating assumptions that in practice are simplistic and even a bit unrealistic, but which nevertheless illuminate all the basic principles involved. The oversimplicity assists in a clearer explanation of them. Only a Manufacturing Forecast (budget) is provided, for instance, rather than complicating our example with the other operating department budgets.

All the statements of our tiny company are presented in a natural forecasting sequence, in Tables 28 to 38, in this and the next chapter. They trace *cash* from its primal generation in the Manufacturing Forecast to its final disposition in the Forecast of Liquidity Velocity (or cash productivity and reinvestment).

The development of each statement is described in its Explanation column at the right. So our comments in the text will be brief, and confined to the less obvious items and relationships. The lines (items) at the left are numbered continuously from 1 to 157, to connect all the tables in a continuous and logical sequence.

Statements that are additive or supplementary, rather than in the main line of development, are numbered parenthetically. For instance, Cash Velocity (Table 31) is merely a variation of the preceding statement of Net Cash Impact (whose numbering ends with line 43); so it starts as 43.1. The Income Statement later continues the main line of development; so its numbering starts with 44.

THE FUNCTIONAL FORECAST

We begin with a Manufacturing Forecast in Table 28. The sales forecast (line 1) is the shipments forecast arrived at jointly by the Sales Department and the Manufacturing Department. It was probably based in part on a scatter diagram or statistical correlation over time between the company's sales and industry sales, Gross National Product, and other pertinent aggregates. And more specifically, the sales forecast was based on a comparison with previous periods of the size and profitability of our backlog of unfilled orders, by customers and products. The sales and profits generated by previous backlogs indicate what we can get from our present one.

The *unit forecast* (line 2) is based on the selling price for our product of $12 per unit. We have assumed that *starting inventory* (line 3) will always be 60% of anticipated unit sales. So in January we start with 3000 units of inventory (60% of 5000).

We therefore need 2000 units of inventory (line 4), plus an ending inventory (line 5) of 3600 units (60% of February's sales forecast of 6000 units (line 2 of February).

We must therefore produce *5600 units* (line 6)—the unit forecast of 5000 less the starting inventory already on hand of 3000, plus the ending inventory required for next month of 3600.

The example assumes that management has not yet converted to direct costing, advocated in Chapter 13, and is on a full-absorption basis. Readers who depend on full absorption in their firms will find this helpful. Those who do not, internally, can simply skip the additional full-absorption details, which are confined mainly to the table's footnotes.

The *standard cost* (line 7) of producing the 5600 units is $8/unit, or $44,800. The $8 is derived from the standard manufacturing cost computation in footnote *a*, based on standard output of 5000 units/month.

The $8 of manufacturing cost includes standard overhead charged to production of $10,000/5,000 units, or $2 (line *a*.5). For 5600 units of required output, overhead thus totals $11,200. But standard overhead charged to production is only $10,000, regardless of production volume. So $1200 will be *overabsorbed*, reducing cost of goods from $44,800 (line 7) to $43,600 (line 9). This computation is summarized in footnote *b*.

The $1200 of overabsorbed overhead (line 8) is the reduction of fixed cost per unit due to the higher unit production (5600, rather than 5000 at standard), which is now spread over the *same* $10,000 of standard overhead. Dividing the reduced cost of goods manufactured of $43,600 (line 9) by the 5600 units of production, gives us an adjusted cost per unit of $7.80 (line 9.1).

Our ending inventory (line 10) will therefore be valued at $28,100, or 3600 units of ending inventory (line 5) multiplied by the adjusted cost per unit of $7.80.

This will now affect our material purchase needs. The 5600 units of production require 3 pieces/unit of direct material, at $1 each (*a*.1), or $16,800 (line 11). The required ending materials inventory (line 12) is February's 7200 units of production (line 6) multiplied by 3 pieces at $1, or $21,600. So we will need $38,400 of material ($16,800 plus $21,600), on line 13, less the $16,800 of beginning inventory (line 14), or required materials purchases (line 15) of $21,600.

FORECASTING NET CASH IMPACT AND CASH VELOCITY

Next, Table 30 assimilates the data from the Manufacturing Forecast, Table 28 (and from the other functional forecasts). It shows how they will produce *cash* inflows and outflows in the form of receipts and disbursements.

The cash to be received from the collection of receivables each month (line 16) is based on Table 29, which is a Collection Experience Table. In

Table 28 Functional Forecasting of the Cash Sources

	Line	J	F	M	A	Explanation
1.	Sales forecast	$60,000	$72,000	$96,000	$108,000	Given.
2.	Unit forecast (units)	5,000	6,000	8,000	9,000	At $12/unit selling price.
3.	Starting inventory (units)	−3,000	3,600	4,800	5,400	60% of unit sales, line 2, was previously produced.
4.	Inventory required (units)	2,000	2,400	3,200	3,600	Line 2 less line 3.
5.	Ending inventory (units)	+3,600	4,800	5,400	6,000	60% of next month's sales, line 2.
6.	Production required (units)	5,600	7,200	8,600	9,600	Line 4 + line 5.
7.	Standard cost of goods manufactured[a]	44,800	57,600	68,800	Etc.	Units produced, line 6, ×$8 standard cost per unit (a. 6).
8.	Burden (OH) underabsorbed (overabsorbed)[b]	(1,200)	(4,400)	(7,200)		Units, line 6, ×$2 of absorbed standard OH less $10,000 of standard OH (a. 5).
9.	Adjusted cost of goods manufactured	43,600	53,200	61,600		Standard cost, line 7, less burden overabsorbed, line 8.
9.1	Cost per unit	7.80	7.40	7.15		Adjusted cost, line 9, + units produced, line 6 (rounded).
10.	Ending inventory value	28,100	35,500	38,600		Ending inventory, line 5, × cost per unit, line 9.1.
11.	Material used	16,800	21,600	25,800		Units produced, line 6, ×3 pieces (a.1). Last month's materials purchases, line 15.
12.	Ending materials inventory	+21,600	25,800	28,800		Next month's production, line 6, ×3 pieces at $1/piece (a. 1).
13.	Materials required for production	38,400	47,400	54,600		Material used this month, line 11, + ending inventory required, line 12.

| 14. | Beginning inventory | −16,800 | 21,600 | 25,800 |
| 15. | Materials purchases | $21,600 | $25,800 | $28,800 |

Line 11. This is last month's ending inventory, line 12.

Material required, line 13, less beginning inventory, line 14, × $1/unit.

Standard costs per unit, computed on the basis of *5,000 units per month*:

a.1 Direct material	3 pieces at $1.00	$3.00
a.2 Direct labor	1 hour at $2.00	2.00
a.3 Variable costs	$1.00/unit	1.00
a.4 Total variable costs		$6.00
a.5 Fixed costs	$10,000/month	2.00
a.6 Standard cost per unit		$8.00

^bBurden overabsorbed in January (line 8):

Explanation

b.1 *Standard* cost of goods manufactured	$44,800	Line 7: 5600 units produced, line 6, × $8/unit standard costs, line a.6.
b.2 Burden absorbed by 5600 units of production	11,200	5600 × $2/unit standard burden, line a.5.
b.3 Less: standard burden	−10,000	5000 × $2, line a.5.
b.4 Burden overabsorbed	(1,200)	Burden absorbed by 5600 units at $2, less $10,000 standard burden (5000 units at $2). That is, an additional 600 units (5600 − 5000) × $2 of burden was absorbed, or $1200.

Table 29 Forecasting Cash Collections: Collection Experience Table[a]

Line	O (000)	N (000)	D (000)	J (000)	F (000)	M (000)	Explanation
15.1 Sales (receivables generated)	$60.0	$50.0	$50.0	$60.0	$72.0	$96.0	O, N, and D are actual; J, F, and M are from line 1 forecast.
Collections of receivables							
10% of this month's sales	6.0	5.0	5.0	6.0	7.2	9.6	
70% of last month's sales	—	42.0	35.0	35.0	42.0	50.4	
15% of sales made 2 months ago	—	—	9.0	7.5	7.5	9.0	
4% of sales made 3 months ago	—	—	—	2.4	2.0	2.0	
(1% uncollected)							
15.2 Total cash receipts	6.0	47.0	49.0	50.9	58.7	71.0	
15.3 Net receivables outstanding	54.0	3.0	1.0	9.1	13.3	25.0	Sales less cash receipts, line 15.1 less 15.2.
15.4 Cumulative net receivables	54.0	57.0	58.0	67.1	80.4	105.4	Receivables outstanding, cumulated.

[a] A useful alternative method of estimating receivables collections is to apply last month's receivables/sales experience (or that of the same month last year) to next month's estimated sales. For example:

Estimated *February* cash collections (000)

Sales, January	$ 60	
Receivables, January 31	67.1	
Receivables/sales, January	112%	
Days sales outstanding (112% of 31 days in the month)	34.7	days
Receivables, January 31	67.1	
Plus: forecasted sales, February	+72.0	
Plus: gross receivables on February 28	139.1	
Less: estimated receivables on February 28 112% (January receivables/sales), or 34.7 days/31 days, of $72 February sales	−81.0	
Plus: estimated bad debts	58.1	
Less estimated cash discounts		
Total	$ 58.1	

This compares with $58.7 of February cash receipts, in the table.

297

Table 30 The Forecast of Net Cash Impact (NCI)

	Line	J	F	M	Explanation
	Cash Inflow				
16.	S: Collections of receivables	$50,900	$58,700	$71,000	Forecast based on Table 29, line 15.2.
17.	− A: Disposals of assets, etc.	—	140,000	—	Sale of idle plant. From Capital Budget (not shown).
18.	+ L: Long-term borrowing	—	—	—	None.
19.	+ E: Sale of stock to key employees	—	—	20,000	Quarterly purchase plan.
20.	Total cash *inflow*	$50,900	$198,700	$91,000	Sum of lines 16 through 19.
	Cash Outflow				
21.	C: Payment of trade payables	$20,000	$21,600	$25,800	Materials purchases last month, line 15. Direct materials.
22.	Direct labor	11,200	14,400	17,200	Units produced, line 6, × $2 direct labor per unit, line *a*.2.
23.	Variable costs	5,600	7,200	8,600	Units × $1 of variable costs.
24.	Fixed costs	2,000	2,000	2,000	Assumed (supervisory, insurance, rents, excises, etc.). (Burden − fixed costs = noncash charges and accruals.)
25.	Selling, engineering, and administrative	13,000	14,000	15,000	From respective departmental forecasts (not shown).
26.	Taxes	—	—	15,000	Quarterly payment.
27.	Total costs	51,800	59,200	83,600	
28.	+ A: New manufacturing equipment	10,000	—	—	From Capital Budget.
29.	New office equipment	—	—	15,000	From Capital Budget.
30.	− L: Principal payments on mortgage	5,000	5,000	5,000	Monthly amortization.
31.	Term loan prepaid		100,000		
32.	− E: Dividend payments	—	—	—	None.
33.	Repurchase of common stock	—	5,000	—	
34.	Total cash *outflow*	66,800	169,200	103,600	
35.	*Operating Cash Impact (OCI)*	(5,900)	(5,500)	(17,600)	Table 29, line 16, less costs (line 27) and fixed outlays (e.g., monthly amortization (line 30).
36.	*Net Cash Impact (NCI)*	(15,900)	29,500	(12,600)	Cash inflow, line 20, less cash outflow, line 34.

Table 30 (*Continued*)

Line	J	F	M	Explanation
Cash summary				
37. Cash, start of month	25,000	20,000	25,000	From line 43.
38. Net cash impact	(15,900)	29,500	(12,600)	Line 36.
39. Cash balance	9,100	49,500	12,400	Line 37 plus (minus) line 38.
40. Required level	20,000	25,000	25,000	Based on estimated sales and cash needs.
41. Cash over (under) required level	(10,900)	24,500	(12,600)	Line 39 less line 40.
42. Short-term borrowing (repayment): +L(−L)	10,900	(24,500)	12,600	To bring cash balance, line 39, up (or down) to required level, line 40.
43. Cash balance, end of month	20,000	25,000	25,000	Cash balance, line 39, plus or minus borrowing, line 42.

February, for instance, the company will generate sales (and therefore receivables) of $72,000 (line 15.1). This produces total cash receipts, in accordance with the collection experience percentages indicated, of $58,700 (line 15.2, which is later carried to line 16). So we will have net receivables outstanding of $13,300 (line 15.3), and cumulative receivables (the extent to which sales exceed collections) of $80,400 (line 15.4).

The NCI Statement, Table 30, is also fed by the Capital Budget (not shown) with $140,000 of cash to be generated in February from the disposal of assets (line 17). And $20,000 of cash will come in March from the sale of stock (line 19). Total *cash inflow* (line 20) is thus the sum of S, −A, +L, and +E (lines 16 to 19).

Cash outflow (lines 21 to 34) is the exact opposite: C, +A, −L, and −E. Total costs (line 27) come directly from the Manufacturing and other functional forecasts. The other cash outlow items (lines 28 to 33) are various assumptions we have introduced to provide some depth of cash experience.

Operating cash impact (line 35) is the portion of cash flow that is operational and recurring. It is the difference between collections (line 16), and costs (line 27) plus recurring outlays such as monthly amortization (line 30).

Net cash impact (line 36) is the *total* cash result of all the company's expected inflows and outflows of cash, recurring and nonrecurring. It is the difference between total cash inflow (line 20) and outflow (line 34).

Now we bring all the cash flows in our forecast down to a convenient

Table 31 The Cash Velocity Forecast (Cash Productivity and Reinvestment, Cash Basis)

43.1	*Cash balance, start*				
	Cash *produced* by				
	Operations:				
43.2	Collections of receivables (S)	$ 58,700			
43.3	Less: Total cash costs (C)	(59,200)		(500)	[0.5]
43.4	− A: Decreases in *long-term assets*			140,000	(100.5)
43.5	+ L: Increases in *current debt*			—	
43.6	+ E: Increases in *equity:*				
	Sale of stock to employees			—	
43.7	Total cash produced				
	Cash *reinvested* in:				
	+ A: Increases in *long-term assets:*				
43.8	New office equipment			—	
43.9	− L: Decreases in *current debt*	24,500	(17.6)		
	Decreases in *long-term debt:*				
43.10	Payments on mortgage	5,000	(3.6)		
43.11	Term loan repaid	100,000	(71.8)	129,500	(93.0)
	− E: Decreases in *equity*:				
43.12	Repurchase of common stock			5,000	(3.6)
43.13	Less: Total cash reinvested				
43.14	Net cash produced (reinvested)				
43.15	*Cash balance, end*				

Cash Summary. Starting with $25,000 of cash at the beginning of January (line 37), we adjust for the net cash impact (line 38), to give the cash balance (line 39). We have estimated our required level of cash to be $20,000 in January and $25,000 in the subsequent two months (line 40). So we will need to borrow or repay short-term loans in the amounts that we are under or over requirements (line 42). This results in our cash balance at the close of the month (line 43), which becomes our starting cash for the new month (line 37).

The Forecast of Cash Velocity, in Table 31, is a valuable supplement to Net Cash Impact, from which it is entirely derived. But it restates NCI in a format that is more usable for purposes of cash strategy.

Starting with February's anticipated NCI cash balance of $20,000 (line 37), it shows cash dissipated in February and March by *operations*, or S − C (line 43.3). It shows cash generated by reductions in *assets* (− A); by increases in *debt* (+ L); and by increases in *equity* (+ E) (lines 43.4 to 43.6).

Table 31 (*Continued*)

February				March		Explanation[a]
$ 20,000				$ 25,000		Line 43
	$ 71,000					16
	(83,600)	(12,600)	[63.0]			27
	—					17
		12,600	(63.0)			42
		20,000	(100)			19
139,500	(100)			20,000	(100)	
		15,000	(75.0)			29
						42
		5,000	(25.0)			30
						31
		—				33
− 134,500	(96.5)			− 20,000	(100)	
$ 5,000	(3.5)			0		
$ 25,000				$ 25,000		Same as line 43

[a] Entirely from *NCI*, Table 30.

They will provide total February cash productivity of $139,500 (line 43.7).

This cash will be *reinvested* in new assets (+A) and in the reduction of debt (−L) and equity (−E), which in February totals $134,500 (line 43.13). We produced $139,500. So the final cash balance will be increased by $5,000 of net cash produced, to $25,000 (line 43.15). This corresponds with line 43 of the NCI statement, showing $25,000 at the end of February.

The Forecast of Cash Velocity also gives the relative percentage *importance* of the various productive sources and reinvestments of cash. Total cash produced is *100%* (line 43.7), of which each item of cash produced and cash reinvested is a percentage.

The $139,500 of total cash to be produced in February will be supplied entirely (100.5%) by the sale of an idle plant for $140,000 (line 43.4). And 93% of this cash will be reinvested in the reduction of debt (43.11).

In March, all the $20,000 of cash produced (43.7) came from the sale of stock to employees (43.6). It was reinvested in office equipment (75%) and a mortgage repayment (25%), on lines 43.8 and 43.10.

The Net Cash Impact and the Cash Velocity Forecasts give us an excellent picture of the company's raw cash potential. They are on a cash basis rather than accrual basis. This is our *bill-paying* ability, which is sometimes the most important thing we can know about our company. But they do not give the complete cash picture; they ignore accrual-basis inflows and outflows that will very quickly add to or subtract from spendable cash.

Sales are ignored, for instance, in favor of a higher or lower amount of cash collections—though the shipments have been made and will soon be collected as cash. Cash statements do not include accounts payable, taxes payable, accrued expenses, and other noncash liabilities. But they do include a note payable that produced immediate cash. They do include asset increases that were paid for with cash, such as receivables and inventory. These were accounted for in the operating section, as total cash costs (lines 27 of NCI and 43.3 of Cash Velocity).

We gain much by converting the Manufacturing Forecast and the other functional budgets into these narrower cash-basis forecasts. This is dramatized by operating cash impact and net cash impact (lines 35 and 36 of NCI), and by the operations section of the Cash Velocity Forecast (43.3). They are quite gloomy about actual, spendable cash. But our accrual-basis Income Statement, as we will soon see, predicts a highly profitable operating situation. Had we skipped the cash basis analysis—and gone directly from the Manufacturing Forecast to the Income Statement—our very adverse operating cash impact (line 35) would have been missed completely.

What the cash-basis forecasts are telling us, which the accrual-basis Income Statement is not, is that receivables collections will be too low. Soaring monthly sales mean that collections will trail costs, and cash flow will be negative. For any month, that is, collections will be related to previous months' *lower* sales. So this month's collections will be less than its sales. But costs are geared to *this* month's sales. So the cash impact this month is negative.

Any company, but especially one that is growing, therefore ignores cash-basis forecasts at its peril. They are a crucial decision-making tool for anticipating when and by how much our cash will be tight or excessive. We can then take proper corrective steps, and we can accurately forecast seasonal borrowing and repayment. Also, we can see *where* cash will flow during each month—inventory, advertising, or wherever—so that our delivery and payment schedules can be timed efficiently.

PROJECTING BALANCE SHEET CASH

The Projected Balance Sheet in Table 32 is a valuable supplement to Net Cash Impact, whose accuracy it also verifies.

We simply take the forecasted sales at a seasonal or long-term date when cash requirements will peak, and construct the balance sheet needed to produce those sales. A first approximation is to compute the present *percentage of sales* of each asset and liability, and apply that percentage to the projected sales volume. This gives us the projected balance sheet asset and liability items.

Column 1 starts with the company's February Balance Sheet (derived later, in Table 34) and its annual sales of $860,000. We then compute the percentages of $860,000 for each asset and current liability (column 2).

Finally, each percentage is applied to the $1,400,000 of *projected* sales next year (column 3), to give the assets and liabilities needed to produce those sales. It is next February's Balance Sheet.

Current receivables of $80,000, for example, are 9.3% of sales. Applying 9.3% to next year's $1,400,000 sales forecast results in projected receivables of $130,000. Fixed assets and long term debt are derived from plant engineering estimates and the debt amortization schedule.

We now refine and adjust these broad percentage-of-sales estimates, such as for indicated changes in the receivables/sales ratio. The inventory requirement might be tightened up by means of a specific computation: present inventory + purchases up to the forecast target date + value to be added in manufacturing − cost of goods sold = inventory value at the target date (at cost, not selling price). And an alternative fixed assets estimate might be: present net fixed assets + expected additions − depreciation.

We also refine or adjust liabilities projected to the target date, before giving effect to external financing. Accounts payable are closely geared to our purchase schedules and terms, less the estimated payables liquidated during the period. And accruals such as wages payable are tightened up against known production schedules and other budgets.

The Projected Balance Sheet needed to produce sales of $1,400,000 thus has total assets of $620,000, against which are total liability and equity claims of $450,000. So we will need additional cash of $*170,000*.

The *Net Financing Summary* at the end of the table reconciles this $170,000 cash requirement. Total assets will have actually increased (+ A) by $195,000 (that is, $620,000 then less $425,000 now). But not all of it must be financed externally through long-term capital. This is because increased sales generates *automatic financing* in the form of higher current liabilities (+ L) and retained earnings (+ E), which will total $85,000.

Table 32 The Projected Balance-Sheet Forecast of Cash

		February (000) 1	% of Sales 2	February, Next Year (000) 3	Explanation
43.16	Sales (annual)	$860	100.0%	$1400	
	Assets				
43.17	Cash	25	2.9	41	
43.18	Receivables	80	9.3	130	
43.19	Inventory	61	7.1	99	
43.20	Current assets	166		270	
43.21	Net fixed assets	259		350	Engineering estimate.
43.22	Total assets	$425		$620	
	Liabilities				
43.23	Accounts and notes payable	$32	3.7%	$52	
43.24	Taxes payable	10	1.2	17	
43.25	Accruals	7	0.8	11	
43.26	Current liabilities	49		80	
43.27	Long-term debt	90		30	From debt amortization schedule

43.28	Total liabilities	139		110
43.29	Common stock	195		195
43.30	Retained earnings	$91 + 54$	6.3	145
43.31	Equity	286		340
43.32	Total claims	$425		$450

% of sales estimate: 54/860.

43.33	Additional cash required		$170

Total assets (net of depreciation) less total claims: to be financed externally (Net Financing Summary).

Net Financing Summary

43.34	Increase in total assets (+ A)		$195

Line 43.22.

Automatic financing (sales related)

43.35	Increase in current liabilities (+ L)	$31		Line 43.26.
43.36	Retained earnings (+ E)	54		Line 43.30.
43.37	Gross financing required		$110	
43.38	Interim debt repaid (incurred)		-85	
			$+60$	
43.39	Net financing required		$170	

This would have left only $110,000 to be financed ($+$A of $195,000 − $85,000), of the original $170,000 of additional cash required. But $60,000 of debt will have been amortized during the months covered by the forecast, so we are back to a cash requirement of $170,000.

The crux of balance-sheet cash forecasting is thus the arithmetical difference that develops over time between the *sales related* and the *independent* items. Those that are sales related are items like cash, receivables, inventory, fixed assets, accounts payable, income taxes, various accruals, and retained earnings. Independent of sales are fixed items such as investments, nontrade notes payable, long-term debt, preferred stock, and common stock.

The difference that develops between sales-related and independent items is the additional financing we will need.

THE FORECASTED INCOME STATEMENTS AND BALANCE SHEETS

We construct our forecasted *Income Statement* in Table 33 at the same time as the others. All the items are taken from the previous statements, as shown in the Explanation column. Cost of goods sold (line 45) is the adjusted cost of goods produced—line 9 of the Manufacturing Forecast, which amount is net of overabsorbed burden—minus the month's increase in ending inventory (line 10). This is computed in footnote *a*.

In February, for instance, adjusted cost of goods produced is $53,200 (line 51). To this we add beginning inventory of $28,100, which is the ending inventory of the previous month (line 52). Then we subtract the ending inventory (line 53) of $35,500, giving us an adjusted cost of goods sold of $45,800. This is the amount we subtract from sales (line 44) to give us gross profit (line 46).

In *Table 34* we construct the forecasted *Balance Sheets*, from the Manufacturing Forecast and NCI, and from the Income Statements.

THE CRE BASIS OF CASH FORECASTING

From the forecasted monthly Balance Sheets we get variances against corresponding Plan balance sheets—of assets ($\pm$A), liabilities ($\pm$L), and equity ($\pm$E). And the forecasted Income Statements (Table 33) give us variances for sales ($\pm$S) and costs ($\pm$C). All such variances converge— and have their specific favorable or unfavorable impact—on CRE.

And below the surface of these general statements: the original Manufacturing Forecast (Table 28), and the other functional forecasts or bud-

Table 33 The Income Statement Forecast

	J	F	M	Explanation
44. Sales	$60,000	$72,000	$96,000	Line 1.
45. Cost of goods sold (adjusted)[a]	−38,500	45,800	58,500	Adjusted cost of goods produced, line 9, less the month's increase in ending inventory, line 10.[a]
46. Gross profit	21,500	26,200	37,500	Line 44 less line 45.
47. Selling, engineering, and administrative expenses	13,000	14,000	15,000	NCI statement, line 25.
48. Pretax net income	8,500	12,200	22,500	Line 46 less line 47.
49. Taxes	4,250	6,100	11,250	At 50% rate: half of line 48.
50. Net income	$4,250	$6,100	$11,250	

[a]

	J	F	M	Explanation
51. Adjusted cost of goods produced	$43,600	$53,200	$61,600	Manufacturing Forecast, line 9.
52. Add: beginning inventory	23,000	28,100	35,500	Ending inventory of previous month, line 10.
	66,600	81,300	97,100	
53. Less: ending inventory	28,100	35,500	38,600	Line 10.
Adjusted cost of goods *sold*	$38,500	$45,800	$58,500	

Table 34 The Balance Sheet Forecast

| | (Month-End) | | | |
	J	F	M	Explanation
Assets				
54. Cash	$20,000	$25,000	$25,000	NCI, line 43.
55. Receivables	67,100	80,400	105,400	Table 29, line 15.4.
56. Raw materials inventory	21,600	25,800	28,800	Manufacturing Forecast, line 12.
57. Finished inventory	28,100	35,500	38,600	Same, line 10.
58. Other current assets	—	—	9,450	Assumed.
59. Current assets	$136,800	166,700	207,250	
60. Net fixed assets	400,000	259,000	273,000	Net of depreciation at $1000/ month. Asset changes are from NCI, lines 17, 28, and 29.
61. Total assets	$536,800	425,700	480,250	
Liabilities and Equity				
62. Accounts payable	$21,600	25,800	28,800	Materials purchases, Manufacturing Forecast, line 15.
63. Notes payable	30,900	6,400	19,000	Original $20,000 loan ±L as shown in NCI, line 42.
64. Taxes payable	4,250	10,350	21,600	Cumulated Income Statement, line 49.
65. Accrued expenses	(50)	6,950	8,400	Assumed, including interest. This is a balancing item.
66. Current liabilities	56,700	49,500	77,800	
67. Mortgage payable, $100,000	95,000	90,000	85,000	NCI, line 30.
68. Term loan, $100,000	100,000	—	—	Same, line 31.
69. Long-term debt	195,000	90,000	85,000	
70. Common stock, $200,000	200,000	195,000	215,000	NCI, lines 19 and 33.
71. Retained earnings	85,100	91,200	102,450	Cumulated, Income Statement, line 50.
72. Equity	285,100	286,200	317,450	
73. Total liabilities and equity	$536,800	$425,700	$480,250	

gets, provide us with much more specific variance control. This is the variance *detail* into which we must dig—to isolate and analyze the subsurface causes of the general statement variances from Plan CRE.

The Net Cash Impact and Cash Velocity Forecasts (Tables 30 and 31) give us pure cash variances against Plan. But here too the underlying purpose—and that of Working Capital and Liquidity Velocity to be discussed in the next chapter—is to forecast cash return on equity. In our expression $CRE = S/C \times S/A \times L/A$, these statements are saying that

$$+CRE = +S - C - A + L$$

And they are constructed accordingly. Cash inflow is $S - A + L + E$ (lines 16 to 19), which tend to have a positive impact on CRE apart from being cash sources. Cash outflow is $C + A - L - E$ (lines 21 to 34), which tend to have a negative impact on CRE.

All three tiers along which the control process makes its way, in fact, converge on CRE. (1) This is true here at the *forecasting* level, as noted, all statements being constructed around (and variances measured against) the SCALDER cash forces that determine CRE. (2) It is true at the *analysis* level, as we will see, all analytical ratios converging on CRE. And (3) it is true at the *prevention* level, all cash variances being corrected back to the point of maximum CRE.

But all that we have done so far to forecast variances is only prelude. It is an indispensable foundation, but no more, of the control task that is central to the strategy of cash—the control of *liquidity velocity*.

To this we can now proceed.

CHAPTER 23

CONTROLLING THE VELOCITY OF CASH AND LIQUIDITY

To isolate cash variances that alter CRE, we have forecast our basic financial statements against the corresponding Plan statements. Now we zero in especially hard on the balance sheets, and the liquidity story they tell.

The underlying purpose of balance-sheet forecasting is in fact the liquidity analysis. It enables us to construct indispensable forecasts of working capital velocity and liquidity velocity. That is, the succession of forecasted balance sheets tells us precisely what is happening to the flow of funds and cash—and to the quantity, composition, liquidity, sources, and uses of working capital.

THE LIQUIDITY ANALYSIS

Table 35 is a rudimentary *liquidity analysis*, derived from our balance sheets (Table 34) for January, February, and March. It begins by telling us what will happen to working capital between January and February, and between February and March (lines 74 through 82). The dual columns denote the sources of funds and the uses of funds: they are *produced* by $-A$, $+L$, and $+E$ (sources). They are *reinvested* in $+A$, $-L$, and $-E$ (uses).

Going down the February balance sheet, we insert the *changes* from January into the proper column: *Uses* of working capital include current-asset increases ($+A$) of cash, $5000; receivables, $13,300; raw material inventory, $4200; and finished inventory, $7400. And notes payable decreased ($-L$) by $24,500.

Table 35 The Liquidity Analysis

	J – F Sources	J – F Uses	F – M Sources	F – M Uses
	+L	–L	+L	–L
	–A	+A	–A	+A
	+E	–E	+E	–E
1. *Working Capital (WC)*				
74. Cash		$5,000		—
75. Receivables		13,300		$25,000
76. Raw material inventory		4,200		3,000
77. Finished inventory		7,400		3,100
78. Other current assets		—		9,450
79. Accounts payable	$4,200		$3,000	
80. Notes payable		24,500	12,600	
81. Taxes payable	6,100		11,250	
82. Accrued expenses	7,000		1,450	
2. *ATL (across-the-line)*				
83. Net fixed assets	$141,000			$14,000
84. Mortgage payable		5,000		5,000
85. Term Loan		100,000		
86. Common stock		5,000	20,000	
87. Retained earnings	6,100		11,250	
88.	$164,400	$164,400	$59,550	$59,550

Sources of working capital included an increase in accounts payable (+L) by $4200. Taxes payable increased (+L) by $6100. And accrued expenses increased (+L) by $7000.

Having allocated the working capital items, we do the same for long-term assets and liabilities, and equity. These are the *across-the-line (ATL)* items that occur on the balance sheet below (across) the line separating working capital from everything else.

The first ATL item on the balance sheet is net fixed assets (line 60). It declined from $400,000 in January to $259,000 in February, or by $141,000. This is an ATL asset reduction (–A), and is allocated in our liquidity analysis to the sources column (the first one) on line 83. The other source of funds in February (from line 71) is an increase in retained earnings (+E) of $6100.

Across-the-line (ATL) *uses* of funds (the second column) from the February balance sheet include a reduction in mortgage payable (−L) of $5000; a term-loan reduction (−L) of $100,000; and a decrease in common stock (−E) of $5000. We allocate these accordingly on lines 84 to 86.

The identical procedure is now followed in the *March* balance sheet. Each change from February is allocated to the appropriate February-March columns of the liquidity analysis, depending on whether it is a source or use of funds. Each pair of columns must have the same totals, on line 88: for any two connecting balance sheets, the sources of funds must equal the uses of funds, by definition. This is what makes the balance sheet balance.

Our liquidity analysis has now categorized all working capital and ATL items as to whether they were sources or uses of funds.[1] It has illuminated the *dynamics* of the balance sheet, by telling us what has been and is happening to money values and liquidity.

That is, the balance sheet alone is a moderately useful *static* picture of the company's investments (A), and the financing sources of those investments (L and E) frozen at a point in time. The liquidity analysis exposes the dynamic interconnections *between* successive balance sheets. It thus isolates in an extremely useful way the *flows* of funds that management produced and reinvested.

The best way to study this flow of funds is by *reconciling working capital*, which we will now do. After that we can move forward in our analysis from the idea of funds flows to *working capital velocity*, which is an intermediate position or level of comprehension. And then we will be strongly situated to tackle the cash dynamics of *liquidity velocity*—which, in control terms, is what the strategy of cash is all about.

RECONCILING WORKING CAPITAL AND THE ATL SOURCES OF CASH

The raw data of funds produced and reinvested, in our pairs of columns for each month, are now reorganized into a funds flow arrangement called a *Reconciliation of Working Capital* (Table 36).

Lines 89 to 91 give us the increase in working capital between the two months. This is computed directly from the balance sheets by subtracting current liabilities from current assets. For February, working capital will increase by $37,100, which is the change to be reconciled. We must know what will happen internally to the composition and liquidity of working

---

[1] "*Funds*" is a generic term that can mean money value, liquidity, working capital, or cash, depending on the context and type of analysis in which it is applied. It is therefore not a very useful word, and will be discarded as we get into the more specific areas of cash analysis.

capital, during that $37,100 increase. And we must know what net changes in *ATL* (across-the-line) items will produce that increase.

So on lines 92 to 100, we post and total the working capital items that were previously allocated according to sources and uses on lines 74 to 82. In February, we get $54,400 of funds *used* or invested in the various increases in working capital (line 96). They are both increases in current assets and decreases in current liabilities.

And we get $17,300 of items that decreased working capital (line 100), which are *sources* of funds. These all happen to be increases in current liabilities (+L), but could as easily have included reductions in current assets (−A).

It should be noted that we are using the word "funds" in the generalized sense, to mean money value. An increase in working capital, such as higher current assets or lower current liabilities, is an investment or use of money value. A reduction in working capital, caused by lower current assets or higher current liabilities, is a *source* of money value to the company. This is money value in the accrual sense: Accrued items such as taxes payable and accrued expenses are sources of money value in that we are using somebody else's money in our own business until such time as we repay them.

In our reconciliation of working capital, the items that increased working capital (absorbed money value) exceeded the items that decreased working capital (produced money value)—by $37,100 (line 101, agreeing with line 91).

We have thus subjected working capital to an *internal* analysis as to the vital changes in its composition and liquidity that coincided with the increase of $37,100. Now let us perform an analysis *external to* working capital, to determine exactly where the increase came from.

Changes in working capital, up or down, are caused *only* by across-the-line (ATL) changes of the same net amount and direction. ATL items, again, are simply those that are not included in current assets and current liabilities. Working capital items are convertible into cash within one year, but ATLs will be liquidated only over a period of years, if ever.

They include fixed assets, long-term debt repayable after one year, and the various equity accounts. But since they are *anything* that is not working capital, they also include investments, miscellaneous assets, intangibles, reserves, and all the other noncurrent balance sheet categories. The ATL items (lines 83 through 87) are posted in the Reconciliation as either sources or uses of working capital (lines 102 through 106).

The $37,100 increase in working capital could not have been produced by anything that happened *within* working capital itself. It could only have been caused by what took place *between* working capital and the ATL

Table 36 The Reconciliation of Working Capital

		F			M[a]
1. Increase (Decrease) in WC					
89.	February WC	$117,200	March WC		$129,450
90.	January WC	−80,100	February WC		−117,200
91.	Increase in WC	$37,100	Increase in WC		$12,250
2. WC Increases (Uses of Funds)					
92.	Cash (+A)	5,000	Cash	$ 0	
93.	Receivables (+A)	13,300	Receivables (+A)	25,000	
94.	Raw materials (+A)	4,200	Raw materials (+A)	3,000	
95.	Finished inventory (+A)	7,400	Finished inventory (+A)	3,100	
96.	Notes payable (−L)	24,500 54,400	Other current assets (+A)	9,450	40,550
WC Decreases (Sources of Funds)					
97.			Accounts payable (+L)	3,000	
98.	Accounts payable (+L)	4,200	Notes payable (+L)	12,600	
99.	Taxes payable (+L)	6,100	Taxes payable (+L)	11,250	
100.	Accrued expenses (+L)	7,000 −17,300	Accrued expenses (+L)	1,450	28,300
101.	Increase in WC	$37,100	Increase in WC		$12,250

3. *WC Supplied by ATL Items*

Sources of WC

102.	Net fixed assets (−A)	141,000		Common stock (+E)	20,000	
103.	Retained earnings (+E)	6,100	147,100	Retained earnings (+E)	11,250	31,250

Uses of WC

104.	Mortgage payment (−L)	5,000		Net fixed assets (+A)	14,000	
105.	Term loan paid (−L)	100,000		Mortgage payment (−L)	5,000	19,000
106.	Common stock (−E)	5,000	110,000			
107.	*Increase in WC*		$37,100	*Increase in WC*		$12,250

*a*Explanation

89. Balance Sheet, line 59, less line 66.
90. Same.
92. Liquidity analysis, line 74.
    Etc.

section of the balance sheet. This is the crucial point. For instance, a $10,000 increase in raw material financed by a $10,000 increase in accounts payable does not change working capital. Nor would it change if a $10,000 increase in receivables were financed with a $10,000 lesser reduction of notes payable—say by only $14,500 rather than the $24,500 reduction (line 96). This would have resulted in both a current asset and a current liability being $10,000 higher, leaving working capital unaffected.

There is also no direct effect on working capital from changes among *ATL* items, such as a $100,000 addition to the manufacturing plant financed by a $100,000 increase in long-term debt. Nor would working capital have been touched if an idle plant were sold for $100,000 and the cash proceeds used to pay down long-term debt. But suppose the proceeds of the plant sale were used to pay down current liabilities, or the increased long-term debt paid for inventory or eliminated a seasonal bank loan. Then there would be an immediate and equivalent impact on working capital.

Working capital changes are thus explained and measured solely by *across-the-line* changes. It is an arithmetical truism and beyond dispute, yet repeatedly and sometimes disastrously ignored. Time and again, managers produce destructive changes in working capital through ATL transactions that originated with the very best of intentions. This is the company, for instance, that draws down cash or incurs current debt (thus draining working capital) to pay for production machinery that over many years will indeed generate tremendous labor cost savings.

Returning to our Reconciliation, in February, *ATL sources* of working capital are net fixed assets (−A) of $141,000 (line 102) and retained earnings (+E) of $6100, totaling $147,100 (line 103). *ATL uses* were the investments that absorbed and reduced working capital: repayments of long-term debt (−L) and the repurchase of some of the company's common stock (−E), totaling $110,000 (line 106).

Working capital produced by ATL items thus exceeded working capital absorbed by ATL items by the same $37,100 net increase in working capital (line 107). Reconciliation 3 therefore agrees with reconciliations 1 and 2: +*$37,100*.

In March, ATL items produced $31,250 of working capital (line 103) from the sale of common stock (+E) and the increase in retained earnings (+E). ATL items absorbed $19,000 of working capital, from an increase in fixed assets (+A) and a reduction in the long-term mortgage (−L). The net effect was an increase in working capital of $12,250 (line 107). This, too, agrees with reconciliations 1 and 2.

WORKING CAPITAL VELOCITY

This liquidity analysis and reconciliation is now used to compute working capital velocity in Table 37 and liquidity velocity in Table 38.

Table 37 tells us how fast our stock of working capital is turning over—how rapidly we are producing and reinvesting it. So it is a quantitative concept and tool. But it is also a *qualitative* tool: it helps us to decide whether the turnover of working capital, regardless of the rate, is beneficial or harmful, benign or malignant.

In Table 37 the forecast of working capital velocity for February starts with January's month-end balance of $80,100 (line 108). This is from line 90 of the Reconciliation. Then we list all the sources of working capital, totaling $147,100 (line 112).

The various *uses* to which that newly produced working capital was put total $110,000 (line 115). The difference between $147,100 of working capital produced and $110,000 reinvested is *$37,100*. This of course is the same increase in working capital we just computed and reconciled (lines 91, 101, and 107).

So we add the $37,100 increase to February's starting working capital of $80,100 (line 108), to get the ending working capital of $117,200 (line 116). This is February's month-end working capital, agreeing with the Reconciliation (line 89).

Working capital was produced *solely* by ATL items (lines 109 to 112), and was reinvested solely in ATL items (lines 113 to 115). Cash from operations (lines 109 and 110) is of course an ATL item: net income increases equity and depreciation reduces fixed assets, both coinciding with the production of working capital.

The *velocity percentages* next to each item, computed from the *starting* working capital (line 108), are more important than the dollar amounts. February's working capital velocity was very high: the $147,100 of additional working capital (line 112) was a whopping 184% of the starting working capital. This came mostly from the sale of fixed assets (line 111), which alone was 175% of the starting amount. Cash from operations (line 110) generated only 8.9%.

On the reinvestment side, 125% of our starting working capital was absorbed by the repayment of a term loan (line 114). The other items that absorbed working capital were unimportant by comparison.

March working capital velocity is more normal, being undistorted by major nonrecurring items on either the production or reinvestment side. ATL transactions (line 121) produced $32,250 of working capital, or 27%

Table 37 Working Capital Velocity

108. *Working capital, start*
     Produced by:
109.   Net income (+E) $ 6,100   (7.6)
110.   Depreciation (−A)   1,000   (1.2) $ 7,100   (8.9)
111. −A: Reductions in long-term assets   140,000 (174.8)
112. Total working capital produced

     Reinvested in:
113. −L: Mortgage payments $ 5,000   (6.2)
114.   Term loan repaid   100,000 (124.8)   105,000 (131.1)
115. −E: Stock repurchase   5,000   (6.2)
116. *Working capital, end*

117. *Working capital, start*
     Produced by:
118.   Net income (+E) $ 11,250   (9.6)
119.   Depreciation (−A)   1,000   (0.8) $ 12,250   (10.4)
120. +E: Sale of common stock   20,000   (17.1)
121. Total working capital produced

     Reinvested in:
122. +A: Increases in long-term assets   15,000   (12.8)
123. −L: Reductions in long-term debt   5,000   (4.3)
124.
125. *Working capital, end*

of the starting amount. They absorbed $20,000 of this, or 17% (line 124). Nonrecurring items were moderate: the sale of common stock (line 120) was 17% of the starting amount of working capital, and fixed assets (line 122) absorbed only 12.8%.

The $12.250 of working capital produced (line 124), added to the $117,200 at the start (line 117), results in $129,450 of March month-end working capital. Again, this corresponds to the amount shown in the liquidity analysis (line 89). The $12,250 was a mere 10% increase over the starting amount (line 124), whereas February's increase was an extraordinary 46% (line 115).

Table 37 (*Continued*)

	February	Explanation
	$ 80,100 (100)	Reconciliation of Working Capital, line 90.
$147,100 (183.6)		February net income, Income Statement, line 50. Balance Sheet, line 60. Reconciliation, line 102, less $1000 depreciation.
110,000 (137.3)	37,100 (46.3) $117,200	Reconciliation, line 104. Same, line 105. Reconciliation, line 106.

	March	
	$117,200 (100)	Reconciliation, line 90.
$ 32,250 (27.5)		March net income, Income Statement, line 50. Balance Sheet, line 60. Reconciliation, line 102.
−20,000 (17.1)	+12,250 (10.4) $129,450	Reconciliation, line 104, +$1000 of depreciation. Same, line 105.

High working capital velocity is usually, but not necessarily, associated with a high rate of profits and growth. Such a company is presumably managing its working capital and ATL transactions intelligently and dynamically, so as to maximize cash return on equity. Otherwise, why all the activity? The question takes us from the quantitative fact of high working capital velocity to the *qualitative* question: will the rapid working capital turnover in fact benefit profits and growth?

A commanding virtue of the working capital velocity forecast is that it directs us to the proper *areas* of qualitative inquiry. Will February's production of $140,000 of working capital from the sale of a plant—and its reinvestment mostly in the reduction of long-term debt—be a good thing or a bad thing for potential CRE? Or suppose we will produce working capital by expanding long-term debt, and then invest much of it in various long-term assets. Quantitatively, again, velocity will be very high.

But basic qualitative questions are raised at the same time. Will the increase in debt be beneficial, or might it strain our debt service capability and badly distort debt ratios? Will *these* particular fixed assets help us on balance? Will they create an unsupportable ratio of fixed assets-to-net worth, or superimpose a net burden of asset-carrying charges on the heavier debt service burden? And so forth. In thus directing us to the right areas where we can ask the right qualitative questions, the working capital velocity forecast performs an important and probably a unique service.

But apart from giving us the quantitative rate of velocity and exposing the areas of questionable quality, its key role remains clear. Working capital velocity tells us at a glance *why* a particular increase or decrease in working capital will take place, in terms of specific ATL sources and uses of that working capital. It is especially in this application that it becomes a powerful tool of analysis and decision-making in the strategy of cash, directing us within a clearly defined liquidity framework to the maximization of CRE.

LIQUIDITY VELOCITY: FOCUS OF THE STRATEGY OF CASH

Our conclusive analytical weapon in the strategy of cash is the Forecast of Liquidity Velocity (Table 38). It is the logical and final extension of the entire sequence of statements that have preceded it. Liquidity velocity encompasses and exposes *all* the sources of cash produced by $-A$, $+L$, and $+E$, and reinvested in $+A$, $-L$, and $-E$.

Working capital velocity showed us how changes in ATL items produced corresponding changes in working capital. "Across-the-line" referred to the line separating working capital from everything else: it meant anything that was not working capital. This enabled us to analyze changes in the quantity and composition of working capital in terms of the changes in long-term ATL items that produced them.

But in the Liquidity Velocity Statement, the balance sheet line of demarcation separating cause and effect is raised to the point separating *cash* and everything else. "Across-the-line" now means anything that is not cash (and the equivalent), changes in which are produced entirely by changes throughout the remainder of working capital plus the ATL items.

The Liquidity Velocity Statement thus reflects changes in working capital velocity *plus* changes in current assets (except cash) and current debt, all of which are "ATL" items in their impact on cash. It is the ultimate and precise analytical expression of the strategy of cash, focusing as it does on the dynamic interaction between cash and the *entire* balance sheet.

Let us examine liquidity velocity in Table 38, in comparison with working capital velocity in Table 37. February Liquidity Velocity begins with a cash balance of $20,000 (line 126), derived from the NCI statement (line 43), whereas Working Capital Velocity began with working capital of $80,100 (line 108). Next we list, in both statements, the same cash-producing ATL items: $7100 from operations (line 128 vs. line 110), and $140,000 from the reduction in long-term assets (line 129 vs. line 111).

But now Liquidity Velocity introduces as a source of cash the $17,300 of increases in current debt (line 132), taken from the Liquidity Analysis (lines 98 to 100). Total *cash* produced is $164,400 (line 133). This exceeds the $147,100 of total working capital produced (line 112) by the additional $17,300 of cash provided by current debt.

In the reinvestment section of Liquidity Velocity (but not Working Capital) are increases in current assets of $24,900 (line 136), and the decrease in notes payable of $24,500 (line 137). These two reinvestment items absorb a total of $49,400 of cash. It is precisely the amount by which total cash reinvested of $159,400 (line 140) exceeds total working capital reinvested of $110,000 (line 115).

Liquidity velocity tells us that we will generate $164,400 and reinvest $159,400 of *cash*, producing a net gain of $5000 (line 140) over the starting balance of $20,000. We thus end the month with a cash balance of $25,000 (line 141), which corresponds to Net Cash Impact (NCI), line 43. This becomes our starting balance (line 142) for the March Liquidity Velocity Statement.

Working capital velocity was the percentage of each item to the *starting* balance of working capital—the relative extent to which the various items produced or reinvested that initial balance. But in liquidity velocity, we are not interested in the inconsequential starting cash balance or what happens in relation to it. This balance is kept as small as possible anyway, in the interest of effective cash management. What is important is the amount of cash *produced* during the period—$164,400 in February (line 133)—and the relationship to it of the various items of cash produced and reinvested.

The 100% anchor from which all liquidity-velocity percentages are computed, is therefore the total cash produced. February's liquidity velocity will be significantly distorted by the sale of fixed assets (line 129), to account for 85% of total cash produced. And in the reinvestment section, it will be distorted by the channeling of 79% of cash produced into debt

Table 38 Liquidity Velocity

		February		Explanation
126. *Cash balance, start*			$20,000	NCI, line 43.
Produced by:				
127. Net income (+E)	$6,100 (3.7)			Income Statement, line 50.
128. Depreciation (−A)	1,000 (0.6)	$7,100 (4.3)		Balance Sheet, line 60.
129. −A: Decreases in long-term assets		140,000 (85.1)		Reconciliation, line 102, less $1,000 of depreciation.
+ L: Increases in current debt:				
130. Accounts payable	4,200			Same, line 98.
131. Taxes payable	6,100			Same, line 99.
132. Accrued expenses	7,000			Same, line 100.
133.		17,300 (10.5)		
			$164,400 (100)	Total cash produced.
Reinvested in:				
+ A: Increases in current assets:				
134. Receivables	$13,300			Reconciliation, line 93.
135. Raw material inventory	4,200			Same, line 94.
136. Finished inventory	7,400			Same, line 95.
	24,500			
137. − L: Decreases in current debt		$24,900 (15.1)		Same, line 96.
Decreases in long-term debt:				
138. Mortgage payments	5,000			Same, line 104.
139. Term loan repaid	100,000	129,500 (78.8)		Same, line 105.
140. − E: Stock repurchase		5,000 (3.0)		Same, line 106.
		159,400 (97.0)		
141. *Cash balance, end*		5,000		
			$25,000	

			$March^a$
142. *Cash balance, start*			$25,000
Produced by:			
143. Net income (+E)	$11,250 (18.6)		
144. Depreciation (−A)	1,000 (1.6)	$12,250 (20.2)	
+ L: Increases in current debt:			
145. Accounts payable	3,000		
146. Notes payable	12,600		
147. Taxes payable	11,250		
148. Accrued expenses	1,450	28,300 (46.7)	
149. + E: Sale of common stock		20,000 (33.0)	$60,550 (100)
Reinvested in:			
+ A: Increases in current assets:			
150. Receivables	$25,000		
151. Raw material inventory	3,000		
152. Finished inventory	3,100		
153. Other current assets	9,450	$40,550 (67.0)	
154. Increases in long-term assets		15,000 (24.8)	
155. − L: Decreases in long-term debt		5,000 (8.3)	
156.			− 60,550
157. *Cash balance, end*			0
			$25,000

[a]Same explanation applies as for February, above.

323

reduction (line 139). Increases in current debt (line 132) will supply 10%, but increases in current assets (line 136) will absorb 15%, of total cash production.

Liquidity velocity during March will be more normal: operations (line 144) will supply 20% of cash produced, compared with only 4% in February. March increments in current debt (line 148) will produce 47%, but increments in current assets (line 153) will absorb 67%, of total cash.

The differences between Liquidity Velocity and the *Cash Velocity* Forecast in Chapter 22 (Table 31) is also worth noting. Cash Velocity is a cash basis device, having been computed entirely from the Statement of Net Cash Impact. It therefore suffers from the limitations of cash-basis statements that we noted, which are not imposed on an accrual-basis statement such as Liquidity Velocity.

Comparing February's liquidity velocity (Table 38) with its cash velocity (Table 31), we see that both statements start with the same cash balance of $20,000, and arrive at the same $25,000 ending cash balance. But in-between they show different amounts of total cash produced and reinvested. While February's Liquidity Velocity produced $164,000 of cash and reinvested $159,400, Cash Velocity produced only $139,500 and reinvested only $134,500. Liquidity Velocity's accrual-basis cash production thus exceeded Cash Velocity's bill-paying cash by $24,900 (that is, $164,400 less $139,500). And cash reinvested on Liquidity Velocity's accrual basis was also higher by $24,900.

This is because the accrual-basis computation included $17,300 of current debt (line 132) and $7100 of "cash" from operations (line 128), neither of which is in the cash-basis statement. And it was not reduced by the $500 cash deficit incurred in the cash basis statement that was caused by total cash costs exceeding collections (line 43.3).

That is, sales were higher than collections. So Liquidity Velocity accrued the entire $7100 of "cash" generated from operations and was not penalized by the actual operating cash loss of $500. And it accrued $17,300 of *noncash* current obligations (+L) on line 132 which the cash-basis statement ignored. So $17,300 plus $7100 plus $500 equals the $24,900 by which Liquidity Velocity cash generated on the accrual basis exceeded Cash Velocity cash generated on the cash basis.

On the reinvestment side, the $24,900 excess of accrual-basis "cash" over cash-basis is accounted for entirely by the $24,900 increase in current assets (line 136). These included higher receivables, and manufacturing value added to raw and finished inventory, none of which represented outlays of cash.

Liquidity velocity does not give us as tight a hold on immediate bill-paying ability, as we have noted. But it provides a much more complete picture of the company's cash position in terms of short-term realizable and expendable dollars. Cash velocity simply narrows the definition of cash too severely for purposes of cash strategy (but not for bill-paying and solvency purposes).

Another way of looking at liquidity velocity is as an *adjusted earnings* method of forecasting cash. Going downward from February's forecasted net income (line 127) of $6100, which is our starting point, all the items beginning with depreciation *increase cash but not profits*, and we arrive at total cash produced of $164,400. And in the reinvestment section are all the items that *decrease cash but not profits*.

We could have varied the procedure or terminology somewhat, such as calling the increase in receivables (line 134), excess of sales over collections. But the basic principle remains the same. We have adjusted net income (line 127) for cash inflows and cash outflows that *do not affect* that net income, which adjustments combine to forecast an increase in cash by $*5000* (line 140).

Management as investment manager of the balance sheet—charged with maximizing the liquidity velocity and payback of its assets and liabilities—has no more potent analytical tool than liquidity velocity. More than any other, it compresses everything we must know and do to maximize CRE.

We have now journeyed through the first tier of control—*forecasting* the Plan's financial and velocity statements, whereby we isolate potential variances.

Next we traverse the second control tier: *analyzing* the statement forecasts and their variances to determine their impact on future CRE. Only then can we intelligently *prevent* those variances from occurring, on the third tier.

CHAPTER 24

RATIO AND TREND ANALYSIS
OF CASH CONTRIBUTION

We now have a potentially valuable collection of *absolute* variances, which are the amounts by which forecasted financials differ from Planned financials. If the inventory forecast is $600,000 but Planned inventory is $500,000, we have a negative inventory variance of $100,000. If the sales forecast for the same period is $900,000 but Planned sales are $1,000,000, we have a negative sales variance of $100,000.

These raw or absolute variances must now be analyzed creatively and evaluated for their true impact on CRE.

RELATIVE VARIANCES: THE CASH SYSTEM INTERNAL ENVIRONMENT

Absolute variances are compared to one another in *ratio* computations, and to themselves backward or forward through time by means of *trend* computations. Such ratio and trend (relative) variances are far more meaningful than the absolute variances, and direct us more readily to the most workable preventive solutions.

In the example just noted, Plan called for $1,000,000 of sales and $500,000 of inventory, or an inventory turnover ratio of 2. But forecasted inventory is $600,000 and forecasted sales are $900,000, or a turnover of 1.5. The $100,000 absolute variances in both inventory and sales are of course significant. But the *relative* variance of 2 versus 1.5 is much more significant. This is so both analytically, and in terms of the type and the effectiveness of solutions to which it will give rise.

In the first place, 1.5 is a drastic 25% decline from 2. It is a much more urgent danger signal than either of the $100,000 absolute variances. Furthermore, suppose that inventory turnover is now 1.7. The decline in forecasted turnover to 1.5 is an ominous trend, quite apart from the variance against Plan's 2. And this downtrend in forecasted turnover would be even more ominous if Plan was in an *uptrend* as to turnover.

The point, learned as a bitter lesson by so many managements, is obvious: the *relative* ratio and trend variances are the important ones to determine as soon as we know what the absolute variances are.

This ratio evaluation of forecasted financial statements can be conducted fruitfully only within the entire analytical *framework* of ratios, rather than in terms of only a few of them. We are exploring the internal environment of a living cash system, in which all functions are delicately and inextricably entwined. So it is an analysis *among* ratios and trend calculations in a framework where all are functionally interdependent. The interpretation of any one ratio depends in some degree, directly or indirectly, on all the other ratios.

To use a possibly simplistic example, if the sales/inventory ratio is too low, the inventory slowness may not adversely affect bill-paying ability if the inventory/working capital ratio is not excessive but normal. But just what is "normal" may depend on how restrictive is the ratio of current assets/current liabilities. And so forth. This is *direct* interdependence among clearly related ratios. Indirect interdependence now fans out in ever-widening circles, in a much more complex way.

Each ratio is not just a component of an organically interrelated cash system of interacting ratios. It is also identifiable as being either in a causal relationship to most of the other ratios or one that is mainly an effect or resultant. The ratio analysis must distinguish between cause and effect, digging down deep to the ultimate and real cause of the condition being diagnosed.

If we have a high inventory/working capital ratio, for instance, it may not mean that too much inventory is on hand. Perhaps an excessive sales/equity ratio has swollen trade payables and depleted working capital. Then the wrong solution would treat the malady as an inventory problem. The right solution would treat it as a liquidity problem—perhaps by refinancing short-term debt into longer maturities while additional equity is brought in. In the overall ratio scheme, therefore, the correct solution was made to emerge from the verifiable cause, not the effect: the cause was inadequate working capital and equity for the volume of sales generated, of which excessive inventory/working capital was merely a symptom and effect.

It points out as well that we cannot be certain whether a ratio's numerator or denominator caused the problem until we analyze the surrounding ratios. Suppose that fixed assets/equity is excessive. To diagnose it properly, we must at least examine the ratio of sales/fixed assets. If it is too low, our problem is an excess of fixed assets. But if it is normal or better, we are not in any operating sense suffering from too heavy fixed assets. So our high fixed assets/equity ratio was produced by insufficient equity.

And in our interacting framework of ratios, we must investigate *any* significant variance from the corresponding Plan ratio, above or below. Excessive sales/fixed assets is no less a threat to profits than inadequate sales/fixed assets.

There is yet another advantage to examining ratios in terms of a meaningful totality of interacting components. Adverse or weak ratios may require entirely different types of solutions if there are very strong offsetting ratios, than if there are none in the surrounding environment that provide such compensating advantages.

Of course, we must allow for seasonal and other off-center influences on our ratios, in the way we interpret them. A very high inventory/working capital position is normal in the high season but abnormal or dangerous in the slow season.

And it is not enough to analyze ratios within their mutually interdependent spacial framework, at a point in time. We also must see them within their crucially important *trend* framework, as noted, over successive points in time. The cash system is not only an interdependent spacial framework, but a *temporal* or chronological framework as well. The entire array or gamut of ratios may present a healthy picture as of a given moment. But in relation to seasonally comparable earlier dates, it may reveal pathological trends.

We calculate trend percentages simply by choosing an appropriate base period, and dividing the base figure into each succeeding figure:

	Base Year 1	Trend %	Year 2	Trend %	Year 3	Trend %
Sales/ inventory	2.50	100	2.70	108	3.10	124
Inventory/ working capital	0.70	100	0.86	123	105.00	150

Sales/inventory is in a comfortable uptrend: the 3.1 ratio in year 3 is 124% of the base year ratio of 2.5. But inventory/working capital rose from 0.70 in the base year to 105 in year 3, or to 150%. Despite improving inventory turnover, the liquidity of working capital deteriorated because of the sharp increase in inventory/working capital.

EXTERNALIZING OUR ANALYTICAL ENVIRONMENT

Implied in what has already been said is that our ratio analysis must be conducted from the *outside* looking in. We *externalize* our internal environment, and see ourselves as others see us. It is true that we analyze from management's internal vantage point, with all the necessary inside information at our fingertips. But we should *forget* our inside knowledge for the purposes of ratio analysis. We must look at ourselves as does any credit officer in our bank or supplier company, or any 100-share stockholder studying our Annual Report.

We always "place ourselves in the shoes" of our outside creditors and stockholders. Our interpretation of the statements must be the one *they* arrive at, looking at us externally but not internally.

Turned inside out, the principle affirms that we must run our company so that the resulting financial statements present a healthy and vigorous analytical picture to outside creditors and stockholders. Only then is it in fact a healthy and vigorous business. The worst management mistakes spring from neglect of the external statements—believing we know so much about our business that we can let them run down or become overextended.

Our business *is* what the external statements show the creditors and stockholders it is, To delude ourselves that there is a conflict between outside statement and inside condition—however intimate and sophisticated our inside knowledge—is to court disaster. Besides, the business *is* the stockholder's and creditor's. They supplied and will supply the capital on which our future totally depends. *They* have to be content.

So we must always be certain to conduct the ratio analysis from *their* side—"in their shoes." We leave their shoes for ours, analytically, only at our peril.

RELATIVE VARIANCES: THE BEST-COMPETITOR EXTERNAL ENVIRONMENT

And the ratio analysis of our internal cash system must be done not only *from* the outside looking in, but also with reference *to* the outside environment. It must be conducted within an industry or other group framework of *BC* (best-competitor) comparisons. This is the *external* analytical environment of our cash system, on which the internal analysis heavily depends for its meaning and value. We simply do not have a useful fix on our own ratio performance unless it is geared into industry (BC) ratio performance.

The above-average competitor ratios were of course fully considered when the Plan was constructed in the first place, as discussed in Chapter 19. There, to formulate the Guide Plan, we first delineated our planning environment in terms of BC ratios. And based on these ratios, we made a study of BC Cash Availability. This helped us decide how much total excess cash we could release—companywide, form costs and assets—if we operated as efficiently as the best competitor companies.

But now a ratio analysis of anticipated performance against Plan is an evaluation in much finer detail than could be made when the Plan was formulated. So we again determine the industry reference points of above-average CRE performance, and break them down to the CCRs (S/C and S/A) at all levels and in every corner of the company.

As noted in the Planning chapter, ratios on comparable companies in our industry are available from many published sources (in addition to the complex private sources and what can be uncovered by one's own imaginative sleuthing): our industry trade association; releases of publicly traded companies; the U.S. Department of Commerce; Dun & Bradstreet; Robert Morris Associates; various public accounting firms; and government agencies such as the FTC, SBA, and SEC. In developing comparative ratios of our competitors, the timeless rule can be applied with particular force and advantage: where there is a will, there is a way.

THE CRE FOCUS OF ANALYSIS AND CONTROL

Ratio analysis and control of the forecasted financial statements have but one purpose: to determine how effectively we are producing *cash return on equity*, in accordance with Plan. Since management's only operating function is to maximize CRE—within the framework of $CRE = S/C \times S/A \times L/A$ *(R)*—all the control ratios should be cataloged and used in accordance with the five components of this expression.

The various ratios in the first component, CRE, are resultant measurements—the effects of the active ratios. And the *active* ratios are grouped into their S/C, S/A, L/A, or R components, which combine to produce the total impact on CRE.

Our entire control-ratio discussion in the next few chapters will follow this CRE format. The five categories and subcategories of ratios that converge on CRE are as follows:

1. *CRE* ratios (CRE).
2. *Cost* cash ratios (S/C).
3. *Asset* cash ratios (S/A).

    4. *Leverage* cash ratios (L/A).
       Current liquidity ratios.
       Asset debt capacity ratios.
       Operating debt capacity ratios.
    5. *Reinvestment* cash ratios (R).

The four categories of active ratios are *cash generating* in their impact on CRE, because the cash contribution ratios with which they coincide are cash generating. Let us therefore briefly review the basic cash relationships.

The *cost cash*, or profit margin, ratios (S/C) measure the rate of cash inflow from sales. This inflow is caused by a given amount of cash outflow into *costs* that we incurred to produce those sales.

The *asset cash* ratios (S/A) generate cash through turnover. They compare the cash inflow from sales with the cash outflow into *assets* acquired to produce those sales.

And the *leverage cash* ratios (L/A) are cash generating in that they compare the cash inflow from leverage with the cash outflow into assets (financed mostly with that leverage).

In terms of our CRE expression $S/C \times S/A \times L/A$, the numerators S and L are thus the company's *primary inflows* of cash.[1] And the denominators C and A are the *primary outflows* of cash.

Secondarily, we have cash inflows from $-A$ and $-C$, in the absolute sense or relative to sales. These are our *secondary inflows*. They reduce the cash-outflow denominators, thereby increasing the ratios and their relative cash productivity: $+S/C$, $+S/A$, or $+L/A$. And we are back again to S and L as the basic cash inflows.

That is, cash productivity is the *relationship* between cash inflow from sales or leverage and cash outflow into costs or assets. It is increased whether the sales or leverage inflows are increasing relative to cost and asset outflows, or the cost and asset outflows are decreasing relative to the sales or leverage inflows.

And debt reduction $(-L)$ is a *secondary outflow* of cash (supplementing C and A, as the primary outflows). But this merely gets us back to the primary cash outflow of an increase in assets relative to debt (or $-L/A$). Cash flows out to the extent that L/A decreases, whether the decrease is caused by $-L$ or $+A$. And $-S$ is also a secondary "outflow" $(-S/C$ and $-S/A)$, for the same reasons. So we are back again to C and A as the basic cash outflows.

---

[1]Given the fixed quantity of equity implied by the CRE relationship, E is not a source of cash in this context.

Thus, since all the active analytical ratios we will now talk about are classifiable according to $S/C \times S/A \times L/A$ (R), they are cash generating in their impact on CRE.

Let us therefore look at all five categories of ratios.

THE CRE RATIOS

The following are *resultant* ratios, or effects, that define and measure the all-important return on equity.

> Cash flow/equity (CRE)
> Retained cash flow/equity
> Net income/equity
> Cash flow/total assets

Retained cash flow/equity is the payback that remains after dividends; it is the money we use to build the business (directly, and as the basis of leverage). To our creditors it is more important than cash flow/equity in gauging the company's capacity to service longer-term debt: it measures cash retention in the business out of which debt is serviced (operating protection). And it also measures in economic value terms (and after depreciation, in book value terms) the internal buildup in our equity cushion that further protects lenders (asset protection).

An excessive return on equity means substantial earnings. But it is usually also a harbinger of serious problems from inadequate equity capital or too much leverage. Or it could mean an overvalued ending inventory that overstates net income and equity by the same amount, thereby artificially increasing CRE. Both an abnormally low and an abnormally high CRE are danger signals to be investigated. But the latter is the more urgent of the two.

ANALYZING THE COST CASH RATIOS (S/C)

The following profit margin ratios measure the production of cost cash, or the control of costs in relation to sales.

> Cash flow/sales
> Net income/sales
> Gross profit/sales

Cash flow/sales, or the profit margin (S/C), has a powerful causal impact on virtually all the other ratios. It increases the all-important CRE ratio, cash flow/equity. It increases current assets/current liabilities by adding to the numerator or whittling down the denominator. And because it builds working capital and equity, it reduces beneficially those ratios that have these elements as their denominators: current liabilities/equity; total debt/equity; fixed assets/equity; inventory/working capital; and long-term debt/working capital. The benefits of a high profit margin are immediate and all-pervasive, there being almost no performance ratio that does not reflect cash flow and net income in either its numerator or denominator.

Gross profit/sales is the essential supplementary ratio to the profit margin. The difference between sales and the cost of goods sold, it is the manufacturing source of earnings that profoundly influences the profit margin.

One of the best ways to analyze cost cash and the various operating margins that produce it, is a trend analysis of successive income statements. Table 39 covers three successive years. Index numbers for each item were computed by dividing its base year number into its successive years' numbers.

Gross sales moved up briskly to 115%, but net sales rose only to 113%. The difference was returns and allowances, which jumped abnormally to 353%. It suggests a defective product or a customer relations problem, and deserves our prompt attention.

Cost of goods sold (line 4) is under excellent control, rising to 111% in year 3 compared with the net sales increase to 113%. So gross profit (line 5) jumped to 118%.

Selling, general, and administrative expenses (line 6) are less effectively controlled, rising to 118%. But they involve much smaller dollar amounts than does cost of goods. Operating profit (line 7) is therefore not adversely affected, and it soars to 122%. Nonoperating charges and rapidly rising taxes (line 10) hold the gain in net income to 110%.

Performance is summarized by the dynamic gross profit/sales ratio (line 13). In year 3 it was 104% of its base-year level. But net income/sales (line 12) declined slightly to 97%. The company has three areas to investigate and correct, if its strong gross profit performance is to filter down to the profit margin: returns and allowances (line 2), S G & A (line 6), and soaring tax payments (which are a controllable cost like any other).

ANALYZING ASSET CASH RATIOS (S/A)

The following are *turnover* ratios that measure the sales generated by a given amount of assets, or the assets needed to produce a given amount of sales.

> Sales/equity
> Sales/working capital
> Sales/receivables
> Average collection days/terms
> Sales/inventory
> Sales/fixed assets

Sales/equity is the central definition of turnover, toward which all other turnover ratios converge. Given the profit margin (cash flow/sales), a higher sales/equity ratio will produce a proportionately higher return on equity. It is thus a massive contributor to CRE. And like its sister ratio cash flow/sales, sales/equity has a powerful and all-pervasive impact on the other ratios.

Overtrading is the prevalent and dangerous condition of excessive sales/ equity. It is the success story that ends in tragedy, whenever its sinister

Table 39 Trend Analysis of Cost Cash

	Base Year 1 (000)	Year 2 (000)	Index (Year 1 = 100)	Year 3 (000)	Index
1. Gross sales	$24,790	$27,860	112%	$28,570	115%
2. Returns and allowances	201	479	238	710	353
3. Net sales	24,589	27,381	111	27,860	113
4. Cost of goods sold	16,435	18,279	111	18,198	111
5. Gross profit	8,154	9,102	112	9,662	118
6. SG&A expenses	6,700	7,539	112	7,889	118
7. Operating profit	1,454	1,563	107	1,773	122
8. Other income (charges)	(26)	(25)	—	(73)	—
9. Pretax net income	1,428	1,488	104	1,700	119
10. Taxes	651	669	103	842	129
11. Net income	$ 777	$ 819	105	$ 858	110
12. Net income/sales	3.16%	2.99%	95	3.08%	97
13. Gross profit/sales	33.2	33.2	100	34.7	104

implications are fulfilled. A marketing-oriented management achieves a long string of sales records, and profits and CRE are soaring. So too is its sales/equity ratio. The company is automatically generating excessive trade payables and other current liabilities in response to soaring volume, to finance bulging inventories and receivables. The more dramatic its sales achievements, the more financially vulnerable it becomes.

Management then discovers it cannot bring in long-term capital to alleviate the current strain because current liabilities are already equal to the equity (current liabilities/equity is 100%). Long-term lenders would consider their position in the capital structure to be unprotected by an equity cushion. Their debt instruments would be seen as equity, sharing its risks but none of its potential rewards. And it is now probably too late to entice equity money. So more current debt is piled up, at escalating interest rates, and the situation spirals out of control.

Excessive sales growth can be harmful, therefore, because it produces a financially disruptive chain effect: the burgeoning sales/equity ratio generates excessive receivables/working capital and inventory/working capital. It thereby depletes current liquidity, reducing the current and quick ratios. And excessive current liabilities/equity prevents a badly needed injection of permanent capital. Profits finally deteriorate under the weight of mushrooming asset and interest charges. Yet, the potentially fatal conditions could have been signaled and prevented by careful attention to the sales/equity ratio.

If additional equity is unavailable, or even if it is, a drastic but workable solution to overtrading may well be to cut sales volume. It may indeed be a welcome opportunity to eliminate our least-profitable customers—those who pay the slowest, cost us the most freight, buy only small ticket items, cause the most fuss, take undeserved cash discounts, and so forth. We can lop them off and help *both* our profit and the balance-sheet strain.

RECEIVABLES AND INVENTORY CASH

The most potent analytical components of sales/equity are sales/receivables and sales/inventory. Receivables plus inventory are far and away the largest dollar amount of equity in the typical corporation, which would be reason enough. But they are also the most volatile and unpredictable. And they are the ones on which cash flow mostly depends: Nothing undermines it more quickly and surely than a pernicious slowdown in either of these turnovers. They generate financing charges, carrying and storage costs, and losses from the writedown of bad receivables and depreciated or worthless inventory. And we have seen that they increase current liabilities/equity to the detriment of our borrowing ability.

Sales/receivables is a quantitative ratio that measures the amount of receivables. It carries no necessary implication as to their quality or collectibility. Translating it into qualitative language requires that we consider the credit terms under which the sales were made that generated the receivables.

We must use the ratio, *average collection days / terms*: First we divide 360 days by sales/receivables, to get the average number of days receivables were outstanding (average collection days). Then we divide average days outstanding by the terms of sale, or the time within which payment is required.

If a company has credit sales of $2,000,000 and receivables of $200,000, sales/receivables is 10×. So 360/10 equals *36 days*, the average time that receivables are outstanding. Or we could have divided $2,000,000 by 360 to get $555 of sales per day. Then, dividing receivables of $200,000 by $555 would give us 36 days of average time required to collect them.

Now we compare average collection days with the terms of sale, which is 30 days: 36/30 = *120%*.

If receivables rose from $200,000 to $250,000, sales/receivables would drop to 8×. So 360 days/8 would lengthen average collection time to 45 days. And 45/30 lifts our collection days/terms to *150%*.

If all receivables were collected promptly according to the 30-day terms, we would have only $*167,000* of receivables on our books. That is, $\scriptstyle 5\text{\textchar}/(2,000,000/167,000) = 30$ days. This is a sales/receivables ratio of 12×, and collection days/terms would be *100%*

A quick rule of thumb is to consider dangerous a ratio of collection days/terms of more than 133%. In this example, it is anything over 40 days (133% of 30 days). Apart from the heavy financing or opportunity cost of carrying uncollected sales, the *collectibility* itself tends to decline as we go above 133%. The longer an account is past due, on the average, the less likely that it will be collected. As the collection period lengthens, receivables drop in quality and liquidity. It is this qualitative deterioration that collection days/terms seeks to measure in a general way, supplementing the quantitative sales/receivables ratio.

We can of course do internally what an outside observer of our company cannot, when he becomes alarmed at the slowdown of collections: We age our receivables according to those not yet due; 30 days past due; 31 to 60 days past due; 61 to 90 days past due; and so forth. Then we take a very hard look, and perhaps a scary one, at what we have got in the way of collectibility on the longer end.

Practically everything said about sales/receivables and collection days is applicable to sales/inventory (or, really, cost of goods sold/inventory).[2] Like sales/receivables and collection days, inventory turnover has a powerful impact throughout the business. When it is either too low or excessive, almost all the other ratios suffer. It is a rough indicator of the liquidity and quality of inventory, especially when compared with previous accounting periods or competitor companies.

A low inventory turnover, like slow receivables, suggests slow-moving or obsolete items that must be investigated. Slowness could mean we will have to take markdowns chargeable against income, because of obsolescence or physical deterioration; theft; unusable material; or lower material prices. And a bloated inventory, like receivables, produces excessive current liabilities and interest charges. It also costs us money to maintain, store, and protect or secure the inventory items.

Inventory slowness necessarily has the same adverse effects on the other ratios as excessive receivables: the abnormally high inventory/working capital ratio that undermines current liquidity; excessive current liabilities/equity; and usually an even worse deterioration in the profit margin than is caused by receivables slowness. Not only are interest charges increased, but carrying-costs themselves multiply as more and more inventory must be maintained and protected.

The following trend analysis illustrates an easy way to compare turnover of receivables and inventory:

	Period 1	Period 2	Index	Period 3	Index
1. Cash	$ 622	$ 218	35%	$ 194	31%
2. Receivables (000)	2,940	3,010	102	3,006	102
3. Inventory (000)	2,811	3,260	116	4,001	142
4. Sales (000)	24,589	27,381	111	27,860	113
5. Sales/receivables	8.4×	9.1×	108	9.3×	111
6. Sales/inventory	8.7	8.4	96	7.0	80

In period 3, sales (line 4) had risen to 113% of those in period 1. Receivables (line 2) were kept under tight control, at only 102%. The sales/receivables ratio (line 5) therefore moved up to 111%. But inventory

[2]Cost of goods sold is of course valued at cost and not at the higher markup to sales price. It is directly comparable to inventory, which is valued at lower of cost or market. Therefore, cost of goods sold/inventory is the meaningful ratio. Sales/inventory is not, because sales includes the markup and inventory does not. For external purposes of intercompany or industry comparison, however, sales/inventory must be used because this is the way inventory turnover is generally presented and published.

(line 3) soared to 142%, driving down sales/inventory (line 6) to 80% of period 1. The slowdown of inventory is a severe problem that demands major corrective action. And it is complicated further by an accompanying cash drain (line 1) of no less serious proportions (index down to 31%).

This type of asset trend analysis dramatizes relationships that are usually overlooked when the ratio analysis is confined to a single year.

SUPPLEMENTARY CASH PRODUCTIVITY RATIOS

Sales/working capital is a very useful supplementary asset ratio. It double-checks such primary ratios as sales/equity and fixed assets/equity (to be discussed soon). Sales/equity may be normal, for instance, but sales/working capital is too high. This means the culprit is working capital, which is too low in relation to sales. Current liabilities have become excessive, to the detriment of the current ratio and perhaps to our ability to finance externally.

Since the overheated sales/working capital ratio occurs against a normal sales/equity ratio, we should look across the line. Perhaps one of the long-term ATL assets or liabilities are undermining working capital. The problem is often an excessive fixed assets/equity ratio, suggesting that fixed assets grew at the expense of and by draining working capital.

Sales/fixed assets is also supplementary rather than primary. The more sales we generate per dollar of plant and equipment, the better our profit margin. More sales are covering fixed overhead, so per-unit charges against sales are lower. And working capital is probably in good supply compared with fixed assets. But low sales/fixed assets may well mean excessive fixed assets. It suggests high overhead costs per unit of sales and a drain on working capital, to say nothing of excessive debt to finance the fixed assets in the first place.

Sales/fixed assets is a useful supplement to the crucial fixed assets/equity ratio: what would otherwise be excessive fixed assets/equity may not be hurting profits and working capital if sales/fixed assets is high.

An abnormally high sales/fixed assets ratio usually means plant and equipment are being worked too hard and therefore inefficiently, at or above capacity. Or else it could be due to all the property and equipment we are leasing, which would completely reverse the interpretation.

We are traversing the second tier of the control process. Our analysis of the forecasted financial statements has probed into the ratios measuring CRE itself, and into those of cost cash (S/C) and asset cash (S/A) that determine CRE.

It now moves ahead to the crucial ratios of leverage cash (L/A).

CHAPTER 25

LEVERAGE CASH:
SAFEGUARDING CURRENT LIQUIDITY

Everything we do to manage balance-sheet liquidity, involving the SCALDER forces converging on Pi, either originates in or simultaneously determines current liquidity. This was pointed up sharply in our Statement of Liquidity Velocity. As the focal point of balance-sheet liquidity, therefore, current liquidity tends to be the focal point of the strategy of cash.

Our control analysis of current liquidity is done here in the context of leverage cash because, to a considerable extent, current liquidity is both determined *by* and *determines* leverage. The amount and liquidity of working capital is strongly affected by the amounts and relative proportions of current and long-term debt. And the amount of our sustainable debt is strongly affected by the amount and liquidity of our working capital.

We have therefore grouped the leverage ratios into three subcategories, which we will discuss in this and the next chapter: the ratios of current liquidity, asset debt capacity, and operating debt capacity. But mostly we will be talking about current liquidity—its origin, behavior, and impact.

CURRENT COVERAGE AND THE BALANCE SHEET ANALOGY

The ratios of current liquidity are mainly the following:

Current coverage (current liabilities/current assets)
Quick coverage (current liabilities/quick assets)
Net coverage (total liabilities/current assets)
Receivables/working capital
Inventory/working capital
Fixed assets/equity
Fixed assets/long-term debt

For analytical purposes, we should think of the current sector of the balance sheet as a microcosm of the entire balance sheet: the company has only current assets and current liabilities, and the difference between the two is no longer working capital but equity.

The current creditors therefore can look only to current assets for coverage of their liabilities. The ratio of their current liabilities to working capital is the debt/equity ratio. And their equity cushion (equity/total assets) is working capital/current assets. This is the percentage by which current assets can decline before the equity cushion (working capital) is wiped out. On any further decline, current creditors must look to sources of repayment other than current assets—presumably earnings, since there are no other assets. For example:

Current Section	Balance-Sheet Equivalent	Amount
Current assets	Total assets	$2,500,000
Current liabilities	Total debt	1,250,000
Working capital	Equity	1,250,000
Current liabilities/ working capital	Debt/equity	100%
Working capital/ current assets	Equity/total assets	50%

Current liabilities/working capital is our debt/equity ratio: 1250/1250 = 100%. And working capital/current assets is equity/total assets, or the equity cushion: 1250/2500 = 50%. So a 50% decline in current assets, from $2,500,000 to $1,250,000, would wipe out the $1,250,000 working capital (equity) cushion. Then $1,250,000 of current liabilities would no longer have asset protection over and above the remaining $1,250,000 of current assets.

We thus analyze our current position by putting ourselves into the shoes of our current creditors, and look at our company as though the current section were the entire balance sheet in miniature. This is the asset and working capital coverage that our current creditors are receiving. If they are getting too much coverage, we are overliquid and not fully utilizing our current borrowing capacity. If they are too thinly covered, we are heading for financial strain. The health and profitability of our current position are thus measured by the other side of the coin, the health and well-being of our creditor's investment.

Table 40 traces an imaginary company's *coverage ratios*—current coverage, quick coverage, and net coverage.

Table 40 Evaluating Current Liquidity (000)

	1	2	3	4	5
Current Coverage					
1. CA	$ 250	$225	$325	$225	$325
2. CL	100	125	225	125	125
3. WC	150	100	100	100	200
4. CL/CA (asset coverage)[a]	40%	56%	69%	56%	38%
5. CL/WC (debt/equity)	67	125	225	125	62
6. WC/CA (equity cushion)	60	44	31	44	61
Quick Coverage (Inventory $50,000)					
7. QA	$200	$175	$275	$175	$275
8. CL	100	125	225	125	125
9. NQA	100	50	50	50	150
10. CL/QA (asset coverage)[a]	50%	71%	82%	71%	45%
11. CL/NQA (debt/equity)	100	250	450	250	83
12. NQA/QA (equity cushion)	50	29	18	29	54
Net Coverage (LTD $50,000)					
13. CA	$250	$225	$325	$225	$325
14. TL	150	175	275	175	175
15. NCA	100	50	50	50	150
16. TL/CA (asset coverage)	60%	78%	85%	78%	54%
17. TL/NCA (debt/equity)	150	350	550	350	117
18. NCA/CA (equity cushion)	40	22	15	22	46

[a]The asset coverage ratios are the reciprocals of the current ratio, CA/CL, and the quick ratio, QA/CL. That is, CL/CA of 40% is a current ratio of 1/40%, or 2.5×.

In *column 1* current assets are $250,000, current liabilities $100,000, and working capital $150,000 (lines 1 to 3).

Current liabilities/current assets (line 4) is our asset coverage of $100, 000/$250,000, or a comfortable 40%. This ratio is the reverse of the current ratio, of course, which is 250/100 or 2.5×. Though useful for external comparative purposes, the popular current ratio is arithmetically clumsy:

its normal values are up around 200% and 300% (2× and 3×). And it reverses the usual L/A pattern in which a leverage ratio increases and cash is generated as leverage increases. For internal purposes, current liabilities/current assets is therefore more convenient.

Current liabilities/working capital (line 5) corresponds to the debt/ equity ratio of the balance sheet: At $100,000/$150,000, it is a comfortable 67%.

Working capital/current assets (the equity cushion) is $150,000/$250,000, or 60% (line 6). That is, $150,000 of working capital is 60% of $250,000 of current assets—which can therefore decline 60%, or by $150,000, before they eliminate working capital. Then our current creditors must start looking to sources of repayment other than current assets. We can summarize their present and potential position as follows:

	CA (000)	CL (000)	WC (000)	WC/CA
Now	$250	$100	$150	60%
− CA of 60%, or − $150	100	100	0	0

For the present, the $100,000 of current liabilities have a $150,000 working capital cushion on which to rest comfortably. It is 60% of the $250,000 of current assets.

Of course, *CL/CA* (40%) and *WC/CA* (60%) are two sides of the same coin. When one is 30%, for instance, the other is 70%; and vice versa. But this in no way detracts from the analytical value of using *both* ratios, as we will see.

In *column 2* current assets (line 1) decline moderately to $225,000 and current liabilities increase to $125,000, so that working capital drops from $150,000 to $100,000. This sharply increases current liabilities/current assets to 56% (a drop in the current ratio to 1.8×, from 2.5×).

Current liabilities/working capital (debt/equity) jumps to 125%. And the equity cushion of working capital/current assets falls to 44%: it narrows to 44% the amount by which current assets can decline before current liabilities are left without any excess asset coverage. That is, if current assets of $225,000 declined by 44%, or by $100,000, they would be equal to current liabilities of $125,000. The current creditors' working capital cushion would be eliminated.

In *column 3* inventory and receivables increase by $100,000, financed by an additional $100,000 of current liabilities. So current assets are now

$325,000 and current liabilities $225,000, leaving working capital unchanged at $100,000. But current liabilities are now a much higher percentage of current assets, having jumped to 69% (current ratio down to 1.4×). And the debt/equity ratio of current liabilities/working capital soars to 225%.

Current creditors therefore have an investment in the "company" of more than twice that of the stockholders' $100,000 of working capital. And the cushion of working capital/current assets has plummeted to 31%: A drop of only 31% in the $325,000 of current assets, or by $100,000, would bring it down to the level of current liabilities. The company's current position has thus deteriorated markedly on all three counts—current asset coverage, debt/equity, and the working capital cushion.

In *column 4* we liquidate $100,000 of current assets to pay off $100,000 of current liabilities. It does not change working capital, but the liquidity of our current position improves. And we are back to our situation in column 2. Finally, in *column 5*, we borrow $100,000 long-term to restore current assets to $325,000. Since this does not affect current liabilities, working capital doubles to $200,000.

This $100,000 cash infusion improves our current ratios materially: current liabilities/current assets drops to a well-covered 38%, and current liabilities/working capital to 62%. And our equity cushion jumps to a fat 61%: The injection of cash that increased current assets and working capital by the same $100,000 has *doubled* working capital, from $100,000 to $200,000. So the cushion is thicker on which our current creditors can rest their weary heads.

EVALUATING CURRENT COVERAGE

Current liabilities/current assets is a more enlightening analytical device than its ever-popular reciprocal, the current ratio. But it is not very useful when used alone. Arbitrary rules of thumb—such as under 50% is good and over 50% is bad—are as useless and even misleading as the two-to-one popular mythology and silliness that surrounds the current ratio. Nor are intercompany comparisons of much help. A safe level of current asset coverage of liabilities in one company might be very risky in another.

It helps if we use all *three* current coverage ratios. When current liabilities/current assets climbs from 40 to 56% (column 2, line 4), we should be alerted. And when it soars to 69%, we had *better* be alerted. But we are being alerted only to dig deeper analytically. Current liabilities/working capital (column 3, line 5) then tells us that "debt/equity" has climbed—from a comfortable 67% position for our creditors to 125%, and then to 225%. As soon as it rose above 100%, they were no longer protectively covered by working capital.

Even this would not be critical, though bad enough, if it were not that their working capital cushion (margin of safety) sank to 31%. Given the volatility of the typical business—both seasonal and cyclical—working capital below one-third of current assets may threaten current creditors. Either (or both) a shrinkage in assets or increase in liabilities could swiftly wipe out their cushion, forcing them to seek repayment elsewhere than from current assets. This is virtually the definition of critical current stringency, which is the treacherous shoal to be avoided.

The proper interpretation of CL/CA thus requires the other two ratios, if only to establish its broad limits and tell us if it is too high. When it reached 69% (column 3, line 4), the figure was significant because CL/WC (debt/equity) at 225% was far above its prudent 100% line of demarcation —and because the WC/CA cushion was getting scrawny at 31%. It is true that by subtracting 69% from 100%, we get the same 31% as from WC/CA. But then we miss the depth of analysis—the underlying reasons—that the "cushion" concept summarizes so effectively.

We are not helped by the absolute *amount* of working capital, which analytically is a minor consideration. Between columns 2 and 3, where the severe stringency developed, working capital remained unchanged at $100,000. It is the *relationship* between current assets and current liabilities, not the arithmetic difference between the two, that makes or breaks a company's health or the company itself.

QUICK COVERAGE AND INVENTORY RELIANCE

The current coverage analysis tells us all we need to know about current liquidity, except for one troublesome detail: current assets include inventory, which is not particularly marketable or liquid. So we do not know what either our current liquidity or position is until we go through the same exercise with inventory eliminated from current assets. This we call *quick assets*. They consist mostly of cash and receivables—which are much closer to cash than are inventories, both in point of time within the seasonal cycle and in salability. *Quick coverage* is thus a more strenuous test of current position and liquidity than is current coverage.

We have $50,000 of inventory. This we eliminate from the $250,000 of current assets, in column 1, to give us quick assets of $200,000 (line 7). Deducting the same current liabilities of $100,000, we have net quick assets of $100,000 (line 9). So *current liabilities/quick assets* (line 10) is 50%, compared with the more favorable current liabilities/current assets of 40% (line 4).

Current liabilities/net quick assets (line 11) is now our debt/equity reference point, which is 100%: $200,000 of quick assets (no inventory) less $100,000 of current liabilities equals $100,000 of net quick assets—which is now our "equity." So, CL/NQA is 100%. The current creditors' $100,000 is as large an investment in the $200,000 of quick assets as is the owners' $100,000 of net quick assets.

Net quick assets/quick assets (line 12) is the equity cushion, or 50%. This is the percentage that quick assets of $200,000 can shrink before the current creditors must look to the sale of *inventory* for repayment. A 50% decline in quick assets would bring them down to the $100,000 of current liabilities, and the cushion is eliminated:

	QA (000)	CL (000)	NQA (000)	NQA/QA
Now	$200	$100	$100	50%
− QA of 50%, or −$100	100	100	0	0

Until the NQA cushion is wiped out, there are ample quick assets continually turning into cash to satisfy maturing current liabilities. So there is no need for current creditors to concern themselves about inventory at all, let alone its liquidity.

The company's quick coverage proceeds through its five stages to column 5, with quick assets and net quick assets (lines 7 and 9) $50,000 below current assets and working capital (lines 1 and 3). So it has higher (less favorable) ratios of current liabilities/quick assets (line 10) and current liabilities/net quick assets (line 11), and a thinner equity cushion of net quick assets/quick assets (line 12).

In *column 3*, whether we are in trouble or not with our thin current coverages (lines 4 to 6) depends on the liquidity of current assets as now revealed by quick coverage. A safe relationship between current assets and current liabilities depends heavily on how liquid the current assets are— how quickly and easily they could be turned into cash. If the $325,000 of current assets (line 1) consists mostly of inventory and some slow receivables, management has indeed reason to take fright over a working capital cushion of only 31% (line 6). But if it is mostly cash and good receivables, 31% may not cause trouble.

So we look at quick coverage, and see that current liabilities/quick assets (ex inventory) is 82% (line 10). In other words, creditors have an 18%

NQA cushion for current liabilities (line 12) before they will have to look to inventory as a source of repayment. We are not quite as badly off as we thought.

But the safe level of current liabilities/quick assets really depends on the liquidity of receivables, which are the noncash portion of quick assets. It is the parallel of saying that a safe current ratio depends on the liquidity of inventory and receivables. Net quick assets/quick assets of 18% *is* a cause for alarm if our $275,000 of quick assets (line 7) includes $60,000 of overdue receivables. They.may have to be written down or written off as uncollectable. Then our realizable quick assets would be only $215,000, leaving no net quick assets (after $225,000 of current debt) and no "quick" cushion for creditors. They would have to rely on inventory for repayment of $10,000 (that is, $215,000 of QA less $225,000 of current liabilities).

The *inventory reliance ratio*, in fact, can be very helpful in determining the liquidity of our current position. It is the ratio of our NQA deficit (or $10,000 in the example above) to inventory—the percentage of inventory that current creditors must rely on for repayment.

Suppose that we have current assets of $250,000 and current liabilities of $125,000, or a current coverage of 50%. Our position is comfortable except that inventories have climbed to $150,000. Subtracting them from current assets of $250,000 gives us quick assets of only $100,000. After current liabilities of $125,000, we have net quick assets of ($25,000). This NQA deficit is the amount by which current creditors are relying on $150,000 of inventory for repayment. Our inventory reliance ratio is $25,000/$150,000, or *17%*.

Business improves and we buy an additional $50,000 of inventory, financed with current liabilities. So current assets climb from $250,000 to $300,000, of which $200,000 is now inventory. So quick assets (CA − inventory) remain at $100,000. But current liabilities have increased by $50,000 to $175,000, leaving us with an NQA deficit of $100,000–$175,000, or *$75,000*. Our inventory reliance ratio has more than doubled to $75,000/$200,000, or *37%*. Current creditors must rely on 37% of our inventory for repayment.

As with current coverage and quick coverage, how high is high depends largely on the liquidity of the pivotal asset. In this case it is inventory. Suppose that its stated value will not be realized because some important items are lost, damaged, or obsolete. To rely on 37% of inventory for repayment may leave our current creditors in an exposed position. Being "in their shoes" throughout this entire analysis, we ourselves have an identical risk exposure. But if our inventory is highly liquid and marketable, and promises to remain so, an inventory reliance ratio of 37% may even be conservative.

Trend comparisons are helpful in studying the relationship between current coverage and quick coverage. We have seen that current asset liquidity is a function of *current liabilities/current assets* versus *current liabilities/quick assets*. If the trend in one diverges from the other, there is a specific liquidity implication. For example, suppose that current liabilities/current assets remains in a level trend, but current liabilities/quick assets rises (quick assets are declining). A subsurface inventory problem may be gathering force. It is therefore essential that we continually monitor the *trend* relationship between the ratios of current coverage and quick coverage.

NET COVERAGE

Net coverage (lines 13 to 18) is the same series of calculations made under the same assumptions as before—except that current assets are compared to *total liabilities* (line 14), to give us *net current assets* (line 15).

We compute *total liabilities/current assets* of 60% (column 1, line 16). *Total liabilities/net current assets* (line 17), or 150%, is now our debt/equity. That is, current assets of $250,000 less *total* liabilities of $150,000 is net current assets of $100,000. Our creditors' $150,000 of total debt is a much larger stake in the $250,000 of current assets than is the owners' $100,000 of net current assets.

The equity cushion now becomes *net current assets/current assets*, or 40% (line 18). That is, net current assets is now the creditors' cushion: they would lose it in the event of a 40% decline in the $250,000 of current assets. That would reduce current assets by $100,000, or the entire amount of NCA. And creditors would then have to look elsewhere than to current assets for repayment.

Net coverage is a balance-sheet concept that straddles current liquidity and total liquidity. Later we will apply it also to the long-term sector in the form of such tools as FARR (the fixed asset reliance ratio).

Our diagnostic and analytical probing into current liquidity has gone about as far as it can within the confines of current coverage, quick coverage, and net coverage. We should now look into two key liquidity ratios for further enlightenment: receivables/working capital, and inventory/working capital.

THE LIQUIDITY THERMOMETERS: RECEIVABLES AND INVENTORY

Receivables/working capital is a telltale ratio, or thermometer, that reveals overheating when its companion ratios may be normal. It is symptomatic of the liquidity forces flowing through the current position, rather than itself exerting an independent impact. The ratio simply tells us whether receivables are too large (or small) a proportion of working capital, in relation to the size and character of sales volume.

In this way it provides a double check on sales/receivables and average collection days. They may be normal. Yet subsurface problems have given rise to excessive receivables/working capital, which may be constricting current liquidity. It often happens in a period of rapid sales growth, when receivables keep pace with sales and therefore sales/receivables remains constant.

When receivables/working capital has thus overheated, the larger amount of receivables probably contains a larger amount of poor customer accounts. So we are exposed to an inordinate risk of writedowns. It also may have generated too many current liabilities to finance the receivables glut, to the detriment of our credit position. But excessive receivables/ working capital can also mean that our problem is in the denominator: working capital has become deficient. This is a different type of problem and calls for different types of solutions.

Inventory/working capital overheating is more dangerous because inventories are notoriously illiquid as soon as they enter production, which is where they mostly are. The ratio is therefore a crucial thermometer of general overheating, and a sensitive barometer of future trouble.

We saw that receivables/working capital is a warning of problems not revealed by sales/receivables. So too does excessive inventory/working capital tell us that sales/inventory is not to be relied on. Without inventory/working capital, we could muddle into excessive trade payables generated to finance the excessive inventory. This is to say nothing of the bloated inventory itself—its heavy carrying and financing costs and the substantial risk of writedowns to which it exposes us.

Rules of thumb are superficial and by themselves hazardous. But when inventory/working capital climbs above 75%, the burden of proof should be on those who argue against remedial measures to bring it down again. Over 100%, we are in more trouble than we think, even at the top of the season. And we should be alerted if it fails to decline normally as the seasonal cycle moves to receivables and then to collections and cash.

Since inventory is the most illiquid component of working capital, the ratio can increase only at the expense of current liquidity. This is why the quick coverage analysis is an indispensable supplement to current coverage. Current ratios may be fine, as we have seen, but quick coverage (working capital liquidity) is being undermined by inventory/working capital. Once this is known, we must raise our minimum acceptable current coverage ratios to satisfy our minimum liquidity requirements.

The quick-coverage supplementary analysis thus tips us off to the mushrooming inventory, by presenting a deterioriating quick ratio picture. But plugging inventory/working capital into the analysis gives us the more complete liquidity picture, and helps us evaluate it in terms of bill-paying ability.

ACROSS-THE-LINE (ATL) FORCES CONVERGING ON LIQUIDITY

Thus far we have been diagnosing the symptoms (not the causes) of working capital inadequacy: we do not have enough (1) working capital *quantity*, (2) current asset *coverage* of liabilities, or (3) *liquidity* of current assets.

But rarely is either the cause or solution of the inadequacy found within the working capital area itself. They are found, rather, down in the *ATL* (across-the-line) section of the balance sheet: It was mainly here that the insufficient quantity, coverage, and liquidity had their origin—in oversized fixed assets, excessive or too-costly long-term debt, or insufficient equity (including poor earnings). So it is mainly here that they are solvable.

Fixed assets/equity and *fixed assets/long-term debt* together include all three ATL components.[1] Their combined impact on working capital, from both the numerator and denominator sides, is therefore decisive and all-pervading. They are also crucial in the debt-capacity analysis, as we will see. So they are the connecting ratios between current liquidity and total liquidity.

We are in fact starting to move, in our discussion of leverage control, from current liquidity to long-term debt capacity, via the ATL phenomenon that connects them. Current and fixed leverage are linked both structurally and functionally by ATL. Structurally, on the balance sheet, ATL is the line of demarcation separating the working capital province of current liquidity from the fixed or long-term province of overall debt capacity. Functionally, as we have seen, ATL forces determine the ebb and flow of funds from the fixed to the current province and back again.

So we will talk first about this critically important ATL transition zone, and then delve into debt capacity proper.

Probably the best way to begin is with a concise summary of the ATL-working capital relationship, as in Table 41.

[1] *Fixed assets* are here defined as all *non*current assets, including miscellaneous assets. And throughout the entire discussion, assets and debt include the amounts by which rent paid on financial leases has been capitalized (as described in Chapter 6 on leverage cash).

Lines 1 to 3. This summary first presents the five ATL and working capital *uses* of funds (columns 1 and 2), and the five ATL and working capital *sources* of funds (columns 3 and 4).

Then it traces the impact on working capital of changes in each of the uses and sources of funds. Let us begin with the *ATL uses* of funds (column 1).

Table 41 ATL-Working Capital Liquidity

	Uses of Funds		Sources of Funds	
	ATL 1	WC 2	ATL 3	WC 4
1.	$+FA^a$	$-CL$	$-FA$	$+CL$
2.	$-LTD$	$+CA$	$+LTD$	$-CA$
3.	$-E$		$+E$	
	ATL Uses		Zero WC Impact	Negative WC Impact
4.	$+FA$		$+LTD; +E$	$+CL; -CA$
5.	$-LTD$		$-FA; +E$	$+CL; -CA$
6.	$-E$		$-FA; +LTD$	$+CL; -CA$
		WC Uses	Positive WC Impact	Zero WC Impact
7.		$-CL$	$-FA; +LTD; +E$	$-CA$
8.		$+CA$	$-FA; +LTD; +E$	$+CL$
	Zero WC Impact	Positive WC Impact	ATL Sources	
9.	$-LTD; -E$	$-CL; +CA$	$-FA$	
10.	$+FA; -E$	$-CL; +CA$	$+LTD$	
11.	$+FA; -LTD$	$-CL; +CA$	$+E$	
	Negative WC Impact	Zero WC Impact		WC Sources
12.	$+FA; -LTD; -E$	$+CA$		$+CL$
13.	$+FA; -LTD; -E$	$-CL$		$-CA$

^{a}FA includes miscellaneous assets.

Line 4. An increase in fixed assets (+FA) produces no working capital impact (zero WC impact, column 3) if it is financed by an increase in long-term debt (+LTD) or equity (+E). But it reduces working capital (negative WC impact, column 4) if financed by an increase in current liabilities (+CL) or a reduction in current assets (since they are ATL transactions).

Line 5. A reduction in long-term debt (−LTD) is an investment of funds (ATL uses, column 1). It has no working capital impact (column 3) if the sources of funds are the sale of fixed assets (−FA) or a new issue of common stock (+E). But there is a negative working capital impact across-the-line (column 4): the long-term debt was reduced with funds provided by increased current liabilities (+CL) or reduced current assets (−CA). And so forth for line 6 (−E).

As for *working capital uses* of funds (column 2), *line 7* shows that funds used to reduce current liabilities (−CL) have no working capital impact (column 4) if they are derived from a reduction in current assets. But −CL *increases* working capital (column 3) if the funds come from across the line —from the sale of fixed assets, or additional long-term debt or equity financing. And so forth for line 8.

So much for the ATL and WC *uses* of funds. Let us now look at the *sources* of funds (columns 3 and 4).

Line 9. The liquidation of fixed assets as a source of funds (column 3) has no working capital impact (column 1) if they are used to reduce long-term debt or equity. But it increases working capital (column 2) if the funds are used to reduce current liabilities or increase current assets across-the-line.

And the same type of analysis can be traced through lines 10 and 11.

Line 12. The *working capital source* of funds (column 4) is an increase in current liabilities, which does nothing for working capital if used to buy current assets (column 2). But it reduces working capital (column 1) if used to buy fixed assets, repay long-term debt, or reduce equity (such as a dividend payment or the retirement of stock). And so forth for line 13.

THE SUMMARY RATIOS OF ATL LIQUIDITY

Fixed assets/equity and *fixed assets/long-term debt* define and summarize all these ATL relationships, as noted. Together they provide the total ATL-working capital impact.

These summary ratios of ATL liquidity, FA/E and FA/LTD, must act in concert to supply or drain working capital. When they move in opposite directions, their working capital impact is neutralized. For instance:

	ATL ratio	$-WC$	$+WC$
1.	$+FA/E$ $+FA/LTD$	$+FA\ -E$ $+FA\ -LTD$	
2.	$-FA/E$ $-FA/LTD$		$-FA\ +E$ $-FA\ +LTD$
3.	$+FA/E$ $-FA/LTD$	$+FA\ -E$	$-FA\ +LTD$

Line 1. The two ATL ratios together can increase only at the expense of working capital, which is thereby contracted $(-WC)$.

Line 2. They can decline only at the enrichment of working capital.

Line 3. But if one ratio changes and is not supported by the other, their impacts cancel out. That is, $+FA/E$ is a use of funds (applied to $+FA$ or $-E$) that is not now supplied by working capital (as in line 1), but by $-FA/LTD$ (either by $-FA$ or $+LTD$). So the working capital impact is neutralized. And $-FA/LTD$ is a source of funds—which are now applied to $+FA/E$, not to $+WC$ as in line 2. So there is no WC impact.

Equity and long-term debt together constitute the company's *capital fund*, or its source of permanent capital $(LTD+E)$. So the one all-encompassing ratio for measuring the ATL-working capital impact is *fixed assets / capital fund*, or $FA/(LTD+E)$.

An increase in this ratio reduces working capital, as in line 1, and a reduction increases working capital (line 2). It does not matter in either case whether the fixed asset numerator or the capital fund denominator caused the change in working capital. *As in line 1*, to the extent that the increase in fixed assets was not financed out of capital fund $(+LTD$ and $+E)$, the money had to be supplied by working capital. And to the extent that a reduction in capital fund was not replenished from the liquidation of fixed assets, funds had to be drawn from working capital.

Fixed assets/capital fund is valuable as a single, all-inclusive ATL measuring stick. But it is *too* compact for most analytical uses. It conceals the very important transactions *within* the capital fund, between debt and equity, or between either one and working capital. So we should rely mostly on FA/E and FA/LTD, but stress the *causal* component, FA/E.

THE CRUCIAL LIQUIDITY ROLE OF FIXED ASSETS

The *fixed assets / equity* relationship is critically important. A normal to low ratio enhances profits and liquidity, and an excessive ratio is destructive of profits and liquidity. This is because fixed assets are costly both to finance and maintain, as we have seen. And it is because they can increase only at the expense of overall balance-sheet liquidity.

That is, if assets are financed by long-term debt, such ratios as debt/ equity and debt/working capital are forced higher. Debt capacity is used up to that extent. But if we finance fixed assets out of working capital, short-term liquidity is undermined seriously and perhaps dangerously.

The amount and density of fixed assets on the balance sheet—their "weight" among all the other items—is in fact central to an analysis of balance-sheet health and liquidity. As we have seen earlier, they exert a preponderant influence on the size of our long-term debt and of working capital. Both are usually healthy-looking if the balance sheet is "light" on fixed assets. But if assets are so heavy as to encroach on working capital and require excessive liabilities, we usually have an unhealthy-looking patient on our hands.

Analyzing fixed assets thus goes to the root *cause* of things. So it is even more fruitful than analyzing working capital and long-term debt, however crucial they may be as resultants or effects.

Let us assume, for instance, the simplistic situation depicted in Table 42.

Line 1. We are in a too-easy balance-sheet position as to the profitable utilization of available liquidity: working capital is $300,000 (column 3), with current liabilities only 40% of current assets (column 4). Subtracting *total* liabilities (TL) of $300,000 from current assets (CA) of $500,000, leaves net current assets of $200,000 (column 5): *All* our creditors can thus be serviced and repaid entirely from current assets, with $200,000 of net current assets to spare. Moreover, fixed assets are only 50%, and total debt 75%, of equity (columns 6 and 7).

But volume is soaring. So we acquire a second plant and the equipment to bring it into production, for *$300,000.*

Line 2a. The additional facilities are financed entirely with long-term debt. Adding the $300,000 to each side, we now have on our balance sheet $500,000 of fixed assets and $400,000 of long-term debt. Working capital (column 3) and current liabilities/current assets (column 4) remain unchanged, and ample.

But net current assets (column 5) sink to ($100,000), with current assets of $500,000 now exceeded by *total* debt of $600,000. So our creditors must rely for repayment on the conversion of $500,000 of current assets, *plus* $100,000 of fixed assets. [2]

---

[2]This of course is balance-sheet protection of debt, not cash flow protection.

Table 42 The Liquidity Impact of Fixed Assets/Equity

Assets[a] (000) 1		Liabilities (000) 2		WC (000) 3	CL/ CA 4	NCA (000) 5	FA/ E 6	TL/ E 7	LTD/ WC 8	FARR 9
1. CA	$500	CL	$200							
FA	200	LTD	100							
		TL	300							
		E	400							
	$700		$700	$300	40%	$200	50%	75%	33%	0%

2a. New $300,000 plant, debt financed:

CA	$500	CL	$200							
FA	500	LTD	400							
		TL	600							
		E	400							
	$1,000		$1,000	300	40	(100)	125	150	133	20

2b. New $300,000 plant, financed
half from CA and half from debt:

CA	$350	CL	$200							
FA	500	LTD	250							
		TL	450							
		E	400							
	$850		$850	150	57	(100)	125	112	167	20

[a]For simplicity, we ignore the earnings impact on E, CA, etc.

This is measured by our *fixed asset reliance ratio* (FARR):

$$FARR = \frac{(TL - CA)}{FA}$$

$$= \frac{\$600,000 - \$500,000}{\$500,000} = 20\%$$

Creditors must rely on 20% of the fixed assets for repayment. FARR is comparable to the inventory reliance ratio, $(CL - QA)$/inventory, which was the percentage of *inventory* our current creditors rely on to satisfy their claims.

The culprit is obviously *fixed assets/equity* (column 6). It jumped from 50% to 125%, with fixed assets of $500,000 now exceeding the $400,000 of equity. The $300,000 increase in assets generated an equal amount of long-term debt, which caused the $100,000 deficit in net current assets (column 5). It produced an excessive debt/equity ratio (column 7) of 150%. And long-term debt/working capital (column 8) skyrocketed from 33 to 133%.

In *line 1* the stockholders' equity of $400,000 "owned" the $200,000 of fixed assets plus $200,000 of the current assets (after total debt claims of $300,000). But in *line 2a* the $400,000 of equity has a claim on $400,000 of the $500,000 of fixed assets, and on nothing else. The $600,000 of total debt has a prior claim on the remaining $100,000 of fixed assets plus all $500,000 of current assets. A mere plant acquisition has turned liquidity upside down and inside out.

Only *fixed assets/equity* is responsible: It materially increased our debt burden; reduced the liquidity protection of our creditors, who now must rely on some fixed assets; and downgraded the liquidity composition of our equity (in terms of fixed vs. current assets). The stockholders' position has thus been weakened because the asset liquidity of his equity claim has been diminished, and his debt load has soared.

And the creditor's position has also weakened. He now relies not only on current assets—which were more than sufficient in situation 1—but also on operating *cash flow*. That is, he is relying now in 20% of the fixed assets (FARR) to help service his debt. In effect it means he must now rely on cash flow—including the new plant's hoped-for profitability.

The creditors and stockholders thus have an identity of interest in the liquidity of equity, as measured by *fixed assets/equity*. Upon this core ratio, virtually all the debt utilization and capacity ratios and the working capital ratios heavily depend.

One alternative is *line 2b*: Finance the new facilities partly out of current assets and the remainder with long-term debt. Each source thus provides $150,000 of the $300,000 facility cost. It reduces current assets from $500,000 to $350,000, and increases long-term debt to $250,000 (not to $400,000 as in line 2a).

This is a $150,000 ATL drain on working capital (column 3), which line 2a was not. Current liabilities/current assets (column 4) jumps to 57%. Net current assets (column 5) is again $100,000 in the red ($350,000 of current assets less $450,000 of total debt). And fixed assets/equity (column 6) is again at a lofty 125%.

Debt/equity (column 7) at 112% is now less badly off, because half the financing was supplied by working capital rather than new debt. But for this very reason, long-term debt/working capital (column 8) shot up to an untenable *167%*. This came from the higher LTD numerator and the lower working capital denominator.

FARR—the creditors' reliance on fixed assets—is $(TL-CA)/FA$, or $(\$450,000-\$350,000)/\$500,000$. So it is the same *20%*: it does not matter whether the new plant is financed entirely with debt, or partly with debt and partly current assets. The increase in fixed assets produces the same increase in creditors' reliance on a portion of those assets to protect their debt. The single determinative factor, again, is the increase in *fixed assets/equity*.

THE QUALITATIVE RATIONALE OF FIXED ASSETS/EQUITY

Fixed assets/equity is crucial also because a move above 100% is a *qualitative* event, and signals a new ballgame, in the analysis of current liquidity and debt capacity.

This stems from the fact that the balance sheet balances: by the exact amount that fixed assets[3] exceed equity, total liabilities exceed current assets. That is, $FA-E=TL-CA$. By the exact amount that fixed assets exceed equity, creditors (TL) have run out of CA and must look to *those fixed assets* for repayment.

So as FA/E climbs above 100%, a qualitative debt-capacity distinction between assets and earnings replaces the quantitative one of asset size: Net current assets have gone into the red. Creditors now rely not only on current assets but on *fixed assets* as well (FARR). So they are relying on *earning power*, in effect, because fixed assets are not especially liquid. Such assets do not really support debt by their liquidation value, but by their cash-flow contribution.

The following summarizes our three situations in Table 42:

	FA	− E	= TL	− CA	$\dfrac{FA-E}{TL-CA}$	FA/E	FARR
	(000)	(000)	(000)	(000)	(000)		$[(5)\div(1)]$
	1	2	3	4	5	6	7
1.	$200	$400	$300	$500	$(200)	50%	0%
2a.	500	400	600	500	100	125	20
2b.	500	400	450	350	100	125	20

$FA-E=TL-CA$ is arithmetically true (column 5). *Line 1*: While FA is

[3]That is, noncurrent assets.

less than E, TL is less than CA. NCA is positive (CA–TL). So creditors *need* look no further for repayment than the seasonal liquidation of current assets (column 4). This is the happy liquidity situation in which FA/E is less than 100% (column 6). And there is no reliance on FA, so FARR is 0% (column 7).

Line 2a. We buy a new plant with $300,000 of long-term debt. FA/E jumps to 125%. FA – E and TL – CA are both $100,000 (column 5). Our creditors (column 3) must now look to the $500,000 of current assets (column 4) *plus* $100,000 of fixed assets (column 5). So the fixed asset reliance ratio (FARR) is:

$$\frac{TL-CA}{FA} \quad \text{or} \quad \frac{FA-E}{FA}$$

$$100/500 \quad \text{or} \quad 100/500 \;=20\%$$

Creditors must rely on 20% of fixed assets, whether computed in terms of TL – CA *or* FA – E.

Line 2b. We take $150,000 out of current assets (column 4). And we add $150,000 to total liabilities (column 3)—which rise from $300,000 to $450,000—to buy the $300,000 plant. FA/E again jumps from 50% to 125%, and FARR is also 20%. The situation is much like line 2a. Nothing mattered—not even the form of financing—except the increase in fixed assets.

This is the prime mover and independent variable. And debt is the passive financing requirement, dependent on the gap between dynamic assets and static equity. So FA/E is a bull in the china shop, in response to which debt skips gingerly. When FA/E is below 100%, total debt is below current assets. When it is over 100%, debt exceeds current assets. The liquidity situation is reversed, with creditors now relying on fixed assets and necessarily operating cash flow. The debt-capacity ballgame has changed qualitatively, and we are playing with a new set of rules.

EVALUATING THE FIXED AND MISCELLANEOUS RATIOS

Thus far we have defined fixed assets as *all* noncurrent assets. Now let us revert to its usual balance-sheet definition of plant, land, and equipment. This distinguishes it from the other noncurrent assets, miscellaneous assets.

When fixed assets (thus conventionally defined) climb toward 100% of equity, we often detect rigidities and structural illiquidity—and a weakening of our creditors' asset or cash-flow protection. The excessive assets may have sapped working capital in the first instance, when they were bought. Or they drain it secondarily, as the costs and debt servicing of the new facilities absorb cash prior to reaching breakeven volume. Meanwhile, the additional sales from the facility are deprived of sufficient working capital, which produces distortions.

An excessive fixed assets/equity ratio may therefore cause overheating in sales/working capital, and in inventory/working capital and receivables/working capital. It overextends long-term debt/working capital and total liabilities/equity. Its impact on current liabilities/current assets is usually also unfavorable: cash assets are drained while liabilities bulge in response to the increased shipments. And net income/equity tends to be adversely affected, at least until the additional assets become profitable.

Miscellaneous assets/equity is analyzed the same way as fixed assets/equity; it has a similar impact on working capital, long-term debt, and net income. Miscellaneous items have nothing to do with the seasonal cycle and should never be included in current assets (which become cash within one year).

Miscellaneous *cash* includes cash restricted, pledged or segregated; the cash surrender value of life insurance; and so forth. Miscellaneous *receivables* are slow but eventually collectable trade receivables, those from officers and employees, from subsidiaries, and so forth. Slow but eventually usable *inventory*, and supplies, are miscellaneous rather than current assets. And *investments* in subsidiaries, and all prepayments and deferred charges, are miscellaneous rather than current.

Miscellaneous assets must be separated analytically from fixed assets because they serve a different purpose, and are the most vulnerable to markdowns or writeoffs. They prevent cash from going into productive fixed and current assets. And they increase our total debt requirement, like any other asset. Yet miscellaneous assets/equity is often ignored in the analysis, and becomes an unrecognized source of financial and profit deterioration.

It is thus mainly in the control of *current liquidity*, on which balance-sheet liquidity focuses, that we safeguard the fruits of total cash strategy. It contributes more than anything else to the viability and profitability of the business.

But the overriding source or destroyer of current liquidity are the *ATL* forces standing across the line, which are dominated by fixed assets in a manner best described by fixed assets/equity. Sales-supporting *assets* are what makes ATL the bull in our corporate china shop, powerfully influencing current liquidity on the one hand and debt capacity on the other.

It therefore serves our strategic purposes best, on this second tier of the control process, to conclude with an analysis of anticipated debt capacity. Long-term leverage reconnects the ATL and current areas, and closes the liquidity circle.

CHAPTER 26

LEVERAGE CASH:
SAFEGUARDING DEBT CAPACITY

We can now pass from the realm of ATL-current liquidity, on which debt capacity so vitally depends, to the analysis of debt capacity itself.

These brief comments will supplement, from the control standpoint, our extended discussion of leverage cash in Chapter 6. Then we can talk for a moment about controlling reinvestment cash utilization. And we will conclude the chapter with some third-tier recommendations on the prevention of cash variances: It is only in variance prevention that we keep the strategy of cash on track, moving inexorably forward to the maximization of CRE and Pi.

ANALYZING DEBT CAPACITY AND UTILIZATION

The key balance-sheet leverage ratios are the following:

Current liabilities/equity (CL/E)
Total liabilities/equity (TL/E)
Long-term debt/working capital (LTD/WC)

They are dependent ratios, as noted, largely the resultants or effects of fixed assets/equity. Sales, and the assets needed to sustain them, are the cause of which liabilities are the effect.

The three debt utilization ratios—CL/E, TL/E, and LTD/WC—are in fact thermometers. But they measure the temperature of the dynamic *sales-assets* organism, rather than of debt itself (which is passive and a symptom). On the cool end, these thermometers gauge underutilization—a dearth of assets and the consequent failure to borrow sufficiently, to the detriment of CRE. On the warm end, they are quick to reveal overheating from excessive assets that constrict liquidity and force up debt to hazardous levels.

Solutions to inadequate or excessive debt are therefore rarely found in the passive debt area itself, but in the dynamic assets and sales areas: Underutilization of debt is not corrected by borrowing if we have no sales-productive assets to invest in. And overutilization of debt is normally solvable in the dynamic sales-assets sector, or not at all—such as asset or cost cuts (or trimming sales themselves) to relieve the balance sheet of its more pressing current obligations. We can then bring in permanent financing on terms that are not more harmful than the problems we were trying to correct in the first place.

It is in the symptomatic or thermometer sense, therefore, that *current liabilities/equity* tells us whether we are incurring too much early-maturity risk for the size of our equity. And it warns us that bulging current debt is crowding out of our financial structure, and keeping out, sound long-term financing.

Current liabilities/equity is especially important because of balance-sheet leverage, which makes current liabilities so volatile. The large and dynamic quantity of total assets (use of cash) is juxtaposed against the small, fixed quantity of equity (source of cash). So the assets cause wider percentage swings in total liabilities (source of cash) than they themselves experience, as we have discussed. But because long-term debt is fairly stationary, *current* liabilites are volatile by comparison. This volatility is the financing response to a corresponding volatility in current assets. But current liabilities are smaller and more volatile even than current assets, so they are the most unstable sector of all.

Underestimating the perils of CL/E is therefore to underestimate the most unstable risk factor to which the business can be exposed. This volatile indicator, in fact, bares the Achilles' heel of our business. A ratio as high as 75% urgently requires our perceptive probings into the asset cause of the malady.

Nor should a ratio of *long-term debt/working capital* as high as 100% ever leave us complacent. Heavy debt must now be serviced out of an overtaxed pool of working capital. The larger the fixed debt in relation to working capital, the more overtaxed and strained the pool. When it is less than debt, which now is its sole financing source, we are operating day-to-day entirely on long-term borrowings. No current funds were supplied by stockholders' equity, which is frozen solid in fixed (slow) assets.

Excessive long-term debt/working capital thereby squeezes current liquidity while it undermines *total* balance-sheet liquidity for both long-term lenders and stockholders. It often happens in somewhat like the following two-step sequence:

		($000)						(%)		
	CA	CL	WC	FA	LTD	E	CL/ CA	CL/ E	FA/ E	LTD/ WC
1.	2000	1000	1000	1000	500	1500	50	66.7	66.7	50
2.	2000	1000	1000	2000	1500	1500	50	66.7	133	150

Line 1. We are in good shape, with CL/CA of only 50%, CL/E of 66.7%, FA/E also at 66.7%, and LTD/WC of only 50%. Business is good and will get better.

Line 2. We have therefore added to and modernized plant and equipment, to $2,000,000 (FA), financed by a first mortgage (LTD). Nothing else changed, and our position seems fine: CL/CA is still a comfortable 50%. And even the capricious CL/E ratio remains at a satisfactory 66.7%. We have only one problem, and it is critical: FA/E has doubled to an untenable 133%, which is bad enough. But as the crucial determinative influence, it drove up LTD/WC to *150%*.

Our working capital is now subject to heavy demands by *both* the higher fixed assets and debt, unless and until the assets become profitable. But that is almost beside the point. With an excessive ratio of LTD/WC, we could be out of the market for additional financing without even knowing it, or be subject to ruinous borrowing costs and terms. The ratio is too high because sales/equity and fixed assets/equity are too high, which force up the LTD numerator while they undermine the WC denominator.

Total liabilities/equity (or simply debt/equity) tells us which group of financiers paid how much for the company's assets. It can do little more than that by itself, nor can it by itself carry much weight in the debt capacity analysis. Let us imagine the following alternative situations:

	Situation 1	Situation 2
L	$1,500,000	$2,500,000
E	2,000,000	2,000,000
A	3,500,000	4,500,000
L/E	75%	125%
L/$ of E	$0.75	$1.25
E/$ of L	1.33	0.80
L/A	43%	56%
E/A	57%	44%

In situation 1 we have total debt (L) of $1,500,000 and equity (E) of $2,000,000, which together finance $3,500,000 of total assets (A). Debt/ equity is 75%. To the stockholder, per dollar of his equity (L/$ of E), there are only $0.75 worth of debt claims. To the creditor, per dollar of debt (E/$ of L), there is $1.33 of equity. The stockholder has a small liability risk, and the creditor has a large equity cushion.

We also see this in *total liabilities/total assets*, at a modest 43%, or in the ample *equity/total assets* cushion of 57%: total assets can decline 57% before eliminating the equity margin of safety for total liabilities.

But in situation 2 we borrow an additional $1,000,000: total debt rises to $2,500,000, equity remains at $2,000,000, so that total assets are $4,500,000. There is now a hefty $1.25 of debt for each dollar of stockholders' equity. And each $1.00 of liabilities has an equity cushion of only $0.80.

The $1,000,000 of additional debt has weakened the balance-sheet position of *both* the stockholder and the creditor. In terms of the companion ratios: total debt/total assets jumped to 56%, which means the equity/ total assets cushion narrowed to 44%.

THE DEBT/EQUITY CHESTNUT: EFFECTIVE USE AND MISUSE

These companion ratios remind us that debt/equity is essentially a philosophical exercise, as suggested in Chapter 6. Its timeless folklore and philosophy is that the creditor's investment in the company should never exceed the owner's investment, though no one seems to ask why not. The answer, if the question were to be asked, would probably be expressed in terms of morality and fairness. This is fine, but it does not really get us very far into the guts of the business process.

Perhaps the answer could be illuminated with a logical exercise such as the following. It is not only wrong for the creditor's investment to exceed the owner's, but it is also impossible for this to happen. Debt cannot exceed equity, by definition: Any excess is in fact *equity*, because it is exposed to all the risks of equity (but does not share in the profit opportunities that equity enjoys). The excess of debt over equity is *de facto* equity. Though borrowings are legal debt, the protections that ultimately define debt are fictitious to the extent that the debt lacks an equity cushion. A ratio of total debt/equity in excess of 100% is therefore a definitional if not a logical absurdity.

However, the balance-sheet cushion for total liabilities is not equity at all, but *total assets*—and the liquidity of those assets. With debt/equity of 125% in our second example, we still had an equity/total assets cushion of 44%. And the creditors' legal and practical claim to the $4,500,000 of total assets was far stronger than the stockholders' equity claim on those assets. So the larger total-asset coverage of equity than of debt—equity/total assets of only 44% versus debt/total assets of 56%—is of little practical consequence.

At the very least, therefore, debt/equity should be analyzed together with the equity/total assets cushion. This is shown in the following example: Our equity (E) is $2,000,000. But we increase debt (L) during five successive periods from $1,000,000 to $3,000,000:

	1	2	3	4	5
Debt (L) (000)	$1000	$1500	$2000	$2500	$3000
Equity (E) (000)	2000	2000	2000	2000	2000
Total assets (A) (000)	$3000	$3500	$4000	$4500	$5000
Debt/equity (L/E)	50%	75%	100%	125%	150%
Equity cushion (E/A)	67%	57%	50%	44%	40%
A per $ of debt (L)	$3.00	$2.33	$2.00	$1.80	$1.67
L per $ of E	0.50	0.75	1.00	1.25	1.50

Debt/equity (L/E) increases from 50% to 150% (columns 1 to 5). The creditors' cushion of equity/total assets (E/A) therefore declines from 67 to 40%.

And as debt/equity increases, the proportion of the assets contributed by liabilities increases, while the proportion contributed by equity decreases. In *column 1, with L/E of 50%*, debt of $1,000,000 contributed only 33% of total assets (A), while equity of $2,000,000 contributed 67% (E/A).

But in *column 5, with L/E of 150%*, debt contributed 60% (3000/5000) and equity (E/A) only 40% of asset financing. The percentage of the assets contributed by equity *is* the equity cushion (E/A) for the creditors, which has narrowed.

Assets per dollar of debt summarizes the *creditors'* position: it deteriorates from $3.00 to $1.67, as debt/equity rises. And debt per dollar of equity is the *stockholders'* position: it rises from $0.50 to $1.50, indicating the heavier debt risk to which equity is being exposed.

But the creditor comes out second best: his risk increases while his amount and proportion of the total capital supply increases. But he gets no share in the larger profit potential created by his larger supply of leverage —as do the stockholders, who now have proportionally *less* capital at risk (though each of their dollars is more highly leveraged). The stockholders are playing the game of "heads I win, tails you lose, " and up to a point on the risk-reward curve, the creditors play it with them.

Whether debt/equity of 150% (column 5) is in fact risky depends on the condition of our $1.67 of assets per dollar of debt. From the balance-sheet standpoint alone, that is, what our creditors (and therefore we) consider safe asset coverage depends on the *liquidity* of that $1.67 of assets. This is the same as saying that a safe current liabilities/current assets ratio depends heavily on the liquidity of current assets (inventory), or that a safe current liabilities/quick assets ratio depends on the liquidity of quick assets (receivables).

The maximum safe level of debt/equity not only depends on the liquidity of assets, but on the liquidity of *debt* as well. Debt liquidity is the dependability of our supply of leverage cash, mostly the length of time it will be available for our use. The larger the percentage of current liabilities that make up total liabilities, for instance, the lower is the safe ratio of total liabilities/equity. This is usually true, though long-term debt has its own perils in its fixed interest and after-tax (nondeductible) amortization requirements. The schedule of debt maturities nails down refinancing and refunding requirements, ranging from near to long-term, compared to forecasted cash flow. So it tells us much about our debt liquidity.

Only when *all* the influences on asset and debt liquidity have thus been isolated can we determine the safe level of debt/equity.

But the closest approximation we will make to the safe level of debt/equity—building upon those we have been discussing—is not in the balance sheet at all. It is in the analysis of debt capacity *operating* ratios, as we will now see.

EVALUATING OPERATING DEBT CAPACITY

The key operating ratios of debt capacity include the following:

> Cash flow/total charges
> Current liabilities/sales
> Total liabilities/sales
> Earnings/charges
> Debt/market equity

Debt capacity is a *cash* concept. It is our potential ability to service debt out of cash, derived *both* from the balance sheet and from the income statement. Balance-sheet cash depends on the amount and liquidity of assets ($-A$), and on the liquidity of debt ($+L$). Income-statement cash depends on the amount, dependability, and duration of operating cash flow $(S-C)$.

Over the long life of a profitable corporation, the bulk of the cash will come from the income statement. So operating cash flow is far more important in the debt capacity analysis. As discussed in Chapter 6 on leverage, it is probably best computed in terms of *pretax cash flow coverage of total fixed charges*. This is our *depression-recession* level of cash flow, which we suffered in the last one and will suffer in the next one.

Other operating debt-capacity ratios include the following:

1. *Current liabilities/sales* and *total liabilities/sales*, which we examined fully in the chapters on asset cash and leverage cash.

2. *Earnings/charges*. Dividing the minimum after-tax earnings of the past decade by interest charges (plus preferred stock dividends multiplied by 2) plus all or part of financing rentals.

3. *Debt/market equity*. Total debt (at par) plus preferred stock at market, divided by the total common stock capitalization at *market*. It is a useful double-check on the debt/equity ratio computed at book value. A sizable discrepancy between debt ratios computed at book value and those at market value can mean serious potential problems that the market is already recognizing but we are not. A severely depressed common stock capitalization raises *operating* questions about the validity of debt capacity ratios computed from balance sheet numbers.

With this, we have completed a debt-capacity analysis of the forecasted financial statements. So we can start to make appropriate preventive adjustments in our financial position to maintain a sound balance sheet.

REINVESTMENT RATIOS AND CASH UTILIZATION

These are mainly the following:

Capital expenditures/depreciation
Capital expenditures + dividends / cash flow
Dividends/cash flow

We now move from the debt capacity ratios $(+L)$ to those that control the *utilization* of the cash $(+R)$ that we generated from all sources. In the context of $CRE = S/C \times S/A \times L/A$ (R), the portion of cash that we will plow back into capital items (or dissipate in dividends) is evaluated on a long-term basis with such ratios as the following:

1. *Capital expenditures/depreciation.* This is the extent to which cash represented by depreciation $(-A)$ will be invested in capital items $(+A)$ over a period of years. A ratio below 100% suggests an inadequate flow of depreciation funds into capital assets. A ratio above 100% may suggest excessive investment, or inadequate book depreciation.

2. *Capital expenditures + dividends/cash flow*, or funds expended/funds generated. This is the relationship between funds to be disbursed for capital items and dividends, and those generated by depreciation plus net income.

3. *Dividends/cash flow.* This measures cash leakage—the extent to which cash that could be reinvested profitably for the benefit of stockholders is being dissipated as dividends taxable *both* to the corporation and the stockholder.

This is our final exercise in forecasting cash variances against Plan, whereby we anticipate and can prevent adverse cash-productivity and CRE developments. *How* we prevent the problems, and where and by whom, raises questions that can only be answered on the *third tier* of the control process.

TIER THREE: CASH VARIANCE PREVENTION

Having *forecasted* the Statement variances against Plan, and analyzed them for CRE impact, we now make preventitive *course corrections*: Primarily by means of such tools as Cash Variance Reports (CVRs), the forecasted variances do not occur and we are back on target (Plan).

The CVR, as recommended in Chapter 20, is *automatically* prepared and submitted up the line. This is done by the responsible man in whose area the forecasted variance against Plan has occurred. It may be a quantitative, nonfinancial variance occurring against one of his objectives. It may be a CCR variance of his department's S/C or S/A. Or, farther up the line, it may be a significant financial variance of profit-center sales, costs, or assets.

The man's Cash Variance Report is designed around the familiar journalistic categories: who, what, where, when, why, and how. So they tell us, specifically, everything we want to know about the problem and its solution. The CVR works best as a blend of strategy and tactics. The *strategy* questions are what, why, where, and when. And the *tactical* questions are who, and how.

CASH VARIANCE REPORT (CVR)

Strategic analysis:
1. *What* is the anticipated variance or problem: exact description of the problem, reason for the variance, its type or category, amounts involved, its nature and characteristics, seriousness or priority versus other problems, etc.
2. *Why* will it happen: exact origin of the problem, steps leading to it, etc.
3. *Where* will the problem really hit us: exact *area* to be primarily affected.
4. *When* will the variance occur: exact *time* at which the problem will hit the affected area.

Tactical solution:
1. *Who* is personally responsible for effecting the proposed solution and preventing (correcting) the variance?
2. *How* will he solve the problem (prevent or correct the variance):
    (1) *What* is the best solution?
    (2) *Why* is this the best solution (quickest, least expensive, least disruptive, most permanent, etc.)?
    (3) *Where* is it best to implement and effect the solution?
    (4) *When* will the solution be launched and the variance corrected (problem solved): timetable and target date, and condition of the affected area when finally corrected or solved.

Financial variances are best controlled *cumulatively*, in terms of the Plan's "base zero to date," as advocated in the Planning chapter. We do not want to initiate massive preventive action against a variance, such as sales, if it is a one-month aberration that will correct itself fairly soon. But if our forecast shows that, month after month, sales will vary cumulatively from Plan, a determined program of variance prevention must be launched immediately. It is then to these cumulative variances that CVRs address themselves, promptly and forcefully, in launching preventive course corrections.

Variance prevention is absolutely crucial to a successful strategy of cash, whereby we maximize CRE and Pi. It transfers our energies from the problems of the moment—from putting out fires—to *ancticipated* and *analyzed* problems and variances.

In this way do we make the most constructive transition that can ever be accomplished by a company which is determined to grow dynamically and profitably: Precisely here in the control process—on the preventive third tier—we truly implement, or not, the strategy of cash.

The ATL-liquidity analysis of fixed assets, equity, and long-term debt evaluated the profound influence of these balance-sheet forces both on working capital liquidity and on debt capacity. And the debt capacity analysis described how debt influences and is influenced by current liquidity. As L/A, these ratio analyses thus filled in the *complete* liquidity picture being presented together with the profit margin and turnover ratios (S/C and S/A).

That is, the S/C forces materially affect current liquidity through operating-cash contribution to working capital. And the S/A forces also either benefit, distort, or harm working capital and its liquidity. In so doing, they also enlarge or diminish our total balance-sheet liquidity and our debt capacity. Upon these liquidity foundations are superimposed L/A.

So all three categories of CRE ratios—S/C, S/A, and L/A—are *liquidity* ratios in their impact on cash productivity, working capital, total liquidity, and debt capacity. And they are CRE ratios within the three-dimensional cash-productivity (CPF) expression $S/C \times S/A \times L/A$.

Liquidity and CRE are thus identical forces in the realization of Pi. To harness liquidity is to harness the company's total available striking power for maximizing profits and growth. It is to implement the strategy of cash.

GLOSSARY

A (Asset Cash: +S/A)

Asset cash is generated when we refrain from investing funds in asset expansion to support higher sales. This control of assets (A) in relation to sales (S), or +S/A, produces usable liquidity in two forms: (1) the cash and borrowing power that were *not* used to buy new assets and (2) the *expanded* borrowing power from increased cash flow that results from savings of asset-carrying and interest costs.

That is, to the extent of the asset control, liquidity and cash that otherwise would have been invested in assets to produce that incremental amount of sales, are *not* invested in those assets. So they are free to be invested elsewhere to produce *additional* sales and profits. Asset control thus creates asset cash in the form of this free and investable liquidity. In addition, asset control *expands* our borrowing capacity to the extent of the higher cash flow stemming from reduced asset-carrying and interest costs.

ATL (Across-the-Line)

ATL items occur on the balance sheet below (across) the line dividing working capital and everything else. They are chiefly long-term assets and liabilities, and equity. Changes in working capital, up or down, are caused *only* by ATL (across-the-line) changes of the same net amount and direction—by what took place *between* working capital and everything on the balance sheet external to it (i.e., the ATL section).

ATL Liquidity

The impact that variations in ATL (across-the-line) magnitudes have on current and total balance sheet liquidity.

BC (Best Competitors) Cash Availability

The amounts of cash we could generate from sales increase ($+$S), cost reduction ($-$C), and asset reduction ($-$A) if we ran our company as efficiently as the average of our best competitors (BC). This BC cash availability can be estimated by comparing our S/C and S/A ratios, in every corner of the business, with the corresponding ratios of the most profitable companies in our industry (the BC companies).

BV (Breakeven Volume)

BV is that level of sales (S) which produces just enough sales cash (Sc) to pay for constant costs (KC), leaving zero profit (P). The level of BV therefore depends on (1) the amount of constant costs (KC) that must be paid for and (2) the percentage of sales cash (Sc) generated by sales (S)— or %Sc—which sales cash pays for KC. Hence the formula to determine breakeven volume is BV = KC/%Sc.

Cash Availability (Liquidity)

Our company's total liquidity, or its capacity to generate cash from all seven sources: $+$S$-$C$-$A$+$L$+$D$+$E$+$R. When our cash contribution ratios (CCRs) are low—specifically S/C, S/A, and L/A—we have a high cash availability from sales increase (S), cost reduction (C), asset reduction (A), and additional borrowing (L). We may also have a large cash potential from neglected reinvestment opportunities (R), from equity sources (E), and from acquisitions (D).

Cash Consciousness

For virtually all our operating people, this means cost conscious-ness: a total awareness of the existence and reality of *cost cash* ($-$C), which are cash dollars, or savings opportunities, masquerad-ing as costs. It is the recognition that costs, everywhere, are cash potentials.

Cash Creativity

For virtually all our operating people, this means cost creativity: the relentless searching out and implementing of cost-reducing improvements, everywhere by everyone. Cash creativity is the link between cost control and cost reduction, taking us from the control of costs against standards to the tightening up and toughening of the standards.

Cash-Generating Strategies

The broad methods and procedures for generating cash from each of the seven SCALDER sources. Strategies identify the company's major cash-generating problems and opportunities, for which tactical solutions are developed and implemented.

Cash Improvement (CI)

For virtually all our operating people, this means cost reduction. Best achieved in an organized way by means of a dynamic cash improvement (CI) capability.

Cash Margin (CM) Chart

A recommended variation of the conventional breakeven chart: directs our attention specifically and forcefully to the firm's two profit-creating forces, the cash margin (CM) and sales cash/sales (%Sc). The CM Chart is a formidable decision-making tool because it is thus entirely rooted in the profit formula itself, $P = CM \times \%Sc$. It thereby helps compress for us the *entire* profit picture—the causes, quantity, quality, and future of cash flow and profits.

Cash Margin (CM) Factors

The six cash margin (CM) factors are the total cause of profits, in the general profit equation $P = CM \times \%Sc$. The *sales* factors ($+S$) are (1) number of *products*, (2) unit *volume* of each product, and (3) *price* per unit. The *breakeven* (BV) factors are (4) *volume costs* (VC) per unit, (5) *mix* (product distribution of %Sc), and (6) *constant costs* (KC). The CM factors thus increase sales (S) and lower breakeven volume (BV)—widening $S - BV$, or CM—and they increase sales cash/sales (%Sc).

Cash Productivity

In the expression $S/C \times S/A \times L/A$, cash productivity is increased by an increase in the numerators S or L in relation to the denominators C or A. It is the *relationship*, that is, between cash inflow from sales or leverage, and cash outflow into costs or assets. Cash productivity is increased whether the sales or leverage inflows are increasing relative to cost and asset outflows, or the cost and asset outflows are decreasing relative to the sales or leverage inflows. In the broader sense, cash productivity is the output or flow from all seven SCALDER sources that constitute the company's liquidity environment. To maximize cash productivity and profits within this environment, we maximize liquidity velocity— the force, speed, and payback at which cash circulates.

Cash Synergism

The mutually reinforcing interaction of primary and secondary (or derivative) cash productivity. This interaction produces a more-than-proportional increase in total cash productivity.

Cash Velocity

The percentage that each source of cash inflow $(S - A + L + E)$ and each application of cash outflow $(C + A - L - E)$ is of the total cash produced during the period. As a cash-basis financial statement, Cash Velocity modifies the Net Cash Impact statement to show the *relative* cash impacts of each source and use of cash. In the broader sense, cash velocity refers to the speed at which cash circulates within the corporate system, from productive sources to productive uses and back, ad infinitum. It also implies minimizing the elapsed time between reinvesting the cash inflow from receivables and debt, and the payback of cash from investment projects.

C (Cost Cash: $+S/C$)

Generated by reducing the amount of cash invested in cost expenditures while maintaining the same level of sales, or by increasing the level of sales without increasing our cash investment in cost expenditures. Cost cash is thus produced by $+S/C$, whether through an increase in the numerator or a decrease in the denominator.

CCRs (Cash Contribution Ratios)

The S/C and S/A ratios that apply to each man's area of supervision or work, and for whose performance he alone is personally responsible. The head of Manufacturing, for instance, is evaluated by such CCRs as sales/material costs, sales/direct labor, sales/manufacturing inventory, and many others. CCRs accurately measure his contribution to cash productivity, and cash return on equity (CRE), because together they *define* CRE—profit margin (S/C) multiplied by turnover (S/A).

That is, CRE=CCRs: the company's growth, defined by CRE, is determined solely by the sum of all the CCRs throughout the organization, at every level. Cash productivity is increased by an increase in the numerators S and L, or by a decrease in the denominators C and A. And cash productivity declines if the numerators S and L decline or if the denominators C and A increase. So if a man's CCRs are rising, he is contributing to CRE; if they are declining, he is undermining CRE.

CM (Cash Margin)

The excess of actual sales (S) over that level of sales at which we break even (BV), or S − BV. Also expressed as the percentage by which sales exceed breakeven volume: (S − BV)/S, or CM/S, or %CM. In the relationship S = BV + CM, BV is the KC-absorbing portion of sales: as sales rise above this no-profit breakeven volume (BV), the CM surplus (S − BV) is the *profit-generating* portion of sales.

CPF (Cash Productivity Factor)

A substitute or proxy for cash return on equity (CRE), more versatile and revealing, which exposes all the cash forces converging on and producing CRE. Expressed as CPF = S/C × S/A × L/A, which means in effect that CRE is produced by the cumulative force of cost cash (S/C), asset cash (S/A), and leverage cash (L/A). CPF quantifies and measures the combined (unweighted) cash impact of these three ratios on CRE, by thus computing their products in simple multiplication. Because of this three-dimensional causal influence which cash productivity exerts on CRE, we measure the impact of cash strategy primarily in terms of the cash productivity factor (CPF)—and only residually in terms of CRE. Three-dimensional cash productivity is the cause, of which unidimensional CRE is the effect—albeit the all-important effect.

CRE (Cash Return on Equity)

The CRE ratio *cash flow/equity* totally defines management's internal operating purpose and objective. It is the product of two component ratios:

cash flow/sales (*profit margin*) × sales/equity (*turnover*)

CRE is the internal half of Pi (the percentage increase in equity), in which equity is created by retained earnings. External equity formation is ECO and ECA—from public offerings and acquisitions.

D (Developmental, or Acquisition, Cash)

An acquisition or merger generates equity per share, which is potential cash, (1) when it occurs (Transaction ECA), because we acquired more equity per share than we paid out for the company; and (2) as we subsequently develop the SCALDER cash-generating potential present in the acquired company (Liquidity ECA). A developmental acquisition (+D) is one that generates equity and plays a constructive economic role in the company's development and growth— as opposed to a nondevelopmental acquisition which is typically the mere swapping of paper between two groups of stockholders.

Direct Standard Costing

An accounting system that meshes with volume budgeting to separate out volume costs (VC), or direct costs, from total costs— thereby generating indispensable sales cash (Sc) data. That is, $S - VC = Sc$. It differs from conventional full-absorption costing in that no constant costs (KC) are capitalized into product inventory, all of KC being charged directly against earnings. Product inventory therefore contains only direct costs.

E (Equity Cash)

External cash provided directly by the private or public sale of stock, or indirectly (as a potential further source of cash) by the per-share equity formation caused by a public offering (ECO) or an acquisition (ECA).

ECA (Equity Created by Acquisition)

The automatic increase in our equity per share from a merger or acquisition transaction (Transaction ECA), or from subsequently developing the acquired company's SCALDER liquidity potential (Liquidity ECA).

ECO (Equity Created by Offerings)

In the typical public offering which is priced above equity per share, we gain more equity from the proceeds of the underwriting than we give up in the form of equity per share of the stock we offer.

Equity (E)

The primal source of corporate liquidity and cash productivity. Equity (assets minus liabilities) is the stockholders' *net investment* at depreciated book cost, and is also called book value, net worth, or net asset value. This ownership investment (E) is the underlying basis of SCALDER cash productivity, because it finances the asset (A) and cost (C) investments from which sales (S) are generated. The resulting cash flow supports leverage (L) and acquisitions (D), and the total stream of cash is channeled into profitable reinvestments (R). To generate equity per share by whatever means, internal or external, is therefore always to generate liquidity (potential cash): equity = liquidity = potential cash = cash productivity = profits.

Expression

An entirely valid description of relationships that neither makes arithmetical claims nor needs to. The Pi expression, for instance,

$$CRE = \left(\frac{S}{C} \times \frac{S}{A} \times \frac{L}{A} \right)(R)$$

$$Pi = CRE \times ECO \times ECA$$

has no mathematical pretensions, yet is an invaluable conceptual, or idea, framework for describing the total corporate purpose. The same is true for many other expressions (not formulas) used throughout the book, such as $CSA = MCP$; $CRE = -C + S - A + L$ (R), and so forth.

External *versus* Internal Cash

External cash is supplied by leverage (+L), developmental acquisitions (+D), and equity (+E). Internal cash is supplied by cost reduction (−C), sales increase (+S), and asset reduction (−A), and the reinvestment (R) of all previously generated cash.

KC (Constant or Capacity Costs)

The steady "overhead" costs that are a function of time, not of sales volume (such as volume costs, or VC). KC provides the resource capability and capacity—human, physical, financial, technological, and so forth—to create, make, and market our products. It is made up of irreducible *fixed* or cadre costs, project or *payback* costs, and *optional* or staff costs. For the company to make a profit, we must generate more than enough sales cash (Sc) to pay for KC. That is, $S - VC = Sc - KC = P$.

L (Leverage Cash: +L/A)

External cash provided by all creditors and owners senior to the common stockholders—but chiefly by creditors (debt securities) in the typical company.

Leverage Cash Availability

Our capacity to generate cash from borrowings and other senior securities. This depends on our present quantity of leverage, and on such leverage-supporting factors as the amount of future expected cash flow and the size and liquidity of our assets.

LICO (Leverage-in, Cash-out)

The LICO effect produces cash when we invest in a company that enjoys sizable borrowing power, have it borrow (leverage-in), and then sell it or some of its shares (cash-out).

Liquidity (Cash Availability)

A company's total potential for generating cash, or its cash availability, from all seven SCALDER sources. Expressed as

$$CRE = \left(\frac{S}{C} \times \frac{S}{A} \times \frac{L}{A} \right)(R)$$

$$Pi = CRE \times ECO \times ECA$$

A liquid company is typically one with a low or negative CRE and Pi, in which there is substantial room for improvement of cash productivity from all the SCALDER sources. This usually means comparatively low cash contribution ratios of S/C, S/A, and L/A for its industry group; neglected reinvestment opportunities (R); and an unutilized equity-formation potential from public offerings and acquisitions (ECO and ECA). Conversely, a low-liquidity company is *already* at a high rate of CRE and Pi, with high cash contribution ratios (CCRs), having harnessed and employed (used up) its available SCALDER liquidity.

Liquidity is fundamentally grounded in equity formation, CRE being cash flow/equity and Pi the increase in equity from all sources. Anything we do to increase equity per share increases liquidity—our potential for generating more cash from the increased equity, via the SCALDER sources. Stated the other way, an increase in equity is an increase in the denominator of our CRE ratio cash flow/equity. This reduces CRE—and the product of the three cash contribution ratios locked into CRE—thereby increasing the *liquidity* we have available for generating additional cash and earnings.

Liquidity Analysis

Identifying the sources (−A, +L, +E) and uses (+A, −L, −E) of funds in the current and long-term areas of a succession of balance sheets.

Liquidity ECA (Equity Created by Acquisition)

The growth of our equity per share as we develop the SCALDER liquidity potential present in an acquired company, especially one whose balance sheet at the time of the acquisition is more liquid than ours.

Liquidity Environment

Expresses in static terms what "maximum liquidity velocity" expresses in dynamic terms: The manager's entire operating responsibility is to maximize the velocity of balance-sheet liquidity—maximize the force, speed, and payback at which cash circulates within the corporate system. By so doing—and because changes in liquidity velocity precisely determine changes in profits—he maintains and nourishes a liquidity environment of maximum profit and growth.

In the maximum-velocity liquidity environment, CRE is maximized via three simultaneous processes:

1. Generating a pool of internal cash from $-C + S - A$, or $+S/C$ and $+S/A$.

2. Adding to the cash pool with externally generated leverage cash $(+L)$.

3. Recirculating the cash $(+R)$ at maximum velocity among maximum-cash-return projects.

Such a liquidity environment is described by $CRE = (S/C \times S/A \times L/A)\,(R)$.

The productivity of our liquidity environment is also influenced strongly by cash synergism, or the mutually reinforcing interaction of primary and secondary cash productivity. An increase in the primary cash productivity of our liquidity environment generates secondary productivity, and thereby tends to produce a more-than-proportional increase in total cash productivity. The ideal liquidity invironment is thus one of maximum liquidity velocity *and* synergy, in which CRE is maximized.

Liquidity Velocity

Narrowly defined, as "cash velocity," it is the speed and efficiency with which cash circulates within the corporate system—from the productive $-C + S - A + L$ sources of cash to its reinvestment (R) at maximum return, and back to cash production, ad infinitum. High velocity means there is no dilution of cash productivity from dividend payments (leakage), idle cash, low-return temporary investments, or other losses or delays in putting it to work at maximum return.

Broadly defined, liquidity velocity also includes two other crucial elements of cash productivity: the *force* with which our business is now producing cash, especially because of high ratios of S/C, S/A, and L/A; and the *payback* profitability of the projects in which the cash is invested. Hence liquidity velocity in its broad sense means the productive force, speed, and payback at which our cash circulates. We increase CRE and profits by stepping up any one or more of these three components of liquidity velocity.

"Maximum liquidity velocity" thus expresses in dynamic terms what "liquidity environment" expresses in static terms. Management is charged above all with maintaining and nourishing a liquidity environment—generating cash with maximum force from all sources, and simultaneously reinvesting it in those applications that will produce the highest cash payback.

Liquidity Velocity, Statement of

Analyzes the sources and applications of cash, showing the relative impact that each balance-sheet item has on cash production. The change in each current and noncurrent (across-the-line, or ATL) item is set forth as a percentage of total cash produced during the period. The Statement of Liquidity Velocity is the ultimate analytical expression of the strategy of cash, focusing as it does on the dynamic interaction between cash and the entire balance sheet.

MCP (Maximum Cash Productivity)

Describes the ideal liquidity environment: Cash is produced at the maximum rate (force) and reinvested promptly, according to the dictates of liquidity velocity, at the highest possible rate of return. Such a company is growing at its highest possible compounded rate, and is at the point of MCP. Here, costs and assets are held to a minimum in relation to sales volume, leverage is at the point of maximum profitability, and reinvestment sources of cash are being maximized. That is, $S/C \times S/A \times L/A$ (R).

Mix

Each product has a different profitability ratio of sales cash-to-sales (Sc/S, or %Sc), compared with the others. So we can improve the cash productivity of our product mix, and our company's profits, by increasing the proportion of total sales accounted for by high-%Sc products relative to low-%Sc products. A given total sales volume, that is, will be more profitable if it is composed mostly of high-%Sc products. The strategy objective here is to maximize the weighted-average %Sc of all the products making up our total sales volume. Improving mix (%Sc) thus lowers BV (breakeven volume) and increases profits, in the formula

$$BV = \frac{KC}{\%Sc}$$

Net Cash Impact (NCI)

Cash flows into the firm mainly from the collection of receivables (S), the disposal of assets $(-A)$, borrowings $(+L)$, and the sale of stock $(+E)$. It flows out via cash costs (C), the purchase of assets $(+A)$, repayment of debt $(-L)$, and equity reductions such as dividends and stock repurchases $(-E)$. The difference between these cash receipts $(S-A+L+E)$ and cash disbursements $(C+A-L-E)$ is *net cash impact* (NCI).

Pi (The Percentage Increase of Equity)

The gain in net worth or book value per share from *all* sources: internal sources, notably retained earnings; and external sources, notably ECO and ECA. Pi is maximized when equity that is increasing at the maximum rate from external sources generates earnings (retained equity) at the maximum rate. Thus Pi combines cash return on equity (CRE) and equity formation into a total growth concept which is the heart of the strategy of cash. It is expressed as $Pi = CRE \times ECO \times ECA$.

Pinpoint Costing

A process that helps to achieve cost control and reduction by monitoring the cost *detail*—by the meticulous pinpointing of cost origin, cause, location, responsible individual, time of incurrence, and so forth.

Primary Cash Productivity

Cash generation from the original SCALDER sources, which in turn supports the generation of secondary cash. For instance, cost reduction $(-C)$ increases primary cash flow, which then supports increased leverage $(+L)$ as a secondary or derivative source of cash.

R (Reinvestment Cash)

Internal cash supplied by the reinvestment, for maximum cash payback, of all the cash we generated from the six preceding SCALDE sources. When we direct cash into either cost or capital outlays for a stated return over a stated period of time, a reinvestment source of cash has been created.

Reinvestment (R) is the climactic event in the comprehensive liquidity process, whereby the liquidity velocity—or cash recirculation—ring defined by $+S-C-A+L+D+E+R$, is closed.

Retained Cash Flow (RCF)

Net income after taxes and dividend payments, but before deducting noncash charges such as depreciation. RCF is the accrual-basis cash from operations that management finally has available to reinvest. It is therefore a more meaningful and useful internal measurement than "net income," which is distorted by adjustments for depreciation that do not correspond to real-world conditions.

S (Sales Cash, External)

The external dollar volume of sales to customers, from which we derive our initial inflow of operating cash in the form of receivables collections. In per-unit terms, S is our product's price (Pr).

Sc (Sales Cash, Internal)

The cash left over after deducting from sales (S) all variable or volume costs (VC) that *fluctuate with* sales. When sales go up or down 10%, VC such as direct material tends to go up or down 10%. What remains is sales cash (Sc), the "net" or internal cash derived from sales. This sales cash pays for our fixed overhead (constant costs, or KC), and what we have left over is profit (P). Hence

$$S-VC=Sc-KC=P$$

SCALDER

The seven sources of corporate cash and liquidity:

$+S$: *sales* cash
$-C$: *cost* cash

$$-\text{A:} \quad asset \text{ cash}$$
$$+\text{L:} \quad leverage \text{ cash}$$
$$+\text{D:} \quad \text{developmental } acquisition \text{ cash}$$
$$+\text{E:} \quad equity \text{ cash}$$
$$+\text{R:} \quad reinvestment \text{ cash}$$

To burn this cash-productivity acronym into our memory, we might tell ourselves that a *scalder* is a device or tool used for burning: It sprays boiling liquid or superheated steam on surfaces such as those of industrial metals and public buildings, to smooth or clean them.

Secondary Cash Productivity

Additional or derivative cash sources that originate from and are supported by the primary cash sources. Example: additional (secondary) debt cash that is supported by additional (primary) operating cash flow.

Stockholders' Wealth

The present cash-realizable value of the shares of stock in our company, to the enhancement of which all corporate energies are necessarily directed.

Transaction ECA (Equity Created by Acquisition)

The initial and automatic increase in our equity per share at the time, and as a result, of an acquisition. It depends not on the nature of the company we acquire, but solely on the way we construct the securities package offered to the selling stockholders. That is, we receive more equity per share in the form of the acquired company than we give up in the form of the securities package we offer for it.

VC (Volume Costs)

The "variable" costs such as direct material and direct labor that fluctuate proportionately with sales volume (S). Sales cash (Sc) is what remains after deducting volume costs from sales: $S - VC = Sc$.

Volume Budgeting

An accounting method of separating volume costs (VC) from total costs, whereby we can deal only with the sales cash $(S - VC)$ of each product. It thus forecasts and controls cash for *any* level of sales that materializes. Unit costs now contain only volume costs (VC), which fluctuate with sales and so are *fixed per unit* regardless of unit volume. Unit costs do not now include fixed costs (KC), which *vary* per unit depending on the level of unit volume. Volume budgeting therefore enables us to forecast closely what our unit costs will be at *any* future volume level, since those costs will not be affected by volume changes. It is best used in parallel with an accounting system of direct standard costing, which charges VC but not KC to product inventory.

Working Capital Velocity, Statement of

Shows the percentage that each across-the-line (ATL) increase or decrease is of our starting working capital. Only ATL items—fixed assets, long-term debt, and equity—generate or use up working capital. The Statement of Working Capital Velocity thus reveals the relative impacts of each ATL item on current liquidity, and tells us how fast our stock of working capital is turning over—how rapidly we are producing and reinvesting it vis-a-vis the ATL sector of the balance sheet. In short, it is an analysis of changes in the quantity and composition of working capital in terms of the changes in (long-term) ATL items that produced them.

INDEX